RAISED TO OBEY

The Princeton Economic History of the Western World

JOEL MOKYR, SERIES EDITOR

A list of titles in this series appears in the back of the book.

RAISED TO OBEY

The Rise and Spread of Mass Education

AGUSTINA S. PAGLAYAN

PRINCETON UNIVERSITY PRESS
Princeton and Oxford

Copyright © 2024 by Princeton University Press

Princeton University Press is committed to the protection of copyright and the intellectual property our authors entrust to us. Copyright promotes the progress and integrity of knowledge created by humans. Thank you for supporting free speech and the global exchange of ideas by purchasing an authorized edition of this book. If you wish to reproduce or distribute any part of it in any form, please obtain permission.

Requests for permission to reproduce material from this work should be sent to permissions@press.princeton.edu

Published by Princeton University Press

41 William Street, Princeton, New Jersey 08540
99 Banbury Road, Oxford OX2 6JX

press.princeton.edu

All Rights Reserved

ISBN 978-0-691-26126-3
ISBN (pbk.) 978-0-691-26127-0
ISBN (e-book) 978-0-691-26177-5

British Library Cataloging-in-Publication Data is available

Editorial: Bridget Flannery-McCoy and Alena Chekanov
Production Editorial: Jill Harris
Production: Lauren Reese
Publicity: William Pagdatoon
Copyeditor: Karen Verde

Cover illustration by Jared Nangle

This book has been composed in Sabon Next LT Pro

1 3 5 7 9 10 8 6 4 2

PARA MARTÍN

CONTENTS

List of Figures ix
List of Tables xiii
Preface xv
Acknowledgments xvii

1 Education and Social Order 1
2 Two Centuries of Mass Education 38
3 Why Do Governments Regulate and Provide Mass Education? 87
4 Internal Threats and Mass Education in Europe and Latin America 123
5 Teachers, Inspectors, and Curriculums as Instruments of Social Order 183
6 Limits and Possibilities of the Argument 218
7 Indoctrination in Democracies 247
8 Does Education Promote Social Order? 283
9 The Future of Education 310

References 325
Index 345

FIGURES

1.1. Percentage of countries in the world where the central government monitors primary school enrollment, 1820–2010   9
1.2. Percentage of countries in Europe and Latin America where the central government intervenes in primary education, and type of intervention, 1800–2010   10
1.3. Average primary, secondary, and tertiary enrollment rates around the world, 1820–2010   13
1.4. Average primary school enrollment rate before and after civil wars and democratization, 1828–2010   15
2.1. Primary school enrollment rates in Europe, the Americas, and the rest of the world, as a percentage of the population ages 5–14 years and as a percentage of the school-age population, 1820–2010   44
2.2. Historical evolution of primary school enrollment rates, as a percentage of the population ages 5–14 years, in four European and four Latin American countries   46
2.3. Timing of democratization and timing of state intervention in primary education in Europe, the Americas, and the rest of the world   49
2.4. Distribution of primary school enrollment rates, as a percentage of the school-age population, five years before the first democratization in countries that ever democratized, 1820–2010   51
2.5. Average primary school enrollment rates around the world and by region, as a percentage of the school-age population, before and after democratization, 1820–2010   52

2.6. Timing of industrialization and timing of state intervention in primary education in Europe and Latin America 66
2.7. Average primary school enrollment rates, as a percentage of the school-age population, before and after the First and Second Industrial Revolutions, in Europe and the Americas compared to non-Western countries, 1820–2010 67
2.8. Average primary school enrollment rates, as a percentage of the population ages 5–14 years, before and after the onset of interstate wars in Europe and the Americas compared to non-Western countries, 1830–2001 74
2.9. Average primary school enrollment rate, as a percentage of the population ages 5–14 years, before and after the onset of civil wars in Europe and Latin America, 1828–2010 79
2.10. Primary school enrollment rates, as a percentage of the population ages 5–14 years, before and after select civil wars in France, Finland, Colombia, and El Salvador 83
2.11. Differential growth of primary school enrollment rates between countries in Europe and Latin America that experienced civil war versus countries that did not 85
4.1. Public primary education expenditures, number of primary schools, and primary school enrollment in France, 1810–1900 147
4.2. Percentage growth in primary school enrollment and in the number of primary schools after the Guizot Law of 1833 in French departments that experienced high, low, or no violence between 1830 and 1832 150
4.3. Public primary schools maintained by the Chilean central government, and primary school enrollment, in Atacama and the rest of Chile, 1859–1878 163
4.4. Public primary schools maintained by the Chilean central government in the mining provinces of Atacama and Coquimbo, 1859–1878 166
4.5. Primary school enrollment rates in Argentina and in Latin America, as a percentage of the population ages 5–14 years, 1860–1960 168
4.6. Number of primary schools and primary school enrollment rates in Buenos Aires compared to the Interior provinces of Argentina during the oligarchic regime, 1885–1912 179

5.1. Certification requirements for primary school teachers according to the first national primary education laws of European and Latin American countries   190
5.2. School inspection policies according to the first national primary education laws of European and Latin American countries   193
5.3. Compulsory schooling provisions included in the first national primary education laws of European and Latin American countries   196
5.4. Mandatory subjects in the curriculum for lower primary schools according to the first national primary education laws of European and Latin American countries   200
6.1. Average education indoctrination index around the world across different types of non-democratic regimes, 1946–2010   234
7.1. Indoctrination and critical thinking in the education systems of democracies and autocracies, 1950–2021   278
8.1. Chilean statistics of convicted criminals by literacy status   303
9.1. Frequency of student exposure to diverse viewpoints, by country, 2021   316

TABLES

5.1. List of mandatory subjects in the national curriculum for primary schools and for Normal Schools in Argentina and Chile, circa 1880   210

PREFACE

I grew up in a family that put my education before everything else. My grandfather would insist on its importance while he recounted with great sadness the fact that he could not go to secondary school because he needed to support his family. My mother, who managed to raise five children on her own without the income and career opportunities that a college degree would have afforded her, paid for an expensive education even though that meant neglecting more basic needs. The sacrifices they made for me were rooted in their conviction that education would open up a world of opportunities.

Growing up in Argentina, I began to sense contradictions between what I observed and the narratives we tell ourselves about education systems at a young age. I was ten years old when I saw how teachers failed to support my brother as he struggled to concentrate, eventually leading him to drop out of high school. That same year I discovered the arbitrariness of school rules when our fifth-grade teacher prohibited me from going to the bathroom while we were dissecting a fish—a terrible decision on her part, which resulted in my throwing up right there. If schools weren't available when struggling kids needed their support, for whom exactly would they open up a world of opportunities? Who ever thought it was acceptable for a teacher to keep a child with an upset stomach from going to the bathroom?

Despite the contradictions I observed, I bought into the mainstream narrative about the promise of education in the same way that my mother and grandparents did. What I learned in primary school reinforced this narrative. Our education system, we were told, was created by Domingo F. Sarmiento, whose importance in Argentina's history is such that a national holiday is dedicated to commemorate him. In school we learned that

Sarmiento, "the father of education," wanted every individual to have access to education. He zealously established primary schools all over the country, founded the first teacher training institution, and traveled to Europe to learn what the most developed nations of the world were doing to educate children. He wrote the country's first national primary education law, thanks to which a public primary education system was created. And Argentina's education system became a model for all other Latin American countries because it helped promote social mobility like no other.

And then I read Sarmiento's *Facundo: Civilización y Barbarie*. In this book, his most famous written work, Sarmiento blames the recurrence of civil wars in nineteenth-century Argentina on the upbringing of the "barbarian" and "savage" population living in rural areas. This barbarism, he argues, could be eradicated by changing the environment in which these children were raised, using schools to reform their morality and manners so as to resemble the "elegant" and "civilized" children of Buenos Aires.

Sarmiento's *Facundo* should have given me a clue about the questions that had troubled me growing up. But it wasn't until much later, when I started reading about and researching the history of education systems in other countries, that I began to put the pieces together. This book reflects that journey.

ACKNOWLEDGMENTS

This book is the joint product of my long-standing interest in education issues, several years working on education reform and international development, and a decade of research on education systems. Throughout that time, many colleagues and friends engaged with my ideas, asking probing questions and offering thoughtful comments that helped improve the book and made the process of writing it a great joy.

The initial intuition for the argument I advance in this book emerged—unbeknownst to me at the time—from reading *Facundo: Civilización y Barbarie* as part of the admissions process at Universidad de San Andrés. Thanks to a generous scholarship, an intellectual environment that welcomed my inquisitive nature, and the mentorship of political economist Mariano Tommasi and economic historian Roberto Cortés Conde, the years I spent there sowed the seeds for a career as a researcher and educator.

Still, I took a rather scientific approach to choosing a career: While I knew that I would enjoy working at a university, I decided to try other paths to see if I liked anything else better. I tested and discarded various paths before being truly convinced that becoming a professor was indeed the best path for me. Each of those alternative paths, from the years I spent as a macroeconomist in Argentina to the years I worked on education reform alongside Emiliana Vegas at the World Bank, shaped how I think about the world in general and about education systems in particular.

The first serious steps toward this book began when I was working on one of the three studies that formed part of my doctoral dissertation at Stanford University. Ken Scheve, Jeremy Weinstein, James Fearon, and David Laitin in the Department of Political Science, and Susanna Loeb at the Graduate School of Education, helped me advance my research agenda by providing the right mix of enthusiasm and straightforward criticism. Above all, Ken, Jeremy, Jim, and David embraced my interest in education systems—even if this was not their area of expertise—and encouraged me to follow my gut. Everyone should be so lucky.

I began to put pen to paper only after I became a professor at the University of California, San Diego. Many colleagues at UCSD read and commented on different portions of early drafts, provided feedback during presentations of the book project, connected me with resources, or helped me navigate the mysterious process of publishing a book, including Claire Adida, John Ahlquist, Sam Bazzi, Renee Bowen, Lawrence Broz, Karen Ferree, David Fortunato, Francisco Garfias, Peter Gourevitch, Stephan Haggard, Thad Kousser, Sean Ingham, Federica Izzo, David Lake, Megumi Naoi, Gareth Nellis, Simeon Nichter, Lauren Prather, Sebastián Saiegh, Christina Schneider, and David Wiens.

A one-day book workshop in December 2021 led to a significant revision in the scope and ambition of the book. Christina Schneider hosted the workshop and Ben Ansell, Thad Dunning, Beatriz Magaloni, David Stasavage, and Daniel Ziblatt participated as discussants. I thank them all for carving out precious time to read and discuss the initial manuscript and for their perceptive ideas on how to improve it. A subsequent revision also benefited from excellent suggestions from Pablo Beramendi and six anonymous peer reviewers.

In the course of conducting the research for this book, I had the privilege of presenting my work and receiving valuable feedback from political scientists, economists, historians, and sociologists at Boston University, Columbia University, a joint Duke-UNC workshop, Emory University, Harvard University, Johns Hopkins University, the London School of Economics, MIT, New York University, Oxford University, Stanford University, UC Berkeley, the University of British Columbia, the University of Gothenburg, the University of Michigan, the University of Pennsylvania, USC, the University of Virginia, Universidad Católica de Chile, Universidad de los Andes, Universidad de San Andrés, and Yale University, as well as APSA, CIES, RIDGE Economic History, the Ibero-American Economic History Webinar, the Latin American Network in Economic History and Political Economy, Brookings Institution, the Center for Global Development, the Inter-American Development Bank, and the World Bank. I thank seminar participants at these institutions, as well as Ran Abramitzky, Katharine Baldwin, Hoyt Bleakley, Carles Boix, Patricia Bromley, Rachel Brule, Manuel Cabal, Alberto Díaz-Cayeros, Alexandra Cirone, Volha Charnysh, Mark Dincecco,

Nick Eubank, Tulia Falleti, Leopoldo Fergusson, Vicky Fouka, Adriane Fresh, Jeffry Frieden, Daniel Gingerich, Jane Gingrich, Guy Grossman, Anna Grzymala-Busse, Allison Hartnett, Florian Hollenbach, John Huber, Kimuli Kasara, Alan Jacobs, Steven Levitsky, Johannes Lindvall, Shelley Liu, David Lopez, Isabela Mares, John Marshall, Daniel Mattingly, Cathie Jo Martin, John Meyer, Gerardo Munck, María Victoria Murillo, Tomás Murphy, Harris Mylonas, Tine Paulsen, Melina Platas, Macarena Ponce de León, Leandro Prados de la Escosura, Adam Przeworski, Didac Queralt, Nicolas Rodriguez Hedenbratt, Pia Raffler, Francisco Ramirez, Martín Rossi, Arturas Rozenas, Hillel Soifer, Pavithra Suryanarayan, Tariq Thachil, Omar Wasow, Htet Thiha Zaw, and Yang-Yang Zhou. I also thank the *American Political Science Review* for allowing me to use materials I previously published in that journal, and the *APSR* editors and anonymous reviewers for helping me identify key questions that a broader book on the political history of mass education should address.

The book reflects my own original research and also builds on the important work of many historians who have studied the education systems of their home countries. I have done my best to give them credit in these pages, but because I began reading history of education books well before it ever occurred to me that I would write my own book on this topic, I did not initially keep track of all the historians whose work has shaped my own thinking. For that, I apologize.

The case study of Argentina in chapter 4 benefited from historical statistics that were digitized and generously shared by Roy Elis. The cross-national analysis in chapter 7 draws on the Varieties of Political Indoctrination in Education and the Media Dataset, which I coauthored. I thank Anja Neundorf, who led the creation of this dataset, for giving me early access to it.

For funding that enabled the research for this book, I thank the Stanford Interdisciplinary Graduate Fellowship, the Stanford King Center on Global Development, the Freeman Spogli Institute for International Studies, the Europe Center at Stanford University, the Center for Global Development, the Hellman Fellowship, and UCSD's Yankelovich Center Book Improvement Grant, the School of Global Policy and Strategy, the Department of Political Science, and the School of Social Sciences.

I am also indebted to my students, including those who provided invaluable research assistance—Audrey Byrne, Leonardo Falabella, Tomás Lavados, Katy Norris, Lindsay Van Horn, and Samuel Williams—and many others who have helped me improve my ability to promote critical thinking in the classroom. I hope this book will give them a better understanding of why I put so much emphasis on this.

At Princeton University Press, I want to thank Eric Crahan, Alena Chekanov, and especially Bridget Flannery Mc-Coy for their enthusiasm for this project, for helping me understand the book publication process, and for their guidance and excellent suggestions on how to improve the manuscript. I also thank Jill Harris for ensuring a smooth production process and Karen Verde for careful and timely copyediting. Finally, I was fortunate to receive brilliant feedback from Joel Mokyr, to whom I remain grateful for including the book in a series I hold in the highest regard.

I am grateful to friends from all walks of life—scattered across Argentina, Canada, Chile, the United States, Uruguay, and Europe—for their constant encouragement. Their interest in reading the book provided a boost of enthusiasm and disciplined me to write it in a clear and accessible way.

My family, too, supported me through this adventure. My sister Emilia, Dona, my mother, her parents, my brothers, Fafi, my in-laws, and my nieces and nephews have all contributed to this book in more ways than they know.

My deepest gratitude goes to Martín, who in addition to helping me improve this book with his sharp mind and careful read of every draft, is the most loving, patient, and supportive husband. There is no one else with whom I would rather share this precious journey. This book is dedicated to him.

RAISED TO OBEY

CHAPTER ONE
EDUCATION AND SOCIAL ORDER

Education can be a powerful policy tool to reduce poverty and income inequality. This much is widely conceded. Yet in many countries around the world, the schools that low-income families access fail to teach children the skills they need to escape poverty. Although most countries have attained universal access to primary education, about one-third of children with four years of schooling are unable to read a simple sentence. The most common explanation for such dismal learning is that governments simply do not know how to promote skills among children. This line of thinking has spurred hundreds of expensive studies designed to identify which education policies work best to promote skills. I depart from this approach by looking at the political history of public primary education systems to determine what motivated governments to provide education to the lower classes in the first place. Were these systems set up to reduce poverty and inequality, or did they seek to accomplish a different set of goals?

Two major historical transformations that took place in the last two centuries have shaped the character of modern education systems. First, breaking with the tradition of leaving the upbringing of children entirely to parents, local communities, and churches, central governments in the nineteenth century began to intervene directly in the education of children, establishing rules about educational content, teacher training, and school inspections, and mandating children to attend state-regulated schools. Second, these state-regulated primary education systems expanded in size and eventually reached the entire population. While in the early twentieth century only a handful of countries had universal access to primary education, today this is the norm virtually everywhere. What prompted the expansion of primary education systems, and why did states become involved in regulating them?

Much of what has been written in the last half century points to democratization, industrialization, and military competition as key factors that prompted governments to expand primary education largely to improve the literacy, numeracy, or other skills of the population. These explanations, we will see, do not adequately account for why the Western societies of Europe and the Americas led this expansion. What's more, many existing explanations either forget or ignore where education systems come from. They assume, for instance, that because education systems today have the potential to reduce income inequality, promote economic growth, or contribute to military strength, they must have become popular among policymakers for these reasons—and must have been designed to accomplish these goals. Or they assume, alternatively, that because education systems today often seek to inculcate nationalism, they must have emerged for this reason. I do something different by going back in time to examine what the long history of state-regulated primary education can tell us about the systems we have today.

Looking at history teaches us that central governments in Western societies took an interest in primary education first and foremost to secure social order within their territory. Fear of internal conflict, crime, anarchy, and the breakdown of social order, coupled with the perception that traditional policy tools such as repression, redistribution, and moral instruction by the Church were increasingly insufficient to prevent violence, led governments to develop a national primary education system. Central governments went to great lengths to place the masses in primary schools under their control out of concern that the "unruly," "savage," and "morally flawed" masses posed a grave danger to social order and, with that, to ruling elites' power. The state would not survive, education reformers argued, unless it successfully transformed these so-called savages into well-behaved future citizens who would obey the state and its laws.

State-regulated primary education systems, then, emerged fundamentally as a state-building tool. State-building, understood as the process of consolidating the power of a centralized political authority commonly known as the state, is a multifaceted process that unfolded over many centuries. Wars between different rulers played a role in driving this process, leading rulers to invest in creating a centralized taxation apparatus that could be used to finance a permanent army.[1] But external threats were not the only factor affecting the consolidation of central rulers, and armies were not the only mechanism by which they sought to enhance political control. Mass violence *within* the boundaries of a central ruler's territory also posed a challenge to the ruler's effort to develop a monopoly over the legitimate use of violence. While rulers deployed the army, and later, police forces, to repress the disorderly masses, internal threats also motivated them to invest in primary education systems designed to forge social order through indoctrination.

Key to this state-building endeavor was the effort to inculcate a set of moral principles that exalted the value of obedience and rejected the individual use of violence. Every aspect of primary education systems was crafted to teach children to obey existing rules and authorities, and accept the status quo. National curriculums emphasized moral education more than they emphasized skills or the cultivation of nationalist sentiment. Teacher training and certification policies focused on recruiting teachers of exemplary moral character who could model good behavior in the classroom and local community. Centralized inspection systems attempted to safeguard a general atmosphere of discipline and order in schools.

Primary education systems, then, were conceived as part of a repertoire of policy tools used by the state to consolidate its power. The ability to promote social order and prevent violence lies at the core of what defines a state and what gives it legitimacy, so much so that societies afflicted by recurring internal conflict are usually termed "failed states." Throughout human history, those with political power have turned to three main strategies—repression, concessions, and indoctrination—to maintain and consolidate not only social order but also *the existing political order*—the status quo, so to speak, in terms of who holds political power and who is subjected to that power. Physical repression is the most obvious of these strategies: the threat or actual use of force can often persuade people to do or refrain from doing something. It is no coincidence that in premodern societies, and in many societies today, political power has often been concentrated in the hands of those who have the greatest capacity to repress others.

Concessions are another common strategy used to promote social order and acquiescence. Concessions—material, institutional, or symbolic—seek to reduce the reasons for fighting against the status quo by directly

1. Levi (1988); Tilly (1990); Dincecco (2011); Queralt (2022).

addressing the problems and injustices that prompt people to fight. An extreme form of concession entails redistributing political power—changing the status quo—but there are many other less radical concessions that can promote social order without fundamentally altering the balance of power. Redistributing economic resources to less affluent sectors of society or improving the quality of people's lives by providing public services they value are examples of concessions that can reduce the incentives to fight, at least in the short term.

Because public education today is often highly prized by families seeking to improve their children's job prospects, its provision is usually conceptualized as a progressive policy tool that governments use when they want to improve the lives of less affluent members of society. Indeed, one of the reasons why the United Nations advocates for education provision in post-conflict settings is to address economic grievances that, if left unaddressed, could lead to a recurrence of violence.[2] However, during its early stages, mass education was rarely conceived as a concession to appease rebellious sectors of society or address societal demand. In fact, many central governments made efforts to expand education *despite* their perception that parents largely objected to sending their children to school.[3]

The emergence of public primary education systems targeted at the masses—not secondary education or universities, which until recently were limited to elites—fits into a third type of strategy used to promote social order: indoctrination. If physical repression seeks to reduce the probability that those who fight against the established order will succeed, and concessions seek to reduce the probability of conflict by addressing the grievances that make people angry, mass education systems emerged to convince people that the status quo was actually okay, that there was no reason to rebel against it, and that accepting and respecting the status quo would elevate them morally and earn them praise from others. These systems were designed to fulfill a task that churches had been fulfilling for centuries: to mold children's hearts and minds to make them loyal subjects—but loyalty to God was replaced by loyalty to the state, the priest became a teacher certified by the state, and the temple became a school regulated and inspected by the state.

---

2. UNESCO (2011), pp. 160–171.
3. Andersson and Berger (2019); Squicciarini and Voigtländer (2016); Cinnirella and Hornung (2016); Baker (2015); Tapia and Martinez-Galarraga (2018); Cvrcek and Zajicek (2019).

The idea that primary education systems in Western societies were originally designed to indoctrinate may be difficult to fathom for some readers. Today, the word "indoctrination" has a strongly negative connotation, especially in developed democracies, where it is usually reserved to describe the brainwashing that takes place in totalitarian communist or fascist regimes. But in the nineteenth and beginning of the twentieth centuries, education philosophers and reformers in the United States would routinely and openly talk about the important indoctrination goal of schools. It was only after World War I that they gradually stopped using the word to describe their own systems and started talking instead about the "socialization" function of schools.[4] What they meant by socialization, however, was precisely what indoctrination means according to the *Oxford American Dictionary*, which defines indoctrination as "the process of teaching a person or group to accept a set of beliefs uncritically." This is the definition I adopt. It implies that one can indoctrinate children to believe that their ruler was chosen by God and therefore deserves absolute obedience, to believe that they belong to a superior group that should exterminate all others, or to believe that they should give all their property to their ruler. But it also implies that one can indoctrinate children to believe that poverty can be overcome through hard work, that one should only express discontent through nonviolent means, or that democracy is the best political system in the world. What makes something indoctrination is not the *content* being taught; what characterizes indoctrination is that the *process* of teaching this content leaves no room for questioning or critical thinking.[5]

This characterization of education as a policy tool deployed for social control will surely encounter initial resistance from those who believe that schools should give us the power and capabilities to pursue our goals and

---

4. The *Oxford American Dictionary* defines socialization as "the process of learning to behave in a way that is acceptable to society." But who decides what constitutes behavior that is acceptable "to society"—is it members of society at large or only a few elites? For example, when oppressed groups who have no formal voice in politics are taught that they should not use violence to make demands, is the "acceptable behavior" that is being taught one that serves societal interests or one that serves the interests of powerful elites who benefit from the status quo?

5. For a summary of how the usage of the word "indoctrination" has changed over time in the United States, see Gatchel (1959). See also the influential speech delivered in 1932 before the Progressive Education Association by George S. Counts, Columbia University professor and former president of the American Federation of Teachers (Counts 1932). A more recent discussion of how indoctrination is defined by philosophy of education experts—supportive of how the word is used in this book—appears in Callan and Arena (2009).

dreams. I should therefore clarify at once that there is no doubt in my mind that schools *should* seek to empower us to lead autonomous lives. But the main question that this book examines is not a normative one. I am not asking what goals *should* guide the design of education policies. I am asking what goals *actually* guided the design of primary education systems. Was an interest in empowering ordinary people what usually motivated states to promote primary education for the lower classes? Historically, the answer has been no. When central governments in Western societies decided to take over and increase the provision of primary schools for the poor, in general they were not particularly interested in equipping them with the capabilities to live autonomous, prosperous lives. In fact, it was not uncommon for national elites who supported primary schooling to argue that primary schools should *refrain from* promoting social mobility. What usually brought elites together around proposals for mass education was a deep fear that their power was at risk and a conviction that they could mitigate that risk by teaching the masses what to believe and how to behave.

As a strategy for maintaining social order, indoctrinating children to accept the state's unquestioned authority had primarily long-term goals. Six-year-olds who quarreled with each other, rolled their eyes at the teacher, or spoke without permission were not themselves considered an imminent threat to society. What elites feared was the danger that these children would pose as adolescents and adults if their habits and manners were not reformed. The bet that elites made was that investing in children's moral education today would lessen the need for repression and concessions tomorrow, simply because there would be fewer episodes of social disorder to begin with.

The argument that education systems have social control goals will be familiar to some readers. However, this argument never had much influence outside of sociology, and even there, it lost ground in recent decades.[6] Some critics dismiss it as a "cynical" interpretation of history.[7] The heavier blow, however, has come from critics who claim that social con-

---

6. Pierre Bourdieu, Michel Foucault, and Émile Durkheim are among the most influential writers associated with social control theories of education. For a synthesis of these and other sociologists' contributions, see Nash (1990); Filloux (1993); Jasper (2005); and Van den Berg and Janoski (2005).

7. Lindert (2004), p. 99.

trol theories suffer from "evidentiary failure."[8] This book revives these theories by providing a wealth of evidence that social control goals were, in fact, at the heart of the rise and spread of primary education systems in Western societies. Furthermore, the book refines this class of theories by bringing back and clarifying the important role that *states* played in designing and deploying this policy tool—shedding light on *when*, *why*, and *how* states advanced social control goals through mass education.[9]

Why should we care about the origins of state-regulated primary education systems? Perhaps most important, because they remain deeply embedded in the character of modern education systems. The World Bank has decried that the developing world faces a "learning crisis" characterized by the failure of education systems to teach basic literacy and numeracy skills, while the OECD has warned developed countries of the need to abandon rote learning and encourage critical thinking skills. Donors have invested millions of dollars in studies that seek to identify which education policies can address the problem of limited skills acquisition among students.[10] Departing from this focus on the limitations of current education policies, this book offers a broader perspective that highlights the deep historical roots of modern education systems' lackluster performance with teaching skills. It suggests that a key reason behind this phenomenon is that central governments did not create or design primary education systems with the aim of improving the basic skills of the population, much less their critical thinking skills. While the goals of education have expanded over time, and many education systems today do have the explicit goal of promoting skills, the political motivations behind education reform have changed less than we might think. Today, like in the nineteenth century, classrooms remain organized in similar ways—centered around the authority of the teacher rather than the interests of the child—with docility and obedience remaining important goals of mass schooling.

---

8. Boli, Ramirez, and Meyer (1985), p. 154. Interestingly, these critics rejected social control theories of education without providing any evidence against them.

9. The state is notably absent from Bourdieu's work (Van den Berg and Janoski 2005). Foucault, despite writing extensively about the disciplinary function of schools, famously argued for the need to move away from a focus on the actions of the state (Foucault 1995). Norbert Elias's influential book, *The Civilizing Process*, surprisingly neglects the effort that states made through primary education to teach children to self-regulate their emotions and behavior in order to reduce violence in public spaces (Elias 1994).

10. World Bank (2018).

THE EMERGENCE AND EXPANSION OF MASS EDUCATION SYSTEMS

The history of mass education systems can teach us a lot about why these systems look the way they do today. By examining when these systems emerged, why they expanded, and what shape they took, we will be able to say something about why mass education systems became a feature of modern states and why a teacher-centered approach to education became the norm.

EMERGENCE OF MASS EDUCATION SYSTEMS

To understand why state-regulated primary education systems emerged, we need data that enable us to track *when* central governments around the world began to intervene in primary education. Intervention often takes many different forms, including regulation, funding, and monitoring of primary education. I use two different datasets to identify the timing of various types of intervention. The first dataset covers 111 countries and includes information about the year when the central government of a sovereign country or its preceding colonial regime began to monitor primary education systems and, in particular, student enrollment. Monitoring enrollment allows governments to track the progress made in promoting primary education and can be used to inform decisions about where to fund or construct new schools. To complement this information, for a subset of thirty-three countries in Western Europe and Latin America I also collected detailed data about other forms of intervention, such as the year when central governments began to fund primary schools, regulate the curriculum and teacher certification, mandate universal provision, and establish compulsory schooling.

As a way of introducing the data, figure 1.1 shows the percentage of countries in Europe and the Americas on one hand and in the rest of the world on the other, where the central government monitored primary school enrollment from 1800 to the present. From the picture we can see that, while in 1800 no central government in the world made systematic efforts to collect information about primary school enrollment rates, all of them do so today. The figure also shows that in Europe and the Americas, central governments took an interest in monitoring primary education much earlier than in other parts of the world. Indeed, while all central governments in Europe and the Americas were already collecting information about pri-

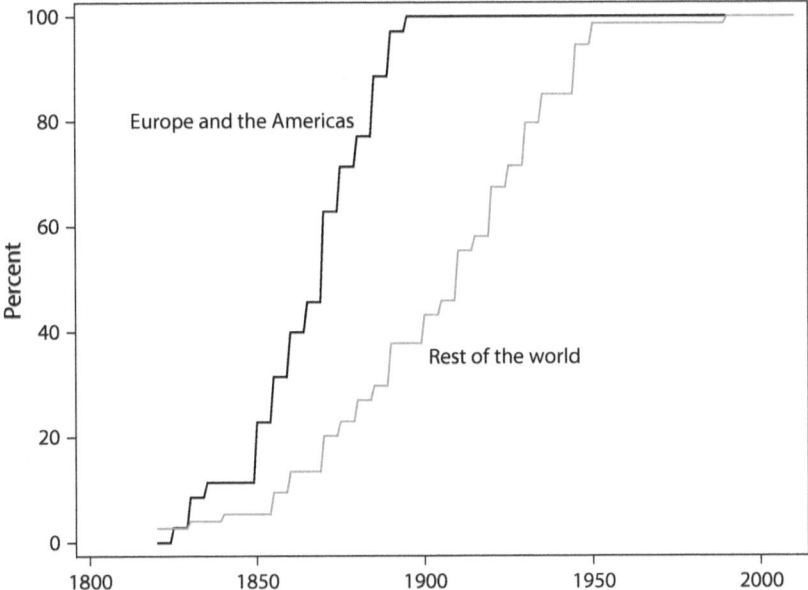

Figure 1.1. Percentage of countries in the world where the central government monitors primary school enrollment, 1820–2010. See text and footnotes for sources and methodology.

mary school enrollment before the end of the nineteenth century, it took until the mid-twentieth century for the rest of the world to catch up.

In addition to monitoring the progress made in promoting primary education, the nineteenth century saw the emergence of additional forms of central government intervention in primary education in Western societies. In figure 1.2 we can see what percentage of central governments in Europe and Latin America provided funding for primary education, imposed a national curriculum, became involved in certifying and/or directly training teachers, and passed a compulsory education law, again from 1800 to the present. The figure also shows what percentage of central governments regulated primary education in *any* of these or other ways such as monitoring enrollment, mandating local governments to provide universal access to primary education, or abolishing school fees for the poor. While in the United States and Canada most of the regulation of primary education happens at the subnational level, figure 1.2 shows that by the end of the nineteenth century, all European and Latin American countries not only monitored

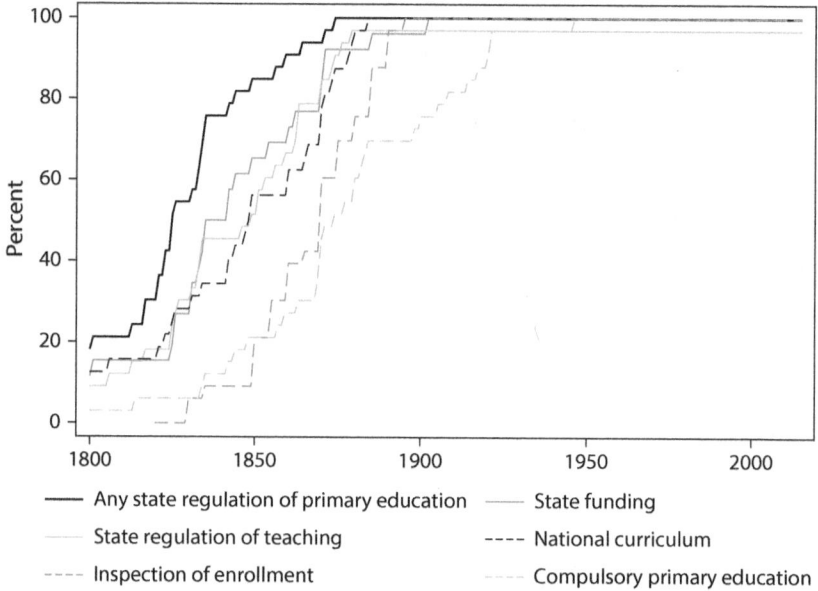

Figure 1.2. Percentage of countries in Europe and Latin America where the central government intervenes in primary education, and type of intervention, 1800–2010. See text and footnotes for sources and methodology.

enrollment in primary schools but also provided funding to promote primary education, regulated the certification and/or training of teachers, and imposed a national primary school curriculum. In fact, each of these forms of state intervention tended to precede central governments' efforts to monitor enrollment. Compulsory schooling laws were the last form of state intervention to be introduced, but by 1900, 70 percent of European and Latin American countries had a compulsory schooling law, and all did so by the 1920s.

While today we take for granted that central governments shape the education of young children in some way, figures 1.1 and 1.2 make it clear that state intervention in primary education is a relatively recent phenomenon in human history. Before states became involved, the task of educating children usually fell under the responsibility of parents and religious organizations. However, starting with a few European countries in the eighteenth century, a major transformation took place: central governments began to play an increasing role in educating children. The move toward the creation of state-regulated primary education systems was led by Europe and the Americas during the nineteenth century, and eventually spread to the rest of the world during the twentieth century.

EXPANSION OF MASS EDUCATION SYSTEMS

The second major educational transformation, one that accompanied the state's emerging regulatory role, was the expansion of access to primary schooling. Access to education is typically measured by enrollment rates—the total number of students enrolled in primary school as a proportion of the population ages 5–14 years or as a proportion of the school-age population. Enrollment rates are not a perfect measure, but they are the most common measure of education provision used to study the history of primary education systems because of their availability: almost all countries have collected and reported student enrollment figures for a long time.[11] The same cannot be said of statistics about the number of schools or the level of public spending on education, whose availability varies a lot more across countries and over time.

To examine how access to primary education changed in Western societies over time, I collected primary school enrollment statistics for forty-two countries in Europe and the Americas from 1828 to the present. Collecting enrollment statistics going far back in time was a major undertaking that involved consulting a large number of primary and secondary sources. This effort yielded a new dataset that covers a longer time period for Europe and the Americas than any other previously assembled cross-country dataset. To compare how enrollment evolved in Western societies and the rest of the world, I complement my original dataset with a dataset on enrollment compiled by economic historians Jong-Wha Lee and Hanol Lee.[12] The main difference between my dataset and theirs reflects the trade-offs that are involved in this type of time-consuming data collection project: While their dataset includes information from 111 countries across all regions, mine has more complete historical coverage of Western countries during the nineteenth century. For example, my dataset contains four additional decades of historical data for Austria, Germany, and Norway; two additional decades

---

11. A child's enrollment in school depends not only on whether there is a school nearby but also on whether families have any reason to send their children to school. Because primary schooling is compulsory everywhere, and has been for a very long time, it is reasonable to assume that any statistics that fall below universal primary enrollment are likely to be driven by limited access.

12. Lee and Lee (2016).

for Costa Rica, Ecuador, France, and Spain; and one additional decade for Argentina, Brazil, and England. On the other hand, Lee and Lee's dataset covers all regions, especially from 1900 on.[13] Together, both datasets enable us to examine global patterns of educational expansion over a longer period than what has been possible when relying on enrollment statistics from UNESCO or other sources.

To illustrate some basic facts about the global history of mass education, figure 1.3 depicts enrollment rates from 1820 on. The graph on the left shows the mean enrollment rate in primary, secondary, and tertiary education around the world.[14] The graph on the right focuses exclusively on primary school enrollment rates, comparing the world mean with the regional means of Europe and Latin America using my dataset.[15]

Three basic facts are worth highlighting. First, the global expansion of primary education unfolded gradually throughout roughly two centuries from the 1800s to the new millennium, a period that also saw other major transformations such as the spread of democracy, the transition of many economies from agrarian to industrial, and the rise of independent postcolonial states in Latin America, Africa, and Asia. While in the 1850s only one in ten children were enrolled in primary schools worldwide, by 1940 a majority of children had access to schooling, and today, almost all countries provide universal or near-universal primary education. Notice how gradual and steady the expansion of primary education was, unlike the spread of democratization, which occurred in waves,[16] or progressive taxation of wealth, which took off after World Wars I and II.[17]

---

13. Although Lee and Lee estimate enrollment rates for all 111 countries from 1820 to 2010, the vast majority of nineteenth-century rates are extrapolated. For example, only nine countries in their dataset have non-extrapolated information before 1870, compared to seventeen countries in my dataset.

14. The data for this graph come from Lee and Lee (2016).

15. The data for this graph come from my original dataset as well as Lee and Lee (2016). I measure primary school enrollment as a proportion of the population ages 5–14 years, whereas Lee and Lee measure it as a proportion of the school-age population. The population ages 5–14 years is usually larger than the school-age population; the latter ranges from ages 6–12, 6–11, 5–11, etc. Therefore, enrollment rates computed as a proportion of the population ages 5–14 years will not only be smaller than those computed as a proportion of the school-age population, but also, they are unlikely to ever reach 100 percent, even when there is universal enrollment in primary education. Enrollment rates as a proportion of the school-age population can be easier to interpret, but they are also less accurate. This is because, while most historical censuses report the number of inhabitants ages 5–14 years, the same is not true for the school-age population, which can only be estimated by making assumptions about the age distribution of the population.

16. Huntington (1991).

17. Scheve and Stasavage (2016).

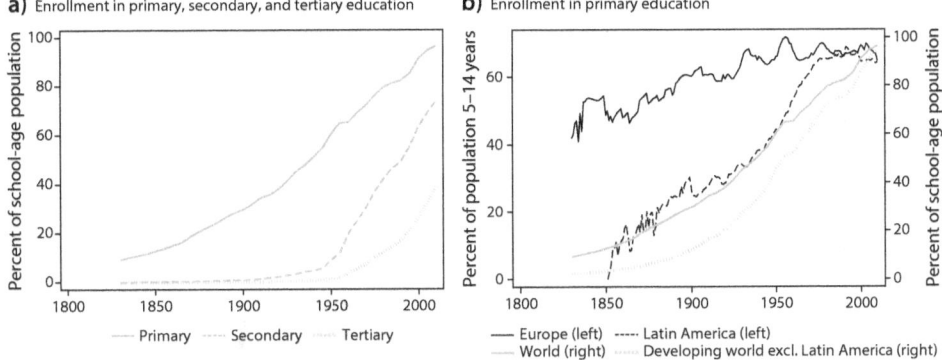

Figure 1.3. Average primary, secondary, and tertiary enrollment rates around the world, 1820–2010. Panel (a) shows average enrollment rates around the world in primary, secondary, and tertiary education institutions, as a percentage of the school-age population. Panel (b) shows average primary school enrollment rates, as a percentage of the population ages 5–14 years and as a percentage of the school-age population, around the world and in Europe, Latin America, and the rest of the developing regions. See text and footnotes for sources and methodology.

Second, primary education became widely available earlier than secondary and tertiary education. While much expansion of primary education took place during the nineteenth century, secondary and tertiary education only began to expand during the second half of the twentieth century. Up until that point, secondary and tertiary education were reserved and intended only for wealthy families; the lower classes only had access to primary education.

Third, in addition to leading the global rise of centralized education intervention and regulation, the Western societies of Europe and the Americas also led the expansion of access to primary education. Europe led the expansion of primary schooling around the world. Several European countries began to regulate and provide primary education to the lower classes already in the late eighteenth and early nineteenth centuries, before statistics became available. The leader was Prussia, which established comprehensive education regulations in 1763 and developed a worldwide reputation for having a model primary education system—all while still maintaining an absolutist regime and an agrarian economy. By around 1850, a majority of children in Europe were already enrolled in primary school, almost a century before the world reached this milestone. The United States and Canada followed Europe's lead in the early nineteenth century and eventually surpassed it in terms of the quantity of provision. Latin America came next: central governments began expanding primary education in the second half of the nineteenth century, several decades after independence. By the 1930s, a majority of school-age children in Latin America had access to primary school. The rest of the developing world lagged considerably behind Latin America.

A PATTERN THAT NEEDS AN EXPLANATION

What drove the expansion of mass education in the Western world? To better understand this expansion, we can look at how primary school enrollment rates evolved *within* countries following important changes in their political, economic, or social conditions. We can ask, for instance: Were transitions to democracy, the rise of an industrial economy, or the need to wage war with other countries followed by increased provision of primary education? How did the provision of primary education change in the wake of internal conflicts that made elites fearful of a breakdown of social order? Knowing when a country's primary school enrollment rate accelerated, stalled, or declined can help us identify which factors drove the expansion of primary schooling, which ones did not, and why.

Assessing the degree to which different political, economic, and social factors drove the expansion of primary schooling in Western societies will be the task of chapter 2, but figure 1.4 previews one of the main patterns identified in that chapter and explained in the rest of the book. The graph on the left-hand side shows how primary school enrollment rates changed on average within European and Latin American countries before and after they experienced a type of internal conflict that is known to bring about considerable political instability and concerns about the state's viability: civil wars pitting the masses against the state. To contextualize the role of internal conflict relative to the role of other factors commonly proposed as triggers of educational expansion, the graph on the right shows how enrollment changed within countries before and after they became democratic.

The pattern that emerges is clear: Violent internal conflict was followed by an acceleration in primary school enrollment rates not seen after transitions to democracy—and, as we will see in chapter 2, not seen either after interstate wars or the transition to an industrial economy. Starting with enrollment rates before and after a civil war took place, we see a marked acceleration in primary school coverage after the occurrence of a civil war. In chapter 2 we will examine these empirical patterns in greater depth and see

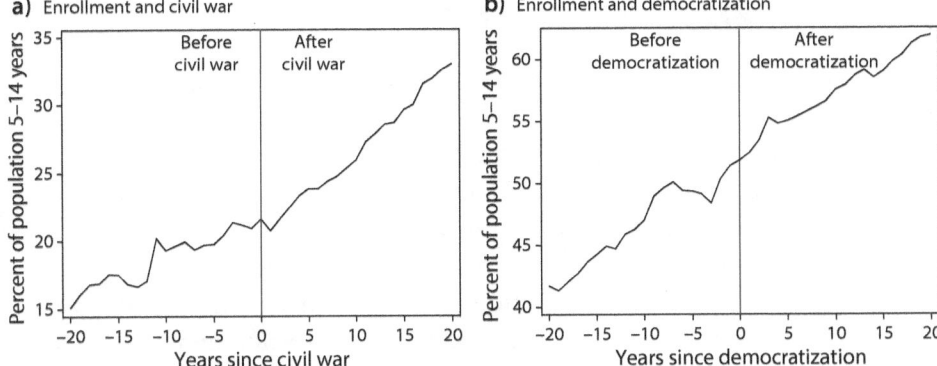

Figure 1.4. Average primary school enrollment rate before and after civil wars and democratization, 1828–2010. This figure reports average enrollment rates as a percentage of the population ages 5–14 years in the twenty years before and the twenty years after a country's first civil war or first transition to democracy from 1828–2010, across all European and Latin American countries that experienced civil war or democratization during that period. See text and footnotes for sources and methodology.

that, indeed, civil wars that pitted one or more groups against the state led to the expansion of mass schooling in Europe and Latin America. By contrast, when we compare education patterns before and after democratization, we see that, in general, there was no acceleration; enrollment rates grew at about the same rate after democratization as they did before.[18]

The main point is not that civil wars *specifically* were a key driver behind the expansion of mass schooling. The occurrence of civil wars simply provides us with a straightforward way to identify situations in which central governments felt threatened by the power of mass violence to upset the status quo. But there are many other situations where governments can feel this threat, too. Throughout the book we will consider a wide range of additional types of internal conflict, from food riots and mass protests to peasant revolts and revolutions, that also prompted the expansion of mass schooling, the introduction of a new curriculum, or some other centralized education intervention expected to pacify the population. The general story that all this evidence points to is the crucial role that elites' fears about the breakdown of social order have played in catalyzing education reform.

18. The effect of democratization on primary school enrollment rates is not the focus of this book, but I have published an in-depth study on this effect elsewhere; see Paglayan (2021).

MASS EDUCATION AS A STATE-BUILDING TOOL

Understanding why Western states led the world in creating and expanding primary education systems requires unpacking the goals of these systems and the conditions under which they became a priority. Although primary education systems pursue multiple goals, I argue that the main goals guiding their creation and expansion were political, not economic. And while schools can pursue many political goals, from teaching a specific partisan ideology to cultivating nationalist sentiments of superiority over other countries, I show that a key goal guiding the development of primary education systems was to promote internal peace and order and, with that, preserve the political status quo and consolidate the state's authority.

Education can in principle pacify disadvantaged members of society by imparting knowledge and teaching skills to obtain better jobs, thus addressing the economic inequalities that might otherwise lead people to rebel against the status quo. I argue that this was not the main goal of primary education systems in Western societies. These systems sought to pacify the population by instilling in people the importance of behaving well and accepting their place in society. If people learned to respect rules and authority figures from a young age, education reformers reasoned, they would continue doing so when they were adults. Because children's minds were believed to be a tabula rasa, imprinting them with proper manners and behaviors was considered a more effective long-term strategy for promoting order than waiting until they were adults to shape their behavior with physical repression or concessions.

From today's perspective, expanding primary education may seem like a counterintuitive policy to ensure that people stay put. That is because we often have in mind a liberal conception of education—one that equips us with useful capabilities to overcome early barriers and live prosperous, empowered, autonomous lives. Moreover, primary education today is often thought of as just the first stage in a longer educational career encompassing secondary schooling and higher education. However, this is not how state-regulated primary education systems were originally envisaged or designed. In the nineteenth century, when these systems first emerged in Europe, elites were often explicit that primary education should teach people to accept their material condition and place in society, and refrain from encouraging people to develop aspirations for social mobility. Nor was primary education during these foundational stages a stepping stone to further education. Recall that secondary schools and universities were reserved for elites until well into the twentieth century. Primary education, often called "popular instruction" or "popular education," was the one and only type of education commonly available to the lower classes.

The idea of placing all six-year-olds in a school to teach them a common set of beliefs and behaviors as part of a strategy of social order was popularized under absolutist Prussia in the late eighteenth century. We will devote much of chapters 3 and 4 to tracing the autocratic roots of primary education in Prussia and the arguments made in favor of schooling the population, precisely because of the influence that Prussian ideas had in other countries. Indeed, the autocratic origins of these ideas did not prevent them from traveling to more democratic countries too, including the United States. Horace Mann, the U.S. politician and education reformer who in an 1848 Report to the Massachusetts State Board of Education coined the famous phrase that education can serve as "the greater equalizer," also argued in that very same report that children should receive a moral and political education to prevent them from taking up arms or rebelling against the status quo.[19]

Ideas about the social control function of education may sound conservative today, but in the eighteenth and nineteenth centuries, when state-regulated primary education systems began to develop in Western societies, both conservatives *and* liberals agreed that the central goal of primary schools was to teach children obedience, discipline, and good behavior to support the stability of the state. Jean-Jacques Rousseau's ideas about the role of education are especially telling given the influence he had on liberals. In *A Discourse on Political Economy*, published in 1758, he articulates that it is in the state's own interest to regulate education in order to ensure that children are taught to be obedient:

> Inasmuch as there are laws for adulthood, there should be laws for childhood that teach obedience to others; and inasmuch as each man's reason is not left to be the sole judge of his duties, the education of children ought all the less to be left to their fathers' lights and prejudices, as that education matters to the state even more than it does to the fathers.[20]

---

19. Massachusetts Board of Education, Horace Mann, National Education Association of the United States (1848), p. 12.
20. Rousseau (2019a), pp. 21–22.

Despite the widespread circulation of arguments for state-regulated primary education systems during the nineteenth century, these arguments often preceded the actual emergence of these systems by several decades. Why? Not all national elites were initially on board with the idea that educating children was a task that the state should take on. While education reformers were convinced that placing the children of the lower classes in state-controlled primary schools was a good idea, oftentimes they encountered resistance from other national elites. The main opposition to these ideas came from elites who claimed that moral education, or the task of teaching people how to behave, should fall exclusively to the parents and the Church, as had been customary for centuries. The state, these elites argued, had no role to play in the upbringing of children. Another, more pragmatic, argument that prevented proposals for state-regulated primary education from coming to fruition was that the state simply lacked sufficient resources to support such an expensive endeavor. Occasionally, some members of the elite would also express their concern that educating the masses could lead to their empowerment and would therefore destabilize the status quo. However, this concern was less common than we might expect precisely because, throughout the nineteenth century, most elites believed that the type of education they would provide to the lower classes would lead them to accept, not question, their place.[21]

How did proposals for state-regulated mass education gain political traction? National elites who had previously opposed or been lukewarm about the idea of placing all children in primary schools regulated by the state became more amenable to this option when their concerns about the efficacy of traditional tools to maintain social order intensified. Of course, while it is safe to assume that elites always want to maintain power and protect the status quo from which they benefit, they have not always turned to primary education to accomplish this. Historically, physical repression, concessions, and the moral education provided by the Church were considered enough to accomplish the goal of pacifying the population. But when these tools were no longer sufficient in the eyes of elites, proponents of a national primary education system designed above all to shape the moral

---

21. England is an exception. There, as we will see in chapter 6, the idea that education could empower individuals was much more common than in continental Europe (Martin 2023). This, I will argue, helps explain why England expanded primary education much later than the rest of Europe.

character and behavior of the masses found a window of opportunity to convince other elites to support their proposal.

One common factor leading to the intensification of concerns about the efficacy of existing tools to pacify the population was the occurrence of crises of internal order. These crises helped forge a large coalition of support for primary education proposals among national elites. Crises of internal order that interrupted a period of relative internal peace and stability led to the diagnosis that existing policy tools were insufficient to promote order and helped convince elites that they needed new policies to prevent future crises. These events increased elites' fear of losing their property, lives, and power to the masses, and often revealed the limitations of existing tools to maintain social order on their own—for instance, when police officers joined hungry rebels in protest or when rebels were willing to risk life and limb to bring about deep change.

This diagnosis in turn helped increase national elites' support for shaping the moral character of children through state-regulated primary schools designed to prevent future citizens from questioning the state or its laws. Some elites who had previously opposed the creation of a national primary education system on the grounds that moral education should be left to the Church no longer argued that the state should not educate children—they argued, instead, that in educating children, the state should use religious doctrine as the basis for teaching morality. Similarly, those who had previously argued that such a system could not be sustained by the state's fiscal revenues now turned to debating alternative ways to finance these systems. Consistently, what emerged after periods of political instability and internal conflict, especially those in which repression failed to bring a quick end to the conflict, was an effort to expand primary schooling to teach children obedience to the state.

A wide range of types of internal conflict motivated central governments to invest in the education of the masses, including mass rebellions, peasant revolts, insurrections, civil wars with popular involvement, social revolutions, and conflicts whose nature ranged from class conflict to center-periphery, secular-religious, or ethnic conflict. The commonality across the diverse types of internal conflict that motivated central governments to invest in mass education was that they were violent and included the participation of the masses, even if not all conflicts were led by them. Regardless of whether the masses were acting on their own, or were mobilized by local elites in the periphery, the Church, or some other actor, mass violence brought together previously divided national elites to support centralized education efforts designed to protect their common state-building project.

To be sure, central governments have not always responded to internal conflict by turning their attention to mass education. Mexico, for example, had persistent internal conflict throughout the nineteenth century and a revolution at the beginning of the twentieth century, yet until the 1920s, access to primary education in Mexico lagged considerably behind the rest of Latin America. Argentina, similarly, had recurrent civil wars that lasted six decades after independence, yet it was not until 1884 that the central government began to regulate primary education. We will spend an entire chapter examining the conditions that must be in place for governments to respond to internal conflict through mass education.

Furthermore, even if central governments respond to internal conflict by expanding primary education, they might do so not necessarily because of an interest in indoctrinating children to obey the state, as the book argues, but for other reasons. First, governments might simply expand access to education to address societal demands for improvements in the standard of living. That is, perhaps the expansion of primary education in the wake of episodes of internal conflict represents a concession to angry citizens rather than an effort in social control. Second, governments might expand access to education in post-conflict settings to increase the skills of the population as part of a broader economic reconstruction strategy. Third, governments might provide education not so much to shape the moral character of future citizens but, more importantly, to promote a common language or religious identity as part of a nation-building project. We will consider each of these possibilities before concluding not only that indoctrination through primary schools was a crucial component of the repertoire of state-building tools used to promote long-term social order, but also that in the history of primary education systems, state-building goals usually preceded redistributive, economic, and nation-building goals.

To understand the emergence and expansion of state-regulated primary education systems in Western societies, we will look beyond school enrollment rates to learn how central governments in Europe and Latin America throughout the nineteenth century designed primary education systems, what goals they were hoping to achieve, and why education became subject to centralized control rather than being left to local parishes or communities as it had been in the past. We will devote several chapters to these questions. Transcripts from parliamentary debates, letters between politicians, special reports commissioned by the central government, and other written materials will give us useful information about the kinds of arguments politicians made in favor of mass education.

The content of landmark national education laws will also help us understand how politicians designed primary education systems. These laws created centralized bureaucracies to regulate primary education, established a common mandatory curriculum, dictated how teachers ought to be trained and certified, and created mechanisms to monitor whether schools were doing a good job at accomplishing the state's goals for primary education. In addition to helping us picture the type of education that elites had in mind, these landmark laws can also help us understand the underlying goals of primary education systems because the shape of these systems reflected these goals.

Both the political debates surrounding the passage of national primary education laws and the content of these laws, we will see, point to the primacy of moral education goals in explaining central governments' effort to regulate and expand primary education. When debating whether the state should intervene in the education of children, the arguments that found most support among national elites were those that stressed how a failure to reform the savage and poor moral character of the masses would lead to enduring problems of anarchy, crime, political instability, and the inability to consolidate the state's power. The importance of moral education is also evident in the first national primary education law passed in each European and Latin American country. Moral education was a pervasive component of national curriculums; typically, a standalone subject was devoted to it, but regardless, moral education was a cross-cutting component of all the subjects taught and of the organization of classrooms and schools. National textbooks used to teach reading and writing taught children about the importance of behaving well and respecting authority, and teacher manuals commissioned and distributed by central governments emphasized that students should learn to sit quietly, comply with rules, and respect the teacher at all times, and that failure to do so should be followed by public humiliation and other forms of punishment. The training of teachers emphasized the development of their own moral character, too. In many countries, state-controlled Normal Schools became the only authorized teacher training institutions, but even when nonstate actors were allowed to train teachers, states usually required aspiring teachers to demonstrate proof of their moral aptitude to teach.

By contrast, the first national education laws placed little emphasis on teaching math or scientific skills, and while some countries introduced a common language of instruction—a common marker of nation-building efforts—this was not the norm. In some, like France, the state promoted a common language of instruction for primary schools from the outset as part of its state-building endeavor to enhance the central government's control over the periphery by ensuring everyone could understand the state's laws and regulations. Still, we will see that, even in France, moral education took center stage in primary schools. Moreover, in several countries, including some of the leaders in primary education provision in Europe and Latin America such as Prussia and Argentina, the moralizing role of primary education emerged several decades before the state made an effort to inculcate a national identity. What the evidence suggests is that nation-building efforts sometimes accompanied and supported state-building goals, but frequently, primary schools pursued state-building goals through moral education *before* they also began to pursue nation-building goals.

In their effort to expand primary education, central governments often took advantage of the existing educational infrastructure that had been put in place by churches. While the Catholic Church made relatively little effort to educate the masses, Protestant churches founded schools, trained teachers, and developed pedagogical methods to teach everyone how to read the Bible in their own language.[22] The ability to rely on this existing infrastructure gave central governments in Protestant countries like Prussia and Norway a clear advantage over Catholic countries like Spain or Italy in terms of the level of access that already existed when they began to regulate primary education.[23]

Despite this greater initial stock, Protestant countries within Europe did not tend to set up state-regulated primary education systems any sooner—or any later—than Catholic ones. Prussia, the birthplace of Protestantism, was among the first states to pass a national primary education law, but England, also Protestant, was among the last, and Spain and Italy passed a national primary education law decades before countries like Belgium or Finland, which had a strong Protestant influence. In other words, what re-

---

22. Woodberry (2012); Gallego and Woodberry (2010).
23. Even *within* Prussia, those regions that had been more exposed to the Protestant Reformation exhibited higher levels of educational attainment than those less exposed to Protestantism; see Becker and Woessman (2009).

ligious denomination predominated does not help explain who led the creation of state-regulated primary education systems.

Moreover, the relationship between the state and the Church varied considerably across countries during the foundational stages of public primary education systems, from conflictive to cooperative. In Argentina, for example, the state's intervention in mass education came into conflict with the aspirations of the Church to maintain a monopoly over moral education. In Prussia and Chile, by contrast, the central government and the Church became allies in expanding access to primary education. In yet other cases, such as France during the July Monarchy, they were neither enemies nor allies: the central government made independent efforts to promote education but, because it lacked the capacity to expand mass schooling as fast as it wanted, anti-clerical politicians made the strategic decision to allow the Church to operate its own schools while subjecting these to centralized regulation. The common thread across these cases, we will see in chapter 4, lies not in the nature of the relationship between the state and the Church, but in the fact that efforts to create a national primary education system emerged out of centralizing rulers' heightened fear of the masses.

Where religious conflict *did* leave an important mark was on the content of the national primary school curriculums that emerged during the nineteenth century, as we will see in chapter 5.[24] Perceptions about the breakdown of social order brought together conservative and liberal elites around proposals for state-regulated primary education to shape the moral character of future citizens. However, the two groups disagreed fervently about whether moral education should include religious teachings or whether it should be entirely secular. The balance of power between them at the time when a national curriculum was introduced played a key role in shaping the outcome of this conflict.[25]

---

24. This argument is similar to Ansell and Lindvall (2013), who argue that the Church-State conflict did not really influence the process of centralization of education but did affect whether education became secular. While their measure of secularization focuses on who controlled the daily operation of schools, I focus on the content of national curriculums.

25. The ability of the Church to influence education policy also depends on the extent to which ruling elites, whether conservative or liberal, need the Church's support to remain in power. Fragile states such as those that rule immediately after a civil war, a democratic transition, or a newly independent country, may provide concessions to the Church such as the inclusion of religious teachings in schools in exchange for the Church's cooperation in promoting primary education in this fragile setting. See Grzymala-Busse (2015, 2016).

COMMON ARGUMENTS ABOUT MASS EDUCATION

Education systems are a heavily studied topic and this book both builds on and departs from what has been written about them by historians and social scientists. To clarify how the book's argument compares with other common explanations of the rise and spread of mass education, it is helpful to classify these explanations into two groups. The first group comprises what I will term *human capital theories* of education. These are theories that conceptualize the provision of mass education as a policy tool that seeks to improve the skills and knowledge of the population. Three main factors have been proposed as triggers for governments' decision to improve skills through mass education: *democratization*, which makes governments responsive to the demands for social mobility of the newly enfranchised masses;[26] *industrialization*, which increases the need for a large, skilled workforce;[27] and *military rivalry* with other states, which creates the need for skilled soldiers.[28]

The book's argument belongs within a second group of theories that I will refer to as *value-centered theories* of education. These theories conceptualize the provision of education as a policy tool that seeks to shape individual values, beliefs, attitudes, and behaviors ("values" for short). The most famous class of value-centered theories are *nation-building* theories of education, which argue that governments became engaged in mass schooling in an effort to construct a nation, using schools to promote linguistic homogeneity and emotional attachment to an imagined national community.[29] Social scientists have proposed four main triggers that prompted central governments to expand primary education for nation-building purposes. One is the *diffusion* of international ideas about the nation-building power of education. According to diffusion theory, governments created and expanded national primary education systems not because of domestic conditions that incentivized them to do so but because of their exposure

---

26. This theory is part of a more general argument that holds that transitions from autocracy to democracy, because they entail an increase in the political power of the newly enfranchised masses to make demands from elected officials, will result in more progressive redistributive policies. See Meltzer and Richard (1981); Acemoglu and Robinson (2006).

27. For a formal model of this common argument, see Bourguignon and Verdier (2000); Galor and Moav (2000, 2006). See also Gellner (1983), who stresses the importance to industrialization of having workers who could read and write in a common language.

28. Aghion et al. (2019).

29. Weber (1976); Gellner (1983); Darden and Grzymala-Busse (2006); Laitin (2007); Darden and Mylonas (2015); Ansell and Lindvall (2013); Alesina, Giuliano, and Reich (2021).

to international ideas in vogue during the nineteenth century that held that having a national primary education system to inculcate a shared national identity was a key element of successful nation-states.[30] Another argument is that governments invested in mass schooling because *industrialization*, and particularly the rise of factories, created the need for factory discipline and docile workers[31]—which presumably required imprinting in children the belief that they and their future supervisors were united by their customs, history, and nationality.[32] A third possibility is that *military rivalry* prompted governments to expand mass education to foster patriotism and nationalism not only among soldiers but also among all future citizens, so as to inoculate them from the territorial and sovereignty claims of foreign states.[33] Finally, a fourth theory holds that governments invested in primary education in response to the arrival of new *immigrants* whose assimilation into a new national identity required them to learn the national language and culture.[34]

It would be inaccurate to characterize these theories as arguing that primary education seeks to promote *only* skills or *only* values—and, by the same token, the argument I advance in this book does not hold that schools seek to shape values exclusively. All schools teach *some* amount of skills and *some* amount of values, and few social scientists would contest this. But social scientists are in the business of simplifying the world by identifying the most essential components of the phenomena they study. In studying primary education systems, they have come to different conclusions about what their essence is: some argue that these systems seek above all to teach knowledge and skills while others, myself included, conclude that they seek first and foremost to mold individual values, beliefs, attitudes, and behaviors.

The extent to which a theory helps explain why the Western societies of Europe and the Americas led the creation and expansion of state-regulated primary education systems is something we can only determine by looking

---

30. Boli, Ramirez, and Meyer (1985); Meyer et al. (1977); Meyer, Ramirez, and Soysal (1992).
31. Bowles and Gintis (1976); Gellner (1983); Mokyr (2002), pp. 120–162. The nineteenth-century economist Alfred Marshall was in favor of using education to develop in workers "a habit of responsibility, of carefulness and promptitude in handling expensive machinery," and to instill punctuality and a strong work ethic (Marshall 1890, p. 261). In contrast, Karl Marx and later Antonio Gramsci denounced the socialization function of schools to produce a class of workers who would respect the power of capitalists.
32. Gellner (1983); Weber (1976).
33. Ramirez and Boli (1987); Darden and Mylonas (2015).
34. Tyack (1974).

at the evidence. Comparing the explanatory power of different theories will be the task of chapters 2 and 5, where I examine the extent to which each explanation is consistent with the patterns of emergence and expansion of primary education systems, and with the characteristics of these systems. Here I preview key findings that will help readers contextualize the importance of the book's argument.

Let's begin by looking at three factors that do not go far in explaining why Western societies led the global expansion of primary education: democratization, industrialization, and interstate military rivalry. Regardless of whether we focus on their human capital or value-centered versions, each of these theories makes predictions that do not align well with the general timing of the rise and spread of primary education systems, or with the characteristics of these systems in Western countries.

Consider, first, democratization theories. If it were true, as economic historian Peter Lindert has asserted in an influential book, that "the spread of democratic voting rights played a leading role in explaining ... the rise of primary schooling,"[35] then we should observe that primary school enrollment rates were low before the spread of democracy and increased considerably as a result of democratization. Much effort has gone into quantifying the precise magnitude of democracy's impact on primary schooling,[36] but these efforts miss the bigger picture: around the world, most of the expansion of primary education took place *before* the spread of democracy.[37] Some autocratic regimes such as the USSR under Stalin are well known for their efforts to educate everyone, but the non-democratic roots of primary education also extend to Western Europe and the Americas. As we will see in chapter 2, in Western countries that were once non-democratic, central governments began to regulate primary education roughly one century before the arrival of democracy. Moreover, close to 70 percent of school-age children in these countries were already enrolled in primary school *before* democracy arrived there for the first time.

Was the expansion of primary education a response to the needs created by industrialization? Let's begin first with the argument that industrialization required a large, skilled workforce. A growing number of economic

---

35. Lindert (2004), p. 105.
36. Brown (1999); Brown and Hunter (1999); Mariscal and Sokoloff (2000); Engerman and Sokoloff (2002); Lindert (2004); Brown and Hunter (2004); Stasavage (2005); Ansell (2010); Paglayan (2021).
37. Paglayan (2021).

history studies show that the First Industrial Revolution required a few "knowledge elites" who could contribute scientific discoveries and technological innovation, and a large *unskilled* workforce—a phenomenon that has led economic historians to describe the first phase of industrialization as a "deskilling" process.[38] The Second Industrial Revolution did require more skilled workers, and its arrival coincided with an acceleration of primary education provision in some Western countries, but in many others it arrived too late to be able to explain the emergence and expansion of primary education systems. On average across Europe and Latin America, central governments created state-regulated primary education systems six decades before the Second Industrial Revolution, and in a majority of Western countries, most children gained access to primary schooling before the second phase of industrialization began to unfold. Moreover, as mentioned earlier, the first national curriculums that governments adopted during the nineteenth century placed considerably more emphasis on teaching moral education than on teaching math, science, or practical technical skills.

The emphasis that curriculums placed on moral education is in principle consistent with the argument that state-regulated primary education systems emerged in response to the industrial economy's need for docile workers, but again, the timing of the emergence and expansion of these systems does not appear to align well with explanations that stress the role of industrialization. In addition, many national curriculums initially allowed instruction in multiple different languages—not the unifying language that Ernest Gellner and others had in mind when they argued that factory discipline required linguistic homogeneity. Moreover, if it were true that governments regulated and expanded primary education because industrialization created the need for a docile working class, then we should see more governmental efforts to expand primary education in industrial areas than in rural regions. Three pieces of evidence are at odds with this prediction. First, although industrialists eventually came to view mass schooling as a desirable policy, many of them initially opposed it because it conflicted with their ability to rely on child labor.[39] Second, as we will see in chapter 4,

---

38. Mitch (1999); Allen (2003); Clark (2005); Mokyr (2005); Squicciarini and Voigtländer (2015); De Pleijt (2018); Montalbo (2020).

39. The tension that existed between central governments and industrialists regarding mass education is carefully documented by Anderson (2018), who argues that governments in Europe adopted child labor laws because industrialists' reliance on child labor hindered their efforts to improve children's moral character through primary schooling.

in countries that led the expansion of primary education in Europe and Latin America, central governments tended to prioritize the expansion of primary education in *rural*, not urban, areas. Third, as I document in chapter 5, central governments often imposed different curriculums for rural and urban schools precisely to prevent the children of peasants from learning skills that could be useful for industry.

Military rivalry theories do not do well either when trying to explain the expansion of access to primary education in Western countries. Proponents of these theories often cite the comprehensive education regulations adopted in Prussia in 1763, immediately after the end of the Seven Years' War, and the 1880s Ferry Laws in France, adopted after the Franco-Prussian War of 1870. Yet, as we will see in chapter 4, the timing of these cases is often misunderstood. In Prussia, in fact, the king had approved similar education regulations *before* the outbreak of the war. In France, the centralization of primary education began in the 1830s and led to a rapid expansion of primary schooling such that, even *before* the Franco-Prussian War, France had already attained near universal primary education. Moreover, when we examine evidence from a larger set of countries, as I do in chapter 2, what we see is that while Western countries experienced a marked increase in primary school enrollment rates after interstate wars, this increase was merely a rebound to recover from the decline in enrollment observed during periods of war.

None of this is to say that democratization, industrialization, and military rivalry *never* explain the emergence and expansion of primary education systems. There is some evidence, for example, that democratization played an important role in driving the expansion of primary schooling in Sub-Saharan Africa.[40] There is also evidence that industrialization contributed to the expansion of mass education in some European and Latin American countries, even if there is no consistent pattern linking these two processes. Finally, in non-Western countries, both industrialization and interstate wars were followed by an acceleration in primary school enrollments. Still, for a consistent predictor of the emergence, expansion, and characteristics of primary education systems in Western societies, we need to look elsewhere.

Immigration waves also do not go far in explaining why governments intervened and invested in primary education. Two of the countries with the

---

40. Stasavage (2005).

greatest number of immigrants during the nineteenth century, the United States and Argentina, both provided high levels of primary education, yet in both cases, immigrants retained the right to send their children to schools whose language of instruction was not the national language. In the United States, for example, public schools during the nineteenth century taught not only English but also German, Dutch, Swedish, French, Polish, and Italian, depending on the composition of the local community.[41] Moreover, the arrival of immigrants prompted governments to adopt compulsory schooling laws especially in those states that received immigrants from countries that lacked a compulsory schooling law.[42] The fact that states were less interested in educating immigrant children if they or their parents had already gone to school abroad, even though, of course, the education these immigrants had received did not instill an American culture or identity, is a clear indication that inculcating a national identity was not a central goal of education intervention during the Age of Mass Migration.

That leaves us with the diffusion theory of education, which provides some helpful clues, and the argument I advance in this book builds to some extent on this theory. We will see in chapter 3 that, before the eighteenth century, the idea that the state could or should educate children was virtually inconceivable. But during the eighteenth and especially in the nineteenth century, mass education came to be conceived as a policy tool that could strengthen the state. The diffusion of this idea, I argue, was a precondition for the emergence and expansion of state-regulated primary education systems. Still, the circulation of these ideas was not enough—education reform proponents also needed to garner sufficient political support to implement these ideas.

This is where the role of crises of internal order proves helpful. Diffusion theory flatly rejects the notion that these crises promoted the rise and spread of state-regulated primary education systems.[43] By contrast, this book shows that national elites' fears of social disorder played a central role in giving political traction to the educational ideas that circulated during the nineteenth century, and shaped the patterns of education regulation and expansion. Heightened fears of social unrest help explain, for example, why the central governments of Chile and Argentina, despite being simultaneously

41. Tyack (1974); Fouka (2020).
42. Bandiera et al. (2019).
43. Boli, Ramirez, and Meyer et al. (1985), pp. 154–155.

exposed to European educational ideas since the early 1840s, created state-regulated primary education systems many decades apart from one another; or why the French government during the 1830s prioritized the expansion of primary education in the rural departments of southern France. These are not isolated examples. We will see that internal conflict involving mass violence against the state is a strong and consistent predictor of the expansion of primary schooling in Western countries.

The second key difference between my argument and diffusion theory lies in the types of values that each theory highlights. I emphasize schools' effort to shape moral values and principles—especially those rejecting individual violence—as part of a state-building agenda to consolidate the power of a central political authority. Primary education, I argue, sought to reduce long-term violence against the state by teaching people that killing, fighting, vandalizing, and other forms of violent behavior were wrong, and conversely, that respecting rules and authority was the right thing to do. Diffusion theory, by contrast, belongs to the class of nation-building theories of education that emphasize schools' effort to inculcate a common language and shared national identity. We will see that while some politicians believed that inculcating a national language and identity was complementary to the goal of enhancing the state's authority, many central governments pursued their moral education goals without concurrently advancing a nation-building agenda—at least until later. When state-regulated primary education systems emerged, teaching children good manners and moral principles—turning "savages" into well-behaved future citizens—was a more important educational goal than inculcating a common language or national identity.

Now that we have a fuller understanding of how other theories of mass education relate to the book's state-building argument, I will summarize some appealing characteristics of my argument.

THREE APPEALING CHARACTERISTICS OF THE ARGUMENT

The state-building theory of education reform that I propose has three appealing characteristics: it explains education reform in a wide variety of contexts, it encompasses other existing explanations to provide a more general theory of education reform, and it helps explain current problems facing education systems.

As I will demonstrate in later chapters, conceptualizing education reform as a response to internal threats to the power of ruling elites helps explain education reform in a broad range of political contexts. For example, while the book's argument applies to autocracies, helping explain the puzzling non-democratic roots of primary education systems, it can also explain education expansion and reform in more democratic contexts. Similarly, the argument I propose can help explain not only the emergence and expansion of primary education reform systems during the nineteenth century but also education reform in more recent decades. Nor does the argument apply only to governments that espouse a liberal ideology or, conversely, a conservative one. Finally, the argument I propose is not restricted to any particular type of internal conflict. It applies to conflicts of varying scale and nature, including class conflict, conflict between the center and periphery, and religious or ethnic conflict.

This is not to say that every instance of internal conflict will lead to education reform, or that every instance of education reform constitutes indoctrination—far from it. An important contribution of the book is to clarify the conditions under which we should expect governments to invest in mass education to inculcate obedience, and the kinds of contexts where this is less likely to occur. This is the task of chapter 6.

Another important feature of the book's argument is that it can encompass other common explanations of educational expansion as part of a more general theory of education reform. The spread of democracy, industrialization, interstate wars, and immigration waves are all factors that social scientists have proposed as drivers of the expansion of primary education. Each of these phenomena are distinct and important in their own right, but there is also a commonality across them: they have all been frequently accompanied by considerable social disorder and instability or, at the very least, heightened concern about these issues. Democratization was often a result of social revolutions or mass mobilization, and its arrival engendered deep fear among traditional elites about how the lower classes might behave after acquiring more political rights. Industrialization and urbanization also engendered new fears among elites about the rise of labor strikes, crime, homelessness, and the spread of diseases—all of which elites interpreted as signs of the deficient morality and behavior of the working class. Immigration waves, too, have created concerns about the rise of criminal behavior and the decline of law and order. And interstate wars often give way to internal turmoil not only among losers but also in victorious countries, where the transition from soldier to unemployed civilian can create new social divisions and conflict. In other words, processes of democratization, industrialization, immigration waves, and interstate wars often coincide with crises of internal order and periods of social and political instability. When they do, I argue, states are likely to turn to mass schooling.

Last but not least, the book's emphasis on the centrality of indoctrination goals in guiding the creation, expansion, and features of primary education systems can help us make sense of the failure of many modern education systems to reduce poverty and inequality. The World Bank calls this failure a "learning crisis," alluding to the fact that children are not learning even basic literacy and numeracy skills despite attending school regularly. The traditional explanation of the so-called learning crisis is that education policymakers do not know how to promote more learning, hence the need to produce and disseminate experimental evidence about the efficacy of different education policy interventions. This book points to a different answer. It suggests that a key reason why education systems fail to reduce poverty and inequality is because that is not what they emerged to do. Acknowledging this may be the best step forward.

SHIFTING PARADIGMS: EDUCATION AND POWER

Once we recognize that mass education may reflect social control goals, we are urged to reconsider many influential theories that, implicitly or explicitly, conceptualize it as a policy tool that seeks to promote human capital. The paradigm shift that stems from this book helps us understand, for example, why autocracies provide a lot of mass schooling—despite modernization theory's famous prediction that education brings about democracy.[44] It also explains why state-regulated primary education systems emerged much earlier than the welfare state. And it offers a possible explanation for the frequent but puzzling observation that the spread of democracy has often failed to bring about higher taxes on the rich or other forms of progressive redistribution.[45]

---

44. Lipset (1960).
45. Ross (2006); Ansell and Samuels (2014); Scheve and Stasavage (2016).

But the most important implication of this reconceptualization of mass education is that it puts education back where it belongs: at the center of debates about power. It should hardly be surprising to academics, whose reputation depends so heavily on the influence of their ideas, that shaping how people think about the world can be an important source of power. And yet, some of the most influential theories of how governments consolidate their power minimize or altogether neglect the great lengths to which governments have gone to control the ideas that shape individual behavior in the political, social, and economic spheres. Consider, for example, Charles Tilly's famous theory of state formation and state-building, according to which the state derives its power from a combination of capital (taxes) and coercion (armies).[46] When confronted with the question of how states forged a monopoly of violence *within* their territory, Tilly argues that they relied on the army and, later, police forces.[47] This book shows that, beginning with Prussia under Frederick the Great, central rulers ascribed considerable importance to a third source of power: *ideological conformity*. In their quest to control the population, they made significant efforts to exert ideological power over their subjects as a means of reducing the use of violence by anyone other than the state.[48] The creation of state-regulated primary education systems should be understood as an internal security policy, not a social welfare or human capital policy.

A central question moving forward is whether education does, in fact, promote social order and political stability, and how its efficacy compares to other policy tools like repression and concessions. Exploring the *consequences* of education—how it shapes individual values, beliefs, attitudes, and behaviors, and what consequences it has for social order, political stability, the strength of states, the stability of autocracies and democracies, demands for economic redistribution, etc.—are important questions stemming from

---

46. Tilly (1990).

47. When considering the question of how monarchs secured "the acquiescence of nearly all of his subject population," Tilly argues that "over and over, rulers *sent troops* to enforce the collection of tribute, taxes, and levies of men of materials ... At the level of the state, ... those oriented to control the national population (police) developed only slowly" (Tilly 1990, p. 75; emphasis mine). Only in the nineteenth century, he argues, did European states establish "bureaucratic police forces specialized in control of the civilian population. They thus freed their armies to concentrate on external conquest and international war" (p. 76).

48. While Tilly (1990) does not consider the role of ideological power, Michael Mann's influential *The Sources of Social Power* does acknowledge it but downplays its importance. In his extensive volume, he makes no mention of the state-driven transformation of primary education documented in this book (Mann 2012).

this book, albeit distinct from the book's interest in explaining what *motivates* the provision of education.

Perhaps most important, moving forward we should ask what drives governments to curb some of their zeal to indoctrinate children and instead reform education systems to teach useful knowledge and skills. Understanding this is key for anyone eager to improve the extent to which education systems equip individuals with the capabilities to lead autonomous lives.

PLAN FOR THE BOOK

The plan for the rest of the book is as follows. Chapter 2 provides a comprehensive picture of global trends in primary schooling over the last two centuries, with a special focus on the Western societies of Europe and the Americas that led the creation and expansion of state-regulated primary education systems. Drawing on new cross-country datasets, I document a set of patterns that any theory of mass education systems needs to explain, such as the fact that these systems emerged well before the spread of democracy and reached a considerable portion of the population during nondemocratic and pre-industrial periods. In line with the book's argument, the chapter shows that internal conflict was a stronger and more consistent predictor of the expansion of primary education than democratization, industrialization, or interstate wars.

After establishing this pattern, chapter 3 develops the book's main argument for why internal conflict in general creates incentives for central governments to educate the masses. The chapter begins by surveying the history of ideas about education and shows that, around the eighteenth century, social contract theorists and Pietist (Protestant) reformers converged on the idea that mass education could support state-building by inculcating obedience. It also discusses the diffusion of these ideas among statesmen and education reformers first in eighteenth-century Prussia and then in other parts of Europe and the Americas. Crucially, I note that the diffusion of ideas alone is insufficient to explain the timing of centralized education intervention. To explain this timing, I develop an argument for why and how internal conflict and fears of anarchy, crime, and social disorder gave these ideas the political traction they needed for central governments to regulate primary education and promote its expansion. The chapter concludes by outlining the main predictions of the argument, which are tested in chapters 4, 5, 7, and 8.

Chapter 4 illustrates, through four case studies, why and how internal threats to social order and political stability led central governments to regulate and promote primary education. To do so, I trace the process of adoption, examine the content, and analyze the implementation of the foundational national education laws of Prussia, France, Chile, and Argentina. The analysis draws on a large collection of historical evidence including statistical data on school construction but also parliamentary debates, special reports commissioned by central governments, state-approved school textbooks, and other primary sources, as well as existing research produced by historians. Collectively, these sources show that internal conflict heightened national elites' anxiety about the moral character of the "savage" masses and increased elite support for mass education not to promote social mobility or industrialization but as part of an effort to promote long-term social order by indoctrinating children to become obedient citizens. Where historical statistics are available, I also show that central governments' efforts to expand primary schooling focused mainly on those regions that posed the greatest threat to the state. The four cases demonstrate that internal conflict has played a key role in explaining the rise of modern primary education systems across a wide range of non-democratic regimes, conservative and liberal governments, and types of conflict spanning the long nineteenth century.

How did central governments design primary education systems, and what does this tell us about the goals of these systems? Chapter 5 shows that moral education goals pervaded the design of these systems, as evidenced by the content of the curriculum, teacher training and recruitment policies, and school inspection mechanisms. I reach this conclusion after conducting an unprecedented analysis of the content of the first national primary education laws adopted in twenty-five European and Latin American countries. The same chapter presents the two competing models for teaching moral principles that existed in the nineteenth century, each reflecting a different view about the roots of morality: the conservative model, which viewed religion as the basis of morality, and the positivist liberal model, which viewed reason and scientific laws as the ultimate source of moral principles. A key insight from this chapter is that when the balance of power tilted toward liberal politicians, the curriculum included a good dose of math and science in line with these elites' belief that this was the most effective way to teach moral values. Ironically, in these cases, the effort to moralize the masses may have inadvertently equipped ordinary people with skills to move up the social ladder and, eventually, demand more political power.

After devoting chapters 4 and 5 to the rise and spread of state-regulated primary education systems in Europe and Latin America during the long nineteenth century, chapters 6 and 7 examine the ability of the book's argument to explain education reform in other contexts, too. Chapter 6 provides a conceptual framework for thinking about the conditions under which governments are likely to invest in mass education as an indoctrination tool to create obedient citizens. The framework posits that governments are more likely to invest in mass education when politicians (1) fear the masses, (2) believe that schools can indeed indoctrinate them, (3) expect to be in power long enough to reap the benefits of indoctrinating children, and (4) have sufficient fiscal and administrative capacity to promote education. These are, in political science jargon, the scope conditions of the argument. I illustrate the importance of these conditions through historical examples from England and Mexico, where the absence of at least one of these scope conditions helps explain why primary education provision lagged considerably behind the rest of Europe and Latin America for decades.

Chapter 7, in turn, moves away from the focus on nineteenth-century non-democracies to consider examples of democracies and recent cases where a heightened fear of mass violence led governments to invest in education for indoctrination purposes. Through examples from England, Peru, and the United States, the chapter suggests that, under certain conditions, the book can help explain education reform in a wide variety of contexts—even democratic ones. The same chapter also deploys a new global dataset on the prevalence of indoctrination in education systems to identify key differences and similarities between the education systems of democracies and autocracies from 1945 to the present.

Although the book focuses on the causes, not the consequences, of mass education, some readers may nevertheless want to know whether mass education actually succeeded in promoting social order. This is the focus of chapter 8. Instead of providing a "yes" or "no" answer, this chapter examines the factors that are likely to affect the success of education systems in accomplishing their goal. The discussion builds on the lessons from chapter 5 regarding how education systems were designed. In a nutshell, I argue that some of the national curriculums, teacher training policies, and other education policies commonly used to forge loyalty to the state, can and have backfired. Still, as I explain in that chapter, whether mass education succeeded in promoting long-term order and stability is irrelevant for the book's argument about what *motivated* the rise and spread of these systems. What we should observe if the book's argument is correct—and what we do observe, as I show in chapter 8—is that politicians *believed* that mass schooling could produce social order, regardless of what prior evidence suggested, and regardless of whether their beliefs were later proven correct or not.

Finally, chapter 9 examines how the historical roots of primary education systems continue to shape education today, helping explain current education systems' troubling performance in promoting skills. Understanding these roots is essential for well-meaning educators and education reformers, international organizations, and anyone committed to strengthening democracy and reducing inequality.

CHAPTER TWO

TWO CENTURIES OF MASS EDUCATION

Starting in the nineteenth century, the world experienced an education revolution characterized by the emergence of state-regulated primary education systems and their expansion to an unprecedented scale. The revolution was slow—it lasted about two centuries—and its timing and pace differed across countries. European states, as I anticipated in chapter 1, were the first to create primary school systems regulated by the state, in some cases already in the eighteenth century, and the first to reach high levels of primary education provision. They were followed by the United States and Canada, and later in the nineteenth century, by Latin American countries. The rest of the developing world caught up much later. Explaining why the Western societies of Europe and the Americas led the transformation of the educational landscape during the nineteenth century is one of the main goals of this book. In this chapter, I introduce some basic facts about this transformation and discuss how they do or do not align with common explanations of it.

One of the most pervasive beliefs today is that democratization and the spread of voting rights to the lower classes was a leading driver of the expansion of primary schooling in the West and around the world. Another possibility is that central governments became interested in regulating and promoting primary education—even in the absence of electoral pressure to do so—because of the needs created by industrialization or interstate military rivalry to train a literate and docile workforce or a cadre of skilled and loyal soldiers. We will see that these arguments do not take us very far in explaining why Western societies led the creation and expansion of state-regulated primary education systems. In fact, the evidence presented in this chapter implies that we need a theory of the origins of modern primary education systems that is consistent with the fact that these systems emerged and expanded under non-democratic regimes and in pre-industrial contexts.

The book argues that *internal threats* to the state-building agenda of centralizing rulers played an important role in motivating central governments to educate the masses for the purpose of instilling obedience to the state. As a first piece of evidence consistent with this argument, this chapter shows that internal conflict is a stronger and more consistent predictor of the expansion of primary schooling than democratization, industrialization, or interstate wars. Political rulers were especially likely to expand primary schooling in the wake of violent internal conflicts pitting the masses against the state.

USING EVIDENCE TO TEST THEORIES

Social scientists have put forth many plausible arguments about the factors that drove states to create and expand mass education systems. All these arguments are plausible in that they follow logically from a set of assumptions. However, an argument can be both logical and misleading—for instance, if it builds on false premises. Throughout this chapter, we will put different arguments to the test by assessing whether the claims they make about the patterns of emergence and expansion of primary education systems find support in the data. The goal here is not to explain the process of educational transformation in specific countries—that is something we will examine later in the book—but to see whether these different arguments are consistent with the *broad* patterns of educational transformation seen across Europe and the Americas.

To assess whether an argument indeed explains the emergence and expansion of primary education, in this chapter we will look at the two measures introduced in chapter 1: first, the year when central governments began to regulate primary education, and second, the provision of primary education as captured by primary school enrollment rates at the country level across two centuries. This is just a starting point. To further understand the reasons why central governments invested in educating the population, chapter 4 also presents evidence about the construction of schools, education funding, and other measures of investment in education, and chapter 5 examines what the first primary education laws in European and Latin American countries stipulated about the content of the primary school curriculum, how teachers ought to be trained and recruited, and how schools ought to be inspected.

INITIAL TIMING OF STATE INTERVENTION IN PRIMARY EDUCATION

Explaining the emergence of state-regulated primary education systems requires us to identify when central governments began to regulate primary education. Most states began to regulate and fund primary schools well before they became directly involved in the daily management of schools. When exactly did governments take an interest in regulating primary education? Was it before or after the spread of democracy? Was it before or after industrialization?

To answer these questions, I collected information about the year when central governments in thirty-three countries in Europe and Latin America began to: fund primary schools; manage them; establish a mandatory curriculum for all primary schools; establish certification requirements for primary school teachers; train prospective teachers; mandate local authorities to provide universal access to schooling; mandate free provision for the poor; and establish compulsory primary education.[1] I compiled this information by consulting more than eighty country-specific history of education books, articles, and doctoral dissertations published in English, Spanish, or Portuguese, supplemented by email consultations with history of education experts.[2]

To encompass countries in other regions too, I examine an additional form of governmental intervention that involves the use of official inspections and gathering of school-level statistics to monitor the state of primary schooling. Specifically, for 111 countries, I look at the first year when official statistics about student enrollment in public primary schools became available. This information was compiled by Jong-Wha Lee and Hanol Lee. The timing of these statistics provides a conservative estimate of when central

---

1. This information does not necessarily capture the earliest expression of politicians' interest in education because sometimes subnational governments had begun to intervene in primary education before central governments did, but it allows us to make conservative statements of the form "politicians were interested in primary schooling *at least as far back as X*."

2. Text sources provide 91 percent of the data; expert consultations, conducted when the dates could not be found in texts in English, Spanish, or Portuguese, provide 9 percent of the data.

governments became interested in primary schooling. This is because other forms of state intervention in primary education, such as the funding of education or the introduction of a mandatory curriculum, usually preceded governments' efforts to collect enrollment statistics.

TRACKING PRIMARY SCHOOL ENROLLMENT RATES FROM 1820 TO 2010

Explaining the expansion of primary schooling requires data that enable us to track this expansion across countries and over time. Efforts to track primary school enrollment rates at a global scale began in the 1960s under UNESCO's leadership, but by 1960, two-thirds of children were already enrolled in primary school. This means that if we rely on UNESCO statistics alone, we will miss most of the expansion of primary education. Moreover, by the 1960s, most countries in Europe and the Americas had already attained universal primary education or were close to doing so, had already undergone democratization and industrialization, and enjoyed peaceful relations with neighboring countries. If we want to understand the expansion of primary schooling and the role that democratization, industrialization, and interstate wars played in this expansion, we need data going much farther back in time.

To track primary school enrollment rates from the nineteenth century to the present, I will use two different but complementary datasets. The first is a dataset I constructed that includes annual primary school enrollment rates, measured as a proportion of the population ages 5 to 14 years, for forty-two countries in Europe and the Americas from 1828 to the present. Constructing this dataset involved consulting official statistical reports from individual countries, statistics assembled by local historians, and cross-country data compiled by others. The starting point was annual data compiled by Brian Mitchell on the number of students enrolled in primary school at the country level going back to the nineteenth century.[3] After assessing the reliability of Mitchell's annual data by contrasting it with decennial data from 1870 to 1940 compiled by Aaron Benavot and Phyllis Riddle, I extended Mitchell's series several decades backwards using close to sixty primary and secondary sources.[4] This included official statistical yearbooks published by central governments, datasets produced by historians specializing in a particular country, cross-national data on student enrollment

---

3. Mitchell (2007).
4. Benavot and Riddle (1988).

collected by the U.S. Bureau of Education from 1872 to 1915, and Peter Flora's well-known statistical volume on Western Europe.[5] The result of this effort is a dataset on primary school enrollment rates that covers a longer period for Europe and the Americas than any other existing cross-national dataset.[6] For example, while for nineteen countries the earliest data I found coincided with Mitchell, for twenty-three countries I extended the series backwards by twenty-six years on average.

The second dataset measures primary school enrollments rates as a proportion of the school-age population and was constructed by Jong-Wha Lee and Hanol Lee as part of the same data collection effort mentioned earlier. It has the advantage that it covers more countries and regions—in total, 111 countries in Europe, the Americas, Africa, and Asia. However, the data are quinquennial rather than annual and the period covered is more limited. In particular, although Lee and Lee extrapolated enrollment rates backwards to obtain *estimated* enrollment rates for all countries in their dataset starting in 1820, in reality only nine countries in their dataset have actual (as opposed to extrapolated) enrollment data before 1870, compared to seventeen countries in my dataset. Indeed, most countries in my dataset contain between one and four extra decades of historical data than that in Lee and Lee's dataset. Despite the sparsity of data preceding 1870 in Lee and Lee's dataset, their dataset provides relatively good coverage for the twentieth century: sixty-three countries have enrollment data beginning in 1900 and eighty-five countries have data preceding 1920. This enables us to cover a longer period than if we relied only on UNESCO's data, which begin in the 1960s.

Using two different datasets of primary school enrollment rates enables us to balance a common trade-off that researchers embarking on the time-consuming task of constructing historical cross-national datasets face: the trade-off between breadth (how many countries one chooses to cover) and depth (how well one covers those countries). My dataset provides the most complete available information about how primary school enrollment rates

---

5. Flora (1983).

6. The full list of sources for each country and year is available in the online appendix (https://press.princeton.edu/books/paperback/9780691261270/raised-to-obey). For a few countries, namely France and Spain, the enrollment figures obtained from the work of historians specializing in a given country differed markedly from those in Mitchell's (2007) dataset; in those cases, I opted to use the figures from these expert country historians. For most countries, however, the data in Mitchell and other sources matched closely, but these other sources enabled me to extend the time series backwards.

evolved in Europe and the Americas, but I will complement these data with Lee and Lee's dataset to provide a sense of how the expansion of education in Western countries compared to the rest of the world.

What do the data on the timing of central government intervention in primary education and the expansion of primary school enrollment rates tell us about when and why governments took an interest in primary schooling and expanded its provision? This will be the question at the back of our minds for the remainder of this chapter.

PRIMARY EDUCATION ACROSS COUNTRIES AND REGIONS

Before we explain why the Western world led the creation and expansion of state-regulated primary education systems, let's look at some basic facts and patterns about this educational transformation. Figure 2.1 shows average primary school enrollment rates in Prussia, the rest of Europe, Latin America, the United States and Canada, and the rest of the world from 1830 to 2010. From this graph, we can observe that in most parts of the Western world the rise of primary education systems began during the nineteenth century. Prussia was the precursor and world leader: its first comprehensive primary education law dates back to 1763; by the 1820s, its primary school enrollment rate was already around 70 percent of the population ages 5–14, equivalent to near-universal primary education when enrollment is measured as a percentage of the primary school–age population. In the rest of Europe, the expansion of primary schooling usually lagged behind Prussia, in some cases more than others. Nonetheless, Europe as a whole had much higher levels of primary education provision than most other parts of the world during the nineteenth century. Outside Europe, the United States began expanding primary education at a fast pace in the 1830s, reaching universal primary enrollment among white children in the 1860s, while Canada reached this milestone a few decades later. Latin American countries also began expanding primary education in the nineteenth century. Although the region did not reach universal primary education until after World War II, it did so earlier than the rest of the developing world. This is partly because central governments in Latin America began to expand primary education earlier than Asian or African countries, gaining a considerable advantage during the second half of the nineteenth century.

Although primary school enrollment rates generally exhibited an upward trend from the nineteenth century onward, the rate of expansion varied over

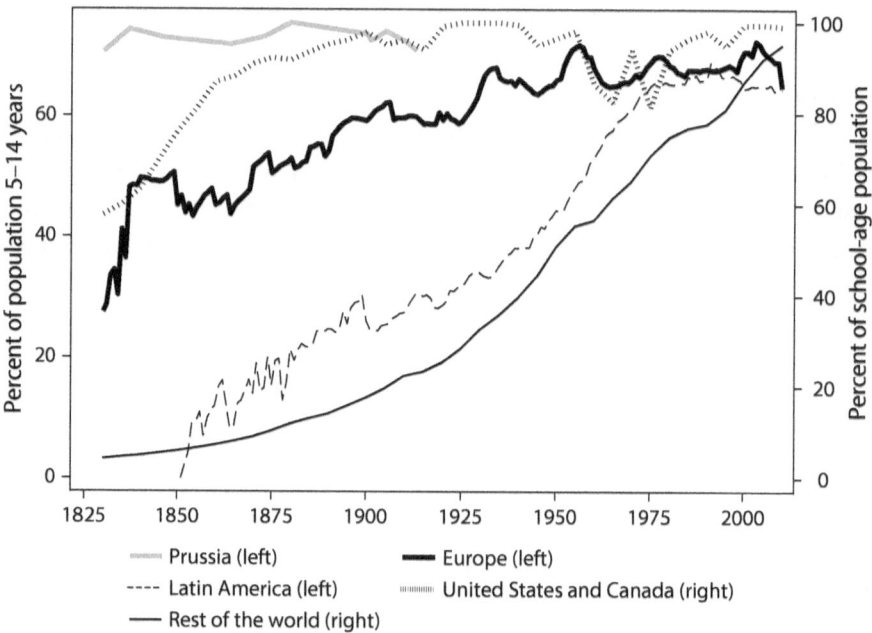

Figure 2.1. Primary school enrollment rates in Europe, the Americas, and the rest of the world, as a percentage of the population ages 5–14 years and as a percentage of the school-age population, 1820–2010. See text and footnotes for sources and methodology.

time, and enrollment sometimes contracted before increasing again. This is true at the regional level and becomes even more noticeable when we look within countries. As an example of this temporal variation, consider figure 2.2, which shows the historical evolution of primary school enrollment rates in four European and four Latin American countries: Prussia/Germany, France, Great Britain, Finland, Argentina, Colombia, Mexico, and Uruguay. Enrollment rates in this figure are measured as a percentage of the population ages 5–14 years; as a result, they lie considerably below 100 percent, especially in recent decades, when children ages 12–14 have typically been enrolled in secondary rather than primary school. What is clear from figure 2.2 is that in most countries, primary schooling had ups and downs despite a common upward trend.

Another important fact evident in figure 2.2 is that different countries began expanding primary education at different times, did so at different speeds, and reached universal enrollment in different years. Within Europe, Prussia and France were regional leaders, while Finland and, notably,

England were laggards. The French government created a state-regulated primary education system in 1833 with the passage of the Guizot Law, which was followed by a rapid expansion of primary schooling that enabled France to reach universal primary education by the 1860s, as shown in figure 2.2. England, by contrast, lagged considerably behind other European powers: it only created a national primary education system with the 1870 Forster Education Act, after which enrollment rates finally caught up with Prussia's and France's rates after decades of lagging behind them. Other European countries took even longer to expand primary education. Finland, for example, began to expand primary education in the 1890s, saw a sharp increase in primary schooling between 1918 and 1921, and had caught up with the rest of Europe by the early 1930s.

Within Latin America, Argentina and Uruguay were regional leaders—along with Chile and Costa Rica—in primary education, while Mexico and Colombia were among the laggards. The Argentine government created a national primary education system in 1884 with the passage of the landmark *Ley 1420*. As in France after the Guizot Law and England after the Forster Education Act, the passage of a comprehensive national law regulating nearly all aspects of primary education was accompanied by centralized efforts to expand the coverage of primary schooling. Starting in the 1880s, Argentina saw a rapid increase in access to primary education, attaining near universal primary education in the early 1940s. In Uruguay, the first comprehensive national law of primary education was passed in 1877, but access to primary schooling only took off after the civil war of 1904. Mexico, on the other hand, lagged behind the region's average throughout the nineteenth century. It was only in the late 1920s that the primary school system began to grow quickly. In Colombia, the expansion of primary education began during the second half of the nineteenth century, then plateaued during the first half of the twentieth century, and finally accelerated from the 1950s on.

The variation in the rate of expansion within countries will be very helpful to us. Much of what we will do in this chapter is to identify which factors predict an acceleration in a country's primary school enrollment rate and which ones do not. It is likely that the factors that drove the expansion of primary education differed across countries, and even within countries over time. The aim of this chapter is not to explain each individual country's trajectory, but to determine whether there were some factors that consistently led to educational expansion in a large number of countries. Our

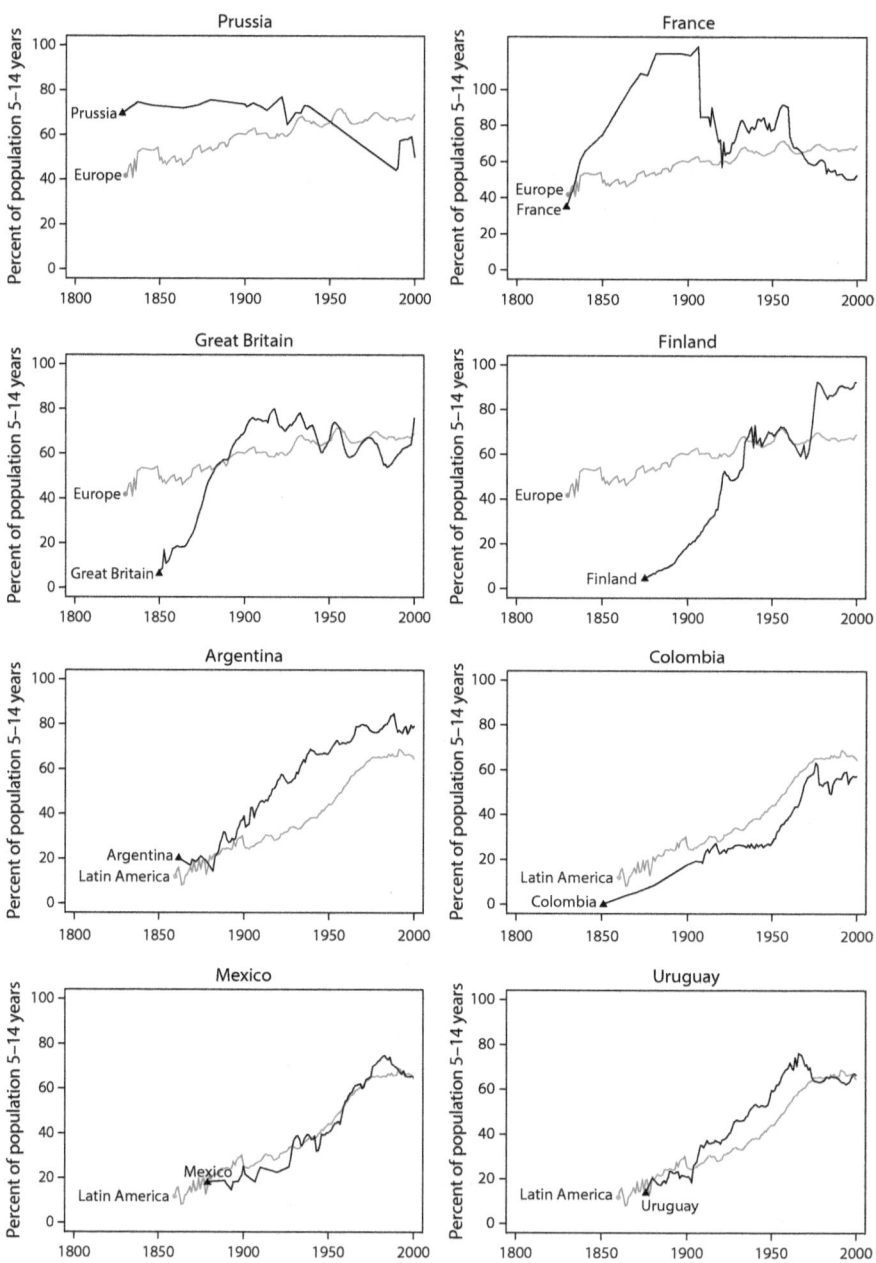

Figure 2.2. Historical evolution of primary school enrollment rates, as a percentage of the population ages 5–14 years, in four European and four Latin American countries.

focus will be on identifying drivers of the expansion of enrollment rates in Europe and the Americas, as these are the regions that led the global expansion of primary education. This analysis is just a starting point. In later chapters we will more closely examine why Prussia and France led the expansion of primary education within Europe, why Argentina and Chile were leaders within Latin America, and why England and Mexico lagged behind.

THE NON-DEMOCRATIC ROOTS OF MASS EDUCATION

Many people believe that the spread of democracy played "a leading role" in explaining the expansion of primary education around the world.[7] Some believe that democracies provide more primary education than autocracies because politicians in a democracy are more likely to listen to what a majority of people want, and presumably, most people want primary education. Others believe that transitions to democracy will be followed by greater provision of primary education not because democracies respond to what voters want but because politicians and traditional elites have an interest in teaching the newly enfranchised classes how to use their political rights responsibly. Whatever the reason, if the spread of democracy played an important role in explaining the expansion of primary education, we should see a large increase in primary schooling after transitions from autocracy to democracy.

History, however, shows that public primary education systems were a non-democratic invention. Barring a few exceptions like the United States, almost all state-regulated primary education systems in the world emerged well before representative democracy was even conceivable. Historians have devoted extensive attention to the case of Prussia because its primary school system, developed under an absolutist regime in the eighteenth century, became a model for the rest of the world. Already in 1717, King Frederick William I signed a royal school ordinance requiring that "in those places where schools exist, parents, under threat of fine, be compelled to send their children to school." Due to a lack of funding and poor enforcement capacity, the order was never implemented, but it was a turning point that marked the moment when the education of children became part of the royal agenda.[8]

---

7. Lindert (2004), p. 105.
8. Melton (2002), p. 46.

The king's successor, Frederick the Great, continued and expanded his father's efforts. In 1753, he allocated an annual grant to train primary school teachers at the Berlin Normal School, imposed a new teacher training curriculum, and signed an order stipulating that all future school vacancies throughout Prussia should be filled with teachers trained in that Normal School. This marked the beginning of the central government's monopoly in training primary school teachers.[9] A new royal school ordinance signed by Frederick the Great in 1763 imposed compulsory primary schooling for children in rural Protestant areas, followed in 1765 by a similar ordinance for rural Catholic areas.[10]

These centralized efforts to regulate and promote primary education were made while Prussia remained an absolutist regime. By the time democracy emerged in 1918—or even by 1848, when a wave of revolutions sought, unsuccessfully, to introduce a democratic constitution—Prussia already had a well-developed primary education system regulated by the central government. In the 1820s, a century before democratization and more than half a century before the introduction of Bismarck's social welfare legislation, 70 percent of children ages 5–14 years were already enrolled in primary school.

Far from being an anomaly, the Prussian case is illustrative of a general pattern: most central governments around the world began to regulate and promote primary education well before democracy emerged. This conclusion comes from comparing the year when a country first transitioned to democracy and the year when its central government first intervened in primary education. Using data from more than one hundred countries across all regions, figure 2.3 shows that governments began to systematically monitor primary schools on average sixty-five years before democratization. The graph adopts a lenient definition of democracy that requires countries to have open and competitive elections and at least 50 percent of males enfranchised.[11] A stricter definition of what constitutes a democracy, such as one requiring universal female suffrage or, at the very least, universal male suffrage, would imply an even larger gap between democratization and central government intervention in primary education.

---

9. Kandel (1910), p. 8.
10. Alexander (1919).
11. This measure of democratization was developed by Boix, Miller, and Rosato (2013). The conclusions hold if we rely instead on other common measures, including the Polity Project's measure of democracy. See Paglayan (2021).

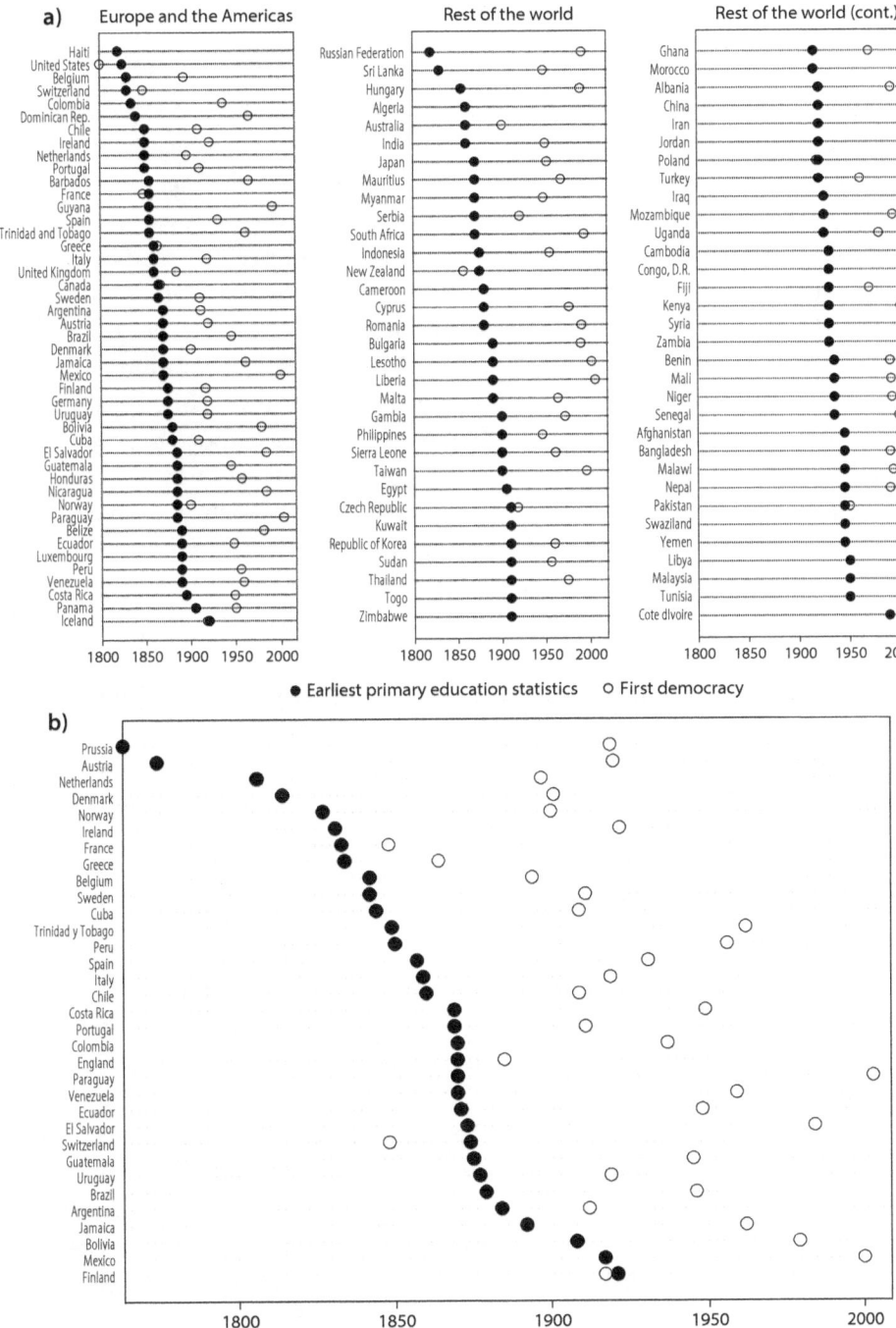

Figure 2.3. Timing of democratization and timing of state intervention in primary education in Europe, the Americas, and the rest of the world. The top graph (a) compares the timing of the first democracy and the first centrally reported primary education statistics in 109 countries. The bottom graph (b) compares the timing of the first democracy and the first comprehensive primary education law in European and Latin American countries. See text and footnotes for sources and methodology.

That central governments began to intervene in primary education may be unsurprising for countries like China, Egypt, or Russia, which have public primary education systems despite never having been democratic. Yet the same is true for regions that experienced democracy relatively early, such as Western Europe and Latin America. There, central governments began to fund and build primary schools, set a mandatory curriculum for all primary schools, and established teacher certification and state-run teacher training institutions more than a century before democratization; and introduced compulsory primary schooling laws—one of the last forms of central government intervention—about seventy-five years before democratization.[12]

The earliest forms of intervention usually came in the form of isolated regulations that targeted only one or two policy areas, such as the curriculum or teacher certification, but eventually central governments adopted a comprehensive national primary education law. These landmark laws occupy a crucial place in the history of education in any country because they created a centralized framework for education systems, regulating multiple aspects of schooling such as the curriculum, teacher training and certification, school construction, funding, inspection, etc. Some examples of these laws include Prussia's 1763 General Rural School Regulations, France's 1833 *Loi sur l'instruction primaire*, Argentina's 1884 *Ley 1420*, and England's 1870 Forster Elementary Education Act. The bottom panel in figure 2.3 compares the timing of the first such education law and the timing of democratization in European and Latin American countries. The data reveal that central governments in these regions adopted comprehensive primary education laws on average sixty-eight years before democratization, thus reinforcing the general conclusion that it was non-democratic regimes that were responsible for the creation of state-regulated primary education systems.

Non-democratic regimes went well beyond the adoption of laws to regulate primary education; they also promoted the expansion of primary schooling. An example of this comes from the history of France. The first French national primary education law, passed in 1833 under the July Monarchy, gave way to the fastest expansion of primary school enrollment rates in French history. By 1848, when universal male suffrage was introduced, two-thirds of children were already enrolled in primary school. What's more, the restriction of political rights imposed when Napoleon III established the Second French Empire in 1851 did not halt the expansion of primary school-

---

12. See the online appendix.

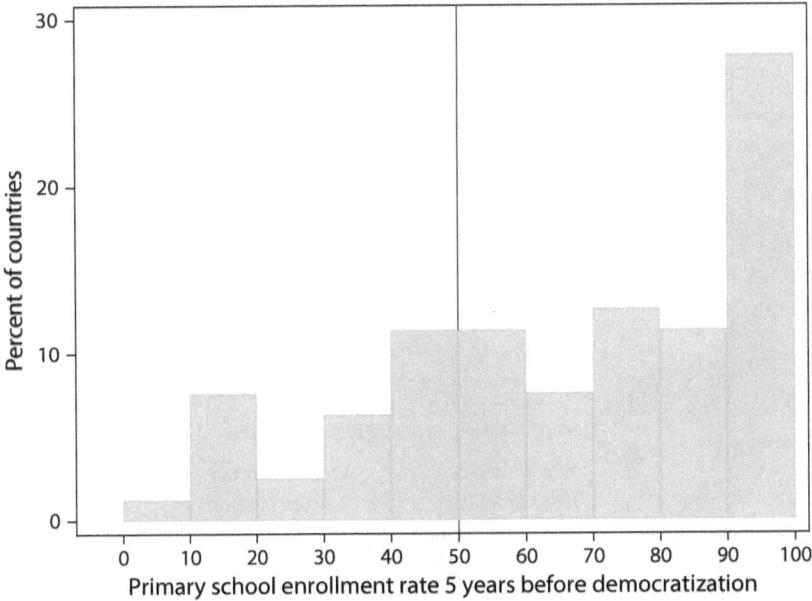

Figure 2.4. Distribution of primary school enrollment rates, as a percentage of the school-age population, five years before the first democratization in countries that ever democratized, 1820–2010. Out of 111 countries with enrollment data, 87 experienced at least one transition to democracy. See text and footnotes for sources and methodology.

ing. In fact, universal primary education was achieved by 1865—*before* the collapse of the second empire and the restoration of political rights under the Third Republic.

The high levels of access to primary schooling attained in France during non-democratic periods are representative of a more general pattern: Around the world, most children gained access to primary schooling before the arrival of democracy, as shown in figure 2.4.[13] The histogram shows what proportion of countries that ever became democratic had reached primary school enrollment rates above 90 percent before they first democratized, what proportion had reached enrollment rates between 80 and 90 percent before democratizing, between 70 and 80 percent, and so on. If

---

13. This statement is true under two different definitions of democracy: (1) universal suffrage, competitive elections, and limits on executive power; and (2) open and competitive elections and at least 50 percent of male adults can vote. The second definition is less demanding than the first. Data for the first definition come from the Polity Project. Data for the second definition come from Boix, Miller, and Rosato (2013).

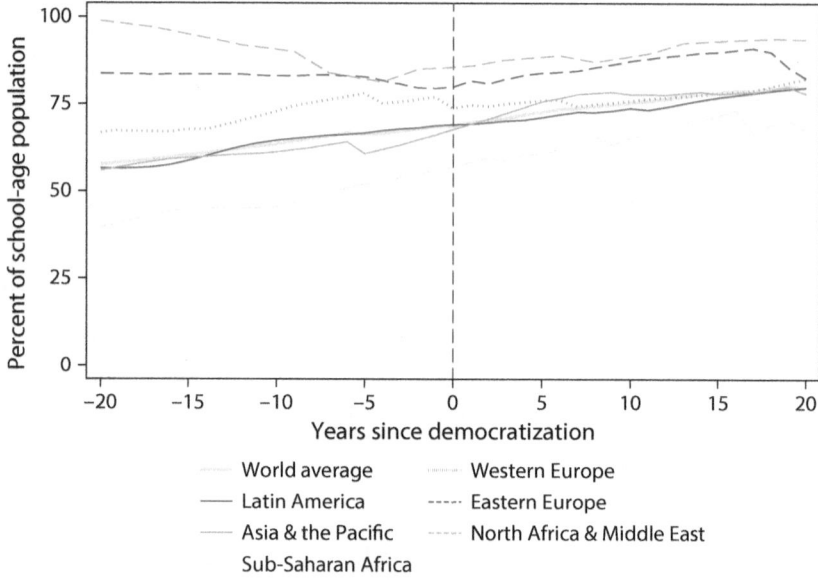

Figure 2.5. Average primary school enrollment rates around the world and by region, as a percentage of the school-age population, before and after democratization, 1820–2010. See text and footnotes for sources and methodology.

we add up all the countries with enrollment rates above 50 percent, that gives us the proportion of countries where a majority of children had already gained access to primary schooling *before* democracy emerged. Seven out of ten countries fall within this group. Put differently, only three out of ten countries that transitioned to democracy were not already providing primary education to a majority of children before they became democratic for the first time.

Another way to understand the magnitude of education provision under non-democratic regimes is to consider how primary school enrollment rates evolved within countries before and after the arrival of democracy. This is shown in figure 2.5. Not all countries that transitioned to democracy did so at the same time, so to be able to compare them, the x-axis normalizes time so that "year zero" for each country is the year in which that country became democratic for the first time. The thick grey line tells us, across all countries that ever became democratic, what was the average primary school enrollment rate in the twenty years before and the twenty years after democratization. The other lines break down this average by region.

An important pattern emerges from figure 2.5: Across all countries that at some point became democratic, primary school enrollment had already reached 70 percent on average before democracy emerged. If we disaggregate the analysis by region, we can see that in all regions except for Sub-Saharan Africa, at least two-thirds of school-age children were already enrolled in primary school before the arrival of democracy. Of special relevance is the fact that in Western European and Latin American countries the bulk of the expansion of primary schooling had already been completed five years before democracy emerged, with enrollment reaching on average 78 percent of school-age children in Europe and 67 percent in Latin America years before the arrival of democracy. This means that the spread of democracy cannot explain why these Western societies led the global expansion of primary education.

Some readers may wonder whether democratization nonetheless led to additional increases in access to primary schooling. This is a question I have examined in great depth elsewhere.[14] The next three paragraphs summarize the results of that investigation.

When people think of democracy as a key driver of the expansion of primary education, a case that often comes to mind is the United States, one of the modern world's oldest democracies and also one of the first countries to attain universal primary education. By 1870, 90 percent of white children in the United States were enrolled in a public primary school, thanks in large part to the common school movement that since the late 1830s set out to establish a public school in every community.[15] But attributing this expansion of education to the fact that the United States was democratic is a big leap. Precisely because the United States had always been more democratic than other countries at the time, at least for white males, we cannot know if the country would have accomplished universal primary education in the absence of democracy—much like France or Prussia did.

To determine how democracy impacts education provision, a better approach is to look at countries that were once non-democratic but eventually became democratic and ask: did the expansion of primary schooling in these countries accelerate after they transitioned to democracy? Figure 2.5 shows that, in most cases, the answer is no: in the average country, primary school enrollment rates increased at the same pace before and after democ-

---

14. Paglayan (2021).
15. Own calculations based on U.S. Department of Education (1993).

ratization. Still, perhaps enrollment rates would have declined or grown at a slower pace if democratization had not occurred. A common strategy that social scientists use to gauge the plausibility of this scenario is to compare how enrollment rates changed in countries that transitioned to democracy relative to countries that remained non-democratic. If democratization enhanced the level of access to primary education either by accelerating or preventing declines in its provision, we should observe that enrollment rates in countries that democratized grew at a faster pace after democratization took place than in countries that during the same period remained non-democratic. Yet this is not what happened: in general, primary schooling expanded just as fast in countries that experienced democratization as in those that remained non-democratic.

There are several potential explanations for why, in general, democracy did not lead to an increase in primary school coverage, but the explanation that finds the most support in the data stems from a point made earlier: In most countries, by the time they became democratic, a majority of people already had access to primary schooling and therefore did not want an expansion of it.[16] In 40 percent of countries that became democratic at some point, including France but also Austria, Denmark, Germany, Sweden, Russia, Japan, Taiwan, Mexico, and many others, access to primary schooling was so far-reaching under non-democracy that there was little room left for expansion after they became democratic. But even in countries where there *was* room for expansion, democracy often failed to bring about an expansion of primary schooling because, while a sizable minority lacked access to it, the majority of voters already had access to primary education. Expanding access to primary education in these countries would probably have helped election-oriented politicians win support from the minority of

---

16. In Paglayan (2021), I considered two additional explanations for the absence of a positive impact of democratization on primary school enrollment rates. First, perhaps most democracies emerged as part of a power-sharing pact between the rich and the middle class, as a result of which institutions were created that gave these groups outsized influence over politics compared to disadvantaged groups who lacked access to primary education. Second, perhaps democracy failed to bring about increased provision of primary schooling when right-wing parties were elected but brought about educational expansion when left-wing parties won elections. While logically plausible, the evidence does not provide much support for these explanations. Democratic regimes were no more likely to promote the expansion of primary schooling when they resulted from social revolutions than when they resulted from intra-elite pacts. Nor have left-wing democratic governments been more likely to expand primary education than right-wing ones.

voters who still lacked access—but minorities don't win elections, and politicians know this.[17]

It is certainly possible that the arrival of democracy did lead to profound changes in the goals pursued by education systems or the quality of education available to citizens. What democracy cannot explain is why Western societies led the emergence and expansion of primary schooling—two transformations that usually preceded the spread of democracy.

LEFT-WING AUTOCRACIES AND MASS EDUCATION

Did non-democratic regimes expand primary education because they embraced a left-wing ideology and relied on the lower classes for political support? Left-wing autocracies have often implemented large land redistribution programs, progressive tax schedules, and other policies that redistribute resources and income from wealthier to poorer members of society. But do left-wing autocracies also explain the rise of mass education? Not consistently.

The argument that left-wing autocracies expanded mass education as part of a bundle of redistributive policies finds empirical support in the twentieth century, when the rise of communist and socialist dictatorships often gave way to an unprecedented expansion of primary education.[18] Indeed, between 1900 and 2010, primary school enrollment rates increased twice as fast in left-wing autocracies as in right-wing ones.[19] Three of the most impressive examples come from Russia, Cuba, and Ghana. In Russia, following the proliferation of public primary schools promoted by Stalin, the proportion of the population ages 5–14 years that were enrolled in a primary school increased from less than 13 percent before the October Revolution of 1917 to 50 percent by 1940. No other country in the world experienced such a staggering expansion of primary education during that period. In

---

17. In line with this explanation, the only region where I find evidence that democratization did lead to an expansion of primary schooling is also the only region where most voters lacked access to primary schooling before democracy emerged: Sub-Saharan Africa. See the online appendix.

18. Manzano's (2017) cross-national study from 1960 to 2000 finds that autocrats who championed a left-wing ideology favoring the interests of the working class were likely to expand access to secondary schooling. Kosack's (2012) study of 1950s Ghana, 1950s Taiwan, and 1930s Brazil similarly finds that non-democratic regimes that relied on the mobilization of poorer sectors of society to assume and retain power made deliberate efforts to expand primary education.

19. The data on the ideology of governments comes from Brambor, Lindvall, and Stjernquist (2017).

Cuba, the establishment of a one-party communist regime in 1959 was followed by a sudden expansion of primary school coverage, which increased by more than ten percentage points within just two years (from 49 percent in 1958 to 62 percent in 1960). In Ghana, under the leadership of socialist dictator Kwame Nkrumah, who introduced the Accelerated Development Plan for Education, primary school enrollment rates increased by thirty-six percentage points (from 24 to 60 percent) between 1950 and 1965. To make sense of the magnitude of this pace, if a country wanted to go from 0 to 100 percent enrollment, it would need sixty-two years to accomplish that at the pace of expansion seen in Russia between 1917 and 1940, forty-two years at the pace seen in Ghana between 1950 and 1965, and fifteen years at the pace seen in Cuba between 1958 and 1960. By contrast, if a country expanded at the average rate of expansion observed around the world between 1820 and 2010, it would take 214 years to accomplish the same goal.

What the rise of left-wing autocracies cannot explain is why the West led the creation of state-regulated primary education systems in the nineteenth century, or why it led the global expansion of primary schooling. Thirty out of the forty-two countries in Europe and the Americas for which we have historical data on primary school enrollment rates never had a left-wing autocracy, and another three countries had short-lived left-wing autocrats who lost power after one or two years. In Europe, almost eight out of ten children gained access to primary schooling as a result of the educational efforts of right-wing, and to a lesser extent centrist, autocratic regimes. In Latin America, the impetus for the creation of primary education systems for the masses developed, and much of the expansion of such systems occurred, under the oligarchic regimes of the late nineteenth and early twentieth centuries, before the emergence of left-wing dictatorships.[20]

Moreover, the rise of populist leaders in twentieth-century Latin America produced mixed results in terms of the level of access to primary education. Brazil's populist dictator Getúlio Vargas, who came to power through a coup in 1930, expanded primary education at the same pace, not faster, than the right-wing government that preceded him. In Argentina, primary schooling under the populist presidency of Juan Domingo Perón from 1946 to 1955 expanded at a slower pace than under the right-wing dictatorship

---

20. Eight Latin American countries had at least one left-wing autocrat who stayed in power for at least five years, but all of them rose to power after 1920, by which time Latin America was already providing twice as much primary education as the rest of the developing world.

that preceded him. In Mexico, the two periods of fastest educational expansion from 1880 to 2010 took place when right-wing factions of the PRI controlled the presidency. The first big increase took place between 1926 and 1929 during the presidency of Plutarco Elías Calles, when primary school enrollment rates increased from 25 to 35 percent, and the second took place between 1958 and 1964, when enrollment increased from 47 to 58 percent under the presidency of Adolfo López Mateos.

In sum, although the rise of communist, socialist, and left-wing autocracies contributed greatly to the expansion of primary education in some parts of the world during the twentieth century, it cannot explain the creation or expansion of state-regulated primary education systems in the West. The absence of left-wing autocracies did not stop the West from being a leader in the regulation and provision of primary education compared to the rest of the world. What else could have prompted central governments to set up primary education systems and promote their expansion?

One possibility is that right-wing non-democracies expanded primary education because they hoped that improving the well-being of the lower classes would prevent mass rebellion against the regime.[21] Yet this explanation is also unconvincing for two main reasons. First, as I document in chapter 4, in the non-democratic regimes that led the creation and expansion of primary education systems in Europe and Latin America and served as educational models for other countries, political rulers and education reformers were explicit that economic redistribution should not be a goal of primary education, and argued, on the contrary, that primary schools should refrain from promoting the social mobility of the lower classes. Second, and crucially, central governments during the nineteenth century were *not* under the impression that parents demanded education for their children. On the contrary, they believed that parents were largely uninterested in sending their children to school because they preferred their children to work at home or in the fields or factories. In part because of this belief, they adopted compulsory schooling laws, as we will see in chapter 5. In other words, governments in Europe and the Americas created and expanded primary education systems *despite* their belief that this was an unpopular policy among the masses.[22]

---

21. For evidence that autocracies have often adopted land redistribution policies to garner political support from land-poor individuals, see Albertus (2015).
22. Andersson and Berger (2019) show that Swedish elites expanded mass schooling even though most parents were uninterested in schooling because it competed with their children's

The remainder of this chapter shows that internal conflict explains the Western rise of primary education systems better than other common explanations, including the diffusion of ideas about the role of education for nation-building, industrialization, or interstate wars.

IDEAS ABOUT THE NATION-BUILDING ROLE OF EDUCATION

Some have argued that the diffusion of fashionable ideas about the nation-building role of education was the main driver behind the rise of mass education systems. According to this view, starting in the late eighteenth century, the idea emerged among European rulers, inspired by Prussia, that in order to build a viable nation-state the state had to provide education to the lower classes to inculcate a strong national identity. This idea then spread to other parts of the world as countries sought to emulate the European nation-state model. Proponents of this view argue that it was the arrival of these international ideas and not domestic forces that led to the creation and expansion of state-regulated primary education systems. Once these ideas arrived in a country, the argument goes, states adopted comprehensive laws to create a unified primary education system, began to expand primary education, and continued doing so at a steady pace thereafter, almost as if on autopilot. From this perspective, the fact that primary education expanded considerably under non-democratic regimes was simply a historical coincidence, driven by the reality that at the time when it became fashionable for central governments to provide education for the masses, most regimes still happened to be non-democratic.[23]

There is no doubt that European ideas about the political role of mass education were an important precondition for the emergence of primary education systems. Europe led the rest of the world in the construction and expansion of primary education systems controlled by the central gov-

---

work responsibilities. In France, too, the national government under the July Monarchy (1833–1848) promoted an unprecedented expansion of primary schooling even though demand for education from the lower classes was low (Squicciarini and Voigtländer 2016). For additional evidence that parental demand for education was low, particularly in rural areas and agrarian economies where families relied on child labor for agricultural productivity, see Cinnirella and Hornung (2016); Baker (2015); Tapia and Martinez-Galarraga (2018); Cvrcek and Zajicek (2019).

23. Paglayan (2021) and the online appendix provide visual evidence that the expansion of primary schooling under non-democracies was not merely a historical coincidence. These regimes appear to have incentives of their own to expand primary schooling as suggested by the observation that reversals from democracy to non-democracy are, on average, followed by an acceleration of primary school enrollment rates that is not observed in countries that remain democratic.

ernment. We saw this already in chapter 1 when we noted that no other region in the world came close to the level of primary school coverage seen in Europe during the first half of the nineteenth century. Central governments in Europe were also precursors in intervening in primary education to fund and monitor primary schools, control the curriculum, and pass compulsory education laws. Prussia in particular introduced compulsory primary education under Frederick the Great in 1763, nine decades before Massachusetts became the first state in the United States to pass a similar law. Indeed, by the time Massachusetts introduced compulsory schooling in 1852, six European countries (Prussia, Denmark, France, Greece, Portugal, and Sweden) had already adopted compulsory schooling laws. European countries also led the way in establishing a system of government-funded Normal Schools to train primary school teachers. Throughout the nineteenth century, Normal Schools became the only institutions allowed to train teachers in most of Europe, the United States, and Latin America. Here again, Prussia blazed a trail, as we saw earlier in the chapter, beginning to fund Normal Schools in 1753. By the time the first state-funded Normal School was established in the United States in 1839, again in Massachusetts, five European countries besides Prussia had already established a system of state-controlled Normal Schools: Denmark (beginning in 1790), Norway (1826), France (1833), Ireland (1834), and Spain (1836). Indeed, when the first state-funded Normal School was created in the United States, there were already 264 Normal Schools throughout Europe.[24]

Hundreds of reports were written in the nineteenth century by government officials who traveled to Europe, and especially to Prussia and France, to learn how to design and successfully run a public primary education system. In 1836, Calvin Stowe was sent by the Ohio State Legislature on an official mission to learn about primary school systems in Europe. In his *Report on Elementary Education in Europe*, he urged Ohio legislators to follow

---

24. This figure comes from Henry Barnard's two-volume report on Normal Schools, which he wrote in 1851 when he was Superintendent of Common Schools of Connecticut. In the preface of volume 2, devoted entirely to the history and characteristics of Normal Schools in Europe, Barnard stresses the importance of learning from Europe to develop public education systems throughout the United States: "This volume . . . embodies information which the author believes can be made available in organizing new, and improving existing systems of public instruction . . . in every State of this Union. Its value does not consist in its conveying the speculations or limited experience of the author, but the matured views and varied experience of wise statesmen, educators and teachers, through a succession of years, and under the most diverse circumstances of government, society and religion" (Barnard (1851, v.2)).

in Prussia's footsteps by sponsoring primary schools and creating state-controlled Normal Schools to train primary school teachers. Horace Mann traveled to Prussia in 1843 and upon his return advocated for the creation of Normal Schools and the development of a primary school curriculum focused, like the Prussian curriculum, on moral education. In Latin America, Domingo F. Sarmiento, who as President of Argentina founded the first Normal School in 1869, had traveled to France, Germany, Spain, Switzerland, the Netherlands, and England in 1845 to learn about these countries' education and immigration policies. In his book *Educación Popular*, published in 1849, Sarmiento not only lays out influential arguments for why Latin American countries should develop a national primary education system, but also provides detailed information on how schools were organized and how teachers were trained in France and Prussia. In its 320 pages, Sarmiento's *Educación Popular* mentions "France" 88 times, "Prussia" 43 times, "England" 29 times, "Holland" 26 times, and "Europe" 78 times. We will devote much of chapter 3 to discussing the role that educational ideas played in driving states to intervene in the provision of primary education.

Despite the undoubted influence of European ideas about education, their diffusion is insufficient to explain the patterns of creation and expansion of primary education systems we have seen so far. Three empirical observations are inconsistent with the diffusion argument. First, countries simultaneously exposed to the same ideas nonetheless created and expanded primary education systems at different times. Take the cases of Argentina and Chile, two neighboring countries that, during the nineteenth century, shared many similarities—independence from Spain in the 1810s, a strong presence of the Catholic Church, a republican constitution, an oligarchic regime, and similar levels of income per capita—and where the same arguments about the importance of having a national primary education system to consolidate the power of the central government began circulating simultaneously during the 1840s. This was in part because Sarmiento, in addition to being the most fervent advocate for a system of mass education in his home country, Argentina, also lived in exile in Chile during the 1840s, during which time he became the director of the first Chilean Normal School and published *Educación Popular*. Despite the widespread dissemination of Sarmiento's ideas in both countries, in turn inspired by his long trip to Europe, the Argentine and Chilean governments began to regulate and promote primary education more than twenty years apart from one another, with Chile passing its first national primary education law in 1860, and Argentina in 1884.

The diffusion argument's prediction that the arrival of educational ideas from Europe triggered a process of steady educational expansion is also inconsistent with the fact that, in most countries, the rate of expansion of primary schooling fluctuated over time. For example, in figure 2.2 we saw that in Argentina primary schooling remained relatively stable throughout the 1860s and 1870s but picked up considerably during the presidency of Julio A. Roca in the 1880s. In Colombia, primary schooling expanded at a relatively steady pace from the 1850s to the 1920s, then stalled for the next three decades, and then expanded at an unprecedented pace starting in the 1950s. France experienced a strong expansion of primary schooling during the early years of the July Monarchy in the 1830s, a deceleration in the 1840s, and a renewed acceleration in the 1850s. These are just a few examples that illustrate a broader point: the expansion of primary schooling did not proceed uninterruptedly as the diffusion explanation predicts; it had ups and downs that differed across countries and that cannot be adequately explained by changes in the circulation of international ideas.

Finally, the diffusion argument is also inconsistent with the evidence presented later in this chapter that the expansion of primary schooling experienced an acceleration after periods of internal conflict. Recall that diffusion proponents believe that domestic forces like internal conflict played an insignificant role in the expansion of primary education. However, as we will soon see, primary school enrollment rates more than tripled in the wake of civil wars, an acceleration that cannot be explained by common global forces. To understand when and why countries expanded mass education, and when the provision of primary education accelerated within a country, we need to look beyond global forces and ideas.

INDUSTRIALIZATION AND MASS EDUCATION

Industrialization is one possible domestic economic condition that could have driven the creation and expansion of public primary education systems. According to Ernest Gellner and other proponents of this argument, the emergence of an industrial economy created the need for skilled and literate workers who could read machine manuals and understand instructions from their supervisors in a common language.[25] Others have argued that the rise of the factory system of production also created the need for docile, punctual, disciplined workers who were predisposed to follow orders. Once

---

25. Gellner (1983); Galor and Moav (2006).

the locus of production moved from the home to factories with expensive machinery, divided but interconnected tasks, and supervisors with whom workers shared no kinship, the need to instill discipline became obvious.[26] Governments, the argument goes, provided primary education to respond to the workforce needs of this new economy.

In theory, three different actors within society could have motivated governments to respond to these workforce needs. One possibility is that the emergence of an industrial economy gave rise to a powerful class of factory owners who used their economic power to pressure the government into expanding primary education. Another possibility is that with the emergence of new job opportunities in factories and cities, ordinary citizens demanded greater public provision of primary schooling so that they and their children could acquire the skills needed to take advantage of these new jobs. A third possibility is that the government, not the private sector, was the main architect of the industrialization process and expanded primary education to create the skilled and docile workforce it needed to support *its own* state-led industrialization goals.

A common objection to the industrialization argument comes from contrasting the histories of England and Prussia: England was an industrial leader and education laggard, whereas Prussia was the opposite. Economic historians have documented that England's First Industrial Revolution, which began around the 1760s, relied not on a mass of literate workers but on a few highly educated people with advanced scientific and technical skills.[27] In fact, despite leading the Industrial Revolution, the government did not make an effort to provide widespread access to primary education.[28] In the early 1850s, many decades after England had begun to industrialize,[29] less than 9 percent of English children were enrolled in primary school. To put this in perspective: of the nine European countries for which we have data in the mid-nineteenth century (Austria, Belgium, Prussia, Spain, France, England, Ireland, Norway, and the Netherlands), England was the only one that had a primary school enrollment rate in the single digits. In Spain,

---

26. Bowles and Gintis (1976); Mokyr (2002), pp. 120–162.

27. Mitch (1999); Mokyr (2005). For similar findings but in the case of France, see Squicciarni and Voigtländer (2015).

28. Green (2013); Mitch (1999).

29. The conventional wisdom is that England began to industrialize in the 1760s. According to Rostow, however, England's industrialization began sometime between 1783 and 1802. In either case, England began to expand primary education more than a half century after beginning to industrialize.

the country with the second lowest primary school enrollment rate, 25 percent of children were enrolled in primary education in 1850. It wasn't until 1870 that England's first national law organizing primary education was passed, the Forster Elementary Education Act, initiating a process of rapid expansion in primary school coverage and convergence with the provision levels seen elsewhere in Europe. In other words, for about one century England was able to sustain the process of industrialization without investing in primary education. By contrast, Prussia became a leader in regulating and providing primary education in the late eighteenth century despite the fact that its economy remained agrarian.

Are the cases of England and Prussia anomalies? That is, was industrialization an important driver of the expansion of primary education in other countries? And was the Second Industrial Revolution perhaps different from the First Industrial Revolution? After all, the type of industrial economy that Gellner appears to have had in mind when he argued that industrialization led to the expansion of mass education was the one characterized by the large, mechanized factories and assembly line production of the Second Industrial Revolution more than with the textile factories associated with the First Industrial Revolution. And economic historians, too, have argued that having a skilled workforce helped boost economic productivity only during the Second Industrial Revolution.[30]

To assess whether industrialization was an important driver of the rise of primary education systems, we would want to know whether these systems emerged before or after the onset of industrialization, and whether industrialization led to an increase in primary school coverage. The problem this presents is that historians and economists are still debating the precise start date of industrialization, even for a country like England that has been extensively studied. One difficulty comes from the scarcity of historical data on the proportion of the workforce employed in manufacturing and, more generally, the composition of the labor force going back to the eighteenth and nineteenth centuries—the period when European countries industrialized.[31] Another difficulty comes from the fact that industrialization

---

30. Galor and Moav (2006).
31. For example, in Banks's commonly used Cross-National Time Series (CNTS) dataset, which contains historical information about the proportion of the labor force employed outside agriculture, only fourteen countries in the dataset have information preceding the year 1900, and of these fourteen, only two countries have a data point below 33 percent, which means that for the other twelve countries, the earliest data point available is one in which one-third of the labor force or more was already employed outside agriculture.

looked different across countries. In some, like England, it went hand in hand with urbanization, but in others the growth of cities occurred without a concurrent process of industrialization.[32]

The approach I take to measure the onset of industrialization is to look directly at the adoption of technological inventions that sparked the First and Second Industrial Revolutions. For the First Industrial Revolution, I measure its onset by looking at the first year when a country had steam ships, trains, or used the mule spindle for textile production, an innovation that required cotton spinning to move from workers' homes to factories.[33] I measure the beginning of the Second Industrial Revolution as the year when a country first produced or incorporated steel into the manufacturing process. Information about the adoption of these inventions was compiled by economists Diego Comín and Bart Hobijn as part of a larger data collection effort on the historical adoption of 104 technological inventions across 161 countries.[34] In addition to providing us with a measure of the onset of industrialization, this dataset covers a larger number of countries than other efforts to measure the timing of industrialization across countries. Combining these data with Lee and Lee's primary school enrollment rates, there are thirty-nine countries with information on primary school enrollment rates both before and after the year of adoption of steel, nine of which are in Western Europe and the Americas;[35] and forty-five countries have enrollment data before and after the First Industrial Revolution, fifteen of which are in the West.

As an additional check on the conclusions I report below, I also use a more holistic measure of industrial takeoff developed by Walt Whitman Rostow, according to whom a country's industrial takeoff occurs in the first year when three conditions are met: (1) the rate of productive investment rises from approximately 5 percent to more than 10 percent of national

32. Gollin, Jedwab, and Vollrath (2016); Jedwab and Vollrath (2015).
33. Mokyr (2002).
34. Comin and Hobijn's (2009) Cross-country Historical Adoption of Technology (CHAT) dataset measures the year when each country first adopted a variety of technological inventions, from the steam engine to the internet. It covers 104 technologies in 161 countries from 1800 to 2000. The dataset is an unbalanced panel. For a given technological invention, whether or not there is information on the degree to which that invention had been adopted in a given year varies across countries. Moreover, there are many countries for which there is no information at all—in any year—on the degree of adoption of some technological inventions.
35. Algeria, Argentina, Australia, Austria, Brazil, Bulgaria, Canada, Chile, China, Czech Republic, Egypt, Finland, France, Hungary, India, Indonesia, Iran, Ireland, Italy, Japan, Mexico, Netherlands, Norway, Peru, Portugal, South Korea, Romania, Russia, South Africa, Sweden, Switzerland, Taiwan, Thailand, Tunisia, Turkey, the United States, Uruguay, Venezuela, and Zimbabwe.

income or net national product; (2) one or more substantial manufacturing sectors develops, with a high rate of growth; (3) existence or quick emergence of a political, social, and institutional framework that exploits the impulses to expansion in the modern sector and the potential external economy effects of the takeoff. The conclusions presented in this chapter remain unaltered when we rely on Rostow's alternative definition and measure of the onset of industrialization.[36]

Beginning first with the emergence of education systems, figure 2.6 compares the timing of industrialization with the timing of landmark education legislation in Europe and Latin America. The circles indicate the adoption of the first comprehensive primary education law in each country for which we also have data on the timing of industrialization. The solid and hollow triangles represent the timing of the First and Second Industrial Revolutions, respectively, as proxied by the adoption of technological inventions, and the squares indicate the timing of industrialization according to Rostow's classification. Notice that there are only two countries (France and Sweden) with data on the timing of industrialization based on all three measures. However, for most countries, we have at least two different measures.

Taking the various measures of the timing of industrialization together, the main conclusion that emerges is the *absence* of a clear pattern linking industrialization and the emergence of a state-regulated primary education system. In nine of the twenty-four countries shown in figure 2.6, central governments adopted landmark education legislation several decades before the First Industrial Revolution. Prussia is well known for making incursions into primary education while its economy was still agrarian, but the list also includes Austria, the Netherlands, Norway, Ireland, Greece, Spain, Venezuela, and Ecuador. In several other countries, the adoption of comprehensive primary education laws occurred after the First and before the Second Industrial Revolution. On average, central governments adopted education legislation six decades before the Second Industrial Revolution.

Given the quality of the data, however, we cannot say with certainty that industrialization and the rise of factories did not play a role in driving the emergence of state-regulated primary education systems in Western countries. By the same token, nothing in the data suggests that it did. There *are* some countries where the central government began to intervene in primary education at roughly the same time as the onset of industrialization.

36. See the online appendix.

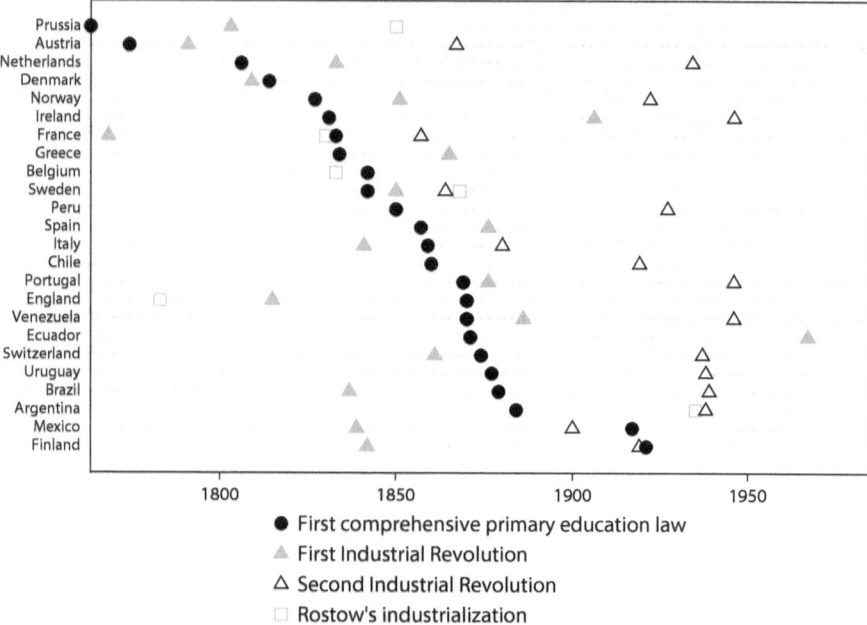

Figure 2.6. Timing of industrialization and timing of state intervention in primary education in Europe and Latin America. See text and footnotes for sources and methodology.

Yet these cases represent only six of the twenty-four countries for which we have data: Denmark, France, Belgium, Sweden, Portugal, and Finland. Moreover, it is not clear whether this concurrence implies that industrialization *led* to the creation of national primary education systems or whether both processes coincided purely by chance. Cathie Jo Martin's investigation into the ideas that shaped Danish education policy suggests that the goals of the 1814 School Acts had little to do with promoting skills for industrialization.[37] In the case of France, we will see in chapter 4 that industrialists at first *opposed* the central government's effort to promote primary education because they thought that schooling children would lead to a reduction in labor supply and, with that, an increase in wages and a reduction of profits.

What about the relationship between industrialization and the expansion of access to primary education? Figure 2.7 suggests that in Europe and the Americas the spread of primary schooling was not associated with the emergence of an industrial economy. The solid black line in figure 2.7 summa-

[37]. Martin (2023).

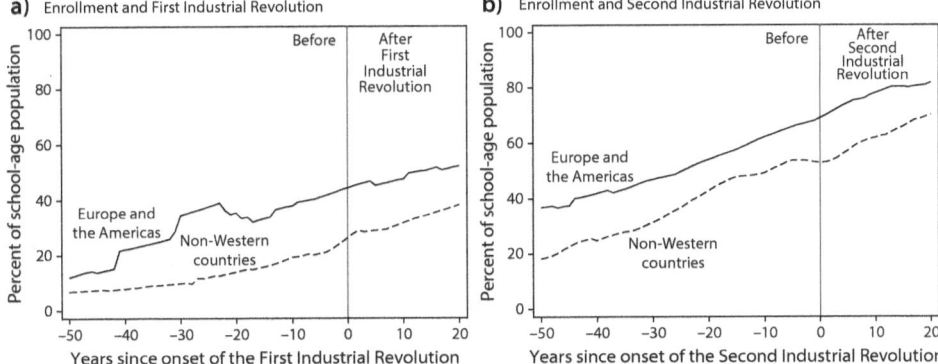

Figure 2.7. Average primary school enrollment rates, as a percentage of the school-age population, before and after the First and Second Industrial Revolutions, in Europe and the Americas compared to non-Western countries, 1820–2010. See text and footnotes for sources and methodology.

rizes how primary schooling evolved in the average Western country before and after the onset of the First Industrial Revolution (on the left) and the Second Industrial Revolution (on the right). In general, primary education began to expand in Europe and the Americas more than a half century before large factories began to appear, maintaining a steady pace of expansion before and after the transition to an industrial economy. Western countries reached high primary school enrollment rates before beginning to industrialize: roughly 40 percent before the beginning of the First Industrial Revolution and close to 70 percent before the beginning of the Second Industrial Revolution. Moreover, the fact that primary schooling in Western countries did not experience an acceleration in the years immediately preceding or following the onset of the First or Second Industrial Revolutions provides evidence against the view that governments expanded primary education to support industrialization.[38]

38. One question is whether primary school enrollment rates in Western countries would have declined or grown at a slower rate in the post-industrialization period had they not industrialized. To assess this possibility, I looked at how enrollment rates evolved in the post-industrialization period in countries that did not industrialize. The analysis, reported in the online appendix, does not provide support for the claim that industrialization led to an increase in primary school coverage. Before industrialization, the enrollment rates of Western countries that eventually industrialized were growing at a faster rate than those of non-industrializing countries. However, after Western countries industrialized, both groups' enrollment rates were growing at the same pace. This suggests that, if anything, industrialization led to a decline in primary school enrollment rates in Western societies.

A potential concern about these results stems from the fact that primary school enrollment rates reflect not only governments' efforts to provide access to schooling but also parents' decision to send their children to school. In principle, it is possible that governmental provision accelerated when countries began to industrialize, but that parental demand for primary education declined as parents wanted their children to take advantage of new job opportunities in factories. Although it is probably true that some parents wanted their children to work in factories, it is unlikely that parental demand declined compared to the pre-industrial period. Many crops and agricultural activities relied heavily on child labor. If anything, economic historians have found that the move away from agriculture led to greater parental demand for education.[39]

Additional evidence that industrialization was not a leading driver of the creation and expansion of primary education systems in the West comes from the content of the curriculum. Prussia is again a useful example to consider given its influence on primary education systems around the world. In the 1760s, when Prussia introduced a mandatory curriculum for rural primary schools for the first time, it emphasized religious and moral education. Not only did the curriculum not impose a common language for primary schools, which according to Gellner was what industrialization required, but it also deliberately sought to prevent children in rural areas from acquiring skills that might be useful in more industrialized areas. The king's concern that if rural schools taught "too much" they might encourage children to "rush off to the cities and want to become secretaries or clerks" led Prussia to impose entirely separate curriculums for rural and urban schools in order to instruct children in rural areas "in such a way that they will not run away from the villages but remain there contentedly."[40]

Many countries followed Prussia's lead in curriculum matters: they imposed separate curriculums for rural and urban areas, focused on teaching moral values and civic education rather than technical or scientific skills,

---

39. Baker (2015) takes advantage of an agricultural pest, the boll weevil, that spread across the South from 1892 to 1922 and had a devastating impact on cotton cultivation, to examine how changes in the production of cotton, a child labor–intensive crop, affected schooling in the early twentieth-century American South. He finds that a 10 percent reduction in cotton caused a 2 percent increase in Black enrollment rates but had little effect on white enrollment between 1914 and 1929. Baker, Blanchette, and Eriksson (2020) investigate the pest's long-run effect on educational attainment. They find that both white and Black children who were young (ages 4–9) when the weevil arrived saw increased educational attainment by 0.24 to 0.36 years. Their results support the view that child labor in agriculture conflicts with school enrollment.

40. Thomas (1919), p. 18.

and allowed instruction in multiple languages rather than imposing a common national language. In Sweden, for example, the 1842 School Act or *folkskolestadgan*, which established a nationwide compulsory primary education system, emphasized religious education, history, and geography—not what we would expect to see in a country seeking to promote industrialization.[41] In Chile, the 1860 primary education law also established a narrow curriculum that was more focused on teaching moral values than useful skills. The greater emphasis on teaching values than skills or a common language is something we will return to in chapter 5 when we examine how the first national school curriculums were designed to accomplish the goals of primary education.

Where the industrialization argument finds stronger support is outside the West, in countries that during the twentieth century expanded primary education as part of a state-led industrialization process. These countries are represented by the dashed line in figure 2.7. The figure shows that non-Western countries had achieved much lower levels of primary schooling than Western countries before they began to industrialize, and that industrialization was followed by an acceleration of primary school enrollment rates. This is especially true for the Second Industrial Revolution: in the ten years following the adoption of steel, primary school enrollment rates increased on average by close to nine percentage points, twice as much as the increase that occurred in the ten years before steel began to be used in the economy.

Russia under Stalin exemplifies this pattern of educational expansion in non-Western countries accompanying a process of state-led industrialization. During the First Five-Year Plan, compulsory schooling was introduced in the countryside and extended in urban areas, and the total number of children enrolled in primary school increased from eleven million in 1927–1928 to twenty-one million—near universal enrollment—in 1931–1932.[42,43]

---

41. Cermeño, Enflo, and Lindvall (2022).

42. On July 25, 1930, the Central Committee introduced three years of compulsory schooling in rural areas and extended compulsory schooling from four to five years in urban areas. The Central Committee also ordered that all children in both rural and urban areas must complete seven years of education by the end of the First Five-Year Plan (Fitzpatrick 1979, p. 170).

43. In Stalin's 1934 *Report on the Work of the Central Committee of the Communist Party of the Soviet Union* to the 17th All-Union Communist Party Congress held in Moscow, January 26 to February 10, 1934, which refers to the period 1929–1934, Stalin writes: "Of all the successes achieved by industry in the period under review the most important is the fact that it has succeeded in this period in training and forging thousands of new men and women, of new leaders of industry, of a whole stratum of new engineers and technicians, of hundreds of thousands of young skilled workers who have mastered the new technique, and who have advanced our socialist industry.

Public primary schools followed the principle of "polytechnization,"[44] which meant that schools must prepare children not just to become efficient workers, but also to understand the scientific basis of production.[45] The Soviet regime's deliberate expansion of mass education in support of industrialization and economic world supremacy was what most impressed the official education missions sent by the United States to the USSR in the 1950s.[46] One of the U.S. mission's reports concludes:

> These aspects were particularly emphasized by the Soviet educational authorities: the basic formation in mathematics, natural sciences, and polytechnic knowledge related to economic production ... From the moment we stepped into the Soviet jet TU-104 in Copenhagen, ... we sensed the technological push that later would be evidenced to us in the educational work going on in the Soviet Union ... In the school classroom and workshop, in the machine building plant, in the countryside, and wherever we went, we felt the pulse of the Soviet Government's drive to educate and train a new generation of technically skilled and scientifically literate citizens.[47]

Another well-studied example comes from colonial Taiwan during the first decades of the twentieth century. Between 1905 and 1935, primary school enrollment rates climbed from a mere 6 percent to 70 percent; by 1940, universal primary education had been achieved. In a detailed study, the historian E. Patricia Tsurumi argues that the Japanese colonial government expanded primary schooling to support the rapid mechanization and commercialization of agriculture. It timed the school terms to align with agricultural seasons and allowed some absences so children could work in the farms but made it compulsory for children to attend classes on agriculture, commerce, and manual work. In these classes, children learned work habits, respect for manual work, and practical knowledge about soil cultivation, livestock, tree and fish farming, and account-keeping. Perhaps surprisingly, because the Japanese colonists feared that imposing their own

---

There cannot be any doubt that without these men and women industry could not have achieved the successes it has, and of which it has a perfect right to be proud" (Stalin 1934, p. 405).

44. Polytechnization should not be confused with vocational education, which only began *after* primary education (Charques 1932, pp. 21–25).

45. King (1937), p. 56.

46. U.S. Department of Health, Education, and Welfare (1959, 1960).

47. U.S. Department of Education (1960), pp. xiv–xv.

culture and language would backfire, they maintained the teaching of written Chinese in primary schools up to 1918.[48]

In sum, although transitions from an agrarian to an industrial economy appear to have been accompanied by an accelerated expansion of primary education in non-Western countries, the same cannot be said about Europe and the Americas. In countries that led the global expansion of primary schooling, primary education provision reached high levels before industrialization, transitions to an industrial economy were not accompanied by a faster rate of expansion of primary education, and the first national curriculums imposed by central governments were more focused on moral and civic education than on teaching a common language or skills relevant to an industrial economy.

MILITARY RIVALRY AND MASS EDUCATION

Interstate wars were commonplace in Europe during the nineteenth century and their occurrence often motivated rulers to protect their borders through investments that contributed to developing a centralized bureaucracy. Much attention has gone into understanding the role that interstate wars played in incentivizing the development of a bureaucratic apparatus capable of collecting taxes to finance the armies needed to wage war. However, social scientists in sociology, economics, and political science have also argued that interstate wars led central governments to expand mass education as a means to defend their territory from foreign threats.[49] Fighting wars with other countries, the argument goes, taught (or reminded) central governments about the importance of investing in mass education as a nation-building tool to instill among new generations the belief that their nation was superior to any other, thereby predisposing citizens to eagerly defend their homeland if it came under attack. In addition, if in school everyone learned a common language, received physical education, acquired basic reasoning skills, and knew enough geography, the national army would be better equipped to win wars against rival countries.

What does the evidence say about the argument that governments expanded primary education in response to interstate wars, seeking to create loyal and skilled soldiers? Proponents of the interstate wars argument often

---

48. Tsurumi (1977).
49. Ramirez and Boli (1987); Darden and Mylonas (2015); Aghion et al. (2019).

turn to the history of Western Europe, especially Prussia and France, to support their argument. A closer look at these cases suggests a different story. In the case of Prussia, Frederick the Great's signing of the General Rural School Regulations of 1763, which extended compulsory primary education to rural areas, coincided with the end of the Seven Years' War that same year. This coincidence has often been misinterpreted as evidence that what spurred the king's interest in mass schooling was foreign military rivalry.[50] However, in his book on the origins of compulsory primary schooling in absolutist Prussia, the historian James Melton notes that already in 1754—before the war broke out—the King had approved education plans similar to those introduced in 1763; they just couldn't be implemented because of the war. This indicates that something else, preceding the war, prompted the king's interest in primary education.

In France, the education laws passed in 1881 and 1882, known as the Jules Ferry Laws, were motivated partly by Prussia's victory in the Franco-Prussian War of 1870 and partly by the working-class insurrection in Paris the following year. A popular saying in France after its military defeat was that the Franco-Prussian War had been won by the Prussian schoolmaster.[51] However, the significance of the Ferry Laws lies not in the creation of a primary school system regulated by the central government, which had already existed since the July Monarchy, nor in what these laws did for access to primary education. The most consequential changes introduced by the Ferry Laws concerned those affecting the structure of education funding, which became more centralized than ever before, and the content of the curriculum. Specifically, the 1882 law removed Catholic instruction from the French classroom and replaced it with a secular form of moral and civic education, hoping thus to strengthen nationalist sentiment.[52] It also introduced gymnastics and, for boys, military exercises as part of the effort to prepare a new generation of patriotic soldiers. In addition to this curriculum reform, the 1880s laws also introduced the principles of compulsory and free primary education. However, France had already achieved universal primary education in 1865, fifteen years before the Ferry Laws and five years

---

50. Ramirez and Boli (1987), pp. 4–5.
51. Reisner (1922), p. 82.
52. Writing soon after France's defeat in the Franco-Prussian War, the French historian Ernest Renan says: "A pupil educated by Jesuits will never be an officer able to compete with a Prussian officer; a pupil of Catholic primary schools will never be able to participate in a scientifically organized war with perfectioned weapons" (Renan 1871, pp. 95–97).

before the Franco-Prussian War.[53] This means that whatever drove the expansion of primary schooling in France preceded the Franco-Prussian War. I will return to this in chapter 4, but for now, it is enough to note that France's first national primary education law was passed in 1833, resulting in an unprecedented expansion of primary schooling at a time of relative peace between France and neighboring countries.

In the Americas, the inability of the interstate war argument to explain the expansion of primary education is more straightforward. In the United States, for example, proposals to develop a system of publicly funded common schools emerged toward the end of the eighteenth century and gained traction among elites starting in the late 1830s—that is, about twenty-five years after the War of 1812 against Great Britain. In Latin America, access to primary schooling expanded during the nineteenth century more than in any other developing region despite the fact that most of the wars affecting Latin America during that century were civil wars, with interstate wars accounting for only one-fourth of the fighting.[54] For example, Argentina and Chile, the top two providers of primary education in Latin America by the turn of the century, passed their first national primary education law in 1884 and 1860, respectively, both during a relatively peaceful period in international relations.

To investigate the role of interstate wars systematically, figure 2.8 graphs how average primary school enrollment rates evolved twenty years before and twenty years after an interstate war in countries that fought interstate wars in the nineteenth or twentieth centuries.[55] The vertical line in the

53. The incorrect view that the Jules Ferry Laws catalyzed the expansion of access to primary education in France is present in Peter Lindert's influential book, *Growing Public*, which claims that France "lagged behind" the rest of Europe in primary education provision until the 1880s (Lindert 2004, p. 100) but that the Ferry Laws of the 1880s helped France "rise to the top of the European schooling ranks." Lindert does not provide any evidence to substantiate the claim that access to primary education increased in France with the introduction of the Ferry Laws. However, the statistics of primary school enrollment analyzed by Raymond Grew and Patrick Harrigan (1991) show that Lindert's assessment is incorrect. The statistics I assembled are consistent with Grew and Harrigan's conclusions: In 1850, 75 percent of children ages 5–14 were enrolled in primary schools in France, compared to 73 percent in Prussia. By 1860, 91 percent of French children ages 5–14 were enrolled in primary school, and by 1865, universal primary education had been accomplished in France.
54. Centeno (1997).
55. The primary school enrollment rates used to construct this figure come from Mitchell because that is the data source used in the main quantitative study of the impact of interstate wars on primary schooling, conducted by Aghion et al. (2019). Aghion and colleagues report that interstate wars led to an increase in primary school enrollment rates. I reproduce their analysis but distinguish between the Western and Non-Western worlds. I find that the patterns differ across

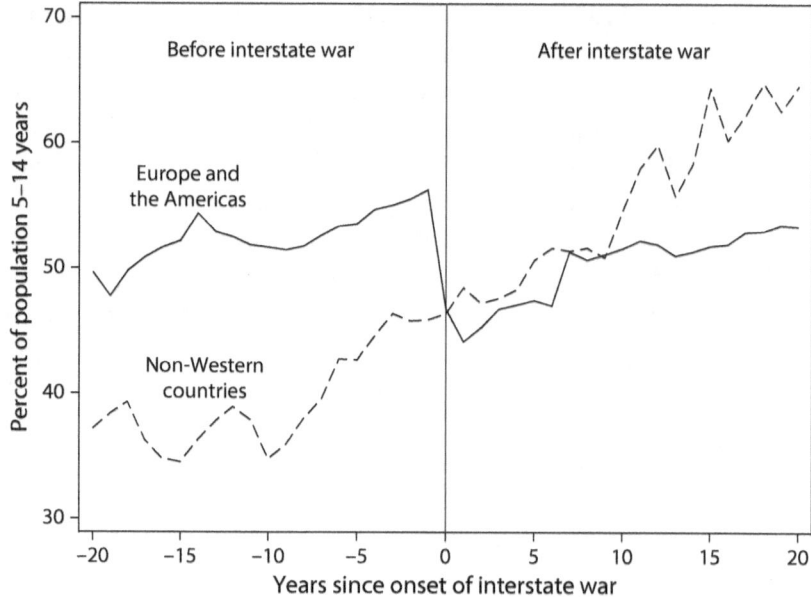

Figure 2.8. Average primary school enrollment rates, as a percentage of the population ages 5–14 years, before and after the onset of interstate wars in Europe and the Americas compared to non-Western countries, 1830–2001. See text and footnotes for sources and methodology.

graph corresponds to the year in which an interstate war began, but the conclusions remain unchanged if instead we look at enrollment rates before and after the end of an interstate war. For any given country, the graph takes into consideration the first interstate war for which data exist on primary school enrollment rates before and after the war.[56] As before, enrollment in Europe and the Americas is depicted by the solid black line, while enrollment in other regions is depicted by the dashed line.

---

regions, and that Aghion and colleagues' conclusion that interstate wars led to an expansion of primary school enrollment rates is driven by non-Western countries. The conclusion that, in the Western world, primary school enrollment rates experienced a drastic decline during periods of interstate war, which was followed by a rebound in enrollment rates, also holds if instead of Mitchell's enrollment data we use my dataset or Lee and Lee's (2016) dataset.

56. For a few countries, this corresponds to a late-twentieth-century war. For example, Argentina fought interstate wars in 1836–1839, 1837–1839, 1851–1852, 1865–1870, and 1982, but we lack data on primary school enrollment rates before 1869, so the war included in figure 2.8 for Argentina is the Falklands War of 1982. Looking at the role of late-twentieth-century wars is a bit removed from the purpose of this book, given our interest in explaining the origins of primary education systems. However, the conclusion remains unchanged if we re-do figure 2.8 focusing only on wars preceding 1950 or 1930.

The data show that in Western countries primary school enrollment rates experienced a sudden and drastic reduction at the beginning of interstate wars, possibly reflecting children's participation in armies or their need to find jobs while older members of their family were away fighting. This initial decline in enrollment was soon followed by a gradual rebound during the first decade after the war. However, the postwar rebound was simply that—a partial recovery back to the enrollment levels that existed before the war broke out.[57] This pattern of decline and recovery does not provide much support for the argument that military rivalry between states explains the Western world's global leadership in primary education. Moreover, additional analyses found in the online appendix (https://press.princeton.edu/books/paperback/9780691261270/raised-to-obey) show that postwar periods have been characterized by educational expansion in all countries, not just those that participated in a war.

INTERNAL CONFLICT: A KEY DRIVER OF MASS EDUCATION

Although many explanations for the expansion of primary education systems have been proposed and investigated, social scientists have ignored or discarded the role of internal conflict as a plausible driver of this expansion. In one influential study, sociologists John Boli, Francisco Ramirez, and John Meyer have gone as far as to argue that expanding the education of the unruly lower classes was "unthinkable" when maintaining order was seen as most problematic. In their view, governments "facing problems of disorder, labor unrest, or failure of social control mechanisms have not resorted to education. They have relied on straightforward repression."[58] In a similar spirit, economic historian Peter Lindert writes that "educating the poor was not viewed as a way to prevent insurrections."[59] These assertions, however, have not been accompanied by an empirical investigation of the

---

57. When we look country by country, the story that emerges is more complicated but, nevertheless, it remains true that there isn't a consistent pattern of acceleration in primary school enrollment rates after interstate wars. In ten countries (Belgium, Bolivia, Brazil, Chile, Colombia, Finland, Italy, Norway, Portugal, and Paraguay) primary school enrollment rates accelerate after interstate wars; in five countries they decelerate (Canada, Cuba, Germany, Netherlands, Peru); in six countries, primary school enrollment rates experience no change in the pace of growth (Argentina, Spain, France, Great Britain, Poland, El Salvador); and in four countries there is a rebound to prewar levels (Ecuador, Greece, Hungary, and Nicaragua).

58. Boli, Ramirez, and Meyer (1985), pp. 154–155.

59. Lindert (2021), p. 49.

relationship between internal conflict and education. In the remainder of this chapter, I show that internal conflicts that brought about considerable political instability were in fact a crucial driver of the expansion of primary education in Western societies.

The common belief that internal conflict does not promote education expansion may stem partly from the fact that, when thinking about how a destabilizing internal conflict impacts schooling, social scientists have found that, in the short term, conflict harms education provision. In times of civil war, for example, schools are often destroyed, and children may drop out of school because roads are blocked, attending school is unsafe, or rebel forces recruit child soldiers. Moreover, governments will often refrain from investing in education during a period of intense conflict. Recall that the attractiveness of education as a peace-building strategy operates over the long term by reducing the probability of rebellion from future, not current, citizens. Politicians who face extremely high levels of uncertainty about whether they will remain in power, as is common for politicians fighting a civil war or social revolution, are likely to focus on their immediate survival, setting aside long-term projects until some level of political stability is temporarily restored.[60] It is not surprising, then, that studies find that civil wars produce a short-term decline in education access and provision.[61]

What social scientists have not considered, however, is the possibility that central governments threatened by a destabilizing internal conflict may later on, as a result of that traumatic experience, become more interested in the education of the masses than they would have been had they not experienced conflict. The long-term educational consequences of internal conflict, then, are also worth examining. Does the occurrence of internal conflict lead to a long-term increase in education provision? The answer is yes, as we will see in this chapter.

Studying whether and how internal conflict shapes education provision presents us with a major challenge—that of identifying periods of conflict and periods of peace. The reason this is a challenge is that, depending on who we ask and what criteria they use to define what constitutes internal conflict, we might conclude that virtually every country at every point in time experienced some instance of internal conflict. And there would be

---

60. Garfias (2018).
61. Shemyakina (2011); Chamarbagwala and Moran (2011); Swee (2015); Leon (2012).

some truth to this conclusion because perfect peace does not exist; there is always some quarrel or dispute going on, no matter how small its scale or how inconsequential in the grand scheme of things. This perpetual presence of internal conflict poses a challenge to our investigation because, in order to assess how internal conflict affects the coverage of primary schooling, we need to have periods of peace interrupted by internal conflict, much like we identified periods of non-democracy followed by democratization or pre-industrial periods followed by industrialization.

I tackle this challenge here by focusing on the consequences of one type of internal conflict that is well-known to be destabilizing: civil wars pitting the masses against the state. The absence of civil war does not imply that there is perfect peace, but the occurrence of civil war does imply an escalation of internal conflict beyond what we may consider normal levels. If the argument I previewed in chapter 1 is true, the intensification of internal conflict that is inherent in civil wars should incentivize governments to invest in mass education. In chapter 4 we will examine other types of internal conflict that, in line with the book's main argument, also played a major role in triggering the emergence and expansion of state-regulated primary education systems in Western societies.

Studying the effects of civil war also makes sense because this constitutes what political scientists would call a "hard test" of the book's theory. Based on everything that has been written so far, we should not expect this type of conflict to have positive effects on education provision. If anything, civil wars have been shown to *depress* education access and provision in the short term. If we can find evidence that civil wars have a positive long-term effect on education provision, that should give us confidence that we are after a more generalizable pattern of education reform triggered by a wide range of types of internal conflict.

Another advantage of focusing on civil wars as a starting point to investigate the role of internal conflict in shaping education provision is that experts have coded the occurrence of civil wars across countries from 1816 to the present as part of the Correlates of War Project. Relying on this external source of information is useful because it ensures that there is no subconscious cherry-picking of what constitutes an episode of considerable internal conflict and what does not. Even the most conscientious and ethical researcher could inadvertently classify what constitutes threatening internal conflict and what doesn't in a way that biases the findings in favor of their argument. The availability of a reputable and widely used dataset that tells us when and where a civil war has occurred guards against this possibility.

In our study of how primary school coverage evolved after civil wars, we will focus on those wars that involve the state as one of the actors. This includes civil wars fought over central control as well as those fought over local issues but with state involvement. We will exclude from consideration regional internal wars or intercommunal internal conflicts in which the state does not participate. This is because we are interested in internal conflicts that are perceived as threatening by national-level politicians. An internal conflict in which the state does not participate is unlikely to be perceived as threatening to national elites; their inaction suggests as much.

To examine the long-term educational consequences of civil war, we will need information about primary school enrollment rates not only after a war but also in the years that preceded it. This implies that we will not be able to analyze the impact of civil wars that occurred before the nineteenth century, or even wars of the nineteenth century that occurred before a country had started collecting education statistics. For example, according to the Correlates of War Project, Brazil had civil wars in 1835–1845, 1893–1894, 1896–1897, and 1932. However, because annual primary school enrollment rates are available for Brazil starting in 1871, we will not be able to analyze the effect of the 1835–1845 war.

Twenty-three countries in Europe and Latin America experienced at least one civil war since 1800 that involved the state as an actor and for which we can observe primary school enrollment rates both before and after the war.[62] Most of these wars began and ended within one year, but some lasted somewhat longer, such as the Spanish Civil War of 1936–1939, and a few lasted much longer, such as Colombia's period of *La Violencia* between 1948 and 1958. Several countries had more than one civil war during the period of study. In the analysis presented below, I focus on each country's earliest civil war with pre- and postwar enrollment data because of the book's interest in explaining the early stages of public primary schooling.[63]

Figure 2.9 replicates a graph from chapter 1 which shows that in European and Latin American countries that experienced civil war, there was a large

---

62. Details by country are provided in the online appendix.
63. The concern that subsequent wars might be endogenous to the provision of education triggered by previous wars is an additional reason for focusing on the first civil war with pre- and postwar enrollment data.

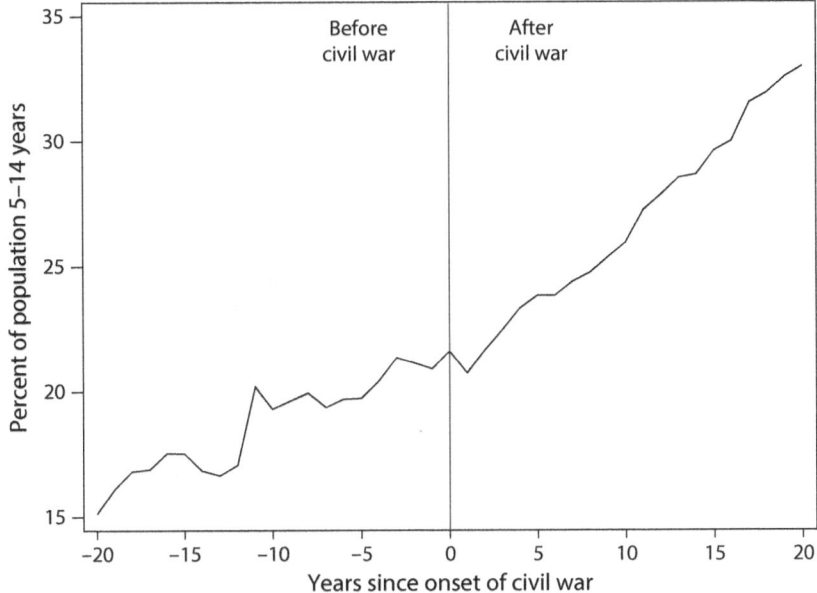

Figure 2.9. Average primary school enrollment rate, as a percentage of the population ages 5–14 years, before and after the onset of civil wars in Europe and Latin America, 1828–2010. See text and footnotes for sources and methodology.

acceleration of primary school enrollment rates in the fifteen years after the war. On average, primary enrollment grew more than twice faster after civil war compared to before. In the graph, the vertical line indicates the onset of civil war, normalized to period zero for comparability across countries, but the results remain unchanged if we look at enrollment trends before and after a civil war ends. While this pattern is consistent with the argument that civil wars led to the expansion of primary schooling, figure 2.9 on its own is not sufficient proof of a civil war's effect on schooling.

One question we may ask ourselves is whether the average acceleration of primary school enrollment rates in the postwar period shown in figure 2.9 is driven by a few isolated but influential cases, or whether it reflects a relatively common phenomenon among conflict-afflicted countries. To answer this question, I looked at each of the twenty-three countries in Europe and Latin America that experienced at least one civil war and for which we have data on primary school enrollment rates. Using simple statistical methods, for each country I assessed whether the slope of the enrollment rate trend became steeper in the postwar period, and whether there was a one-time increase in primary school coverage when the war occurred.[64]

The results of that statistical analysis show that in the majority of countries that experienced civil war, the primary school enrollment rate trend did experience a slope acceleration, a one-time increase, or both, after the war occurred. Figure 2.10 shows a few (though certainly not an exhaustive list of) examples of postwar acceleration in primary schooling from France, Finland, El Salvador, and Colombia. In chapter 4 I will discuss in depth how internal conflict resulted in the centralization and expansion of primary education in four additional cases: 1760s Prussia, 1830s France, 1860s Chile, and 1880s Argentina.

Here, I present briefer examples to give some life to the data. In France, the central government expanded primary education during the first years of the July Monarchy, when a series of violent rebellions in the countryside created a sense of urgency among Parisian elites regarding the need to teach the rural masses to respect the sovereign and its laws. However, in the decade following the impulse of the 1830s, efforts to expand primary education stalled. The Revolution of 1848 renewed national elites' interest in primary education. Conservatives argued that "society is ill," that teachers were to blame for propagating socialist doctrines, and that in order to promote social order, it was necessary that schools teach religious doctrine and "resignation to the order desired by God." After conditioning their support of Louis-Napoleon Bonaparte on the appointment of a pro-Church Minister of Education, a new minister was appointed, and a new law named after him—the Falloux Law—gave new impulse to primary education throughout France.[65]

---

64. Specifically, I estimated a regression model of the linear relationship between primary school enrollment rates and time, allowing for different pre- and postwar linear slopes and an intercept shift at the beginning of the civil war: $Y_{i,t} = \beta_0 + \beta_1(year_{i,t} - t^*) + \beta_2 Treatment_{i,t} + \beta_3[(year_{i,t} - t^*) \times Treatment_{i,t}] + \epsilon_{i,t}$. In this model, estimated separately for each country i, β_1 provides the slope of the primary school enrollment rate trend before the occurrence of civil war, β_2 indicates whether the occurrence of civil war was accompanied by an intercept shift, and β_3 tells us how the country's linear trend in primary school enrollment rate changed after the occurrence of civil war. A total of twenty-three regression tables, one per country, are available in the online appendix. A country is considered to have experienced a *slope acceleration (deceleration)* if the estimated coefficient for β_3 is positive (negative) and statistically significant at least at the 5% level; an *upward (downward) intercept shift* if the estimated coefficient for β_2 is positive (negative) and statistically significant; and *no slope change* and *no intercept shift* if the estimated coefficients for β_3 and β_2, respectively, are not statistically different from zero.

65. Prost (1968), pp. 172–173.

Another example comes from the Finnish Civil War of 1918, one of the most violent civil wars in twentieth-century Europe, with a death toll of 36,000 in only six months. Finland had become an independent state in 1917, but soon after became immersed in a bloody civil conflict between the conservative Whites and the socialist Reds. The Reds' extensive recruitment of peasants and factory workers left the victorious conservative forces with a heightened concern about the education of the lower classes.[66] Soon after the war ended, the government introduced a bill for general compulsory education that emphasized that "civic education would provide society with protection against shocks." Mikael Soininen, the politician who introduced the bill in parliament, presented the events of 1918 as justification for compulsory education. The atrocities of the Finnish Civil War, he argued, would not have taken place if the masses had been enlightened and there had been compulsory education in the country.[67]

El Salvador's civil war of 1932, also known as *La Matanza* ("the massacre") because of the deaths of tens of thousands of rebelling peasants and indigenous communities at the hands of the Salvadoran Army, was followed by a period of sustained expansion of primary education. After the war, the authoritarian central government, led by military officer Maximiliano Hernández Martínez, introduced the first comprehensive primary education law. This law created a centralized primary education system focused on the moral and civic education of children, especially the inculcation of good manners and behaviors consistent with the maintenance of social order, compliance with duties, respect for the state, and patriotism.[68] Under this new centralized system, the coverage of primary schools increased from a relatively stable 13 percent in the decade before the civil war to 21 percent ten years later.

In Colombia also, Bogotá elites blamed the civil war of 1948–1958 on the poor moral development of rural areas. From the 1950s on, the government centralized the provision of primary education, increased the level of funding devoted to education to 10 percent of the national budget, and supported the construction of new primary schools across the territory. After more than a decade of stagnating access to primary schooling, the enrollment rate increased from 27 percent of children in 1950 to 55 percent in 1970.

---

66. For an analysis of the causes, participants, events, and violence of the Finnish Civil War, see Haapala and Tikka (2013).
67. Arola (2003), pp. 141–142.
68. Gómez Arévalo (2012), pp. 101–103.

Alberto Lleras Camargo, president of Colombia in the first four years following *La Violencia*, called for renewed state intervention in education, arguing that the civil war had been caused by the failure of both families and churches to provide a strong moral foundation:

> The insurgency of brutal pressures, the cruelty that characterized this very recent period of our history, would not have caught on so violently on an educated nation, on a civilized country ... The home and the moral and religious education of Colombia failed. That's a historical fact.[69]

These are just some examples that, together with the cases we will examine in depth later in the book, help illustrate a pattern. Of the twenty-three civil wars considered in figure 2.9, fourteen experienced an acceleration of primary school coverage after the war. In the remaining nine countries, seven saw no change in their enrollment trend, and only two countries experienced a decline in primary schooling after the civil war.[70]

One potential objection to the evidence presented in figures 2.9 and 2.10 is that other major political or economic events that coincided with the occurrence of civil wars, and not these wars themselves, may have driven the expansion of primary schooling. For example, the dramatic expansion of primary education in Finland between 1918 and 1922 could have been the consequence of many different factors, including the civil war of 1918, but also, Finland's independence in 1917, the end of World War I a year later, or the consolidation of a representative democracy and the increase in the relative power of parliament under the Constitution of 1919. Indeed, civil wars and social revolutions often catalyze transitions to democracy, and interstate wars often bring about domestic conflict. Could it be that democratization and interstate wars are in fact the key drivers of the acceleration of primary schooling observed in figure 2.9? I considered this possibility by dropping from the analysis any countries that experienced a political regime transition around the time of the civil war, and any countries where the civil war

---

69. Lleras Camargo (1954), quoted in Ramírez and Téllez (2006).

70. In Argentina, Bolivia, Honduras, Peru, El Salvador, Costa Rica, Dominican Republic, and France, enrollment rates experienced a slope acceleration after civil war; in Paraguay and Cuba, an upward intercept shift; and in Uruguay, Colombia, Greece, and Nicaragua, both. Of the remaining nine countries (out of twenty-three), seven countries had no change in their trend (Austria, Chile, Mexico, Brazil, Guatemala, Finland, and Italy), and only two countries saw a deceleration and/or downward intercept shift (Spain and Ecuador).

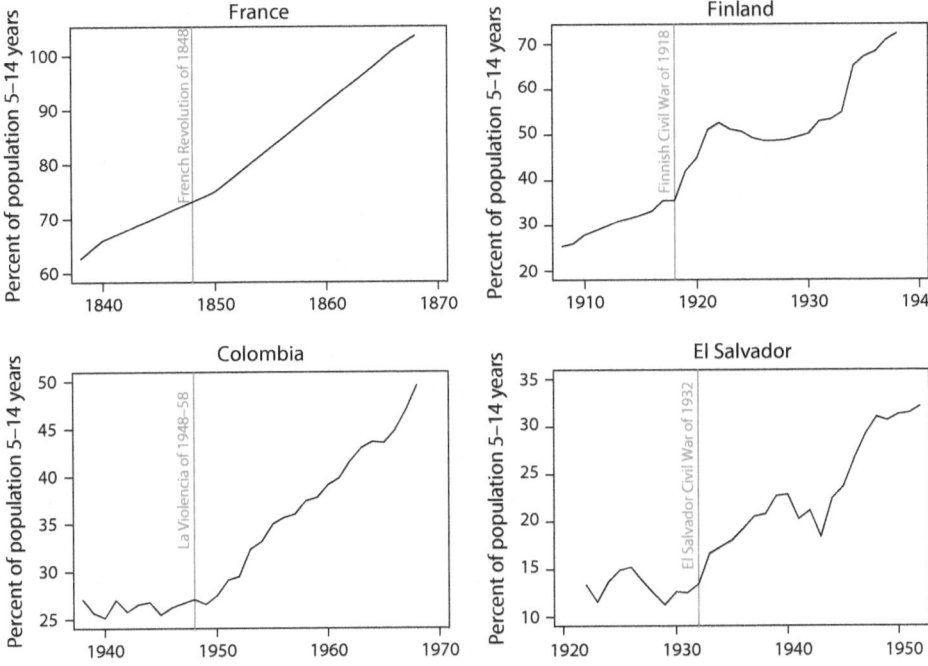

Figure 2.10. Primary school enrollment rates, as a percentage of the population ages 5–14 years, before and after select civil wars in France, Finland, Colombia, and El Salvador.

overlapped with an interstate war. I did not find evidence to support these alternative interpretations. Even if we consider only those civil wars that were preceded and followed by a non-democratic regime and that occurred during periods of relative peace with other countries, we still observe a major acceleration of primary school enrollment rates after civil wars.

A second potential concern is that perhaps civil wars simply coincided with other forces that led to the expansion of primary education everywhere. For example, 1848 was a year of political upheaval in France and many parts of Europe. Even in countries where a revolution did not take place, political elites nonetheless took note of the ideas advanced by revolutionary movements. It is possible that these international ideas, not the occurrence of political upheaval itself, prompted the expansion of primary education. Likewise, from the 1940s through the 1960s, several countries experienced major civil wars that were followed by an acceleration of primary schooling, including Colombia between 1948 and 1958, Greece between 1944 and

1949, and the Dominican Republic in 1965. However, this was a period when many countries redoubled their education efforts even in the absence of civil war, in part because of international competition for economic supremacy during the Cold War and in part because of increased pressure from the United Nations and the World Bank.

To net out the role of international forces that could have led to educational expansion even in the absence of a civil war, I compared how primary school enrollment rates evolved in countries that experienced a civil war vis-à-vis countries where civil war did not occur. This is a helpful comparison because the evolution of the enrollment trends in countries that did not experience civil war can give us an indication of how the trends of countries that *did* experience civil war would have evolved had they not had a war. Figure 2.11 shows this comparison by plotting how much more primary school enrollment rates grew in countries with civil war versus those with no civil war. What figure 2.11 tells us is this: enrollment rates were growing at the same pace in these two groups of countries before civil war broke out, but after it did, conflict-afflicted countries' enrollment rates began growing at a much faster rate compared to countries that did not experience civil war. Averaging across all civil wars, ten years after a civil war the primary school enrollment rate of war-afflicted countries had grown by an additional seven percentage points compared to countries that did not experience civil war. Twenty years later, it had grown by an additional eleven percentage points. This is a large effect not matched by the effect of any other factors.

A third potential concern is related to the fact that social revolutions and civil wars in nineteenth-century Europe and Latin America often brought a liberal coalition to power. It is possible that liberals' ascension to power, and not civil war per se, gave greater voice to those who argued that every individual has the right to education and that, therefore, the state should ensure universal access to schooling. If this were true, we should observe that civil wars that brought liberals to power had a greater impact on primary school enrollment rates than those that did not. Likewise, it is possible that civil wars during the twentieth century brought about educational expansion because they ushered left-wing groups concerned about the welfare of the lower classes into power. However, the data show that this is not what happened. Throughout Europe and Latin America, about half of the wars were won by liberals or left-wing groups, while the other half were won by conservatives or right-wing groups. The impact on primary

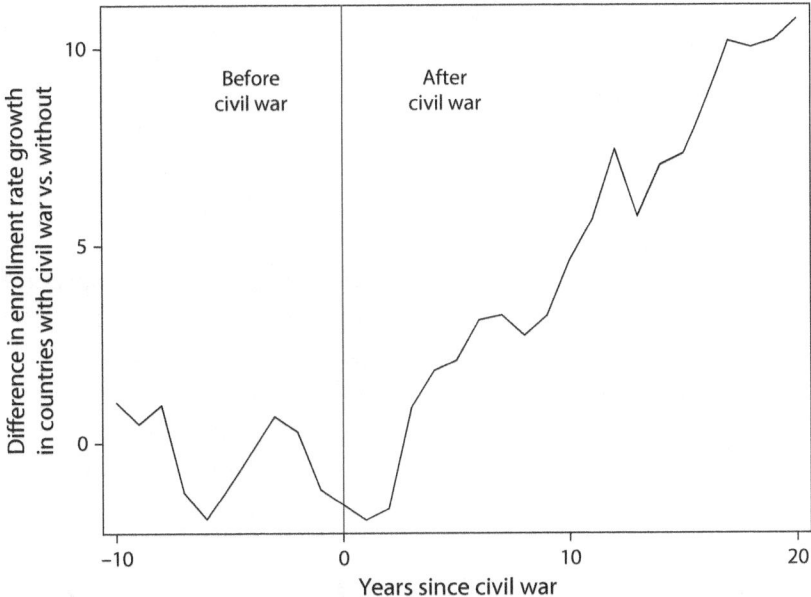

Figure 2.11. Differential growth of primary school enrollment rates between countries in Europe and Latin America that experienced civil war versus countries that did not. Primary school enrollment rates are measured as a percentage of the population ages 5–14 years.

schooling of civil wars did not differ depending on the ideology of the winners.[71] El Salvador in the 1830s and Chile in the 1860s are good examples of postwar state efforts to expand primary schooling by a conservative regime. But even in cases like Finland, where the end of the civil war coincided with an increase in the parliamentary power of the more progressive Social Democratic Party, interest in expanding primary education to prevent a future civil war transcended ideological and party lines, and the conservative National Coalition Party's platform included compulsory education as an urgent task to preserve society by bringing up children and youth to be moral and civilized.[72]

A fourth potential concern is that perhaps the patterns shown in figures 2.9, 2.10, and 2.11 simply reflect the fact that crises in general, including not only crises of internal order such as civil wars but also economic crises, tend to catalyze demand for policy innovation, which could result in

71. See the online appendix.
72. Arola (2003), p. 127.

educational expansion. To consider this possibility I investigated whether banking crises—a common type of economic crisis—that were not accompanied by crises of internal order brought about an acceleration of primary school enrollment rates. I found that they did not.[73] This provides an additional piece of systematic evidence that there is something specific about crises of internal order, and not crises in general, that drove the expansion of primary schooling.

Finally, some readers may wonder whether the effect of civil wars on primary schooling depends on whether the incumbent won the war. Both the cross-national data and the individual cases discussed in greater depth in chapter 4 suggest that the occurrence of civil wars led to the expansion of primary schooling regardless of whether the war was won by the incumbent or brought a new government to power. As I explain in the next chapter, this finding is in line with the book's main argument.

CONCLUSION

Taken together, the evidence presented in this chapter suggests that internal conflict was a stronger and more consistent driver of the spread of primary education in Western societies than democratization, industrialization, or interstate wars. Given these findings, chapter 3 develops an argument to explain why internal conflict in general—not just civil wars—is likely to lead to increased state effort to regulate and expand mass education. Chapters 4 and 5 provide extensive evidence for this argument from non-democratic regimes in nineteenth-century Europe and Latin America. Chapters 6 and 7 show that the logic of conflict-driven education reform travels across time and space and can apply also to modern times and democracies.

---

73. See the online appendix.

CHAPTER THREE
WHY DO GOVERNMENTS REGULATE AND PROVIDE MASS EDUCATION?

Starting in the late eighteenth and especially during the nineteenth century, central governments in the Western societies of Europe and the Americas began regulating, funding, and expanding the provision of primary education for the masses—a sharp departure from a decentralized past in which the education of children had been left entirely up to families, churches, and local governments. In chapter 2 we saw that this phenomenon—the emergence and expansion of primary education systems regulated by the state—preceded the spread of democracy by many decades and was not driven by the needs created by industrialization or external military threats. What explains the emergence and expansion of public primary school systems in the West?

I argue that mass education emerged as a crucial state-building strategy designed to accomplish the state's main function of promoting social order by indoctrinating future citizens to obey the state and its laws. From Thomas Hobbes to Frederick the Great, during the early modern period, primary education came to be viewed by centralizing rulers, philosophers, and education reform advocates as a useful policy tool that could be used to enhance the long-term stability of the state by instilling among the population values and behaviors of discipline, obedience, and respect for the state's authority. Targeting children was considered a particularly effective long-term strategy because children were believed to be more malleable than adults, and impressions made during early childhood, more long-lasting. Still, the idea that the state should play a role in the education of children, especially their moral education, met considerable resistance at first, not only from parents but also from some members of the political elite. What turned the tables in favor of proposals for state-regulated mass education?

The argument I propose highlights the powerful role that fear of the masses played in increasing national elites' support for proposals to create and expand a state-regulated primary education system. Concerns about the threat that mass violence posed to the stability of the state, coupled with the perception that existing policy tools were insufficient to safeguard it, helped convince these elites that their state-building agenda would be better served by an education system designed to instill obedience to the state and its laws.

This chapter fleshes out this theory sequentially. I begin by unpacking both the idea that mass schooling can be used to mold children into well-behaved future citizens, as well as its intellectual history, given that this idea is an important precondition for the development of primary education systems. As we've seen, however, ideas alone are insufficient to explain the rise of mass schooling; threats from below to the state-building aspirations of centralizing politicians played a key role in giving political traction to the idea that central governments should regulate and promote primary education.[1]

Episodes of mass violence that make national elites fear for the stability of the central government, I argue, will help unite these elites behind the idea that the state should play an active role in educating future citizens, and that the main goal of such education should be to shape the moral character of the masses in order to promote orderly behavior and respect for the state and its laws. National elites may disagree considerably about what exactly that education should look like—whether, for example, the moral education provided by the state should be secular or religious. However, underlying this disagreement between national elites we should also find

---

1. I use the terms "centralizing rulers," "centralizing elites," "national elites," and "state-building elites" interchangeably to refer to elites who exert power mainly at the national or central level of government. This includes Paris elites in France, Buenos Aires elites in Argentina, Santiago elites in Chile, etc. The term includes both elites who control the central government and those who form part of the opposition to it at the national level. For example, both liberal and conservative politicians in Santiago comprised the group of centralizing or national elites in 1850 Chile, even though conservatives controlled the presidency and a majority of seats in Congress. National elites, even if they belong to different political parties or factions, all share the goal of protecting and consolidating the central government's power. Crucial to the accomplishment of this goal is the central government's ability to maintain social order and promote widespread acceptance of its authority throughout the territory.

broad agreement about the role of the state in regulating and providing mass education to "moralize" the masses. Concerns about anarchy, crime, peasant riots, strikes, social revolution, civil war, and other forms of internal conflict involving mass violence, to the extent that they are perceived by national elites to threaten the state's viability, will play a crucial role in forging this shared agreement among elites. This chapter explains why.

IDEAS ABOUT EDUCATION, INDOCTRINATION, AND STATE-BUILDING

Before primary education came to be viewed as a useful tool to promote a common national identity or industrialization, the education of the masses by the state came to be viewed as a *state-building* tool that could be used to promote long-term social order by teaching unquestioned respect for the state's authority. Early advocates for the development of such systems argued that primary schools had the power to shape the preferences, beliefs, moral character, and behavior of the masses. The state, according to these advocates, should take control of the provision of primary education because the moral values, manners, habits, and aspirations developed by future citizens had repercussions for the state's stability and its ability to fulfill its main function to promote social order. Educating *children*, they agreed, was especially important because if people learned to respect the state's authority early on, they would continue doing so throughout their lives. By shaping the moral character of children, primary schools could instill respect for the state and its laws, preventing violence, crime, and dissident behavior, and promoting long-term political stability.

Proponents of state-controlled primary education systems argued that these systems would foster long-term order through three main indoctrination mechanisms. First, primary schools could shape behavior by instilling fear of punishment for misbehavior, or conversely, the anticipation of rewards for proper behavior. Stealing, vandalism, quarreling, cheating, lying, and cursing, were typically punished, as were questioning the teacher, speaking out of turn, or disobeying school rules or teachers' instructions. Great thought was given to the type of punishment that was most appropriate for children, with influential education thinkers arguing that disciplining children through physical violence could backfire, leading them to learn violent behaviors themselves. For this reason, other methods of punishment such as public scolding and humiliation or the threat of eternal damnation were considered preferable. By contrast, sitting quietly and completing tasks as instructed were praised publicly. School punishments and rewards sought to teach children that their behavior had consequences, and that obedience, compliance, and respect for existing rules and authorities were in their own best interest.

Second, mass education proponents argued that primary schools could teach the masses from a young age to be content with what they had. The crucial goal here was to teach people that, even if rebellion was costless and punishment for misbehavior was avoidable, they had no reason to rebel against the status quo. Sometimes these lessons were taught by inculcating a love of one's country or nation, but even before cultivating national identity became an important goal of primary education, schools often taught values of moderation and self-sacrifice and tried to instill in children the belief that happiness resulted from accepting one's lot.

Third, proponents argued that schools could cultivate unconscious habits of compliance and deference simply through repetition. The mere act of attending school every day and following schedules, routines, and rituals, such as marching in silence from classroom to breakroom, would develop habits of discipline and obedience and lead individuals to internalize from a young age what constituted good manners and civil behavior.[2] Repetition of specific words, sentences, and paragraphs, as part of the process of learning how to read and write, was also considered a useful means for teaching specific political values and beliefs. An example of this is found in a French primary school textbook authorized by the Royal Council on Public Instruction in 1841 for teaching reading and writing; in the first section of the textbook, the words chosen to exemplify different sounds emphasize authorities like "King" and "God" and values like "kindness," "goodness," "acceptance," and "order." In addition, in this and other textbooks, the passages used to teach children how to read are filled with moral lessons about the importance of obeying one's parents and teachers, fulfilling one's duties toward others, treating others with kindness and respect, staying away from violence, and other messages that the state wanted future citizens to internalize.

The commonality across these three mechanisms, and the reason I call them *indoctrination* mechanisms, is that the educational process left no room for questioning the norms, values, beliefs, habits, and behaviors that

---

2. Firsthand descriptions of routines and their expected effect on children's behavior include, e.g., Sarmiento (1849), Alexander (1919), and Kandel (1933).

schools were trying to inculcate. The norms to be taught in schools were crafted by elites, often to their own benefit, and engaging in a process of critically evaluating the merits of these norms was inconceivable. Whether adults with well-developed reasoning capabilities agree with the desirability of some of these norms is beside the point.

Education reformers were prolific in their writing, devoting many essays, letters, books, and speeches to articulate these three important functions of mass education. One influential example is *Educación Popular*, a book commissioned by the Chilean government to Argentine politician Domingo F. Sarmiento. Published in 1849, *Educación Popular* quickly became a must-read among nineteenth-century Latin American politicians interested in the development of a mass education system. In it, Sarmiento argues that the newly independent states of Latin America have inherited "savage races" characterized by their "hatred of civilization" and "rebellion against culture," and that "the fate of the state" depended on the education it gave to children. *Educación Popular* describes the expected consequences of primary schooling by highlighting its moralizing effects and its ability to instill obedience to a common authority that operates beyond the realm of the family:

> Attending school will have on children a moralizing effect from spending there time that, in the absence of school, would go towards laziness and abandonment; habituating the spirit to the idea of a regular, continuous duty gives the child habits of regularity in his way of operating; adding an authority besides the paternal one, which does not always work constantly toward the moral development of children, begins to form in the spirit the idea of an authority that operates outside the family; finally, the grouping of masses of individuals, the need to contain in them their passions and the opportunity to strengthen relationships built on sympathy put down without them feeling it the first rudiments of morality and socialization, so necessary to prepare them for obligations and duties of life as adults.[3]

There are additional ways in which primary education could serve to promote social order besides the three indoctrination mechanisms discussed above.

The first, highlighted by French philosopher Michel Foucault, is that schools can act as daytime prisons, keeping young children and adolescents

---

3. Sarmiento (1849), p. 57.

off the streets and away from opportunities to engage in any kind of behavior that threatens the public order.[4] The second concerns the use of primary schools as a tool to monitor the individual behavior of children and their parents through teachers who are embedded in their communities and act as loyal agents of the state.[5] This monitoring function of primary schools was certainly of interest to the state as it sought to gather information about the population across the national territory, and the creation of primary school inspection systems also helped to fulfill this informational goal of primary education. However, for the act of monitoring to have an effect on people's actual behavior, and in particular for monitoring to prevent people from rebelling against the state, people must understand the consequences of their behaviors and the costs of rebellion. Teaching about these costs was a central goal of primary education systems.

Targeting *children* to maintain social order was primarily a long-term investment; while schools could keep children from the streets in the short term, their main function was to shape the values and behavior of *future* citizens. The underlying belief behind this targeting was that molding the child's individual character was a more cost-effective way to promote social order than trying to alter the behavior of adults.

Importantly, during the nineteenth century primary education was usually considered a terminal degree for the masses, not a stepping stone to acquire further education.[6] In fact, the terms "primary education," "popular education," and "popular instruction" were used interchangeably. Secondary schools and universities remained reserved for the upper classes well into the twentieth century, as we saw in previous chapters.[7] This conception of primary education as a terminal degree for the masses helps explain why many elites were not fearful of its provision; the masses, they believed, would simply be compelled to attend primary schools in which they would learn how to behave. Primary education would not lead to other kinds of educational opportunities that could expose the masses to subversive ideas, they reasoned, because those opportunities simply would not be available to them.

---

4. Foucault (1995).

5. E.g., Foucault (1995) writes that the school "must not simply train docile children; it must also make it possible to supervise the parents, to gain information as to their way of life, their resources, their piety, their morals. The school tends to constitute minute social observatories that penetrate even to the adults and exercise regular supervision over them" (p. 211).

6. E.g., Guizot (1816); Pigna (2009), p. 286.

7. Brockliss and Sheldon (2012), pp. 91–92.

To explain why national elites set up primary education systems, we need to understand their beliefs about the likely benefits of mass education. The rest of this section delves deeper into the intellectual history of educational ideas as articulated by influential political philosophers, rulers, and their education advisers. To preview the main takeaways, during early modernity, as new ideas for organizing social and political life emerged in the hands of social contract theorists, the education of all children emerged as an important task that *the state* should take over for its own sake, to promote internal social order and the political legitimacy of the state. In the late eighteenth century, these ideas combined with Pietist pedagogical thought to influence the creation of the Prussian primary education system; from there, they traveled to other states that throughout the nineteenth century looked to Prussia as a model for state-building. However, while important, these ideas are insufficient to explain the rise of state-controlled primary education systems—even in the case of Prussia. What often gave political traction to these ideas were violent episodes that heightened national elites' fear of the masses.

EDUCATION IN SOCIAL CONTRACT THEORIES

What should be the goals of education? Who should attend school, and what should be taught there? Should the state be involved in its provision, and if yes, how? These are centuries-old philosophical questions on which thousands of essays and books have been written. Here I will attempt to sketch out the history of those ideas in just a few paragraphs, focusing on the elements that are most relevant for my argument.

The idea that the state should educate children goes back at least to Plato, who in the context of thinking about how to maintain social order in a society where conflicting interests could evolve into dangerous civil wars, argues that lawmakers should take charge of educating all children to create social peace. Plato fears that if a child's "upbringing is inadequate," the child will become "the most savage creature on earth. For that reason," he argues, "the lawgiver must not allow the upbringing of children to be something secondary or incidental."[8] Rulers "must cling to education" in order to "tame" children, "guiding children towards correct reason, *as defined by law*,"[9] directing their souls to "become good," and preventing the teaching of anything

---

8. Plato (2016), 766a, p. 218.
9. Plato (1992), 424b, p. 99; Plato (2016), 766a, p. 218; Plato (2016), 659d, p. 77. Plato highlights that what constitutes "correct" reasoning is defined by the laws established by political authorities. Education should teach children to understand and accept these laws. Emphasis is mine.

"that is counter to the established order."[10] Mass education, in Plato's view, must be compulsory and controlled by a Superintendent of Education.[11]

These ideas notwithstanding, during most of Western history the legitimacy and power of political rulers emanated from their military capacity—that is, their capacity to both defend and repress the population—and from religious doctrines such as the divine right of kings. Such doctrines were spread by the Catholic Church who, along with parents, took on the task of providing a moral education to children, teaching them right from wrong. Religious education, however, was quite limited in scale, content, and frequency: it was neither universal nor compulsory, it focused on the Bible, and church-run schools usually operated on Sundays only.

It was during the early modern period and especially during the Enlightenment, when the power of absolute monarchies and the Church came to be questioned and ideas about a new type of political system based on a social contract started to gain support, that the idea of state-regulated mass education emerged with greater force. Influential political thinkers from Hobbes to Rousseau helped shape the idea that mass education was a central component for promoting social order and political legitimacy, and that this education had to be provided by the state.

One of the most compelling arguments about the need for the state to provide mass education comes from Thomas Hobbes's social contract theory as articulated in *Leviathan*. Given the huge influence of this book, I will first unpack the relevance of education in Hobbes's political thought, before turning to influential ideas by other political philosophers who also place education at the center of theories of social order and political legitimacy. Written during the English Civil Wars of 1642–1651, which forced Hobbes to go into exile, in *Leviathan* Hobbes asks how societies can avoid "the war of all against all." His well-known conclusion is that civil wars can be avoided if everyone agrees to give up the right to govern themselves and instead delegates the authority to govern to one person, the *sovereign*.

What is less well-known today is how central the educational duty of the sovereign was, according to Hobbes. Political theorist Richard Tuck explains that, because of his own training in rhetoric, Hobbes became convinced that almost everything we believe to be "right" or "wrong" is a matter of subjective conviction and is therefore open to debate. "A sovereign is created by men who (in a 'state of nature') are conscious of the fallibility and conten-

---

10. Plato (1992), 424b, p. 99.
11. Plato (2016), 765d-e, p. 217.

tiousness of their own opinions, in order to have a common source of judgement in disputed matters, and thereby to avoid civil strife." The role of the sovereign, therefore, is to judge what is true and what is false, and what is right or wrong. Given this, "the chief enemies of civil order are (on Hobbes's account) any persons who seek to persuade their fellow citizens of the truth of *anything* disputable, without the permission of the sovereign. Since an education system looks precisely like a mechanism for persuading people of certain things, his theory required in principle an extremely close management by the sovereign of what was taught in both schools and universities, just as it required a close management of what was taught by churches."[12]

Hobbes argues that education is what makes man fit for society and what ensures social order.[13] Internal peace, he says, "cannot be maintained by any civil law or terror of legal punishment"; it can only be maintained by educating people.[14] This education, he stresses, is one of the sovereign's main duties; he must define what principles should be learned in school, and then see that they are taught correctly, never renouncing the power of "appointing teachers and examining what doctrines" are taught to ensure these are not "contrary to the defence, peace, and good of the people."[15] People must be taught the grounds and reasons behind the sovereign's rights, he says; otherwise, they become "easy to be seduced and drawn to resist him." The "instruction of the people in the essential rights of sovereignty" by the sovereign is therefore "not only his duty, but his benefit also," because this education provides "security against the danger that may arrive to himself in his natural person from rebellion."[16]

In addition to teaching people the grounds for the sovereign's power, the Hobbesian education system places a major emphasis on teaching obedience to the sovereign because his unquestioned authority, says Hobbes, constitutes the basis of social order. "The people are to be taught, first, that they ought not to be in love with any form of government they see in their neighbour nations, more than with their own, nor ... to desire change. For the prosperity of a people" comes not from whether they are ruled by aristocrats, a democratic assembly, or a king, "but from the obedience and concord of the subjects.... Take away, in any kind of state, the obedience (and consequently the concord of the people) and they shall ... in short time

---

12. Tuck (1998), p. 153.
13. Hobbes (1991), *De Cive* I.2.
14. Hobbes (1994), XXX.3.
15. Hobbes (1994), XXX.3.
16. Hobbes (1994), XXX.6.

be dissolved."¹⁷ Second, says Hobbes, people should "be taught that they ought not to be led with admiration of the virtue of any of their fellow subjects, . . . nor of any assembly (except the sovereign assembly)"; their obedience is "to the sovereign only."[18] Third, the people "ought to be informed how great a fault it is to speak evil of the sovereign representative (whether one man or an assembly of men), or to argue and dispute his power, or any way to use his name irreverently, whereby he may be brought into contempt with his people, and their obedience (in which the safety of the commonwealth consisteth) slackened."[19]

The idea that educating children was crucial to promote good moral behavior gained strength during the Enlightenment, as new ideas about the basis of morality emerged. From Locke to Rousseau, Voltaire, or Kant, Enlightenment philosophers shared the view that human beings are born neither good nor evil; our moral principles, they argued, are molded by our experiences and by the education we receive. This idea of human nature challenged the prevailing Christian doctrine of the original sin according to which we are born with a natural predisposition to evil and ill behavior. From Voltaire's metaphor that we become wolves not because we were born wicked but because we did not receive a proper education,[20] to Kant's argument that man "is merely what education makes of him,"[21] Enlightenment philosophers stressed the power of education to shape our moral character. For Rousseau, "the first education ought to be purely negative" in the sense that it must be focused on preventing vices rather than cultivating virtue; "prevent vices from arising, you will have done enough for virtue."[22] Voltaire highlighted the power of education to develop our conscience so that we will refrain from performing bad actions simply to avoid the consequences that those actions would have on our conscience.[23] For Kant, the first goal of education was to make individuals "subject to *discipline*; by which we must understand that influence which is always restraining our animal nature from getting the better of our manhood."[24] Discipline, Kant wrote, "is merely restraining unruliness."[25]

17. Hobbes (1994), XXX.7.
18. Hobbes (1994), XXX.8.
19. Hobbes (1994), XXX.9.
20. Voltaire (1901b), p. 181.
21. Kant (1900), p. 6.
22. Rousseau (2019b), p. 195.
23. Voltaire (1901a).
24. Kant (1900), p. 18. Emphasis in the original.
25. Kant (1900), p. 19.

Enlightenment philosophers also had something to say about whether the *state* should be involved in educating the masses or whether this education should be left to parents. Rousseau was among the strongest proponents of a state-run education system. In his *Discourse on Political Economy*, he stresses that education is too important a matter to be left in the hands of fathers; like Hobbes, he argues that education should be directed by the state to teach obedience to children:

> Inasmuch as there are laws for adulthood, there should be laws for childhood that teach obedience to others; and inasmuch as each man's reason is not left to be the sole judge of his duties, the education of children ought all the less to be left to their fathers' lights and prejudices, as that education matters to the state even more than it does to the fathers ... Public education under rules prescribed by the government, and under magistrates established by the sovereign is, then, one of the fundamental maxims of popular or legitimate government.[26]

The focus on the education of *children* specifically reflected a belief, substantiated by neuroscience today,[27] that early childhood is the period when human beings are most susceptible to external influence. Investing in molding a child's mind was therefore believed to be a way to secure proper values and behavior among *future* citizens. The idea that children are more "malleable" than adults has a long tradition in political philosophy dating back at least to Plato's *Republic*, where he writes: "You know, don't you, that the beginning of any process is most important, especially for anything young and tender? It's at that time that it is most malleable and takes on any pattern one wishes to impress on it."[28]

Similar ideas about the long-term term benefits of "imprinting" children's minds, to borrow the term used by Hobbes,[29] can also be found among political philosophers during the Enlightenment. Locke refers to the minds of children as a tabula rasa, "as easily turned this way or that way as water itself." For this reason, "great care is to be had of the forming of children's minds and giving them that seasoning early which shall influence their lives always after." Adulthood was too late a stage to discipline people according to Locke: "He that is not used to submit his will to the reason of others when he is young, will scarce hearken or submit to his own reason when he is of

---

26. Rousseau (2019a), pp. 21–22.
27. National Research Council, Institute of Medicine (2000).
28. Plato (1992), 377a–b, 52.
29. Hobbes (1994), XXX.6.

an age to make use of it."³⁰ In a similar vein, Kant argued that "discipline must be brought into play very early; for when this had not been done, it is difficult to alter character after in life."³¹ Rousseau also emphasized that the training of future citizens must begin early in their lives: "To form citizens is not the business of a single day, and to have them be citizens when they are men, they have to be taught when they are children."³²

There was also among several of these influential philosophers a concern about the use of physical coercion to straighten children's behavior. Plato believed that "Forced bodily labor does no harm to the body, but nothing taught by force stays in the soul.... [D]on't use force to train the children in these subjects; use play instead."³³ Some Enlightenment philosophers had an even more extreme view. Locke, for example, thought that if "rough methods" were applied, children would pay attention to and learn from those methods, and this would "introduce a contrary habit."³⁴ Essentially, Locke was arguing that we teach by example; if children are disciplined through physical force, they will learn to use force themselves to obtain what they want, which is contrary to the goal of education to promote a well-ordered society.

The preceding ideas about how children ought to be educated, stressing discipline and obedience from a young age, are perhaps unexpected coming from Enlightenment philosophers like Rousseau or Kant. Indeed, the Enlightenment also gave rise to a current of thought that affirmed that human beings have the right and responsibility to deploy their free agency and capability for inquiry to the pursuit of an autonomous life unconstrained by doctrines or traditions.³⁵ This alternative idea is more akin to how we would describe the goals of a liberal education and did in fact make

---

30. Locke (1996), *Some Thoughts Concerning Education*, pp. 32, 36.
31. Kant (1900), p. 4.
32. Rousseau (2019a), p. 20.
33. Plato (1992), 536d–e, 208.
34. Locke (1996), *Of the Conduct of the Understanding*, p. 30.
35. History school textbooks tend to stress these emancipatory ideas when describing the Enlightenment. However, in recent decades historians have criticized this as an outdated and misguided description (De Dijn 2012). One particularly influential historian of the Enlightenment, Jonathan Israel, distinguishes between two competing groups of Enlightenment philosophers and ideas. The progressive ideas that today we associate with the rise of Western liberal democracies and secular politics, writes Israel, stem from what he calls the *Radical Enlightenment*, whose main philosopher was Baruch de Spinoza. By contrast, mainstream Enlightenment philosophers such as Voltaire and Locke emerged in reaction against Radical Enlightenment ideas, espousing conservative ideas and defending the status quo. Voltaire, for example, felt an "inexplicable sympathy toward Louis XV's regime" (De Dijn 2012, p. 799) and expressed that "he was not in the least

its way into the design of secondary schools and universities for members of the elite. However, it had little influence on the foundational debates that shaped the rise of state-regulated education for the popular classes.

Rousseau's work illustrates the different types of education that Enlightenment philosophers envisioned for elites versus the rest. In *Émile, or On Education*, he proposes a child-centered education that nurtures the child's curiosity. *Émile*, however, is not a book about mass schooling; it focuses on the upbringing of a rich man's son by his private tutor. The pedagogy that Rousseau proposes here, with its emphasis on cultivating the child's holistic development, differs from the idea he advances in other works that the state should educate all children for the sake of cultivating obedience. There is a tension in Rousseau and other Enlightenment philosophers' work between their interest in safeguarding the state's legitimacy and authority, and their defense of individual freedom. In Rousseau's case, he reconciles these through the concept of the *general will*, defined as "the collective will of the citizen body taken as a whole. The general will," he argues, "is the source of law and is willed by each and every citizen. In obeying the law each citizen is thus subject to his or her own will, and consequently, according to Rousseau, remains free." The question of how good laws that everyone would willingly obey emerge in the first place presents a problem for Rousseau. To address it, he turns to the role of an authority—the legislator in *Discourse on Inequality* or the tutor in *Émile*—who has the function to persuade others—before they can discern for themselves—to accept that the laws are in their own best interest. Similar to the role he ascribes to mass schooling or even to "the tutor in *Émile*, the legislator has the role of manipulating the desires of his charges, giving them the illusion of free choice without its substance."[36]

A testament to the limited influence that child-centered pedagogies had in the everyday functioning of primary schools is the fact that John Dewey, a proponent of this type of pedagogy, was considered revolutionary for his time. Writing at the beginning of the twentieth century, Dewey reacted to the prevailing model of education, criticizing schools for their "strict disciplinarianism which was the style of education in his day" and teaching methods focused on students' "passive reception of ideas."[37] He proposed,

---

interested in 'enlightening' or emancipating the man in the street, his coachman or any other 'servants'" (Israel 2006, p. 528). See also Israel (2001).

36. Bertram (2023).

37. Cooney, Cross, and Trunk (1993), pp. 134–135.

instead, that teachers take the child's own initiatives and interests into account to promote individual curiosity, inquisitiveness, and autonomy. And he argued that the things learned in school should serve as an instrument not for the maintenance of the status quo but, on the contrary, for social change. There would have been no Dewey, or at least he would not have been considered progressive, if the liberal ideas about education that we associate with the Enlightenment had penetrated the public primary education systems that emerged in the nineteenth century.[38]

It should be clear from this section, but it is worth stressing, that the main arguments that shaped the early stages of mass education ascribed to it a *state-building* role. Nation-building arguments emerged later in the history of mass schooling.[39] Primary education, its proponents argued, should focus not necessarily on teaching a common language or national identity, but should definitely teach moral principles and inculcate obedience to the sovereign and its rules as part of the state's interest and its function to preserve social order and prevent civil strife.

BROUGHT TO YOU BY PRUSSIA

The educational ideas of Hobbes, Rousseau, and others did not just stay within the circle of philosophers; they reached and influenced European rulers and their counselors, providing them with new ways of thinking about how to promote social order. From Europe, they then traveled to the Americas, and later to other parts of the world, shaping there too the development of public primary education systems.

One of the first states to put these educational ideas into practice was Prussia during the eighteenth century, under the absolutist regime of Frederick II, perhaps better known as Frederick the Great. The king was an admirer of Enlightenment political philosophers, with whom he often corresponded, and even granted asylum to Rousseau when he fled France after the publication of *Émile* and *The Social Contract* in 1762. Often referred to as an "enlightened absolutist" for the kinds of reforms he pursued, in 1763 Frederick II signed the General Rural School Regulations, a royal decree that introduced compulsory primary schooling in all Protestant rural

---

38. Cooney, Cross, and Trunk (1993), pp. 133–148. See also Dewey (1916), especially pp. 300–301, where he explains how German philosophy shaped the goals and characteristics of education systems during the nineteenth century.

39. The exception is Rousseau (2019b), who as part of the *Considerations on the Government of Poland* did discuss the usefulness of education to "give souls the national form," turning individuals into loyal, devoted citizens by immersing them in the culture and history of their country.

areas of Prussia, followed in 1765 by a similar decree for Catholic areas. This school law established the basic principles that would guide Prussian primary schooling for the next century and beyond, regulating almost every aspect of primary education—the school day and school year, school fees, discipline, the curriculum, methods of instruction, teachers, and school supervision and administration.[40] Every aspect of schooling was tightly regulated by the state. This marked the beginning of the Prussian primary education system.

The significance of the Prussian case lies in the impact it had on the development of primary schooling worldwide. Prussia's ascendance to the category of "great power" beginning with Frederick II led statesmen around the world to look at Prussia to understand the roots of its success. As they did, a common view emerged that Prussia's power relied in large part on its ability to control its population, which in turn was the result of its educational efforts. As this view gained strength, more and more countries began to send public officials on education missions to Prussia to observe its primary schools and identify lessons that could be applied back home. Education reformers from other parts of Europe and from the Americas borrowed ideas from Prussia. For this reason, looking at the educational ideas that circulated in Prussia can tell us something broader about the ideas that shaped the global rise of primary education systems.

The educational ideas popularized by Prussia starting in the late eighteenth century bear a striking resemblance to those of early modern political philosophers in highlighting that primary schools should be regulated by the state and should focus above all on shaping the moral character of children to teach them discipline, self-restraint, and obedience to rules and authorities. The General Rural School Regulations of 1763 tasked teachers precisely with providing a moral education to all children—which in the case of Prussia was to include the teaching of religion—and placed special emphasis on the inculcation of habits and values of discipline and obedience. The decree explicitly called for educating "the young for the fear of God"[41] and stipulated that "discipline must be done wisely so that ... [the child's] stubbornness, or self-will, are broken ... and lying, cursing, disobedience, rage, quarreling, brawling, etc. are punished."[42]

---

40. Alexander (1919), p. 14.
41. Prussia (1763), p. 1.
42. Prussia (1763), p. 22.

There is virtually no disagreement among historians, says Kenneth Barkin, that compulsory schooling in Prussia was conceived by the state "as a mechanism of social control to indoctrinate children in political submissiveness."[43] Contemporary observers throughout the nineteenth century also highlighted this aspect of Prussian primary education. Consider, for example, what the U.S. intellectual and preacher Orestes Brownson wrote in 1839:

> Let it be born in mind that in Prussia the whole business of education is lodged in the hands of government. The government established the schools in which it prepared teachers; it determined both the methods of teaching and the matters taught. It commissions all teachers and suffers no one to engage in teaching without authority from itself. Who sees not then that all the teachers will be the pliant tools of the government and that the whole tendency of the education given will be to make the Prussians obedient subjects of Frederic the king? Who sees not that education in Prussians is supported merely as the most efficient arm of the police and fostered for the purpose of keeping out revolutionary or, what is the same thing, liberal ideas.[44]

Similar impressions about Prussian schooling persisted through the early twentieth century.[45]

In addition to the influence of Enlightenment philosophers, the Prussian school system's emphasis on teaching discipline and obedience incorporated the ideas of Pietism. Since its emergence in the seventeenth century, Pietists wanted to restore Luther's message that "God judges according to that which lay within the depths of your heart" and "the sincerity of your beliefs." They focused on "inward reflection," not outward manifestations of religiosity, as "the core of all worship and observance," insisting that God's

---

43. Barkin (1983), p. 32. Whether the state succeeded in accomplishing its social control goal, and in particular, the extent to which teachers complied with education regulations, remains a subject of controversy among historians. I return to this point in chapter 8.

44. Brownson (1839).

45. In a book published by Thomas Alexander in 1919 based on his study of the history of the Prussian primary education system as well as firsthand observation of primary schools in Prussia, he concludes: "A careful study of the Prussian school system will convince any unbiased reader that . . . the whole scheme of Prussian elementary education is shaped with the express purpose of making ninety-five out of every hundred citizens subservient to the ruling house and to the state" (Alexander 1919, p. v).

word must "penetrate our hearts" and the individual "must serve God from deep within the temple of his very soul."[46]

Cultivating the individual's heart and inner convictions, Pietists claimed, was important both for spiritual salvation and for maintaining the hierarchical social order. Pietists wanted people to accept their societal role not through external coercion but out of personal conviction that this was the right thing to do. One Pietist educator explained the Christian duty to accept one's place in society through a simple analogy: "The body of Christ consists of different members. Not every member can be a hand, foot, eye, or ear. Each member has its own task. . . . The foot should not desire to become an eye, nor the hand an ear."[47]

Pietist ideas had begun to enter schools at the beginning of the eighteenth century through the work of August Hermann Francke (1663–1727), who stressed that, through inward reflection, individuals could acquire both the self-discipline required to exercise their duties and the calmness to accept their place in society.[48] Obedience to authority was among the most important of such duties, Francke told his students. Foreshadowing the language of the 1763 General Rural School Regulations commanding teachers to break the child's will, in the 1690s Francke wrote that teachers' task was "to break the natural willfulness of the child; the schoolmaster who seeks to make the child more learned had forgotten his most important task, namely that of making the will obedient."[49] Obedience to a master or ruler, Francke told his students and the teachers he trained, must be rooted in an inner conviction: "Genuine obedience is not merely outward, but comes from deep within the soul. It is not rendered out of coercion but with a willing heart."[50]

The two main education advisers to Frederick II, the Protestant Johann Hecker and the Catholic Johann Felbiger, were both admirers of Pietists' pedagogical ideas. Felbiger earned the king's trust when he advised him that teachers should instill in their students not only a sense of their spiritual duties but also secular obligations such as "loyalty, obedience, and devotion to the king."[51] Like Francke and Locke, Felbiger believed that physical force was usually an unadvisable method for disciplining children and should

---

46. Phillip Jacob Spener, quoted in Melton (2002), p. 26.
47. Francke, quoted in Melton (2002), p. 29.
48. Melton (2002), p. 30.
49. Francke, quoted in Melton (2002), p. 43.
50. Francke, quoted in Melton (2002), p. 40.
51. Melton (2002), pp. 185–186.

only be reserved for situations when other methods had failed to induce obedience. According to the king's adviser, children were more likely to comply with rules if they internalized that this was the right thing to do, hence the importance of providing a moral education to children that emphasized the importance of respecting rules and authorities. Moreover, this internalization of the value of obedience among children would provide a safeguard against rebellion once they became adults, too. In Felbiger's own words:

> Human beings are by nature moved by kindness and reason rather than force. Despotic methods will not induce pupils to obey. They must be convinced that it is useful and correct to follow the schoolmaster's wishes. Only then will they learn to obey even in situations where force is absent. In this way, the schoolmaster accomplishes his most important task: his pupils will observe their duties not only in school, but throughout their lives.[52]

A useful method for impressing obedience upon children, claimed Felbiger, was the use of state-approved textbooks including classroom exercises in which children had to repeat and memorize certain phrases and paragraphs that emphasized concepts of obedience, discipline, etc. For example, a school manual for teachers written by Felbiger in 1768 instructs teachers that every student must memorize the following answers:

"Q: Who is subject to the power of the ruler?

A: Everyone . . .

Q: From whence comes the power held by the ruler?

A: This power comes from God.

Q: Whom does God ordain?

A: Everyone who holds authority. Because all who exercise authority are ordained by God, subjects must be submissive, loyal, and obedient, even to a ruler not of our religion . . .

Q: What does it mean to resist authority?

A: To resist authority is to rebel against the divine order.

---

52. Felbiger quoted in Melton (2002), p. 187.

Q: What happens to those who do not submit to authority?

A: They will suffer eternal damnation.[53]

This passage illustrates a common technique used throughout the nineteenth century: the embedding of structured dialogues within textbooks by which children learned, through the power of repetition, that they must respect the ruler's unquestioned authority and obey his laws, or else they would be punished. The specific type of punishment varied, sometimes focusing on "eternal damnation" as in the passage above, other times highlighting more mundane consequences, such as losing the esteem of one's parents, teachers, and friends. By contrast, those who were obedient, children were told, would be rewarded by going to heaven, or by earning the praise and love of others.

If children's moral education was a crucial goal of Prussian primary schools, it is equally clear that promoting social mobility was not. On the contrary, Prussian rulers wanted primary schools to teach children in rural areas to be content with what they had and prevent them from developing aspirations for more. Frederick II himself told his Minister of Education in a letter written in 1779 that "teachers in the countryside [must] instruct the young in religion and morals ... and educate them far enough that they neither steal nor murder." However, concerned that if children learned "too much, they rush off to the cities and want to become secretaries or clerks," the king told his Minister that children "must be taught in such a way that they will not run away from the villages but remain there contentedly."[54] His successor, Frederick William III, also warned that primary education must not promote social mobility but should instead teach common people to accept the social position they were born into: "We do not confer upon the individual or upon society any benefit when we educate him beyond the bounds of this social class and vocation, give him a cultivation which he cannot make use of, and awaken in him pretensions and needs which his lot in life does not allow him to satisfy."[55]

The Prussian education model emphasizing the teaching of discipline, acceptance of one's lot, and respect for the sovereign's authority is significant because it heavily influenced the design of primary education systems

---

53. Melton (2002), p. 186.
54. Alexander (1919), p. 18.
55. Frederick William III quoted in Reisner (1922), pp. 143–144.

elsewhere. Some of this influence was driven by a relocation of Prussian education reformers, including Felbiger. In January 1774, Maria Theresa of Austria asked her ambassador in Berlin if Frederick II would be willing to grant Felbiger a leave of absence, a request to which the king acceded. After arriving in Vienna in May of the same year, Felbiger was appointed to the Commission on Education and given ample authority over primary education, first in Austria, and later in Hungary.[56]

A more important channel for the diffusion of educational ideas were the dozens of visits from government officials who traveled from Europe and the Americas to Prussia to learn about its primary schools. Among them, two of the most famous visitors were Domingo F. Sarmiento, author of the influential book *Educación Popular*, and Horace Mann, who led the Common School Movement in the United States. A fervent advocate for the creation of a national primary education system, Sarmiento agreed with early modern philosophers and education reformers from Prussia that "moral education is precisely the goal of primary instruction"[57] and primary education should especially target the masses, whom he referred to as "undisciplined hordes"[58] in need of restraint. The Prussian primary education system also made a strong impression on U.S. education reformer Horace Mann, who traveled to Prussia in 1843 while he was Secretary of the Massachusetts State Board of Education. The trip convinced Mann that the United States should emulate the Prussian project of using primary schools to teach political values and respect for political institutions to the masses, writing:

> if Prussia can pervert the benign influences of education to the support of arbitrary power, we surely can employ them for the support and perpetuation of republican institutions ... If a moral power over the understandings and affections of the people may be turned to evil, may it not also be employed for good?[59]

I will discuss education reforms in Argentina and the United States further in chapters 4 and 7, respectively, but one point worth highlighting here is that the educational ideas of Prussia found a receptive audience in many different political contexts, including other absolutist regimes, the oligarchic regimes of nineteenth-century Latin America, and more democratic

---

56. Melton (2002), pp. 211–212.
57. Cousin (1833a), p. 4.
58. Sarmiento (1845), p. 140.
59. Massachusetts Board of Education, Horace Mann (1844), p. 23.

contexts.[60] We will illustrate this point in coming chapters when we examine a range of cases that, despite featuring different political regimes, share a common logic underlying their educational reforms.

A similar observation applies to the pervasiveness that these educational ideas had across elites of different political ideologies and different dispositions toward the Church. Considering that Protestant pastors like Johann Hecker, Catholic priests like Johann Felbiger, and anti-clerical Enlightenment philosophers, all advanced a similar idea that the state had an interest in shaping the moral character of the masses, it should come as no surprise that this idea became quite popular throughout the nineteenth century among both conservative and liberal elites, as well as among Protestants, Catholics, *and* Church opponents. To be sure, there were differences between them with respect to the curriculum, something we will examine in depth in chapter 5. But to preview one of the conclusions of that chapter, conservatives and the Church believed that the basis of morality was religious doctrine and, therefore, that the moral education of the masses should be based on the teaching of the Bible and the catechism. Liberals and Church opponents, on the other hand, believed that moral principles could be accessed through reason regardless of one's religious beliefs. They therefore advocated for a curriculum where moral education was secular and where reasoning skills were cultivated to enable people to access these principles. Beneath these differences and struggles over how to teach morality, however, elites from across the ideological spectrum came to view mass education as a powerful moralizing and state-building tool to mold children into well-behaved adults.

AN INCOMPLETE EXPLANATION

The rise of public primary education systems in Western societies was tightly linked to the circulation of ideas about the state-building role of mass education. These ideas provided political rulers with new ways of thinking about the strategies they could deploy to carry out one of the state's most important functions: to promote internal peace and social order. Although

---

60. Most common measures of regime type, such as the Polity Project and Boix, Miller, and Rosato's (2013) database on political regimes, classify the United States as a democracy in the 1830s and 1840s, when the Common School Movement emerged under Horace Mann's leadership. However, the right to vote was limited to white men; in particular, neither women nor enslaved Black individuals could vote during this period. Therefore, by present-day standards, the United States in the 1830s and 1840s would be considered, at best, a limited democracy.

the emergence of a conceptualization of mass education as a policy tool that could be used by the state to indoctrinate future citizens was necessary for the rise of these systems, the circulation of this idea was often insufficient to prompt rulers to expand primary education.

At any given point in time, multiple ideas and policy proposals abound, and not all of them find enough political support. Take the case of climate change: global warming is a well-documented fact, and environmentalists have been incessant in their efforts to educate society and advocate for reforms to reduce climate change, but political support for reforms that would reduce our negative impact on the environment has been elusive. Something similar often happened to mass education advocates in the eighteenth and nineteenth centuries: although they were convinced of the power of public schooling to promote social order, other political elites whose support they needed to advance education reform were not as convinced about the importance of having a state-regulated mass education system.

The rise of public primary education systems, then, required not just the circulation of ideas about the benefits to the state of regulating and providing mass education but also the *popularity* of these ideas among national elites. Explaining the rise of these systems requires understanding what led the educational ideas we have discussed so far to gain sufficient political traction, especially among national elites who had the power to introduce or block centralized education reforms. This is the task for the remainder of this chapter, in which I argue that episodes involving mass violence that heightened national elites' fear of the masses helped increase elite support for state-regulated mass education.

THE CATALYZING ROLE OF INTERNAL CONFLICT

A central argument of this book is that episodes involving mass violence that contribute to an atmosphere of social unrest and political instability are likely to increase national elites' willingness to invest in primary education in order to prevent future threats against the state. The key characteristics of these episodes are: one, they involve mass violence; two, they are perceived by national elites as destabilizing; and three, they lead elites to conclude that repression and redistributive concessions alone are insufficient to prevent social disorder.

Many different types of episodes involving mass violence, of varying scales and driven by different causes, can feel threatening to national elites. Some examples include crime waves, food riots, peasant revolts, labor strikes, civil wars between a peripheral province and the central government, civil wars between an ethnic or religious minority and the group that controls the national government, social revolutions, etc. The nature and roots of the conflict are also not particularly relevant to the argument; social strife may be driven by economic, geographic, political, ethnic, racial, or religious inequalities, to name some common sources of conflict. What the argument does require is that the conflict involve mass violence and that it be perceived by national elites as destabilizing. It would be unlikely for a conflict that does not involve the masses to lead national elites to become more concerned about mass behavior than they were before the occurrence of that conflict. Likewise, the state is unlikely to invest in mass education if the conflict involves mass participation but does not threaten the state's stability.

Why would episodes of internal conflict that involve mass violence increase national elites' willingness to regulate and promote mass education? The starting point of this argument is the assumption that national elites care about maintaining power and promoting social order. This, after all, is arguably the main function of the state—hence the use of the term "failed state" to refer to societies that are trapped in a cycle of recurring civil wars. To accomplish the goal of promoting social order, national elites can choose from a set of policy tools: physical repression, redistribution to buy off potential or former rebels, and mass indoctrination (including primary education). Each of these policy tools operates in a different way.

Repression can restore social order in the short term by jailing or killing unruly individuals and forcing their leaders to go into exile. However, the need to use repression implies that the state has failed, at least temporarily, to accomplish the goal of preventing social disorder. It is possible for the *anticipation* of state repression to prevent rebellion from emerging in the first place. For this to be true, however, people must believe that the expected costs of repression are greater than the expected benefits of rebellion. These costs will depend both on the probability of being repressed and on the consequences should they be repressed—spending two months in jail, losing one's house, a limb, a child, or one's life, are not likely to be perceived as having the same cost.

Concessions that improve the well-being of unruly individuals can also help to restore order in the short term. Whereas repression can help increase the expected costs of rebelling, redistributive policies that address rebels' grievances can help reduce the expected benefits of rebellion. If national elites know that the masses are angry about the level of economic inequality in society and are willing to fight for an improvement in their material well-being, elites can introduce redistributive policies to reduce the reasons for rebelling. These policies can take many different forms, from land redistribution to progressive taxation, labor policy reform, improvements in infrastructure, social welfare programs, or public employment opportunities, to name just some examples. By reducing potential rebels' economic grievances, national elites can reduce the probability of rebellion. From the perspective of elites, though, redistribution comes at a cost: it reduces their relative economic power. Moreover, redistributive policies also come with a commitment problem: redistribution may enable elites to appease rebels in the short term, but once redistribution takes place, what is to prevent people from rebelling again in the future and demanding more concessions?

The indoctrination of children offers an entirely different approach. While redistributive concessions and repression seek to restore social order in the short term through the use of carrots and sticks, indoctrination is a long-term strategy that focuses not on trying to end an existing conflict between elites and the masses, but instead, on preventing *future* conflict from emerging in the first place. Indoctrination efforts seek to promote social order by convincing people that they have no reason to rebel against the state's authority. If people internalize the value of peace, discipline, and obedience to the sovereign and its laws, and develop unconscious habits of deference to authority, this will reduce the probability of rebellion even in the absence of repression or redistribution. Primary education for the masses, as we have seen, was believed to serve precisely this function: to inculcate values and habits that would prevent unruly behavior.

As appealing as this policy tool may sound based on its potential benefits to a ruler, it also has considerable costs associated with it. The creation and expansion of a national primary education system that teaches loyalty to the state is no small task, least because of the resources needed to construct schools and hire teachers in often remote areas, but also because of the centralized bureaucratic infrastructure needed to ensure that what schools teach is in fact aligned with the state's goals. The decision to expand primary education will therefore depend on both expected benefits *and* costs.

Episodes of internal disorder, particularly those involving mass violence and perceived by national elites as destabilizing, can lead elites to recalculate the costs and benefits of mass indoctrination, resulting in increased elite support for educational expansion. During times of internal peace, it is natural for elites to focus on the substantial costs of expanding education (e.g., school construction, teacher training and recruitment, etc.). Although education reformers may insist that the long-term benefits of expanding education will offset these costs, many elites will likely remain unconvinced. The observed internal peace suggests to them that the existing policy mix used to promote order is adequate, and therefore expanding education would be an unnecessary cost. However, when internal disorder tangibly upsets the central government's authority, national elites previously content with existing policies can be persuaded that they need new policies to promote order, including mass education. Elites who experience destabilizing internal conflict may conclude that providing primary education will be more beneficial than they thought before the conflict occurred.

Exposure to internal conflict can lead elites to update their perceptions of the costs and benefits of mass education through at least two informational channels. First, although elites care about the possibility of mass rebellion even in peaceful times, they have imperfect information about the magnitude of this threat. In particular, elites do not know if the masses are moral or immoral. All they observe is mass behavior; based on that behavior, they form beliefs about whether the masses are more likely to be moral or immoral. The occurrence of internal conflict involving mass violence can lead elites to update their perceptions and conclude that the masses are more immoral, dangerous, and prone to rebellion than they previously thought. Alternatively, national elites may know that some individuals in society (call them "radicals") are immoral and are likely to revolt at some point in the future, but they do not know to what extent radicals will have widespread support because they do not know how moral or immoral each member of society is. Here again, experiencing internal conflict can prompt elites to confirm their beliefs about radicals and, more importantly, update their beliefs about the immorality of individuals whom they knew little about before the conflict occurred.

It is also possible for internal conflict to reveal information about the limitations of existing policy tools to promote social order. If elites' diagnosis is that existing policies are insufficient or inadequate, this can create a window of opportunity for new approaches to promote social order. One possible limitation may lie in the state's repressive apparatus. For instance, the unexpected difficulty of accessing rebel regions, or police forces' joining the protesters they were supposed to repress, could suggest that repression can fail to quash rebellion, and that indoctrination to prevent conflict in the first place may be worthwhile. The occurrence of internal conflict again operates by modifying elites' beliefs about the expected net benefit of mass education. If national elites believe they can control the masses easily through repression, then making long-term investments in changing the masses' morality will not be appealing to them—doing so would add a cost that, according to elites' beliefs, is unnecessary given that other efficacious policies are already available. However, if an internal conflict emerges and the central government has difficulty defeating rebels, national elites are likely to update their beliefs about the efficacy of existing policies such as repression and redistribution, conclude that these are less effective than they previously thought, and become more open to investing in costly but potentially more effective long-term tools like indoctrination.

Internal conflict can also reveal information about the inadequacy of existing approaches used to shape the moral character of the masses. If families, local communities, and the Church were previously responsible for the moral education of ordinary people, the outbreak of an internal conflict that threatens the stability of the state may increase national elites' belief that new approaches toward moral education are needed. In particular, internal conflict can heighten elites' concerns about a misalignment between the interests of the state and those of the Church. If traditional moral education was focused on teaching people to obey God's laws only, the occurrence of internal conflict can make national elites become more interested in a type of moral education that teaches obedience to the sovereign and its laws. This again would increase national elites' support for a system of mass education controlled by the state.

Would this pose a threat to the Church and therefore lead the Church to oppose the state's intervention in mass education? Not necessarily. As the case of Prussia illustrates, sometimes public schools teach loyalty to both God and the sovereign, thus helping advance the goals of both the Church and the state. Religious authorities will often welcome increased state promotion of mass education, even if this means giving up some control over moral education, because in exchange they obtain a larger audience of children exposed to religious teachings. Of course, there are other cases where the Church and national elites will come into tension. In some of these cases, Church supporters are too weak politically to prevent the secular state from displacing the Church in education matters. Argentina in the 1880s is an example of this, as will become clear in chapter 4. In other cases, liberal politicians may offer concessions to win over some of the Church's supporters within the national government. This occurred in France during the 1830s, as we will see in the next chapter. Such concessions can take many different forms, such as providing public resources for Church-run teacher training institutions, including religious instruction within public schools, or allowing pastors and priests to retain some school supervision functions. To be sure, these concessions come bundled with greater state intervention in education, and the most fervent Church supporters are unlikely to be swayed by them. Yet what is necessary for the advancement of state-led education reform is not the support of *all* national elites but the support of a majority of them. Fear of the masses in contexts of internal conflict can help move the needle in that direction.

All the channels I have discussed so far are consistent with a view of individual behavior as driven by a rational consideration of costs and benefits. From this point of view, internal conflict can lead to a rational recalculation of the expected net benefits of mass education by providing new information about the morality of the masses, outlier "radicals" and their influence, the efficacy of repression and redistribution, and the success of existing moralizing forces.

In addition to these channels, a more visceral response to internal conflict on the part of elites may also explain their decision to adopt education reform. We know from neuroscience and psychology that personal experience of catastrophes tends to activate primitive brain regions such as the amygdala, generating exaggerated responses due to fear.[61] The vividness of lived experiences can activate responses that would be less likely to emerge if left entirely to the parts of the brain responsible for logical thinking. One area of public policy where the role of lived experiences versus rational reasoning has received considerable attention is climate reform. Educating people about the dangers of global warming has proved ineffective in garnering public support for reform; in fact, even among individuals who do not dispute the fact of global warming and are aware of its dangerous consequences, including wildfires and tsunamis, climate reform is usually not a priority. However, actual exposure to wildfires in one's neighborhood does increase an individual's support for climate reform, pointing to the importance of lived experiences in shaping individual behavior. A similar mechanism could explain the expansion of mass education following internal

61. Weber (2006).

conflict. Even if elites have heard and considered arguments for the expansion of state-controlled mass education as a means to promote social order, it is possible that their support for these policies will only materialize when they have actually lived through a crisis of internal disorder that puts their lives, property, and power at risk. According to this view, fear, not reason, would explain elites' increased support for mass education proposals following episodes of acute mass violence.

Separating rational and visceral responses to internal conflict is unfeasible in historical settings because the tests that scientists typically use to assess the presence of a visceral response involve, for example, measuring the level of skin conductance. What we *can* do, though, is analyze whether the arguments and language used by national elites to discuss education reform changed after experiencing internal conflict. Do elites become more concerned about the masses' immorality or the inefficacy of repression after facing internal conflict? Does their speech become more emotional? These are questions we will examine in the next chapter, but the short answer to both is yes. This should not be surprising. Trying to adjudicate whether rational *or* visceral responses to internal conflict drove the post-conflict expansion of primary education is a futile exercise; although as social scientists we strive for simplicity, the human beings we study are complex and varied. What drives one person may not drive another. Some people may be more inclined to respond to logical and abstract arguments, while others may be more sensitive to lived experience and emotional stimuli. The key point is that, for multiple reasons that may differ across elites, we should see that internal conflict leads to an increase in national elites' support for mass education proposals.

In this way, the occurrence of internal conflict can help forge a sufficiently large coalition of support among national elites to advance the creation and expansion of a primary education system. Some members of the elite will have been convinced about the value of such a system prior to the occurrence of internal conflict—the Felbigers, Sarmientos, and Manns of each country. However, by instilling fear and concern about the masses and the set of existing policy tools used to control their behavior, violent internal conflict can bring additional elites on board, enlarging the coalition that supports mass education. If large enough, this coalition will choose to invest in primary education for the masses under the direction of the state.

The coalition size needed to develop a primary education system will depend on the type of political regime in place. In an absolutist regime like Prussia under Frederick II or Austria under Maria Theresa, the king or queen may move forward with reform unilaterally. In a constitutional monarchy with a limited franchise but some degree of parliamentary politics such as France under the July Monarchy, or in the oligarchies of nineteenth-century Latin America, kings and presidents could in principle introduce education reforms via royal or executive decree; however, the creation of a national primary education system typically requires a comprehensive education law supported by a parliament or congress. Violent internal conflict that threatens the stability of the central government could contribute to forging this coalition by creating a sense of urgency among members of parliament about the need for such a system. The impact of internal conflict in democracies is more difficult to predict. In well-functioning democracies that represent the interests of the electorate, we would expect congressmembers not to respond to mass rebellion by introducing education reforms aimed at indoctrinating the population; in such democracies, congressmembers would likely respond to mass rebellion by addressing the grievances that led to rebellion in the first place. In reality, however, there is often a disconnect between the policy agenda of elected representatives and the policy preferences of the electorate. In such contexts, it would not be surprising to observe national representatives responding to internal conflict by pursuing education reforms that, instead of empowering individuals, seek to control them.

Episodes that involve mass violence against the state are likely to lead national elites to recalculate the costs and benefits of education even if the masses were not the instigators of the conflict. Internal conflicts in which two groups of elites fight against each other—for instance, elites in one province contest the power of the central government, or members of the bourgeoisie fight against the king and aristocracy—can still create incentives to expand primary education when the masses join in the rebellion against the state's authority. Even if the idea of rebelling did not originate with the masses, their participation in it—and the political instability that this engenders—can provide sufficient reasons for national elites to become more interested in teaching the masses to respect the state's authority.

Some readers may wonder whether the theory of conflict-driven education reform I have outlined applies only to cases where incumbent elites come out victorious from the conflict, retaining their position of power within the central government. While the theory may be more intuitive for these cases, we should observe a similar dynamic when a new group of elites comes to power as a result of internal conflict. Consider one of the most dramatic forms of political turnover; that which occurs after a revolution brings a new dictatorship to power. As Steven Levitsky and Lucan Way document in their book, *Revolution and Dictatorship*, revolutionary governments often face an initial period during which counterrevolutionary forces seeking to remove the new government from power become activated.[62] To consolidate their newly acquired and fragile power, these regimes must invest in state-building. While Levitsky and Way focus on new regimes' efforts to strengthen the repressive apparatus of the state, this book provides a complementary argument that highlights the role that mass education can play in enhancing the stability of new regimes. In chapter 2 I discussed evidence in support of this argument when I noted that civil wars led to an expansion of primary schooling regardless of whether the war was won or lost by the incumbent. Later on, we will review specific examples from France and Mexico where new elites turned to indoctrinate the very same popular sectors that had supported their violent ascension to power.

Not all episodes of internal conflict will lead to education reform, and we will spend all of chapter 6 considering the limits of the argument. One thing that must be true for this to occur is that elites must have a sufficiently long time horizon to reap the expected long-term political benefits of educating children. Investments in mass education are primarily a long-term investment; elites are unlikely to incur the costs of expanding primary education unless they expect to be around long enough to reap the benefits. This condition can hold in various types of non-democracies—from absolutist to constitutional monarchies, oligarchies, hegemonic-party regimes, and personalist dictatorships—and sometimes also in democracies, either those captured by an entrenched elite, or those in which a stable and institutionalized party system exists and there is regular rotation between parties in power. Indeed, in chapter 4 I discuss examples from different types of non-democratic regimes where mass rebellion against the status quo led to the expansion of primary education as a means of indoctrination, while in chapter 7 I present evidence of conflict-driven education reforms in democratic contexts.

62. Levitsky and Way (2022).

One interesting question is whether internal conflict must come to an end before education reform takes place. On one hand, during an internal conflict, the state is likely to prioritize allocating resources to activities that can directly help end the conflict; education, from this perspective, may not be a priority. In addition, because the provision of education by the state is a long-term form of investment in social order, national elites who face high levels of uncertainty about their political future may not have incentives to make such long-term investments. This is especially true in countries afflicted by chronic internal conflict; there, elites' short-term concerns about their immediate survival will likely supersede long-term concerns. In these circumstances, an end to the conflict would be necessary for national elites to expand primary education. However, in situations where the state has sufficient resources to fight rebels and expand education *and* national elites anticipate that the conflict will come to an end, they may choose to expand primary education before the conflict ends.

To summarize, proposals for the creation of a national primary education system often encountered resistance from elites who argued that the state lacked the funds to support primary schooling or that moral education was best provided by individual families, local communities, or the Church. A key factor that helped forge consensus among national elites for the expansion of primary education was the occurrence of violent episodes of internal conflict pitting the masses against the state. When acute enough to threaten the state's authority, these episodes made national elites more fearful of the masses and more convinced that expanding primary education was necessary to prevent future mass violence against the state.

USING HISTORY TO EVALUATE THE ARGUMENTS

The theory of education reform I have articulated in this chapter may seem intuitive in retrospect, but it departs sharply from the way most people think about the factors that drove the global rise and spread of mass education. Further, my argument departs from most of what has been written about the consequences of internal conflict for both state-building and education provision. For these reasons, it is crucial to assess whether my theory finds support in the real world.

What should we observe in the real world if the argument I have outlined in this chapter is a good explanation of the rise and spread of state-regulated mass education systems? The theory predicts that, under certain conditions, internal conflict involving mass violence against the state will (1) lead to an increase in state-regulated primary education; (2) lead to an increase especially in those regions where repression was less effective in containing the conflict; (3) increase the salience of arguments about the role of primary education in maintaining social order; and (4) increase the state's efforts to promote moral education in primary schools.

First, the theory I have articulated predicts that internal conflicts involving mass violence and perceived by national elites as destabilizing will tend to lead to an increase in state-regulated primary education. This increase can be manifested in three main ways: (1a) an increase in the level of state regulation of existing primary schools; (1b) an increase in the level of primary education provision in contexts where the state was already regulating primary schools; or (1c) a combination of both an increase in the level of state regulation and an expansion of primary schooling.

Note that an increase in the level of state regulation of primary education does not necessarily imply that the central government will become the main authority in charge of overseeing, funding, constructing, and running the daily operations of primary schools. This would be the most extreme case, but the theory is also consistent with a situation in which schools continue to be run by local authorities and the Church, while becoming subject to more national regulations specifying what they can teach, who can teach, etc., in order to better align these schools with the goals of the state. To ensure that mass education serves the indoctrination goals of the state, and to prevent it from empowering the masses, central governments can introduce comprehensive education laws and regulations that, for example, give the state extensive powers to train and recruit teachers, create centralized inspection systems to monitor teachers and schools, impose a national curriculum to control the content of education, and specify what textbooks can be used. All these forms of central government intervention in primary education are designed to increase the probability that, regardless of who runs the daily operation of schools (e.g., the state, local governments, the Church), primary education serves the state's goals of maintaining power and promoting order.

Besides an increase in the level of state regulation of primary schools (predictions 1a and 1c above), an alternative—or additional—manifestation of the state's increasing interest in mass education following episodes of internal conflict would be an expansion of primary education by the state (prediction 1b). The evidence I presented in chapter 2 is consistent with this prediction; recall that in that chapter I described a pattern of primary education expansion following civil wars in Europe and Latin America. This finding stands in contrast with a common argument that civil wars disincentivize investments in state capacity,[63] and with the finding that civil wars have often led to lower access to education during the war.[64] The source of this difference lies in the fact that, while other studies focus on the *short-term* consequences of civil war for state capacity and education provision, the question I consider in this book is whether, in the *long term*, the occurrence of internal conflict is likely to lead states to promote mass education above and beyond what they would have done if internal conflict had not occurred. To answer this question, in the next chapters I draw on a wealth of historical data spanning two centuries to provide a deep understanding of how internal conflict and elites' fear of the masses led to educational reform in the Western world. While some of the evidence I present comes from contexts afflicted by civil wars, I also provide evidence from additional types of internal conflict such as peasant revolts, food riots, and other forms of social unrest.

The second prediction of the theory is that the expansion of primary schooling by the state will be greater in areas where repression was less effective in containing the internal conflict, as these are the areas where national elites are most likely to conclude that other strategies besides repression are needed to promote long-term social order. Chapter 4 explores this theoretical prediction in two cases, 1830s France and 1860s Chile, where the magnitude of internal conflict varied across departments and provinces. Using historical statistics on educational expansion, that chapter shows that central governments' effort to promote primary education was greater in departments and provinces where the level of conflict was greater. Chapter 7 discusses more recent examples of national efforts to promote educational expansion in violence-afflicted regions.

Third, the theory also implies that ideas and arguments about the role of primary education in maintaining social order will become more salient among national elites who experience internal conflict. This is a crucial implication as it relates to the reasons why internal conflict will tend to lead to educational expansion. I propose that experiencing internal conflict will change the beliefs and arguments espoused by national elites about the costs

---

63. Collier et al. (2003); Besley and Persson (2008); Cárdenas (2010).
64. Shemyakina (2011); Chamarbagwala and Moran (2011); Swee (2015); León (2012).

and benefits of expanding primary education. However, there are alternative reasons why internal conflict could lead to educational expansion. For example, it is possible that, in the aftermath of an internal conflict, political elites expand primary education in an effort to improve the economic well-being of former and potential rebels. This would imply the use of primary education as a redistributive tool more than as a tool to indoctrinate future citizens. Alternatively, perhaps the process of fighting a civil war or other type of acute internal conflict leads to an improvement in the capacity of the state to raise revenue and reach remote areas. This could then lead to an expansion of primary education not because of an increased interest but because of an increased ability among national elites to expand education for the masses. Much of chapter 4 will be devoted to considering these alternative channels behind the post-conflict expansion of primary education.

Fourth, the theory implies that we should observe increased effort by the state to promote moral education in primary schools following internal conflict. Promoting the state's moral education agenda requires, on one hand, that parents send their children to school, and on the other, that schools advance the state's education agenda. Efforts to accomplish the former can include the adoption of compulsory schooling laws, penalties for parents whose children do not attend school, or rewards for those who do. Efforts to ensure the latter can include state intervention in teacher training and recruitment to screen aspiring teachers based on their moral qualifications, the adoption of a national curriculum that emphasizes moral education, and centralized school inspections. As I explain later in the book, the state could approach the design of the curriculum in different ways. First, as previewed earlier and as will become clear in chapter 5, moral education can be secular or religious—an issue on which liberals and conservatives are likely to disagree given their differing views about the roots of morality. Second, moral education can be promoted by requiring all primary schools to teach a specific subject on moral education or by embedding moral lessons across all subjects. For example, textbooks used to teach children how to read and write may be full of moral lessons that the state wants all children to learn. Even science and math textbooks could include moral lessons. The content of national curriculums and additional policy tools by which states can attempt to promote moral education will be the subject of chapter 5.

It is also important to clarify what the theory does not imply. I do not argue that national elites will respond to internal conflict *only* with education; primary education is one of several tools used by central governments to promote order. Repression and redistribution may be used because they are thought (rightfully or not) to help restore order in the short term by quashing rebellion and addressing rebel grievances. By contrast, mass education is mostly used to promote long-term social order by convincing future citizens to accept the status quo and respect the state's authority.

Nor do I argue that internal conflict will *always* lead central governments to invest in mass education as an indoctrination and state-building tool. Four main conditions must be true for this to occur, and we will discuss each one in detail in chapter 6, but to preview the discussion from that chapter: Governments are more likely to invest in mass education to indoctrinate future citizens, first, when social unrest heightens their fear of the masses; second, when they believe that schools can indoctrinate—and not empower—the masses; third, when they expect to be in power long enough to reap the benefits of indoctrinating children; and, fourth, when they have sufficient fiscal and administrative capacity to regulate and promote education. These conditions are not always in place, and when they are not, it is unlikely that internal conflict will result in increased central government efforts to indoctrinate the masses through education.

Finally, the theory does not imply that primary education will succeed in promoting order. My goal is to explain central governments' decision to invest in primary education systems, not the consequences of these investments. In other words, my argument concerns the motivations behind governments' support for primary education, not whether education accomplished the intended goals. What needs to be true for my argument to be valid is not that education in fact succeeded in promoting social order, but that national elites *believed* that education had this power when they chose to invest in it. It is common for education policies not to produce the outcomes reformers had in mind; that is, it is entirely possible that, despite national elites' intentions, primary schooling contributed to social mobility, economic modernization, and political instability. This can happen, for instance, if students and families react in unforeseen ways that defy the state's goals, or if the state fails to ensure teachers' compliance and accurate implementation of education policies. While not the primary focus of the book, in chapter 8 I discuss the conditions under which primary education is likely to accomplish the goal of promoting social order. That chapter also provides evidence that when governments came to believe that an education system had failed to promote social order, they did not stop believing in the promise of education but instead reformed the curriculum or the teaching profession to better realize that promise.

CONCLUSION

In this chapter I have asked what may be behind the patterns we saw in chapter 2 concerning the expansion of primary education in Western societies. To explain this pattern, I have articulated a theory that highlights the emergence of ideas linking state-regulated mass education with the accomplishment of the state's goal to promote social order, and the crucial role that violent internal conflict can play in giving these ideas political traction by increasing national elites' fear of the masses and convincing them that existing policies were insufficient to promote social order. I argue that experiencing internal conflict will likely increase elites' support for the idea that the state should regulate and promote mass education in order to shape the moral character of future citizens and inculcate obedience to the sovereign and acceptance of the status quo.

In the next chapters, I provide a wealth of historical evidence, including primary education statistics, parliamentary debates, and education laws and regulations, to illustrate *why* internal conflict increased elites' support for mass education proposals in Europe and Latin America, and *how* primary education systems were designed to accomplish the state's goals. Chapter 4 shows why and how internal conflict shaped the foundation of a state-regulated primary education system in four non-democratic regimes: 1760s Prussia, 1830s France, 1860s Chile, and 1880s Argentina. Chapter 5 examines how the original design of national primary education systems across Europe and Latin America sought to accomplish the state's indoctrination goals. Chapter 6 discusses the four conditions that must be true for my argument to explain education reform in other contexts beyond those considered in chapters 4 and 5. The absence of one or more of these conditions can explain, for example, why Prussia, France, Chile, and Argentina created a state-regulated primary education system when they did—and not earlier—and why primary education in England and Mexico lagged behind the rest of Europe and Latin America, respectively. Chapter 7 provides concrete examples of the theory's power to explain education reform in democratic contexts.

CHAPTER FOUR
INTERNAL THREATS AND MASS EDUCATION IN EUROPE AND LATIN AMERICA

Internal conflict was a key driver of the expansion of access to primary education in Europe and Latin America, as we saw in chapter 2. The last chapter articulated a theory that explains *why* and *how* internal conflict led central governments to regulate and promote primary education. This chapter illustrates that theory with concrete evidence by tracing the process of adoption and implementation of landmark national education laws in four countries. The analysis provides qualitative and quantitative evidence for three main predictions of the book's theory as developed in the previous chapter. First, episodes of mass violence *heightened national elites' anxiety* about the flawed moral character of the masses, led them to conclude that existing policy tools (e.g., repression, redistribution, and moral education exclusively in the hands of the Church) were insufficient to promote social order, and created a sense of urgency about the need to promote the "moralization of the masses" through a system of state-regulated primary schools. Second, the *main goal* driving the creation of national primary education systems was to shape the moral character of the lower classes to eradicate their "barbaric," "violent," "anarchic" predisposition and thus prevent future episodes of mass violence. Third, central governments *expanded primary schooling* more strongly in those regions where they had experienced greater difficulty restoring social order through traditional policy tools such as repression or redistribution.

The evidence comes from two European and two Latin American cases: 1760s Prussia, 1830s France, 1860s Chile, and 1880s Argentina. The periods correspond to the adoption of the first comprehensive national primary education law in each country: the 1763 General Rural School Regulations in Prussia; the 1833 Primary Instruction Law in France, also known as the Guizot Law; the 1860 General Law of Primary Education in Chile; and the 1884 Law of Common Education in Argentina. For each case, I examine what were the main debates concerning the provision of mass education, how internal conflict shaped these debates, what was the content of the resulting laws, and how the passage of these laws altered the provision of primary education across the territory.

Two main criteria guide the selection of these four cases. First, I chose four cases where the passage of a landmark education law was preceded by acute internal conflict involving mass violence against the state. This would be an inappropriate case selection strategy if the chapter sought to establish *whether* internal conflict shapes primary education, but that was the task of chapter 2. In this chapter, the goal is to understand more deeply *why* internal conflict is followed by greater state promotion of primary education. Choosing cases where a temporal correlation between internal conflict and education reform exists gives us an opportunity to examine what *mechanisms* underlie this correlation: Is the temporal correlation purely a coincidence? Is it driven by the book's argument that crises of internal order can exacerbate elites' fear of the masses and increase their interest in indoctrinating the masses to prevent future violence against the state? Is it driven by something else—for instance, an increase in national elites' interest in addressing economic grievances to promote peace?[1]

Second, I selected these four cases not only to have cases from both Europe and Latin America, but also to have variation across cases in the time period, the type of non-democracy, the dominant political ideology, the scale and nature of the internal conflict, the relationship between the Church and the State, and whether the incumbent elites remained in power after the internal conflict. As explained in the previous chapter, the theory of conflict-

1. The case selection strategy I adopt in this chapter entails choosing cases "on the regression line." According to Lieberman (2005), this strategy "provides a check for spurious correlation and can help to fine-tune a theoretical argument by elaborating causal mechanisms. Although intensive investigation of 'on-the-line' cases may lead to the identification of alternative explanations, the primary goal is to assess the strength of a *particular* model. As such, there is little value to the pursuit of cases that are not well predicted by the model" (p. 444). For a complementary discussion of cases "off the regression line," see chapter 6.

driven education reform I propose should apply regardless of these factors. Indeed, the cases of Prussia, France, Chile, and Argentina presented herein collectively show that the book's argument applies across a wide range of contexts. The cases span more than a century of history and differ from one another in important respects: an absolutist regime with a legacy of Protestantism and ties to Pietist education reformers in Prussia; a constitutional monarchy with limited franchise but active parliamentary politics and a complicated relationship with the Catholic Church in France; a conservative oligarchic regime strongly allied to the Catholic Church in Chile; and a secular oligarchic regime heavily influenced by anti-Church liberals in Argentina. Similarly, the scale of the conflict also differs across cases: peasant revolts in Prussia, rural riots in France, and civil wars in Chile and Argentina. The nature of the internal conflict varies across cases as well, with the conflicts in Prussia and France representing primarily class conflict, and the cases in Chile and Argentina representing primarily center-periphery conflicts. Moreover, while in Prussia and Chile the incumbent government remained in power despite the internal conflict, in Argentina the civil wars had no clear-cut winner, and in France a new political regime and elite assumed power aided by the very same social unrest it sought to suppress. The chapter shows that, despite their many differences, in each of the four cases the landmark moment in the formation of a national primary education system, the pattern of educational expansion, and the characteristics of these systems, all responded to an episode of acute internal conflict that increased elites' interest in educating the masses for the purpose of social control.

PRUSSIA

Prussia's first comprehensive primary education law was issued by Frederick II in June 1763. Known as the General Rural School Regulations (*General-Landschul-Reglement*), the 1763 law applied to all Protestants living in rural areas, thus encompassing the vast majority of the population.[2] The law's long-lasting influence cannot be overstated. When, more than 150 years later, the progressive American educator Thomas Alexander criticized Prussia's primary education system, he described the 1763 Regulations as "the first and last law which Prussia has had that touches all sides of the question,"

---

2. Separate school ordinances for Catholics and urban residents were introduced in 1765.

pointing "very clearly the direction which the German elementary school was to take."[3] Not only did the Regulations compel parents in the countryside to send their children to primary school, they also established a uniform curriculum for all rural primary schools centered around moral and religious instruction, required schools to use state-approved textbooks, charged teachers with cultivating discipline and obedience and breaking the child's will, and required them to track daily attendance to identify and fine noncompliant parents. Rural primary schools were removed from the care of the nobility; pastors were charged with weekly inspection of schools but on behalf of the state, a consistorial inspector was made responsible for conducting an annual inspection, and the provincial consistory was given the final say over the appointment of teachers.[4] The introduction in 1765 of primary school ordinances for Catholics and for urban residents completed the regulatory framework needed to create a Prussian primary education system.

The passage of the General Rural School Regulations in August 1763, just a few months after the end of the Seven Years' War, has led some scholars to conclude that "the union of state and schools ... was sparked by a clear challenge to Prussia's position in the European state system." According to this view, what prompted the rise of Prussia's primary education system were military threats from abroad, its main goal being to ensure a steady supply of loyal and skilled soldiers who could communicate in a common language and who shared a national identity and patriotic sentiments against neighboring countries.[5]

At least three historical facts cast doubt on the nation-building and military interpretations of the rise of Prussian primary schooling. The first is the content of the state-mandated curriculum for rural primary schools. The Prussian education laws of the 1760s allowed schools to teach in German or Polish,[6] and allowed religious teaching according to Protestant or Catholic doctrine.[7] In other words, neither linguistic nor religious homogeneity—

---

3. Alexander (1919), p. 14.
4. To ensure that teachers' character was in line with the state's moral goals for primary schooling, the Regulations prohibited anyone who worked or owned a tavern, or drank heavily, or promoted discord in their community, from working as a teacher. The Regulations also regimented the school day, indicating precisely how many hours should be devoted to the catechism, how many to reading instruction, and how many to writing.
5. Ramirez and Boli (1987), pp. 153–154.
6. Melton (2002).
7. Lamberti (1989), p. 15.

two common markers of a shared national identity—were goals of primary schooling. The inculcation of a national identity that replaced any ethnic or religious identities would not become a goal of Prussia's primary education system until 1808.[8] Further, if the 1763 Regulations had sought to train skilled soldiers, we would expect that goal to be reflected in the curriculum it established. Historically, the main subject used to train soldiers was physical education or gymnastics, which involved teaching military exercises as well as exercises to strengthen the body. Other subjects complemented physical training; geography often taught students how to read maps, while history could inculcate a sense of superiority vis-à-vis other countries. Yet physical education was not among the subjects that rural primary schools had to teach under the 1763 Regulations—nor were geography or history. Under the Regulations, one-third of school time had to be devoted to prayer, chanting, and catechism, a subject designed to instill moral values grounded in religious doctrine; another third was to be devoted to reading, taught using the Bible and other religious texts; and the remaining third focused on teaching writing. In fact, gymnastics and social studies entered the official curriculum for rural areas for the first time in 1872, under Bismarck's administration—more than a full century after the creation of Prussia's national primary education system.

A second problem with the military argument comes from the observation that Prussian military officers usually opposed the 1763 General Rural School Regulations and tried to block its implementation. They considered the recruitment of teachers—at the time primarily men—a threat to their ability to recruit soldiers and preserve the army's strength. Acknowledging these concerns, Frederick II subsequently instructed provincial authorities not to approve the appointment of tall schoolmasters so as not to deprive the army of "giant brigades."[9] We may wonder whether Frederick II himself saw in primary education a means to strengthen the army, even if that view was not shared by military officers. The army's course during the decade following the end of the Seven Years' War does not support this hypothesis: Frederick II reduced the army's total size and increased the proportion of foreign mercenaries, which came to roughly equal that of Prussian recruits.[10] The king's increased reliance on foreign mercenaries,

---

8. Anderson (2013), pp. 94–95.
9. Melton (2002), pp. 177–178.
10. Melton (2002), p. 173.

either uneducated or educated abroad, is inconsistent with the view that he introduced compulsory primary education because he wanted to strengthen the nationalist sentiment, unity, and loyalty of the military.

But the main problem with attributing Frederick II's interest in primary education to military concerns heightened by the Seven Years' War is that the king had already expressed interest in the education of peasants *before* the war started. This lesser-known fact is documented by the historian James Melton, author of a detailed book on the eighteenth-century origins of compulsory schooling in Prussia. In 1754, two years before the outbreak of the Seven Years' War, Frederick II had already approved educational plans very similar to those introduced in 1763, the implementation of which had to be suspended when the war broke out. The 1754 plans had been drafted by Johann Hecker, one of the main advocates—along with Johann Felbiger—for education reform during the 1740s and 1750s. Although the war's outbreak prevented the implementation of these plans, once the war ended Frederick II immediately turned to Hecker for support drafting a plan for primary education. The result of Hecker's work was the General Rural School Regulations of 1763.

What, then, prompted Frederick II's and his advisers' interest in primary education as early as the 1750s? Melton documents that the king's unusual interest in primary education at a time when Prussia was still overwhelmingly rural was tightly linked to the peasant rebellions of the 1740s and 1750s, which signaled the breakdown of traditional sources of authority in the countryside.

Historically, the maintenance of order had relied heavily on the deep, contractual ties that bound peasants and lords living on the same land. The landed nobility protected peasants who lived in their estate from outside threats; in exchange, peasants were required to work on the lord's land for a certain number of days per week. The remaining days could be used for subsistence farming. The lord had the right to prevent peasants from leaving their farms without prior permission, to increase the amount of labor services required of peasants, and to turn to corporal punishment, fines, or imprisonment if the peasants were deemed—by courts controlled by the lords—to have violated their contractual obligations.[11]

Several economic and demographic changes contributed to the breakdown of this social order in rural areas during the eighteenth century.

---

11. Clark (2006).

First, from the beginning of the century, there had been an increase in the number of landless rural workers who worked in the lord's land part-time but also held other jobs, sometimes outside the lord's estate. In Brandenburg in 1743, 52.5 percent of rural households were landless; in East Prussia in 1750, this figure rose to 70 percent.[12] These landless day workers did not feel the sense of duty and deference toward the lord common among peasants brought up under the lord's patriarchal wings. Second, the growth of commercial agriculture and rising grain prices during the mid-eighteenth century led new investors to purchase lands. The increasing frequency with which estates changed hands also contributed to erode peasants' sense of duty.[13] Suddenly, peasants found themselves working for someone they did not know, and not infrequently, for someone who owned but did not live in those lands.

Against this backdrop of eroded seignorial authority, the main trigger of the peasant rebellions that began multiplying across Prussia in the 1740s was the sudden rise in hunger coupled with Prussian lords' untimely increase in the labor obligations of peasants. These two developments were interrelated. Between 1739 and 1742, anomalous weather patterns in much of Western Europe, including Prussia, shrunk harvests and increased grain prices.[14] As starvation and mortality rose, Prussian landowners seeking to capitalize on grain price increases began to intensify the labor obligations of peasants living in their estate.[15] Because estates changed hands frequently, every new landlord tried to exploit peasants to their limit.[16] In parts of Bohemia, Silesia, East Prussia, and Pomenaria, where large-scale commercial agriculture was more common, peasant labor obligations reached as high as six days per week during the 1740s and 1750s.[17] This left peasants no time for subsistence farming—again, in a context where food deprivation was pervasive.

Some peasants responded to the increase in labor obligations by attempting to flee the lord's estate, others turned to lawsuits against the lord, but the most common form of resistance was collective action. This took many different forms including strikes, destroying fields and granaries, abusing

12. Melton (2002), p. 125.
13. Clark (2006).
14. Post (1984).
15. Clark (2006); Ford (1919); Carsten (1989).
16. Carsten (1989).
17. Melton (2002), p. 149.

seignorial farm equipment and cattle, setting fires in the village, rioting in the towns during market day, and violent peasant rebellions, which increased in number and intensity during the middle decades of the eighteenth century.[18] Social banditry multiplied as Prussia entered, in the words of historian Karl Schleunes, "a period of protracted social and political instability." Peasants also responded to food shortages through infanticide, child abandonment, and declaring children illegitimate. Like social banditry and rebellion, the upper classes interpreted these actions as signs of the moral degradation of the rural lower classes. The political consequence of this moral degradation, according to a contemporary observer, was "a propensity toward disobedience and disloyalty."[19]

As peasant rebellions spread, with unrest in one village giving rise to unrest in neighboring ones, the situation in the countryside became "an urgent political issue" for Frederick II and his advisers.[20] The king initially responded to the social upheaval through agrarian reforms that recognized and sought to address peasants' grievances.[21] Compulsory labor services were the most important issue targeted by these reforms. Cognizant that the increase in peasants' labor obligations had been the main trigger behind rural unrest, in 1748 the king ordered a sizable reduction of labor services in Pomenaria, and in 1753 he issued a similar order for Silesia.[22] In addition to limiting labor obligations via royal decrees, additional reforms were introduced that favored peasants, including the 1747 reform of the patrimonial courts responsible for resolving disputes between peasants and landlords,[23]

18. Schleunes (1989), pp. 20–21; Melton (2002), p. 149.
19. Schleunes (1989), p. 18.
20. Melton (2002), p. 151.
21. Other reforms targeted the lords. For example, because it was believed that the frequent sale of estates to new owners was one of the causes of increased peasant insubordination, the king introduced tax concessions and ad hoc gifts to families in financial trouble to reduce their need to sell their land. "When these measures failed," Frederick tightened "state control of land sales, but this proved counterproductive;" limiting the nobility's "freedom to dispose of property" damaged "the dignity and economic stability" of the estate-owning class that this policy was supposed to help. "The quest for a less interventionist and controversial method of supporting the noble interest ultimately led to the foundation of state-capitalized agricultural credit unions (*Landschaften*) for the exclusive use of the established Junker families" (Clark 2006, pp. 158–159).
22. Melton (2002), pp. 152–153.
23. Since 1747, all patrimonial courts were required to employ government-certified, university-trained jurists as judges, effectively placing the courts under the authority of the state instead of the nobility. Some of the most prominent litigation cases reveal that royal judicial officials often sought to restore rural harmony through compromise decisions that provided some satisfaction to peasants as opposed to siding with the traditionally powerful nobility. See Clark (2006), p. 164; Dwyer (2014), p. 119.

and the Edicts of 1749, 1752, 1755, and 1764, which prohibited lords from expropriating peasants' landholdings. As Guy Ford has noted, the very frequency of these edicts demonstrates the king's interest in peasants as a class and his failure to extinguish the disputes between peasants and lords.[24]

Concessions to peasants proved insufficient to promote social order. One example of the inadequacy of concessions comes from the Stavenow estate in the rural district of Prignitz. In 1753, as a result of government mediation, the estate had agreed to reduce peasants' labor services, and peasants, in turn, had agreed to work the newly established (and lower) number of days. However, in 1756, Conrad Kleist, whose family had owned the Stavenow estate since 1717, petitioned the king "for himself and in the name of his brothers ... for remedy against ... insubordination." Peasants were again refusing their labor duties even though, as the exasperated Kleist reminded the king, in 1753 these had been "in various ways infinitely reduced."[25]

Conflict in Stavenow and elsewhere illuminated the commitment problem inherent in using agrarian reform to promote social order: while reducing labor services could placate peasants today, nothing prevented them from making further demands tomorrow. Making concessions to peasants could not solve the ultimate problem of mid-eighteenth-century Prussia, a problem that James Melton aptly refers to as a "crisis of seigniorial authority."[26]

The peasant rebellions of the 1740s and 1750s also revealed the limitations of relying on repression and threats of repression to restore order in the countryside. In 1749, peasants in two districts close to the Lithuanian frontier formed an alliance to demand their freedom. When troops arrived to the area, not only did the armed peasants resist, but they were also supported by soldiers on leave from the army.[27] Although sending soldiers sometimes helped end peasant rebellions, stories of "stubborn" peasant resistance became increasingly common. Conrad Kleist faced his own share of "recalcitrant" peasants. In his petition to the king, Kleist had asked Frederick II for authorization to announce that those who did not accept their labor obligations would be dismissed and replaced with "loyal and obedient children of this land." The king gave the Kleists freedom to "remove insubordinate colonists, if incorrigible, and put others in their place." Although Kleist

24. Ford (1919), p. 366.
25. Hagen (2002), p. 539.
26. Melton (2002), p. 145.
27. Carsten (1989), p. 62.

publicized this ruling in 1757, and subsequently secured support from the sheriff of Prignitz to enforce the order, he faced considerable difficulty removing disobedient peasants from his estate.[28]

Nor were priests and pastors able to contain peasants' insubordination. In the Stavenow estate, for example, "communal insubordination . . . was a susceptibility . . . which the Lutheran pastors could not banish from their flocks' minds and hearts." Although peasants respected pastors' guidance toward Christian salvation, they did not trust them with their secular concerns, as "pastors often appeared captives of their own interests, if not also the lordship's."[29]

It was this context of crisis in rural authority, coupled with the failure of agrarian policies and repression to halt the spread of peasant rebellions, that gave education reformers a receptive audience in Frederick II. According to Melton, proposals to educate the rural lower classes had been circulating since before Frederick II's reign, but the crisis of the mid-eighteenth century, by illuminating the weakness of seigniorial authority and the need for new ways to exercise control in the countryside that did not rely on the threat of coercion from lords, made agrarian reformers more receptive to education reform:

> It was the issue of labor services that brought reformers face to face with the central issue posed by the crisis of seigniorial authority. The paternalist ideal of seigniorial control had presumed the physical presence of an external, coercive force. . . . The issue of labor services became a metaphor for more fundamental changes in the structure of seigniorial authority during the second half of the eighteenth century. In their efforts to reduce the labor obligations of the peasantry, Prussian . . . agrarian reformers grappled with the central dilemma posed by their changing agrarian landscape: How could the lord exact the labor and obedience of his subjects once the coercive mechanisms of seigniorial control had been removed? In the face of economic changes that weakened the direct and personal exercise of seignorial authority, how could one induce rural subjects to perform their social and economic obligations? Schools were to provide reformers with an answer to these questions.[30]

---

28. Hagen (2002), p. 540.
29. Hagen (2002), p. 442.
30. Melton (2002), pp. 151–152.

Proposals for mass education had existed at least since the late seventeenth century, when Pietists began to advocate for the education of the lower classes as a means to cultivate discipline, obedience, and respect for authority.[31] As I explained in chapter 3, in the 1690s, the Pietist August Hermann Francke founded elementary schools that introduced concrete pedagogical innovations to accomplish these goals, including taking roll to monitor children's attendance and behavior, requiring children to raise their hand to ask a question, and constantly monitoring children "whether sitting in class, playing in the schoolyard, eating in the dining hall," or "wherever pupils may be."[32] Pietist reformers were also pioneers in the standardization of elementary school textbooks, and Pietist schools were the first to require formal training for elementary school teachers, giving rise to the first Normal Schools.[33]

In addition to Pietism, the Enlightenment also helped change prior beliefs about mass education. Enlightenment philosophers, as we saw in chapter 3, challenged the historical notion that the lower classes were uneducable, proposing instead that human beings are shaped by their environment and the education they receive. Moreover, like Pietist reformers, Enlightenment philosophers supported soft methods for disciplining students, focusing on students' conscience, not physical coercion.

While Pietism and the Enlightenment proposed new ways of thinking about the role of mass education in promoting discipline and obedience, and Pietism in particular offered concrete education innovations that would eventually become appealing to the state, it was not until the mid-eighteenth century that these ideas found an audience interested in implementing them on a large scale.

One of the first votes of confidence for proposals to create a state-controlled mass education system came in 1750, when Frederick II appointed the Pietist educator Johann Hecker to the Supreme Consistory. Hecker (1707–1768) had taught at one of Francke's schools and then went on to establish his own, introducing several pedagogical innovations. In particular, while teachers in other schools rotated from student to student, teaching

---

31. In the 1690s, the Piestist August Hermann Francke had founded several schools—elementary schools for the poor, vocational schools for the middle class, boarding schools for elites—and the *Seminarium selectum praeceptorum*, the first teacher training institution in Central Europe, established to ensure that future teachers had the training needed to be agents of spiritual and moral reform. See Melton (2002), p. 36.

32. Francke, quoted in Melton (2002), p. 44.

33. Melton (2002), p. xiv.

each one individually, Hecker, building on Francke's idea that unsupervised children had the tendency to become unruly, introduced group teaching, creating a hallmark feature of modern education systems. Seeking to further his educational agenda, in 1750 Hecker convinced Frederick II to create the Supreme Consistory, a state body directly responsible to the king and in charge of the supervision of Lutheran churches and schools. Through this appointment in the consistory, Hecker obtained a new platform to implement his educational ideas. In 1753, the king provided annual funding to Hecker's teacher training institution in Berlin and gave it special status as the preferred institution to recruit teachers, effectively converting it into the first state-sponsored Normal School for training primary school teachers. Frederick II would go on to support Hecker's 1754 comprehensive school reform plans for Minden-Ravensberg, which would then serve as a model for the 1763 General Rural School Regulations, also drafted by Hecker at Frederick II's request.[34]

The king's support of Pietist pedagogy was a strategic choice reflecting not religious conviction but his primary goal of consolidating the state's authority.[35] Contrary to his father's devotion to Pietism, Frederick II was not a religious man; in fact, he held a personal hostility toward Pietism and felt attracted by the ideas espoused by Enlightenment philosophers, several of whom he corresponded with on a regular basis.[36] Yet, like his father, Frederick II became convinced that Pietism could be of strategic use for his goal of buttressing monarchical authority. Pietist religion emphasized a conception of spiritual growth through obedience, discipline, and love of one's neighbor at every waking hour. The latter, according to Pietist reformers like Francke and Hecker, required working for societal good, unconditional service to the state, and blind obedience to the King—principles that any absolutist king would find attractive.[37] But at the same time that he took advantage of Pietist ideas to strength the state's authority, Frederick II advanced four measures that made it clear he had no intention of making Pietism the official state religion: first, he allowed religious pluralism in an effort to reduce religious conflict between Lutherans, Calvinists, Pietists, and Catholics; second, he adopted a separate set of education regulations for Catholic areas which enabled moral and religious instruction

---

34. Vollmer (1918); Melton (2002).
35. Erxleben (1967), pp. 60–61; Gawthrop (1993), p. 275.
36. Gawthrop (1993), p. 275.
37. Gawthrop (1993), pp. 4, 9, 143–146.

to rely on Catholic, not Protestant, doctrine; third, he placed the Supreme Consistory created in 1750 to oversee education under the authority of the Ministry of Justice; fourth, he established through the 1763 General Rural School Regulations that the pastors who supervised the work of teachers had to report to a Superintendent appointed by the state.[38]

While Hecker was the king's trusted adviser on education issues in Protestant regions of Prussia, Johann Felbiger became his main adviser in Catholic areas. Although trained by Jesuits, Felbiger admired Francke's and Hecker's educational work and visited Hecker in Berlin to observe how he implemented his pedagogical ideas. The influence of Pietism on Felbiger's educational ideas is evident in the striking similarity between Francke's arguments about the goals of education and Felbiger's idea that students "must be convinced that it is useful and correct to follow the schoolmaster's wishes. Only then will they learn to obey even in situations where force is absent. In this way, the schoolmaster accomplishes his most important task: his pupils will observe their duties not only in school, but throughout their lives."[39] Like Francke and Hecker, Felbiger believed that schools had to educate not only good Catholics, "creatures of God, instruments of his holy will, and good members of the Church," but also "honest subjects of their ruler, useful members of the state."[40]

The assessment that the rural crisis of social order was fundamental in triggering the rise of state-regulated mass education in mid-eighteenth-century Prussia is further supported by Karl Schleunes's study of the history of Prussian schooling. Schleunes argues that the proposal to introduce compulsory mass schooling for rural areas "was born and nurtured within the womb of gathering social crisis. Those who proposed [it] did so in response to that crisis, not merely because of the notion that peasants had suddenly become educable." While Schleunes acknowledges that notions of crisis are problematic and "any historian worth his salt should be able to find one," he insists that mid-eighteenth-century "contemporaries did perceive a crisis and that they did begin to act accordingly.... Social dislocations ... contributed to the questioning of long-held political and social assumptions. The ultimate question of what it was that held society together

---

38. Erxleben (1967), pp. 60–61, 89, 92–98.
39. Felbiger, quoted in Melton (2002), p. 187.
40. Felbiger, quoted in Melton (2002), p. 102.

drew the attention of an ever-widening circle, reaching far beyond those who ordinarily reflected upon such matters."[41]

The crisis in agrarian relations, and the inadequacy of repression and concessions to deal with it, also helped convince landowning elites to support proposals for the education of the rural lower classes, especially their moral education. Historically, landowners had opposed educating peasants, fearing they would develop greater aspirations. But in the 1750s, an increasing number of economic elites began to support mass education, finding in Pietist pedagogy a promising solution to the problem of peasant disobedience. Support for mass education grew in journals and manuals read by landowners and estate managers. For example, an article published in a Silesian economic journal in 1757 advocated for the establishment of schools focused on teaching moral principles and "inner contentment" to peasants, and claimed that as a result of this education, "disloyalty, laziness, idleness, disobedience, disorder, . . . would all disappear."[42] One vehement supporter was the minister of Silesia, Ernst Wilhelm von Schlabrendorff, who supported compulsory schooling since 1755, and who, after touring Silesia in 1756, became further convinced that the reduction of peasants' labor obligations had to be coupled with mass schooling.[43] Schlabrendorff's views echoed those of Carl Egon von Fürstenberg, governor of Bohemia between 1771 and 1782, who argued that the future stability of society depended on peasant education:

> As long as the peasant's moral character is not reformed, his indolence and resentment toward his lord will persist . . . But if one improves his character before reducing his excessive labor obligations, this education will muffle his discontent and suppress the dangerous impulses bred by constant maltreatment.[44]

In sum, proposals to shape the moral character of the lower classes through mass schooling had circulated in Prussia since the mid-seventeenth century, but only gained support from rulers in the middle decades of the eighteenth century, when peasant rebellions increased in frequency and intensity, creating an urgent problem for social order. As rebellion spread throughout the countryside, it signaled the end of an era in which social

---

41. Schleunes (1989), p. 18.
42. Melton (2002), p. 158.
43. Melton (2002), pp. 153–158, 185.
44. Fürstenberg, quoted in Melton (2002), p. 165.

order had been maintained by the physical, coercive presence of the lord. To promote order in the periphery, Frederick II responded with two policy innovations: agrarian reform to address peasants' immediate grievances, and the creation of a public primary education system to inculcate moral values of obedience among the lower rural classes. State-controlled schooling emerged during a crisis of internal order as a new mechanism to promote long-term order through self-coercion, or the internalization of values of loyalty, obedience, and devotion to the king.

FRANCE

The most impressive expansion of primary schooling in the history of France occurred in the 1830s under the July Monarchy (1830–1848). Previously, the provision of primary education had been the domain of local towns and parishes. Although the revolutionaries of 1789 had passed legislation seeking to ensure universal primary education, the French Revolution had left the state with no resources to implement this vision. Subsequent central governments during both the Napoleonic Era and the Bourbon Restoration were content to leave primary education to municipal governments and the Catholic Church. This changed drastically during the July Monarchy. Between 1830 and 1833, several proposals were introduced in parliament seeking to promote the expansion of primary education in the entire territory and to increase the central government's regulatory power over primary schools. Parliament passed the first comprehensive national law of primary education in June 1833. Named after François Guizot, the Minister of Public Instruction who spearheaded the reform, the Guizot Law of 1833 was considered by contemporaries the "most far-reaching primary education law in French history."[45] Its passage not only created a primary education system regulated by the central government but also, as we will see, was followed by a marked increase in public spending on primary education and by the fastest expansion in the number of primary schools that France has ever seen. The result of this was a massive growth in enrollment rates, which increased from 32 percent at the beginning of the July Monarchy to 71 percent by the end of the regime.

The July Revolution of 1830 had overthrown the Bourbon dynasty, bringing the bourgeoisie to power and replacing the old regime with a new

---

45. Toloudis (2012), p. 41.

constitutional monarchy that constrained the king's legislative powers and reduced the power of the Catholic Church. However, contrary to the Republican party, most of the July revolutionaries opposed the expansion of political rights, including the extension of voting rights. In addition, when it came to Church-State relations, supporters of the regime held varying opinions about how much the power of the Church ought to be reduced, with the more liberal faction of the regime supporting complete Church-State separation and the more conservative faction accepting some level of Church participation in civil affairs as long as the state remained the supreme authority.

The Guizot Law of 1833 was a product of the mass violence that the July Monarchy had to deal with in its early years and reflected the regime's concern about the moral roots of this violence. Although the July revolutionaries had fought with the support of the working class in Paris, once they came to power, workers, artisans, and peasants turned against the government. In the months following the ascension of the July Monarchy, popular unrest reached alarming proportions not only in Paris but also in the countryside.[46]

The popular discontent of the early 1830s had economic roots. The harvest of 1830, the smallest since 1816 due to poor weather conditions, and a tariff policy that restricted wheat imports had led to a 50 percent increase in bread prices. The wine, iron, and textile industries also experienced severe problems, creating widespread unemployment. Riots and attacks on farmers and merchants selling or transporting grain became ubiquitous, reaching peak levels in late autumn and winter of 1830–1831 and in the spring and early summer of 1832. The lower classes blamed the new government for their economic misfortune and demanded price controls—including a "fair price" for bread—as well as more jobs and higher wages.[47]

The level of mass violence that spread throughout France between 1830 and 1832 had not been seen since the Revolution of 1789. Pamela Pilbeam, who has studied this period of French history in great depth, describes the protests as "common, violent and often supported by the forces of order."[48]

---

46. Pilbeam (1976), p. 278.

47. Pilbeam (1976), pp. 279–283; Gonnet (1955); Pinkney (1961).

During the period of violence in 1830–1832, the July revolutionaries accused the Republican party of "exploiting the anarchy" of the lower classes and inciting "violence" and "subversive" behavior to advance their political agenda. The government refused to make concessions. It instead placed restrictions on club meetings and prosecuted many clubs where Republicans met.

48. Pilbeam (1976), p. 288.

Approximately 139 violent protests occurred during those years, involving more than 181,000 participants and resulting in 1,300 deaths and 3,500 wounded citizens.[49] Initially, the violence was confined to Paris and suppressed by the national guard without difficulty,[50] but starting in February 1831, it began spreading geographically, eventually reaching forty-eight different *départements*, with particularly high levels of violence in the rural departments of southern France. The escalation of violence and the central government's rising concern about the "barbaric," "turbulent," and "anarchic" behavior of the lower classes[51] prompted a replacement of the cabinet, which in March 1831 became headed by Casimir Périer, a member of the most conservative faction among the July revolutionaries. Under his leadership, the government redoubled its efforts to suppress the riots by turning to the national guard, the gendarmerie, and other military reinforcements.

However, the limits of relying on repression to maintain social order soon became evident.[52] Not only were the crowds "too numerous for existing police resources to handle," but also, and more problematically, there were a "large number of national guardsmen who participated in popular protests" either actively or by refusing to obey orders to quash the riots.[53] In an episode in Besançon, which like many others was interpreted by the government as an embryonic revolution, a large crowd burst into the streets, insulting grain merchants and smashing the windows of the tax office to destroy its records. Many members of the national guard, ordered to suppress the rebellion, threw down their weapons and joined the crowd, while others deserted.[54]

Guizot had deep first-hand knowledge of the limitations of repression: Before he became Minister of Public Instruction in October 1832, he had been the July Monarchy's Minister of Interior. In his memoirs, he recalls that episodes like the one in Besançon were common. In an entire chapter devoted to the problem of "anarchy" that Casimir Périer's government had to deal with in 1831 and 1832, he highlights that "administrative authority

---

49. The figures are based on data collected by Tilly and Zambrano (2006).
50. In October 1830, recalls Guizot, crowds "belonging to that idle, corrupt and turbulent population that lives deep in Paris ... strolled the streets and came to assail the Palais-Royal with cries: *Death to the ministers! Polignac's head!*" (Guizot 1860 t.2, pp. 124–125).
51. Guizot (1860), t.2.
52. Pilbeam (1991), pp. 177–178.
53. Pilbeam (1976), pp. 288–289.
54. Pilbeam (1976), p. 287.

was ignored" and the intervention of the army in violent disorders "aggravated the evil instead of suppressing it":

> In Grenoble,... in Strasbourg, in Tours, in Toulouse, in Montpellier, in Carcassonne, in Nîmes, in Marseilles, similar disturbances broke out. And it was not only among the people that the spirit of disorder reigned, it penetrated even into the army.[55]

For Guizot and his contemporaries, the mass violence that emerged during the early years of the July Monarchy was caused by moral deficiencies that needed to be corrected through public primary education. Multiple reports published during the early 1830s pointed to the moral deficit of the lower classes as the underlying culprit of unruly behavior. One of the most innovative reports—a real precursor in the use of statistics to study social phenomena—was André-Michel Guerry's *Essai sur la Statistique Morale de la France*, published in 1833. It included choropleth maps of the level of "immorality" in the French departments as proxied by statistics on crime, suicides, illegitimate children, poverty, and illiteracy, and fueled the perception that crimes against persons were particularly high in the south of France, where lack of education was also greater. It was not uncommon for advocates of mass education to cite crime statistics as proof that primary "instruction moralizes the population, since there are relatively more individuals accused of committing crimes among those who are illiterate than among those who have received some instruction."[56] The validity of these conclusions is beside the point; what is relevant is that French political elites argued that schooling was a good idea because it would moralize the masses and thus reduce crime.

There are in principle many reasons why education could reduce criminal behavior and mass violence, and some of these reasons have nothing to do with the role of education in improving the moral character of the masses. It could be, for example, that education enables people to find better jobs, in turn reducing the economic motivation to commit a crime or rebel. Social mobility and financial security aspirations are certainly one of the reasons why people today pursue education degrees, but the question we must ask ourselves is whether in 1833, when the French government proposed and parliament approved the creation of a primary education

---

55. Guizot (1860), t.2, p. 209.
56. M. Allard, quoted in Sarmiento (1849), p. 55.

system, it did so to improve the economic well-being of the lower classes. This is certainly a possibility we must consider. The violence of the early 1830s had been triggered by escalating bread prices and unemployment, and the government made efforts to address these economic grievances: it relaxed the restrictions on wheat imports and adopted redistributive policies including subsidies for bread and the creation of large public works programs. Was the government's effort to promote primary education also a redistributive strategy designed to improve the earnings and job prospects of the poor?

The historical record does not support this interpretation. While some Republican politicians favored an education system that in addition to teaching moral values also helped lift people out of poverty, liberals—who controlled the cabinet and a majority of parliament—were not interested in the redistributive aspect of mass education. In 1831, parliament commissioned Victor Cousin to study the Prussian primary education system, resulting in the publication of two reports that significantly shaped parliamentary debates on primary education. In the first report, Cousin described the Prussian education system in detail as a model to be emulated, highlighting its emphasis on "inculcating in young people obedience to the laws, fidelity and attachment to the prince and to the State so that these combined virtues may early germinate in them the sacred love of the Fatherland." The second report, addressed directly to members of parliament to advise them on how to design a primary education system for France,[57] made no mention whatsoever of social mobility as a goal of mass education. Instead, Cousin wrote that "moral and religious education is precisely the end of primary education." In fact, the entire report focused on the question of how parliament should structure the primary education system in order to accomplish this goal.

Guizot himself was also clear that his priority—and the goal of his primary education bill—was to improve the moral character of the masses, not their economic well-being:

> It has often been said that I did not like the people, that I had no sympathy for their miseries, their instincts, their needs, their desires.... While feeling for the material distress of the people a deep sympathy, I was especially touched and preoccupied by their moral distress, being

---

57. Cousin (1833b).

certain that ... to improve the condition of men, it is first of all their soul that must be purified, strengthened and enlightened.[58]

The state must provide primary education to all families, argued the Minister of Public Instruction, "and in this it does more for the moral life of peoples than it can do for their material condition. This is the true principle on this point, and it was the one adopted by my bill."[59]

In this context of heightened concern about the moral roots of mass violence, the king signed several royal ordinances that sought to increase the state's control over primary education, and two Ministers of Public Instruction before Guizot—Barthe on January 20, 1831 and Montalivet on October 24 of that year—introduced primary education bills to parliament. The bills were similar to Guizot's in many respects, and Guizot in fact integrated many provisions from them into his own bill.[60] However, the Barthe and Montalivet bills were introduced at a time when education legislation was not a priority for parliament. In January 1831, when Barthe introduced his bill in the Chamber of Peers, the "anarchy" had not spread across France yet, and concerns about the moral education of the masses were not salient among parliamentarians. Knowing that the bill would find little support, the minister removed his bill from consideration before it reached the Chamber of Deputies.[61] In October of that year, when Montalivet introduced his proposal, the government did perceive a crisis of social disorder, but its priority at the time was to contain it through repression and a reform of the national guard. As a result, the bill was hardly discussed in parliament and failed to reach the Assembly by the end of 1831. Montalivet himself explained that at the time when he introduced the education bill, the government had to deal with numerous projects on "matters much more important or at least more urgent and requested with much more authority."[62]

By the end of 1832, however, the conservative and liberal factions behind the rise of the July Monarchy were united in agreement that "popular instruction is a need."[63] When Guizot introduced his bill in January 1833, economic conditions had improved and the wave of mass protests had

58. Guizot (1860), t. 3, pp. 54–55.
59. Guizot (1860), t. 3, p. 64.
60. Institut National de Recherche Pédagogique (n.d.).
61. Gontard (1959), p. 469.
62. Gontard (1959), p. 485.
63. Gontard (1959), p. 493.

subsided.[64] In this more peaceful yet still fraught context, despite few substantive differences with respect to Montalivet's bill, Guizot's proposal received overwhelming parliamentary support.[65] As both Guizot and Montalivet recalled many years later, the two years of acute social disorder had helped forge unity within the government. In Montalivet's words, "the anarchic tragedy" of those years "at least had the merit of precipitating the only measure of salvation which could be effective, that is to say, the restoration of unity in the government."[66]

While most of Guizot's original proposal was approved without hesitation or amendment,[67] a long debate emerged in parliament about the distribution of school oversight powers between the central government, municipalities, and the Church. While Barthes's education proposal of January 1831 excluded religious authorities entirely from the supervision of schools, the more pragmatic Guizot, seeking to build a broader coalition of support for his bill, proposed the creation of local school supervision committees consisting of the mayor, three municipal councilors appointed by the municipal council, and the parish priest or pastor.[68] Through an amendment made by the Chamber of Deputies, the final law included two additional members, "a principal, college dean, professor, regent" and "a primary school teacher residing in the constituency," both appointed by the Minister of Education.[69] The inclusion of religious officials on local

64. Only 7,500 protest participants were identified in 1833, compared to 55,000 the year before (Tilly and Zambrano 2006).
65. The debate of the Guizot Law began with Guizot's presentation of the bill on January 2, 1833. The Chamber of Deputies introduced amendments and approved the amended bill on May 3, 1833: of the 256 deputies present, 249 voted in favor and only 7 voted against. The bill was then sent to the Chamber of Peers, which introduced amendments and approved the amended bill, with 114 in favor and 4 against. The revised bill returned to the Chamber of Deputies, where additional amendments were introduced; 219 members voted in favor and 57 against. This version of the bill returned to the Chamber of Peers, where 86 members voted in favor and 11 against. The king signed the bill into law on June 28, 1833.
66. Gontard (1959).
67. Despite the back and forth that took place in parliament during the months of May and June 1833, most of the amendments introduced were simple editing changes that did not alter the content of the law in any way. On issues related to the obligation of municipalities to maintain primary schools for boys, the content of the curriculum, the additional primary education opportunities to be made available in urban areas, departments' obligation to create Normal Schools to train primary school teachers, the remuneration of teachers, and the procedures for certifying and appointing teachers, the original bill remained essentially intact. The issue of girls' education, to which Guizot's original bill devoted one article, was removed altogether from the final law.
68. "Projet de loi présenté par Guizot le 2 janvier 1833 et projet tel qu'il a ete modifié par la Chambre des Deputés dans sa Séance du 3 mai 1833" (1833), Art. 17.
69. France (1833), *Loi sur l'instruction primaire—Loi Guizot du 28 juin 1833*, Art. 19.

supervisory committees helped garner support from conservative members of parliament, while still maintaining the support of liberals in parliament by ensuring that secular authorities held a majority in these committees.

But the more important point about the parliamentary debates is that the main goals of primary education as articulated by Guizot were never questioned by conservatives or liberals. In Guizot's own words, the main goal of primary schools was to promote long-term order and political stability by teaching children to respect the sovereign and its laws:

> When men have learned from childhood to understand the fundamental laws of the country and to respect its sovereign, the sovereign and the laws become a kind of property which is dear to them, and they do not refuse the obligations that it imposes upon them ... Thus the public mind is formed, thus a true patriotism is maintained, thus fortifying and consolidating societies and thrones.[70]

The French historian Antoine Prost notes that "the quarrel" in parliament took place "against a background of unanimity" in which "the need for moral education and the principles of order, authority, property, are beyond debate."[71] This unanimity, argues Maurice Gontard in his seminal book on the history of education in France, reflected a growing and widespread belief among elites in Paris that primary education, if regulated by the state and staffed by teachers loyal to the state, would "teach ordinary people obedience, respect for the law, love of order, thus strengthening social stability and the security of the Monarchy."[72]

Even members of the opposition like Baconnière de Salverte, a member of the Left within the Chamber of Deputies who criticized several provisions of Guizot's proposal,[73] nonetheless agreed with Guizot that the main goal of primary education was to shape children's moral character. Speaking in the session of April 29, 1833, he began: "In the first part of his

---

70. Guizot (1860), p. 86.
71. Prost (1968), pp. 8–9.
72. Gontard (1959), p. 493.
73. Salverte in particular advocated for revising Article 1, which outlined the national curriculum for primary schools. In the session of April 29, 1833, he proposed adding language to specify that children should not only receive "moral and religious instruction," but also learn about their political rights and duties, especially the principles of equality before the law and of just compensation for duties. While other members of the left supported this proposal, center and right-wing members, who held a large majority of seats in the Chamber of Deputies, were aligned with Guizot and the conservative central government in this respect and did not support Salverte's proposal (France. Assemblée Nationale (1871–1942), SER2 V83 1833, p. 246).

speech, the Minister spoke of the importance of morality and religion in primary education. No one, gentlemen, will dispute this importance."

Indeed, a comprehensive analysis of the full transcripts of parliamentary debates on the Guizot Law reveals that no-one disputed that the main goal of primary education was to shape the moral character of children. Precisely because there was widespread agreement on this, the fiercest debates between the left, right, and center were those concerning who should have the power to ensure that primary schools were doing a good job in terms of "the maintenance of discipline" and "the maintenance of good manners and public order."[74]

The Guizot Law increased the central government's control over primary education and promoted its expansion across France. It did not make the central government the only or even the main authority in charge of primary education; under the law, authority to oversee schools was shared between the central and municipal governments and the local priest. But while before 1833 the question of whether to provide primary education and what type of education to provide had been left entirely to municipalities and the Church, the Guizot Law altered this forever. It established a mandatory national curriculum for all primary schools that focused heavily on moral and religious instruction. It also made it mandatory for every town with at least 500 inhabitants to establish and maintain a primary school for boys and required municipalities to raise additional taxes if their ordinary revenues were insufficient to fund primary education. State subsidies were also contemplated by the law, but only after municipal and departmental sources of funding had been exhausted. A crucial provision of the law gave the central government the power to use royal decrees to impose new taxes on municipalities that failed to raise education funds voluntarily, thus giving the state the power to effectively compel municipalities to expand and fund primary education as required by the law.

Beyond regulating the content, supply, and funding of primary education, in the 1830s the central government also increased its regulation of teacher training and recruitment and its oversight of primary schools. The Guizot Law required all departments to establish teacher training institutions and gave the state the final say over teacher certification. In the realm of school oversight, the law required municipalities to provide a "report of the state of affairs for all primary schools under their jurisdiction" to the prefect and

74. France. Assemblée nationale (1871–1942), SER2 V83 1833, p. 296.

the national Minister of Education. In addition, in the fall of 1833 the central government conducted the first comprehensive survey of all primary schools in the country. Known as the Guizot Inquiry (*L'enquête Guizot*), the survey resulted in rich baseline information about the number, location, characteristics, and quality of primary schools. With respect to school quality, Guizot instructed inspectors to concentrate especially on whether schools were succeeding in promoting morality and maintaining order. This effort to monitor primary schools was consolidated in 1835 with the creation of a centralized primary school inspectorate.

The Guizot Law was followed by a marked increase in primary education expenditures and by the fastest expansion in the number of primary schools that France has ever seen. Figure 4.1 illustrates these developments. The top graph displays the evolution of public primary education expenditures from 1820 to 1900, while the bottom graph shows the number of primary schools and students enrolled in them, both adjusted by population size.[75] Beginning with the level of funding, figure 4.1 shows that annual public expenditures on primary education increased markedly after the Guizot Law: during the first year of the law's implementation, expenditures more than tripled compared to the year before, increasing from 49 million francs in 1833 to 160 million in 1834. This marked increase in primary education spending was not driven by an increase in national income or in total public spending. The number of primary schools also increased considerably after the Guizot Law: although the expansion of schooling had accelerated in the early years of the July Monarchy, between 1830 and 1833, during the first years of implementation of the Guizot Law the rate of expansion more than tripled. Accompanying all this was a massive growth in enrollment rates, which increased from 32 percent at the beginning of the July Monarchy to 71 percent by the end of the regime.

Although most of the increase in public expenditures after 1833 came from municipal and departmental coffers,[76] the fact that municipalities and departments increased education funding suddenly and markedly after 1833

---

75. Data on the level of aggregate public and private expenditures on primary education come from Carry (1999). Data on primary education expenditures as a percentage of GDP and as a percentage of total public expenditures come from Toloudis (2012), table 3.1, pp. 43–44. Data on the number of primary schools and student enrollment in primary schools, both adjusted by population size, come from Grew and Harrigan (1991). For the years before 1837, when data about the number of girls schools are unavailable, I use Grew and Harrigan's (1991) estimates of the total number of primary schools, which are based on data about the number of boys' and mixed schools and their estimate of the number of girls' schools (table S.1, p. 251).

76. See the online appendix.

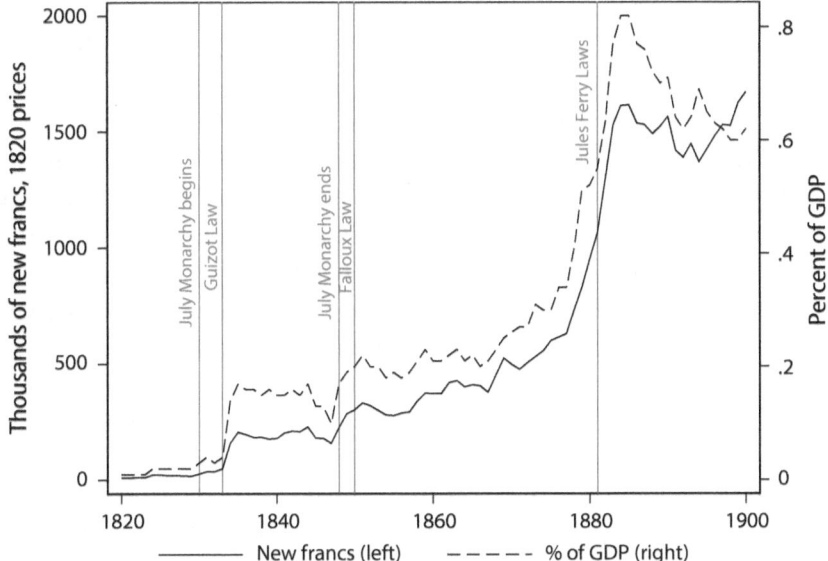
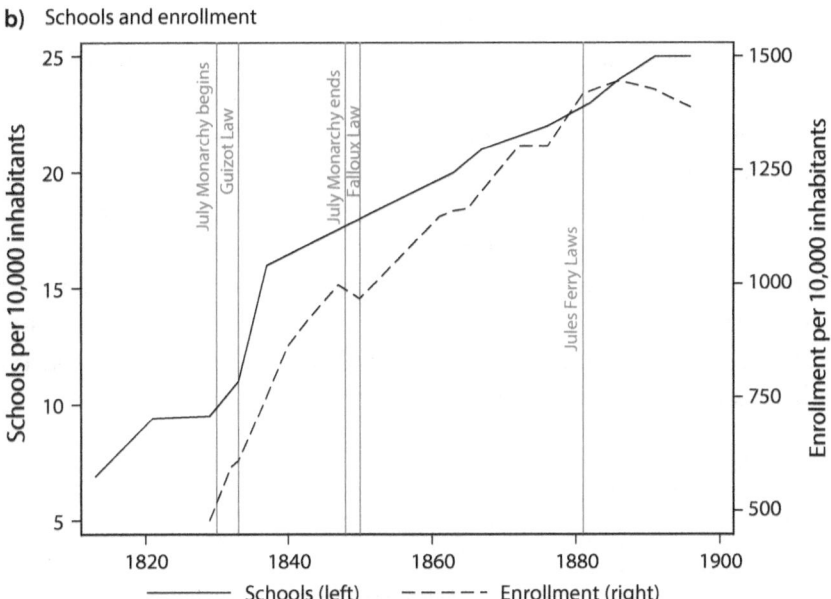

Figure 4.1. Public primary education expenditures, number of primary schools, and primary school enrollment in France, 1810–1900. See text and footnotes for sources and methodology.

suggests that most of the expansion of education funding at these levels was the result of the new national law, which required subnational governments to invest in primary education.[77] My own analysis of how municipalities funded these increases in education expenditures provides additional evidence that the central government played an important role in incentivizing—or outright forcing—municipalities to devote resources to primary education. In the typical French department, only about 21 percent of municipalities were able to comply with the law's funding provisions using ordinary revenues, and another 33 percent established new taxes voluntarily in response to the Guizot Law. However, the remaining 46 percent of municipalities did not take active steps to fund primary education; here, the central government intervened by imposing new taxes via royal decrees, a power accorded to it by the new law.[78] State subsidies for primary education also increased considerably in the first two years after the passage of the Guizot Law to fund school construction and textbook distribution.[79]

In sum, the timing of the Guizot Law of 1833, the concerns about the moral character of the masses that influenced its passage, the increased control over primary education that the law gave to the state, and its consequences for education funding and the supply of primary schools, are all consistent with an explanation of educational expansion promoted by the state in response to the mass violence of the early 1830s.

If mass violence was indeed an important driver of the state's efforts to expand primary education, we should observe not only increased state effort to regulate and expand primary schooling in the wake of internal conflict but also greater effort in regions where the crisis of social order posed a greater threat to political stability. This is an implication of the book's argument that we could not test for the Prussian case given the lack of available statistics on primary education,[80] but French statistics do allow

---

77. Data on whether public expenditures on primary education were funded by municipalities, departments, or the central government, come from Carry (1999). Data on primary education expenditures as a percentage of GDP and as a percentage of total public expenditures come from Toloudis (2012), table 3.1, pp. 43–44.

78. Data on whether municipalities funded primary schools through ordinary tax revenues alone, through a new tax introduced by the municipality following the Guizot Law, or through a new tax imposed on the municipality via royal decree, come from statistics published by the central government for the year 1834. These are available in digital format in: Inter-university Consortium for Political and Social Research (1992).

79. See the online appendix.

80. Prussian official statistics on primary education begin in 1816. In particular, there are no available statistics to examine whether the location of peasant rebellions in the 1740s and 1750s is associated with the intensity of efforts to expand primary education during the 1760s and 1770s.

this type of analysis.[81] Figure 4.2 shows the growth in primary school enrollment and in the number of primary schools (both adjusted for population size) after the Guizot Law of 1833 in three different groups of French departments: those with no registered violent events, those with low levels of mass violence, and those with high levels of mass violence between 1830 and 1832. The latter group, composed primarily of departments in the South, includes the top 25 percent most violent departments based on the number of people who participated in violent events (adjusted for population size).[82] The results should be reviewed with some caution because it is difficult to ascertain the quality of department-level statistics in 1830s France,[83] but they do suggest that primary education after the Guizot Law of 1833 expanded more in departments that experienced more mass violence between 1830 and 1832.

Multiple factors could of course be behind this finding besides the explanation I propose. For example, while it is possible that the expansion of primary schooling in violence-afflicted departments was greater because the central government had a particular interest in expanding primary education due to the violence in those departments, it is also possible that these departments happened to have more local fiscal capacity, more local demand for education, more need for workers who could contribute to industrialization, or a greater presence of the Catholic Church—factors that could also have contributed to the expansion of primary schooling. I considered each of these plausible explanations and did not find support for them.

---

81. For department-level data about enrollment and number of primary schools, I rely on Interuniversity Consortium for Political and Social Research (1992), which digitized information collected by the French central government during the 1830s. For department-level data about violence, I rely on Tilly and Zambrano (2006).

82. Figure 4.2 groups departments based on the level of violence in 1830–1832 as measured by the number of participants in violent events over those three years (adjusted by the department's population size); 36 departments experienced no conflict, 48 departments experienced violent conflict, and 2 departments had missing data. Among the 48 departments with violent conflict, the distribution of violence intensity is not symmetric; most departments exhibit low levels of violence, but some departments exhibit higher levels of violence. Departments with 50 or more participants in violent conflict per 10,000 inhabitants represent the top 25 percent most violent departments; these are the "high violence" departments in figure 4.2. Paris was an outlier, with 1,015 participants in violent conflict per 10,000 inhabitants, and is excluded from the analysis. Tilly and Zambrano (2006) also compiled information about other measures of violence, including the number of violent events and the number of resulting deaths, and these are highly correlated with the number of participants involved in violent events. However, I do not use these other variables in the analysis because they contain more missing data.

83. It is possible that some departments underreported and others exaggerated the number of schools and students. These potential inaccuracies are more likely to cancel out when we aggregate the data at the national level than when we aggregate departments into several groups, hence the need to be more cautious about the conclusions.

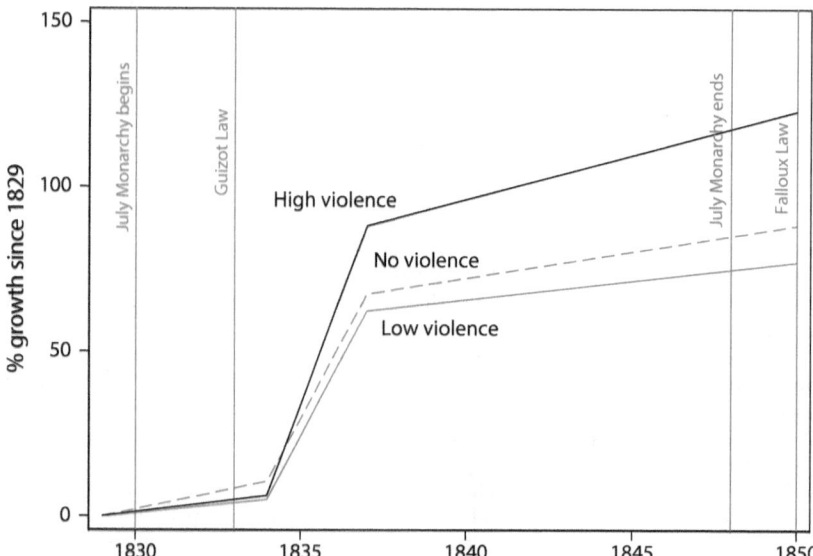

Figure 4.2. Percentage growth in primary school enrollment and in the number of primary schools after the Guizot Law of 1833 in French departments that experienced high, low, or no violence between 1830 and 1832. See text and footnotes for sources and methodology.

With respect to the concern that primary education may have expanded more in violent departments because these departments had more resources, available evidence on the capacity to fund education suggests that this was not true. Municipal revenues were lower, not higher, in those municipalities that had higher levels of mass violence. In particular, while in departments with high levels of conflict, an average 14.5 percent of municipalities had sufficient resources to fund primary education out of their ordinary revenues, this figure rose to 21.6 percent of municipalities in departments with low or no conflict.[84]

Two pieces of evidence suggest that local demand was also not a crucial driver behind the expansion of primary education during the July Monarchy. The first comes from the letters of grievances that the clergy, nobility, and third estate sent to King Louis XVI in 1788; in a systematic study of the content of these letters, economic historians Mara Squicciarini and Nico Voitgländer found, first, that demand for modernization and for education in particular was very low among the lower social classes, and second, that places where this demand was higher did *not* experience more educational expansion during the July Monarchy.[85] The second piece of evidence comes from how primary education was funded in the 1830s. If we believe that a municipality's voluntary decision to introduce a new tax to fund primary education—as opposed to having that tax imposed by the central government via decree—is a good proxy for the level of local demand for education, then what we see is that demand for primary education was lower in municipalities with high levels of violence: In these departments, on average 45 percent of communes were imposed a tax by royal decree after failing to voluntarily impose a tax on their own, compared to 38 percent of communes in departments with low or no conflict.[86]

There is also little evidence that the French government had economic reasons for expanding primary schooling in departments that experienced more mass violence. We have already seen that Guizot, who pushed the bill through parliament and oversaw the initial implementation of the law, had

---

84. My calculations rely on data on education funding in 1834 from Inter-university Consortium for Political and Social Research (1992) and data on violent events from Tilly and Zambrano (2006).

85. Squicciarini and Voitgländer (2016).

86. See the online appendix. My calculations rely on data on education funding in 1834 from Inter-university Consortium for Political and Social Research (1992) and data on violent events from Tilly and Zambrano (2006).

little interest in using primary education to improve the material well-being of the lower classes. Still, we might wonder whether the government had other economic goals. In particular, southern France, where the problem of violence was greater, also tended to be more rural than the rest of the country. Did the government seek to expand primary education in that region to promote industrialization? Two pieces of evidence suggest it did not. First, like in Prussia, French education legislation prescribed different types of primary education for rural and urban areas. In the latter, children had access to "upper" primary schools that taught subjects that might be useful for city jobs, including "geometry and its usual applications" and "notions of physics and natural history relevant to everyday life." However, in rural areas children only had access to "lower" primary schools. "In the most withdrawn countryside and for the most humble social conditions," Guizot insisted that primary schools "must be very simple" and must focus on moral and religious instruction.[87]

Moreover, industrialists themselves—whom we would expect to support policies designed to promote industrialization—were not keen on the state's efforts to expand primary education. In 1833, a group of large manufacturers wrote a letter to the government in which they noted that although the "physical and moral improvement of the working class" could be improved, they were concerned about the impact that the Guizot Law and the expansion of primary education would have on the supply of labor and on their ability to remain competitive.[88]

Finally, the role of the Catholic Church deserves special attention given the prominence of religious conflict in French politics since the 1789 Revolution and the fact that the presence of the Church tended to be stronger in departments that experienced more violence in the 1830s. Was the expansion of primary schooling during this decade the result of the Church's efforts? The answer appears to be no: most of the expansion of primary schooling during the July Monarchy, including the expansion seen in departments with high levels of violence, came from an expansion of public schools,[89] which were predominantly secular.[90]

---

87. Guizot (1860), t. 3, p. 20.
88. Société pour l'Instruction élémentaire (1833), pp. 150–151.
89. Statistics about the number of public and private schools are available starting in 1834; because they were not collected every year, 1850 is the year with available statistics that is closest to the end of the July Monarchy. During this period from 1834 to 1850, the number of public schools increased by about 94 percent, whereas the number of private schools increased by 51 percent.
90. See the online appendix. I estimate that 74 percent of public school enrollment corresponded to public *secular* schools. This estimate was obtained using official data reported by Grew

Did the state make a stronger effort to expand public schooling in places where the Catholic Church was stronger precisely because it wanted to reduce the power of the Church? Again, the answer appears to be no: departments where the historical presence of the Church was stronger, as signaled by a higher share of clergymen who in 1791 confirmed their loyalty to the Catholic Church instead of swearing allegiance to the Civil Constitution promoted by the revolutionary government,[91] did *not* see larger increases in the number of primary schools during the July Monarchy. Indeed, the Protestant Guizot, a pragmatic, saw the Catholic Church's contribution to the expansion of schooling as necessary to accomplish universal provision of primary education because the state simply did not have enough political power or resources to accomplish this goal on its own. Guizot's interest in encouraging the church's cooperation is what led him to give the local priest a seat within the local councils created to oversee primary schools.

Where the influence of the Church was felt the most was not in the expansion of primary education but in the content of primary education. Guizot and most members of parliament were of the opinion that moral education had to include religious teachings because, in 1830s France, the Catholic Church was still the most legitimate authority on matters of morality. Because a crucial goal of primary education was to teach the masses obedience, docility, and respect for authority, moral and religious education was not just a standalone subject; the entire curriculum and school atmosphere was supposed to promote good moral behavior. In a manual for primary school teachers written by central authorities in 1836, the chapter on moral education was by far the longest one; in addition, the manual included chapters about religious education and about the "Moral organization of

---

and Harrigan (1991) and applying the following procedures and assumptions. There were four types of primary schools during the July Monarchy: public secular, public religious, private secular, and private religious. Disaggregated data on the number of schools and student enrollment in each type of school were not collected during the July Monarchy. However, available statistics on the number of teachers working in each type of school (collected for 1834 and 1837) show that the proportion of public school *teachers* in secular schools remained stable during 1834–1837, the period of fastest expansion in the number of primary schools. Based on this stability, I assume that the distribution of public school *students* enrolled in secular vs. religious schools also remained stable during the July Monarchy. Available statistics for students indicate that 74 percent of public school children were enrolled in secular schools in 1850, and the remaining 26 percent of public school children were enrolled in religious schools. Based on the assumption I stated previously, these figures lead me to estimate that in 1834, around 74 percent of public school children were enrolled in secular schools.

91. The choice of this proxy for the historical presence of the Catholic Church follows Squicciarini (2020).

the school: Discipline; moral and religious spirit."[92] Similarly, in *Alphabet des écoles primaires extrait de l'alphabet et premier livre de lecture*, authorized by the Royal Council on Public Instruction for teaching primary school children how to read, write, and pronounce French, the section that teaches vocabulary and pronunciation emphasizes moral values and secular and religious authorities. For example, the sound for "oi" is exemplified with the word "roi," "ieu" with "Dieu," "ia" with "diable," "ié" with pitié, "ien" with "bien." Similarly, the section of the textbook used to teach reading skills is filled with religious and moral content. Children are taught about the importance of obeying God and one's parents and teachers. They are told that those who behave righteously will be on God's good side, while those who misbehave should fear the consequences.[93] Even textbooks designed to teach natural science, like *Des merveilles de la nature, ou Lectures physico-morales à l'usage des écoles primaires*, written by a school inspector, constantly refer to "God" and "morality."[94]

Still, the Minister of Public Instruction—who before assuming his role requested that the phrase "and Worship" be removed from his title and ecclesiastical affairs be transferred to the Ministry of Justice—believed that the Church could only go so far in accomplishing the goals of primary education. Most of his contemporaries viewed the Catholic Church with great suspicion and hostility and wanted the state to constrain and oversee priests' action in primary schools. That was why the Guizot Law delegated the supervision of schools to municipal councils predominantly made up of secular municipal authorities. In addition, the Guizot Law gave the state the final word over teacher certification. It stipulated that the education commission of each department, under the authority of the national Minister of Education, would have the authority to conduct teacher examinations and issue competency certificates to teachers, and that aspiring teachers must also obtain a certificate of morality issued by the mayor and the local municipal council, not the local priest—even if teachers wanted to work in private religious schools.

The reason for constraining the power of the Church over primary education, Guizot and his contemporaries argued, was the belief that primary education should serve the interests of the state, whether or not those were aligned with the interests of the Church:

92. *Nouveau manuel des écoles primaires* (1836).
93. *Alphabet des écoles primaires* (1841).
94. *Des merveilles de la nature* (1838).

The great problem of modern societies is the government of minds.... Formerly the Church alone had the government of spirits. She possessed both moral authority and intellectual supremacy. She was responsible for nourishing intelligences as well as regulating souls, and science was her domain almost as exclusively as faith. This is no longer: intelligence and science have spread and secularized.... The government [must] not remain foreign to the moral development of succeeding generations, and as each new generation appears on the scene the government must establish intimate links between these new generations and the state within which God created them. Large scientific establishments and large establishments of public instruction supported by large public powers, this is the legitimate and necessary role that civil government plays in intellectual affairs.[95]

In sum, the July Monarchy's efforts to centralize and expand primary education through the Guizot Law were deeply shaped by the new regime's experience with mass violence and the national guard's unwillingness to repress the masses. In an attempt to prevent future rebellion against the regime, the national government expanded primary education to teach children to respect the state and its laws, focusing its efforts especially in those areas of France where the level of mass violence had been greater. Industrialists were not particularly supportive of educational expansion, nor were the government's efforts driven by military threats from other states. Although the Guizot Law did not entirely supplant the place of municipalities or the Catholic Church in primary education, neither municipal characteristics nor the presence of the Church can explain why the expansion of schooling was greater in more violent areas. What seems more likely is that the government prioritized educational expansion in formerly violent areas because those were precisely the areas where the problem of morality was deemed to be greater.

CHILE

Within Latin America, Chile was a precursor in creating a centralized primary education system, doing so one year after the civil war of 1859, which has been characterized by historians as "the most acute conflict that the ruling oligarchy faced since the consolidation of its political project in the

---

95. Guizot (1860), t.3, p. 14.

1830s."[96] The proximity of this civil war and the 1860 General Law of Primary Education was not coincidental. Efforts to centralize primary education were driven by a shared fear among conservative and liberal elites in Santiago, heightened by the civil war, that neglecting the moral education of the masses would endanger the power of the central government and the stability of the oligarchic political regime.

When civil war erupted in 1859, it threatened to overhaul the political institutions established in the 1830s. After winning a civil war against liberals in 1830, conservative elites had consolidated their political hegemony aided by the 1833 Constitution. The Constitution concentrated power in the president, established a close Church-State relationship, and established literacy and wealth requirements for voting, yielding an electorate of less than 2 percent of the population. A twenty-five-year period of political stability under conservative, oligarchic rule followed. In 1851, a dispute within the Conservative Party over the succession of incumbent president Manuel Bulnes escalated into civil war, but the conflict lacked mass participation; it was purely a fight among political conservative elites that never threatened to alter the established political institutions.[97]

The 1859 civil war differed from previous civil wars.[98] Led by radical liberal elites in the northern mining province of Atacama, it involved widespread popular participation from peasants, workers, artisans, and other members of the lower classes who joined the Atacama rebel forces. Rebel demands threatened to upend a long-standing balance of political and economic power that strongly favored the conservative and liberal elites in Santiago. On the political front, rebels demanded a new Constitution which, if approved, would have substantially reduced the powers for the central government in Santiago, constrained presidential powers, extended voting rights gradually, and excluded the Church from state matters. On the economic front, rebels also demanded less central government interference and lower taxes on copper and silver exports. At the time, Atacama was a leading mining province, along with its southern neighbor Coquimbo, and the

---

96. Ortega Martínez and Rubio Apiolaza (2006), p. 13.
97. Collier (2003), pp. 98–102; Ortega Martínez and Rubio Apiolaza (2006).
98. Chile also had civil wars in 1829–1830, 1851, and 1891, but the 1859 civil war was the first to meet all scope conditions (see chapter 6) and, crucially, the first with adequate subnational data to assess the second theoretical prediction.

central government's heavy reliance on copper and silver exports was perceived by Atacama's mining owners and workers as unfair.[99]

The war lasted four long months, from January 5, when rebels led by Pedro León Gallo seized Atacama's capital Copiapó, to May 12, when the central government finally removed the rebels from power. In between, Atacama rebel forces temporarily occupied Coquimbo, controlling its capital La Serena from mid-March to the end of April. As news traveled about the "revolution" in Atacama, as newspapers described it, the provinces of Aconcagua, Colchagua, and Talca briefly joined in rebellion, but unlike Atacama, these were quickly suppressed by government military forces.

The central government faced multiple difficulties in defeating the Atacama rebels. At the beginning of the civil war, rebel forces were four- to five thousand strong, while central government troops barely exceeded two thousand, their presence in Atacama minimal. Atacama rebels were also incredibly well-resourced; they controlled the treasury of one of the wealthiest provinces. Atacama's mineral resources and metal industry enabled rebels to mint large quantities of silver coins and, crucially, produce artillery including cannons, rifles, and other weapons. Furthermore, Atacama was remote and inaccessible. Land travel to the capital Copiapó, located 800 kilometers north of Santiago, would have required government troops to travel through long stretches of deserted territory with few looting opportunities or food sources. Travel by sea was similarly difficult. The closest port was Caldera, also controlled by rebels. Indeed, the government attempted to land there on January 16, but soon retreated after realizing its armed forces were insufficient. Inability to defeat the rebels led conservative president Manuel Montt to seek extraordinary powers to expand the government's troops. At the end of April 1859, after many failed attempts and lost battles, and owing to a tactical mistake by the rebels, the central government defeated Atacama's rebel forces, which by then had also occupied Coquimbo. In May, it finally recovered Copiapó.

The war brought together conservative and liberal elites in Santiago, united by their interest to preserve the centralization of political power, oligarchic institutions, and economic policies that benefited them. In particular, Santiago liberals supported conservative president Manuel Montt's efforts to suppress Atacama's radical rebels. Even after the war ended, throughout the 1860s liberals and conservatives remained formally allied via

99. Fernández Abara (2016).

the Liberal-Conservative Fusion. Their main opponent was the new Radical Party formed in 1863 by former Atacama rebels.[100]

In addition to reconfiguring the landscape of political parties in Chile, the 1859 civil war also reshaped primary education provision, which transitioned from a decentralized system controlled by municipalities to a centralized one controlled from Santiago. The 1833 Constitution had given the state a general mandate to promote public education but left the management and funding of *primary* education to municipalities, reflecting national elites' greater concern about promoting secondary and university education to ensure a steady supply of bureaucrats.[101] Beginning in the 1840s, ideas about the political importance of primary education began to spread across national elites. Spearheading this dissemination was Domingo F. Sarmiento, an exiled Argentine politician who, upon arriving in Chile in 1840, became a prolific journalist and writer.[102] Sarmiento argued that primary education would extirpate the violent predispositions of the masses and thus promote social order in newly independent Latin American countries.[103] Other Chilean public intellectuals agreed with his emphasis on the moralizing and civilizing function of mass education, including the liberal brothers Luis and Gregorio Amunátegui. The latter wrote an influential essay on what primary education should look like, where they argued:

> Just attending a school where reading and writing and discipline are taught, actively promotes the education of students' hearts. At school, children, generally speaking, develop habits of order, of submission, ... that later they cannot forget.... They will display the same virtues anywhere else as in school. The student accustomed to completing his homework accurately, ... to suffering a punishment if he does not comply ... will most likely become an honest individual who will never break his word ... The more educated they are, the more they perceive the penalties inherent in the violation of divine and human laws.[104]

Despite the circulation since the 1840s of ideas highlighting the state-building role of primary education, over the next two decades primary schooling expanded largely through municipal and private initiatives. The

---

100. Edwards (1932); Edwards Vives and Frei Montalva (1949); Salazar and Pinto (2018).
101. Jáksic and Serrano (1990).
102. Campobassi (1975).
103. Sarmiento (1845).
104. Amunátegui and Amunátegui (1856).

Chilean government gave Sarmiento and the Amunátegui brothers some space to implement their ideas. For example, in 1842, it appointed Sarmiento as director of the first state-controlled Normal School to train primary school teachers in Santiago, and in 1845, it sent him on an official mission to learn about primary education in Europe and the United States, which resulted in the publication of *Educación Popular*.[105] The government also began subsidizing municipal schools. Still, these initiatives fell short of establishing anything close to the centralized education system that Sarmiento advocated for. In fact, as Chilean historians Sol Serrano, Macarena Ponce de León, and Francisca Rengifo explain, government subsidies were allocated "haphazardly" in response to demands articulated by local elites, lacking any kind of central planning.[106]

Two separate attempts to create a national framework for primary education failed to receive support in Congress before the 1859 civil war. The first proposal, presented by the liberal politician José Lastarria in 1841, did not make it to the floor; Lastarria removed it following feedback that it would never make it through Congress. A second proposal debated by the Chamber of Deputies in 1849 also failed. Among its most controversial provisions were the creation of a dedicated tax to fund primary education and of a Primary School General Inspectorate, which according to most congressmembers gave excessive power to the state in matters of primary education.[107]

Support for the creation of a national primary education system increased dramatically after the civil war. Buttressing the central government's postwar effort to control and promote primary education was national elites' belief that indoctrinating the masses would help prevent future civil wars. The 1859 civil war greatly strengthened this belief, as President Montt's speeches demonstrate. When Montt spoke in 1857 and 1858 during the inauguration of Congress, he began by noting that the previous year had been a peaceful one.[108] In this context, in his 1857 speech, Montt only mentioned primary schooling to express satisfaction with its expansion,[109] And in 1858, he did not mention primary education at all.[110] By contrast, Montt's 1859 speech

---

105. Campobassi (1975).
106. Serrano, Ponce de León, and Rengifo (2012), pp. 156–158.
107. Egaña Baraona (2000).
108. Chile (1859a), pp. 1, 241.
109. Chile (1859a), p. 10.
110. Chile (1859a), pp. 241–252.

to Congress, delivered less than two months after the central government reclaimed Atacama, began highlighting the war, noting that "the order of the Republic has just suffered a difficult test."[111] Montt linked the "anarchy" and "disorder" of 1859 to rebel leaders' ability to mobilize the masses, whom he argued had "evil passions" and poor moral values:[112]

> The rebels ... looked for support in the evil passions and ignorance of the masses ... That way they were able to introduce anarchy ... a state of disorder ... The crisis ... deteriorated the moral values of the masses and weakened their respect for authority.[113]

Whereas before the civil war Montt had not prioritized primary education, by 1859 his diagnosis of the war's moral roots convinced him otherwise. He told Congress that "It is essential for the central government to make an extraordinary effort to ensure tranquility and domestic order,"[114] and urged it to pass a national primary education law to address the moral roots of disorder. Departing from prewar speeches in his assessment of the state of primary education, in 1859 Montt argued that "Primary schooling ... does not satisfy our needs":[115]

> A large part of the evils that affect the public order are rooted in ignorance. Extirpating it through a system of common schools that enlightens the masses by correcting their bad manners is the most urgent task you can devote yourselves to.[116]

In 1860 Congress passed the General Law of Primary Education, the first comprehensive national law regulating primary education, considered by Chilean historians "a political and legislative landmark."[117] This law replaced the decentralized primary education system with a new system in which the central government became the main provider, funder, regulator, and supervisor of primary education. The law prohibited public school tuition, imposed a national curriculum emphasizing moral and religious education,

---

111. Chile (1859b), p. 5.
112. Chile (1859b), pp. 6–7.
113. Chile (1859b), pp. 6–7.
114. Chile (1859b), p. 7.
115. Chile (1859b), p. 10.
116. Chile (1859b), p. 11.
117. Serrano, Ponce de León, and Rengifo (2012), p. 159.

required prospective teachers to be trained in state-controlled Normal Schools, and created a centralized inspectorate.[118]

While in the 1840s national elites had been reluctant to intervene in matters of primary education, conservatives and liberals after the 1859 civil war agreed that creating a national primary education system was an urgent need. They also agreed that the goal of such a system was, in the words of Chilean historian Loreto Egaña Baraona, to act as "a moralizing element and a guardian of order"; and that, because it "constituted a social function, the state should be responsible for its development."[119] Serrano and her colleagues also note that after the 1859 civil war "the political elite in general supported public primary schooling, with the exception of a few isolated" members of Congress. Although a few members expressed "concern that the rural masses' expectations might change" due to their education, "finally these voices did not have much political influence. Among the political elite, what prevailed was a sentiment of the urgency to expand schooling. On this front, consensus among conservatives and liberals existed."[120]

This conservative-liberal consensus was also present in the media. In June 1859, immediately following the civil war, the conservative newspaper *El Mercurio* characterized primary education reform as "a moral reform," and argued that "reforming mass customs" must be "our main objective."[121] The more moderate *El Ferrocarril* concurred. In an article published in November 1859, it argued that "ignorance" is man's worst adviser; "there is no crime" it does not imagine: "The unenlightened classes are the most real, effective, permanent and difficult danger that can have a nation in constant siege."[122]

The 1860 law yielded not only centralization of educational authority, but also expansion of primary schooling under the state's directive. Implementation of the law began in 1863 during the presidency of José Pérez Mascayano, who was elected by a coalition of conservative and liberal politicians in 1861. Pérez Mascayano appointed ultra-conservative politician Miguel María Güemes as Minister of Justice, Worship, and Public Instruction. Güemes issued the 1863 *Reglamento General de Instrucción Primaria*, which established the regulatory details needed to begin implementation. Once

118. Egaña Baraona (2000); Serrano, Ponce de León, and Rengifo (2012); http://www.archivonacional.cl/616/w3-article-28319.html.
119. Egaña Baraona (2000), p. 30.
120. Serrano, Ponce de León, and Rengifo (2012), p. 82.
121. Egaña Baraona (2000), p. 32.
122. Egaña Baraona (2000), p. 34.

the *Reglamento* was in place, Güemes's ministry oversaw a major reorganization of the supply of primary schooling, closing some schools, consolidating others, leaving others untouched, and creating new ones.

As predicted by the book's theory, the central government's decision regarding how many schools to maintain varied considerably across provinces as a function of the threat they posed to the government during the civil war. The largest expansion of primary schooling occurred in Atacama, the bastion of the rebellion and the province where the central government had found it most difficult to restore its power. This is shown in figure 4.3, which uses statistics on the number of primary schools maintained by the central government and the number of students enrolled in these schools, available by province since 1859.[123] These statistics offer evidence that once the 1863 *Reglamento* was issued and the Ministry of Public Instruction began implementing the 1860 law, the number of primary schools maintained by the central government in Atacama increased markedly. The increased availability of primary schools in Atacama following the central government's intervention after 1863 was also accompanied by sharp increases in primary school enrollment, which climbed from around 8 percent of the population ages 5–14 years before 1863 to over 14 percent just by 1865. By contrast, in provinces where the rebellion was quickly suppressed by the central government (Aconcagua, Colchagua, Coquimbo, and Talca) and in provinces that had remained loyal to the government throughout the 1859 conflict, the government did not prioritize the expansion of primary schooling.

In addition to promoting the expansion of primary education, the national government also selected and distributed the textbooks that could be used in primary schools. In line with its educational goals, most textbooks emphasized moral lessons. They sought to instill in children a sense of duty, stressed the value of being obedient, submissive, loving, and respectful of their parents, God, and Chilean laws. One commonly used textbook, *Libro de la infancia* (Book of Childhood), described a good student as someone who "does not laugh or talk with his peers; does not dare play. When the teacher is not looking at him he remains as still as when he looks straight

---

123. The data come from multiple years of the *Anuario Estadístico de la República de Chile*. Statistics for primary education at the provincial level were not systematically collected before 1859. The few data that exist before that year (e.g., for 1853) are of poor quality. For this reason, I do not present trends using these data. However, the conclusion that, following the 1859 civil war, the central government prioritized the expansion of primary education in Atacama remains true even if we were to incorporate these data into the analysis.

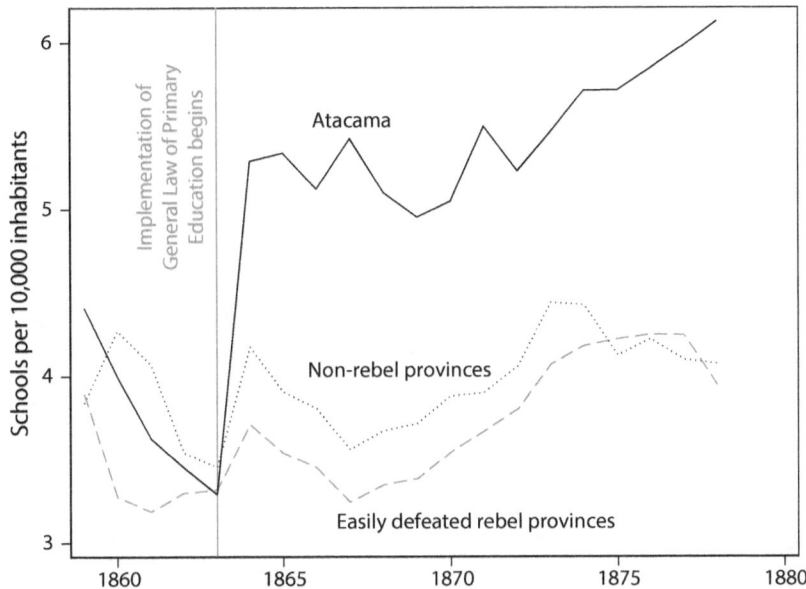
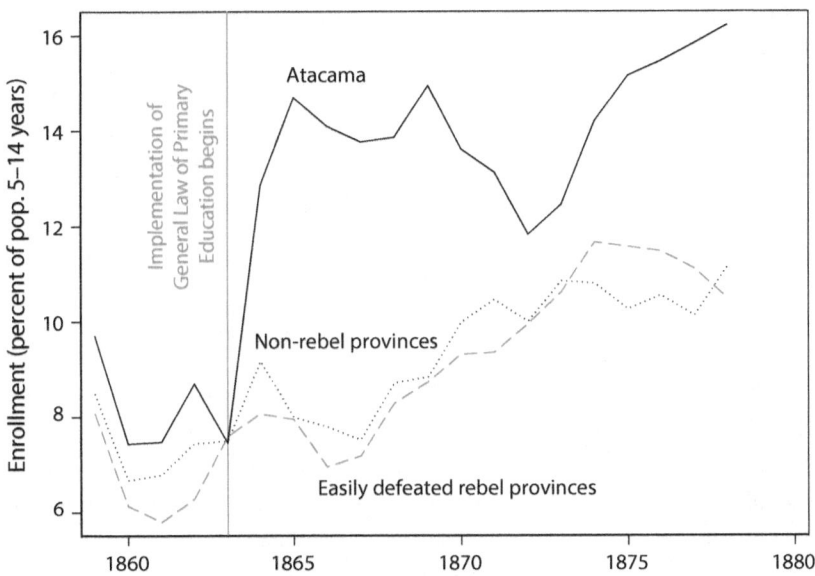

Figure 4.3. Public primary schools maintained by the Chilean central government, and primary school enrollment, in Atacama and the rest of Chile, 1859–1878. See text and footnotes for sources and methodology.

at him." Another common textbook, *La conciencia de un niño* (A Child's Conscience), written in the first person so that the child would internalize its content, taught children to be content with what they had, including passages such as: "I am very happy; I have excellent parents who continually take care of me. Their goodness provides for everything I need." The same book had a chapter titled "What a child must know" which told children: "if you are a subject, you must obey and behave well" and "not judge your superiors based on what you see; they have goals you do not understand."[124]

Still, the patterns of school expansion shown in figure 4.3 could also be driven by other explanations. One question is whether the central government expanded primary education in Atacama to appease rebels through redistribution. The content of primary education offers clues about the plausibility of this argument. Recall that Atacama rebels were liberal and opposed Church intromission in state matters. Had the government sought to appease rebels, it would have promoted secular education, not the heavily Catholic schools it actually promoted. The 1860 General Law of Primary Education established a national curriculum that mandated teaching "Christian Doctrine and Morality," the opposite of what Atacama rebels would have wanted. Moreover, as we saw earlier, the initial implementation of the law was charged to a fervent defender of the Catholic Church's power, Miguel María Güemes, appointed Minister of Public Instruction by Montt's successor. Throughout the 1860s, the Ministry approved and distributed textbooks on reading and writing suffused with religious content. *La conciencia de un niño*, for example, taught reading skills by having children read passages such as the following:

> If I am happy with what my parents give me to eat and drink; ... if I am nice to others, I will sow the seeds of my good behavior ... If I behave well and satisfy God, when I die I will go to Heaven.[125]

The presence of religious content in the national curriculum and school textbooks should not be confused with the notion that the expansion of primary education was driven by the Catholic Church. While the type of moral education prescribed by the 1860 law included considerable religious content, the same law also made it clear that the central government was the supreme authority over education issues, retaining the power not only to alter the curriculum but also a monopoly over teacher training and

---

124. Serrano, Ponce de León, and Rengifo (2012), pp. 309–312.
125. Sarmiento (1844), pp. 32–33, 36.

certification, the authority to determine where to construct schools, and the authority to inspect schools and apply penalties to those that deviated from the central government's education directives.

Nor were the central government's efforts to expand primary education a response to parental demands. On this point, there is ample evidence from primary and secondary historical sources that elites in Santiago generally believed that parents were "indifferent" or "resistant" to primary schooling due to their "ignorance" and "selfish" reliance on their children's labor.[126] These perceptions were informed by the reports that the central government received from school inspectors, who wrote that "parents' general indifference toward their children's education continues to be the most powerful obstacle we face when it comes to disseminating primary instruction."[127] To be clear, the existing evidence does not imply that elites were correct about parents' reluctance to send their children to school. But if unmet demand for primary schooling existed, most members of Congress appear to have not known about it.[128]

Interstate wars also fail to explain the expansion of primary schooling in Chile after the 1859 civil war. The large expansion of schooling observed in Atacama in 1864 occurred during a period when external military threats were not salient.[129] Moreover, the national curriculum established by the 1860 law did not include subjects typically associated with preparing future soldiers and nationalist citizens, such as physical education, geography, and history. The mandatory subjects and the textbooks used to teach children reflected the "moralizing" goals of primary schools, which sought to instill respect for authorities, rules, and norms, and to inculcate, to quote the Amunátegui brothers, "habits of order, of submission, that later they cannot forget."

Another possibility is that the central government expanded primary schooling in Atacama to foster the mining industry. Both Atacama and Coquimbo comprised the *Norte Chico* region, which benefited from copper

---

126. Chile (1860a); Egaña Baraona (2000); Archivo Nacional de Chile.
127. Egaña Baraona (2000).
128. Ponce de León (2010).
129. Chile fought wars against neighbor states in 1836–1839 and 1879–1884, and against Spain in 1865–1866. While it is possible that the expansion of primary education in the late 1860s was partly a response to the war against Spain, it is not clear why the government would have targeted Atacama specifically. Moreover, the sharpest expansion of Atacama's primary education took place in 1864, when international peace prevailed.

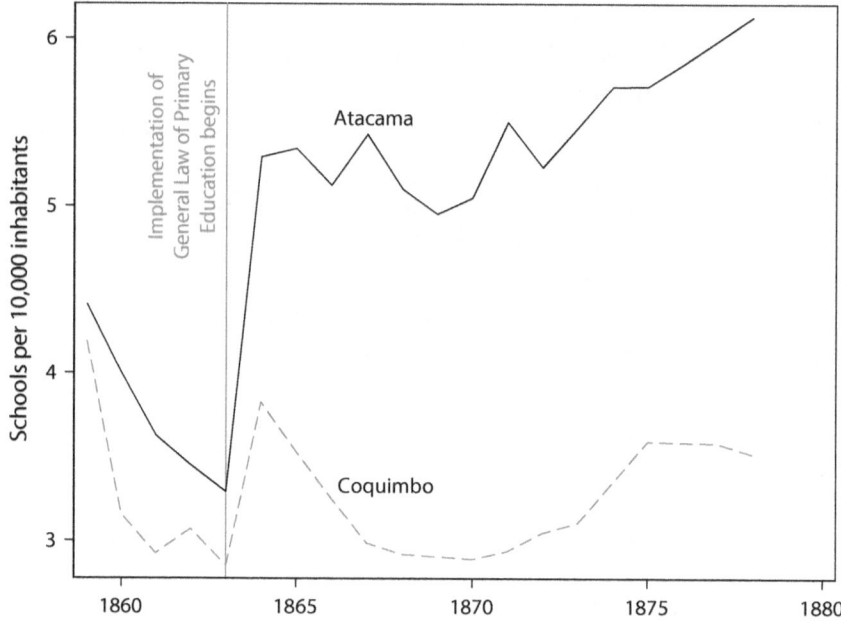

Figure 4.4. Public primary schools maintained by the Chilean central government in the mining provinces of Atacama and Coquimbo, 1859–1878. See text and footnotes for sources and methodology.

and silver booms and accounted for the bulk of Chile's mineral exports.[130] Coquimbo was synonymous with copper, producing one-third of Chile's copper output, while Atacama stood out for silver, accounting for at least one-third of Chile's silver production. These commodities were immensely and increasingly valuable to the Chilean economy throughout the nineteenth century, with silver dominating in the 1830s, and copper leading from the 1840s through the 1880s.[131] If the central government's efforts to promote primary schooling had sought to support the mining industry, we should see similar expansion in both provinces. If instead educational expansion responded to the civil war, we should observe greater expansion in Atacama, since that province represented the main threat to the central government. We observe the latter, as figure 4.4 shows.

Some readers may also wonder whether the patterns shown in figure 4.3 are driven by differences in state capacity. It is important to note that differ-

---

130. Collier and Sater (2004), pp. 76–80.
131. San Román (1894); Pederson (1965).

ences in local capacity are unlikely to explain these patterns because the graphs show the number of schools controlled by the central government. Still, perhaps efforts made by the central government to win the 1859 civil war led to stronger central state capacity, in turn enabling it to implement long-standing educational goals that could not materialize before the war. To investigate this possibility, I examined whether war induced an improvement in central state capacity, measured by national fiscal revenues. The answer is no. In fact, Atacama saw significant growth in primary schools in 1864 despite *declining* national fiscal revenues between 1859 and 1864.[132]

In sum, the 1859 Chilean civil war threatened the state's authority. In response, the central government took over primary education and expanded its provision in former rebel areas. Crucial to the central government's postwar educational efforts was the belief that indoctrinating the masses would help prevent future civil wars and crises of internal order.

ARGENTINA

At the start of the twentieth century, Argentina was viewed as Latin America's leader in primary education provision. Yet four decades earlier, when Chile was rolling out a national primary education system, Argentina's primary schooling levels remained unremarkable. The turning point occurred with the passage of the 1884 Law of Common Education, a national law that would shape primary education for more than a century. This law declared that primary education would be free, universal, compulsory, and secular, established a common national curriculum, a national inspectorate, and state monopoly over teacher training, and granted extensive regulatory and oversight powers to the central government through the new National Education Council.[133] It also initiated a period of rapid growth in primary school coverage, shown in figure 4.5: while enrollment rates had remained

132. See the online appendix. In addition, the fact that population growth between 1854 and 1865 was greater in Atacama than the rest of Chile does not explain the patterns shown in figure 4.3 because the number of schools and students are adjusted by total provincial population.

133. The historical literature on the significance of the 1884 law is too extensive to cite. Some examples include: Tedesco (1966); Puiggrós and Carli (1991); Alliaud (2007). For a shorter but authoritative example, see the Biblioteca Nacional del Maestro's project *Memoria e Historia de la Educación Argentina*, which describes the 1884 law as the "piedra basal" (foundation stone) of the Argentine national education system (Biblioteca Nacional del Maestro, n.d., "Ley de Educación Común 1420"). Similary, Alliaud (2007) writes: "The *creation of the National Education Council and the sanctioning of the Law of Common Education*, in 1881 and 1884, respectively, are two events that mark the emergence and consolidation of a national education system ... The *Congreso Pedagógico*

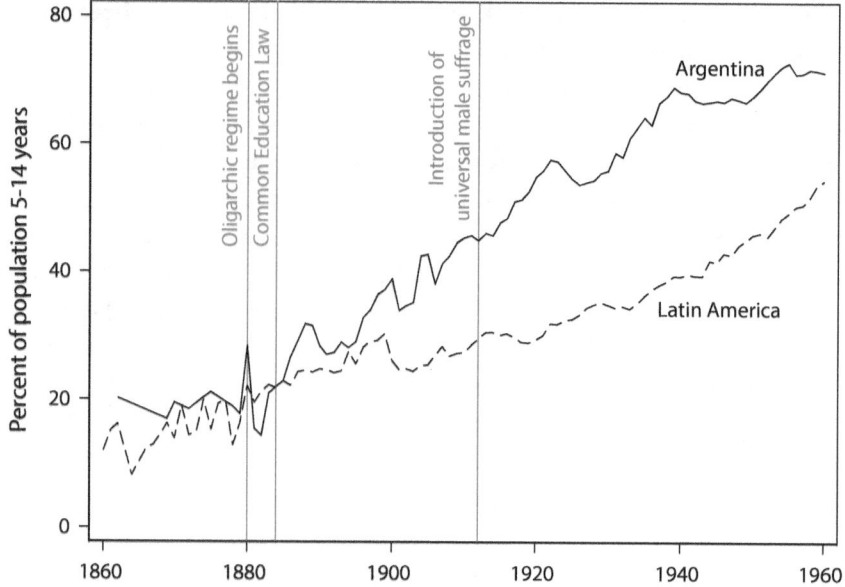

Figure 4.5. Primary school enrollment rates in Argentina and in Latin America, as a percentage of the population ages 5–14 years, 1860–1960. See text and footnotes for sources and methodology.

relatively flat at around 20 percent in the two decades preceding the 1884 law, in the two decades after its passage enrollment more than doubled, placing Argentina on a path that set it apart from the rest of the region. Why did the state make such a considerable effort to control and promote primary schooling during the 1880s?

The creation of a national primary education system was intimately connected to the long history of civil wars that afflicted Argentina since its independence from Spain in 1816 until 1880. This assertion stems from my own investigation and from dozens of studies conducted by Argentine historians. One of the classic books on the origins of Argentina's primary education system, Juan Carlos Tedesco's *Educación y Sociedad en la Argentina (1880–1945)*, notes that education "fulfilled, more than an economic function, a political function"—namely, the "socialization of new generations" into "notions about the legitimacy of the distribution of power." Interest in the "moralizing role of teaching," says Tedesco, stemmed from the failure

---

of 1882, an immediate antecedent of the 1884 law, captured and established the basic organizing principles of education" (Alliaud 2007, pp. 56–57; emphasis in the original).

of the central government in Buenos Aires to assert its authority in the rest of the provinces, known as the Interior:

> First and foremost, the diffusion of education was linked to the achievement of internal political stability.... It was thought that education, to the extent that it massively disseminated certain principles, would effectively contribute to the task of eliminating the pockets of resistance to the central government that remained, especially, in the interior of the country.[134]

The "pockets of resistance" that Tedesco refers to are the rural paramilitary groups who for six decades, from 1820 to 1880, fought against the centralization of authority in Buenos Aires. These armed groups made up primarily of civilians and known as *montoneras* were led by warlords or *caudillos* from the Interior. They demanded a federation of autonomous provinces, equal provincial representation in Congress, restrictions on imports to protect local economies, and shared access to rents from the port and customs located in Buenos Aires City—the main source of revenue in Argentina's export-based economy. These demands clashed with the interests of Buenos Aires elites, who wanted to have direct administrative control of the entire national territory, congressional representation based on population size, monopoly control of the armed forces, an open economy, and crucially, monopoly access to rents from the Buenos Aires port and customs.

Because neither side had sufficient military capacity to clearly impose its will on the other, the violent conflict over the distribution of political and economic power between Buenos Aires and the Interior spanned six decades. In that time, the balance of power tilted in favor of federalists from the 1830s to the 1850s—whose sanctioning of a federal Constitution in 1853 resulted in Buenos Aires's secession for the next ten years—and then gradually shifted in favor of Buenos Aires from 1861 onward, when its military victory led to reunification under a new federal Constitution that gave Buenos Aires greater privileges compared to the other provinces. Throughout the 1860s and 1870s, as three different presidents—Bartolomé Mitre, Domingo F. Sarmiento, and Nicolás Avellaneda—embarked on reforms to consolidate a central authority, including attempts to form a national army and tax collection authority, rural *montoneras* again broke out in rebellion.[135] During

134. Tedesco (1986), p. 64.
135. Rock (1985).

Mitre's presidency alone (1862–1868), there were 107 rebellions and 90 battles which resulted in a death toll of 4,728.[136] The conflict finally ended with the 1880 Revolution, in which centralizing elites emerged triumphant, leading to the designation of Buenos Aires City as the country's capital.

When Roca assumed the presidency in October 1880, consolidating internal peace and the state's authority were his top priorities, encapsulated in his motto, "peace and governance."[137] In one of his first speeches as president, he remarked that "nations preserve their independence and integrity" not by relying on the enthusiasm of the moment, "but with internal peace, the civic virtues of the citizen, and respect for the principle of authority and compliance with the Constitution and the laws."[138] Speaking to congressmen, he repeatedly urged them to "end the revolution and begin the period of order," telling them: "Let this be our public aspiration: peace and order; let's realize this agenda and the light that begins to shine on the Republic will become a bright spotlight."[139]

To consolidate internal order, Roca put forth an ambitious state-building agenda that sought to increase the state's presence in people's lives.[140] Investments in infrastructure contributed to increase this presence and unify the country economically and politically. Aided by foreign loans and rapidly growing tax revenues from grain exports, Roca's administration constructed new public buildings to house the state's expanding bureaucratic apparatus, expanded the number of ports, and promoted the extension of the railroads network. In addition to unifying distant markets, ports and especially railroads were designed to facilitate the national government's ability to access and exert control over the Interior provinces, a crucial need given Argentina's large territory.[141] In 1869, when the first national census was conducted, the railroad network was less than 700 kilometers long and reached less than 20 percent of the population, a proportion that remained similar until Roca assumed the presidency in 1880. Just ten years later, all provincial capi-

---

136. Oszlak (2012), p. 107.
137. Roca's motto in Spanish was "paz y administración."
138. Botana (1971), p. 198.
139. Botana (1971), p. 199.
140. Oszlak (2012).
141. The importance of railroads' political function has been highlighted by Argentine historians and helps explain not only why the entire network converged toward Buenos Aires City, where the national government resided, but also why the government supported the construction of railways reaching some of the most remote and poorest provinces, such as the northern Salta province, which had little to contribute to the national economy.

tals had been connected to a railroad network that reached 50 percent of the population and extended over more than 14,000 kilometers—the longest in Latin America and the ninth longest in the world at that time.[142]

In addition to extending the geographic reach of the state, Roca was also keen to displace the Catholic Church from people's daily lives and replace it with the state. A law passed in 1884 established a civil registry of births, marriages, and deaths in any territory controlled by the national government, ending the Church's prerogatives in these crucial moments of a person's life.

Primary education was another major pillar of Roca's state-building agenda to promote social order by increasing the state's presence in people's lives. In January 1881, less than three months after assuming power, Roca signed a decree establishing the National Education Council (*Consejo Nacional de Educación* or CNE). The decree charged the CNE with primary education provision in Buenos Aires City, and the 1884 Law of Common Education gave it the power to regulate and oversee primary schools in the entire national territory.[143] As head of the CNE, Roca appointed former president and mass education reform advocate Domingo F. Sarmiento, who drafted the 1884 Law of Common Education.[144] Sarmiento's enormous influence on the formation of a national primary education system has earned him the nickname "father of Argentina's education," and a national holiday, Teachers' Day, coincides with the anniversary of his death. To understand what Roca's appointment of Sarmiento tells us about how national elites conceptualized primary education, we first need to make a detour and delve into Sarmiento's trajectory and ideas about the role of mass education.

Sarmiento belonged to the group of politicians who had fought to centralize power in Buenos Aires. He began his fight against Federalist forces in 1829, when at the age of 18 he joined the Unitary Army supporting Buenos Aires. When his native province of San Juan was taken over by federalist *caudillo* Juan Facundo Quiroga, Sarmiento fled to Chile, returning only after Quiroga's death in 1835. Back in Argentina, Sarmiento became deeply embedded in national politics, using his writings to denounce federalist leaders. His most notable target was Juan Manuel de Rosas, the powerful

---

142. Pérez (2018).
143. Campobassi (1956).
144. Pigna (2009), p. 286.

caudillo who between 1835 and 1852 controlled the province of Buenos Aires, forming alliances with other provincial warlords and establishing a highly repressive and dictatorial political regime. Persecuted by the Rosas regime, in 1840 Sarmiento was again forced to exile to Chile. There, he published his most important book, *Facundo: Civilization and Barbarism*, named after his former enemy Facundo Quiroga. In it, he describes with dramatic prose and in vivid detail his traumatic experience fighting against federalist *caudillos* and *montoneras*, and outlines a provocative and deeply influential explanation of the causes behind the Argentine civil wars.

Sarmiento was convinced that the cause of Argentina's civil wars, of its "anarchy," was the "barbarian," "savage," and "violent" character of the rural masses and *caudillos* of the Interior, whose instinct to kill and destroy clashed with and was a threat to the civilized and well-behaved population of Buenos Aires. "Since childhood," wrote Sarmiento, the people of the Interior "are used to killing cattle, and this necessarily cruel act familiarizes them with bloodshed, and hardens their hearts against their victims' groans."[145] Children grow up riding horses, taming savage animals,[146] carrying knives and playing with them "as if they were playing with dice,"[147] and developing a "butcher's instinct."[148] For Sarmiento, this upbringing also explained the ease with which *caudillos* like Facundo Quiroga or Juan Manuel de Rosas recruited the rural "bloodthirsty hordes" into *montoneras* to fight against the civilized population of Buenos Aires, whom they regarded with "implacable hatred" and "invincible disdain."[149]

Locating the root of civil war in the upbringing of the rural population led Sarmiento to advocate for a national system of primary schools controlled by Buenos Aires elites. These schools, he claimed, would "extirpate" the rural masses' violent predispositions by inculcating in children the values, moral norms, and civilized behaviors prevailing in the capital. In time, this would end the cycle of civil wars afflicting the country and consolidate the state's authority. As an indication of the probable efficacy of a national policy, Sarmiento pointed out that in the isolated places where primary schools existed and "moral precepts are inculcated in students with special attention," internal peace prevails. "I do not attribute to any

---

145. Sarmiento (1845), p. 34.
146. Sarmiento (1845), p. 33.
147. Sarmiento (1845), p. 58.
148. Sarmiento (1845), p. 67.
149. Sarmiento (1845), p. 68.

other cause," said Sarmiento, "the fact that so few crimes have been committed" and a "moderate behavior" prevails in these places.[150]

The idea that the Argentine civil wars were caused by a clash of moral and cultural values between the barbarian Interior and civilized Buenos Aires was appealing to centralizing elites but was predictably rejected by federalist ones. The publication of *Facundo* while Sarmiento was exiled in Chile caused a diplomatic rift between the Chilean government and the federalist government of Juan Manuel de Rosas, which Chile de-escalated by sending Sarmiento on a two-year trip abroad to visit primary schools in France, Prussia, and other European countries. The result of that trip was *Educación Popular*, published upon Sarmiento's return to Chile in 1849, in which he further developed his ideas about the need for a national primary education system, writing that "Primary instruction must be exclusively devoted to moral development and to the maintenance of social order,"[151] and citing French statistics to argue that primary education, by moralizing the masses, would lead to a reduction of crime.[152] The following excerpts from this book help illustrate his main ideas about the moralizing role of primary education, the direct benefits to elites of providing mass education, and the superiority of educating new generations compared to relying on repression as a strategy to preserve social order:

> Society at large has a vital interest in ensuring that all the individuals who will eventually come to form the nation have, through the education received in their childhood, been sufficiently prepared to carry out the social functions to which they will be called . . . The dignity of the State, the glory of a nation, . . . can only be obtained by elevating the moral character, developing the intelligence, and predisposing it to orderly and legitimate action.[153]
>
> There is also an object of foresight to bear in mind when dealing with public education, and that is that the masses are less disposed to respect life and property as their reasoning capabilities and moral sentiments are less cultivated. Out of selfishness, then, from those who today enjoy greater advantages we must try as soon as possible to blunt that instinct toward destruction.[154]

---

150. Sarmiento (1845), p. 73.
151. Sarmiento (1849), p. 23.
152. Sarmiento (1849), p. 36.
153. Sarmiento (1849), p. 48.
154. Sarmiento (1849), p. 48.

> The existence of armies for peoples accustomed to not feeling other stimuli of order than coercion is certainly a great need... but public education satisfies another more compelling, less expendable need. It is not entirely proven that without permanent armies, or with less numerous ones, order would not have been preserved in each State, or that there would have been more or fewer revolts... But it is very certain that by not educating the new generations, all the defects that our current organization suffers from will continue to exist and take on more colossal proportions... without the improvement of the moral and rational situation of spirits.[155]

Although Sarmiento's ideas were well-received by centralizing Buenos Aires elites, primary education took a back seat while the civil wars raged, as elites focused on the more urgent problem of quashing *montoneras* led by federalist *caudillos*. During the 1860s and 1870s, when the balance of power began to shift gradually in favor of Buenos Aires, the central government under the presidencies of Mitre (1862–1868), Sarmiento (1868–1874), and Avellaneda (1874–1880) prioritized forming a national army as the main strategy to quash *montoneras*. About 43 percent of the national budget between 1863 and 1880 was devoted to strengthening the army and waging war against internal enemies. In addition to repressing rebels, the government used material concessions to appease *caudillos*, including generous subsidies to the provinces and sponsoring a railroad connecting the provinces of Córdoba and Santa Fé. However, the government soon realized that this approach to maintaining social order had only been made possible by the unprecedented economic growth of the 1860s. When a trade depression hit the country in the 1870s and revenues waned, rural rebellions against the federal government surged, underscoring the frailty of relying on concessions to forge order and unity. In an attempt to prevent future rebellions, Sarmiento's presidency undertook some initial efforts to promote primary schooling, building primary schools and establishing Normal Schools to train primary school teachers. But the pressing need to quash *montoneras* meant that these efforts stopped short of creating a national primary education system and were thus accompanied by only a mild expansion of primary schooling.[156]

---

155. Sarmiento (1849), p. 51.
156. Rock (1985), pp. 118–131.

The end of the cycle of civil wars in 1880 created a more fertile environment for Sarmiento's ideas to be put into action. When Roca assumed power in 1880, in addition to creating the CNE and appointing Sarmiento to it, he charged Sarmiento with drafting a national primary education bill. To inform this bill, Sarmiento organized the 1882 Pedagogical Congress, where top national politicians were joined by national school inspectors, university professors and secondary school teachers, directors of Normal Schools, and delegates from other Latin American countries, to debate the organizing principles of primary education—whether attendance should be compulsory or voluntary, what should be taught in schools, etc. The national government's position on the role of primary education was clearly articulated by José María Torres, appointed a few years earlier to direct the main state institution in charge of training primary school teachers. In his speech to the Pedagogical Congress, this fervent advocate of the disciplining role of education said:

> The Argentine Republic needs to repel the desert's barbarism and has managed, through the intelligent and strenuous effort of its army, to reduce it to relatively narrow regions; but it urgently needs to also reduce to the narrowest limits the barbaric elements of society—which are apathy and ignorance, and their sequel of crimes—through the intelligent and persevering effort of an *army of teachers* who know how to teach, educating the moral nature of the children, so that schools serve effectively to prevent crime [and] consolidate domestic peace.[157]

The emphasis on primary education as a means to reform the masses' barbaric nature and thus promote social order—clearly shaped by Sarmiento's ideas—was a common theme in the education debates of the early 1880s. The president of the 1882 Pedagogical Congress, Onésimo Leguizamón, spoke of the inferior moral values of the lower classes, lamented the disorder that their vices engendered, denounced the masses' passive loyalty to local bosses and *caudillos*, called on the "socially superior" to take charge of addressing these issues, and described teachers as an "unarmed army to whom we trust the civic and moral preparation of the new generations".[158]

> Free and compulsory instruction is simply a matter of national defense. It is necessary to extinguish ignorance, the source of disorder that

---

157. Puiggrós and Carli (1991), p. 106. Emphasis is mine.
158. Puiggrós and Carli (1991), p. 106.

threatens our future. If you do not want to force all parents to instruct their children, prepare to widen our prisons ... The absence of education ... engenders social dangers, because a mass of inadequate beings poses natural resistance to public law, to the improvement of customs, to mutual respect; ... societies have institutions, and a deficient aptitude in the people to practice them engenders great despotisms,[159] or at a minimum, local loyalties, always so fatal for public life ... The ignorance of the people is the greatest of the national dangers.[160]

During the debate of the 1884 Law of Common Education in Congress, the presentation of the bill sponsored by Roca's government was in charge of the Minister of Justice, Worship, and Public Instruction, Eduardo Wilde. In his speech, Wilde emphasized the importance of maintaining order in schools, underscoring that "of course the quarrels and disagreements begin at school, to continue on the street, ... finally sowing indelible divisions in the people." Wilde, himself a medical doctor, viewed the lack of morality of the masses as an illness, social divisions as its symptom, and primary education as a cure.[161] He told Congress:

> The State, which has some rights over adult citizens, also has them over young children. It imposes certain duties on citizens ... It has the obligation to form citizens ... The State, which regulates the transmission of property, which protects the life and honor of citizens, cannot neglect education; and with the same right with which it turns family

---

159. By "despotisms," Leguizamón refers to federalist governments like that of Juan Manuel de Rosas. In a similar vein, when Sarmiento criticized the federalist Rosas in *Facundo*, he wrote, "an ignorant people will always vote for Rosas."
160. Puiggrós and Carli (1991), p. 157.
161. Beginning in the 1880s, medical doctors became heavily involved in the administration and design of primary schooling. In addition to Wilde's appointment to the Ministry of Justice, Worship, and Public Instruction, doctors were regularly consulted on the role of primary education to eradicate alcoholism, prostitution, poor personal hygiene, and other habits and behaviors which at the time were considered "examples of immorality and of the sickness of the masses." For example, in a selection of articles published by the Ministry's official publication, *Monitor de la Educación Común*, doctors argued that these habits and behaviors were caused by a lack of self-repression, and that physical illnesses were a punishment for these poor behaviors. Medical doctors continued exercising considerable influence on primary education in the early twentieth century. Their most visible and influential figure was José María Ramos Mejía, who presided over the National Education Council starting in 1908. Ramos Mejía wrote extensively on the role of early childhood experiences in shaping the structure of the brain. He published a crucial report in 1909 arguing that immigrants posed a social danger due to their biological inferiority, and that primary schools needed to be reformed in order to imprint in immigrant children's minds deep nationalist sentiments. See Puiggrós and Carli (1991), pp. 119–122; Ramos Mejía (1899).

children into soldiers, it can and should impose the obligation to educate them, because this matters for the good of the Nation.[162]

At no point during the congressional debates of the Law of Common Education did either liberal or conservative elites in Congress question the idea that the main goal of primary education was to moralize the masses. They did not agree, however, about what that entailed and, in particular, whether the moral education of the masses ought to be secular or religious—a debate we will return to in chapter 5. The salience of concerns about morality is indicated by a simple word count: across all congressional sessions where the law was debated, the word "moral" was mentioned 269 times; by contrast, words beginning with "industr," "econom," and "trabaj" (work) were mentioned a total of 74 times.[163]

When passed in 1884, the Law of Common Education mandated universal provision and compulsory attendance to primary schools for all children ages 6–14; established that education ought to be free and secular; set teacher certification requirements, including the requirement to prove "moral competence" and to graduate from a Normal School regulated by the central government; established funding mechanisms to expand education; and gave the CNE the responsibility to monitor regulatory compliance through a system of inspectors, implement School Censuses, and regularly gather education statistics. We will look at the content of the national curriculum for primary schools in chapter 5, but the following excerpt illustrates the type of content included in the textbooks approved by the CNE for primary school children:

> To love the homeland is to love freedom, to love the law, to love order, to love authority, to respect it, uphold it, defend it, and sacrifice bad passions. To love the homeland is to detest and fight tyranny; to detest and fight anarchy.[164]

The Law had a steady impact on school construction and enrollment. In line with the predictions of the theory developed in chapter 3, and also with Sarmiento's recommendations, the expansion of primary education during

---

162. Wilde, in Argentina, *Diario de Sesiones (Diputados)*, July 13, 1883, p. 581.
163. The word count is based on Argentina, *Diario de Sesiones (Diputados)* of June 23, July 4, July 6, July 11, July 12, July 13, July 14, July 18, July 20, and July 23 of 1883, and Argentina, *Diario de Sesiones (Senado)* of August 18, September 30, and October 8 of 1881, August 28 of 1883, and July 26 of 1884.
164. Tedesco (1965), p. 62.

Roca's presidency was most pronounced in rural areas of the Interior provinces, which for six decades had challenged the authority of Buenos Aires. This is illustrated in figure 4.6, which shows the evolution of primary school enrollment rates and the number of primary schools in Buenos Aires and the rest of the country from Roca's assumption in 1880 to the introduction of universal male suffrage in 1912. Two main patterns emerge from this figure. First, consistent with Sarmiento's claim that Buenos Aires was more "civilized" than the rest of the country, at the beginning of Roca's presidency the level of school enrollment in the Interior was considerably lower than in Buenos Aires: around 20 percent of school-age children were enrolled in primary schools in the Interior, compared to more than 35 percent in Buenos Aires. Second, starting with Roca's presidency, the oligarchic regime established in 1880 prioritized the expansion of schooling in the Interior of the country, which by the end of the oligarchic regime had reached primary education levels similar to those of Buenos Aires.[165] Between 1885—when education statistics at the provincial level first became available—and 1912, primary school enrollment rates increased by 27 percentage points in Buenos Aires (from 36 to 63 percent) and by 37 percentage points in the Interior (from 22 to 59 percent). The more pronounced expansion of primary schooling in the Interior was not driven by a few isolated provinces: between 1885 and the end of the oligarchic regime, eleven of the thirteen provinces of the Interior saw greater expansion of primary schooling than Buenos Aires Province and Buenos Aires City.

Taking into consideration the goals of primary schooling articulated by national policymakers, one alternative explanation for what led the national government to expand primary education is the influx of immigrants and, with that, the government's potential interest in assimilating them into an Argentine nationality. While plausible in theory, the nation-building explanation is not consistent with the historical record. Sarmiento, Roca, and other elites promoted policies in the 1880s which they hoped would attract highly educated people from France, the U.K., the Netherlands, and other prosperous parts of Europe. In their view, these immigrants would bring

---

165. Although we cannot be entirely sure of what caused the temporary decline in primary school coverage between 1889 and 1892, especially in the Interior, this decline coincided with the financial and economic crisis that began at the end of 1888. The crisis reached its most critical phase in 1890, resulting in the resignation of incumbent president Miguel Ángel Juárez Celman. The crisis affected primary schooling in the Interior provinces the most, as educational expansion in these provinces was more dependent than in wealthy Buenos Aires on the federal government's support (Elis 2011).

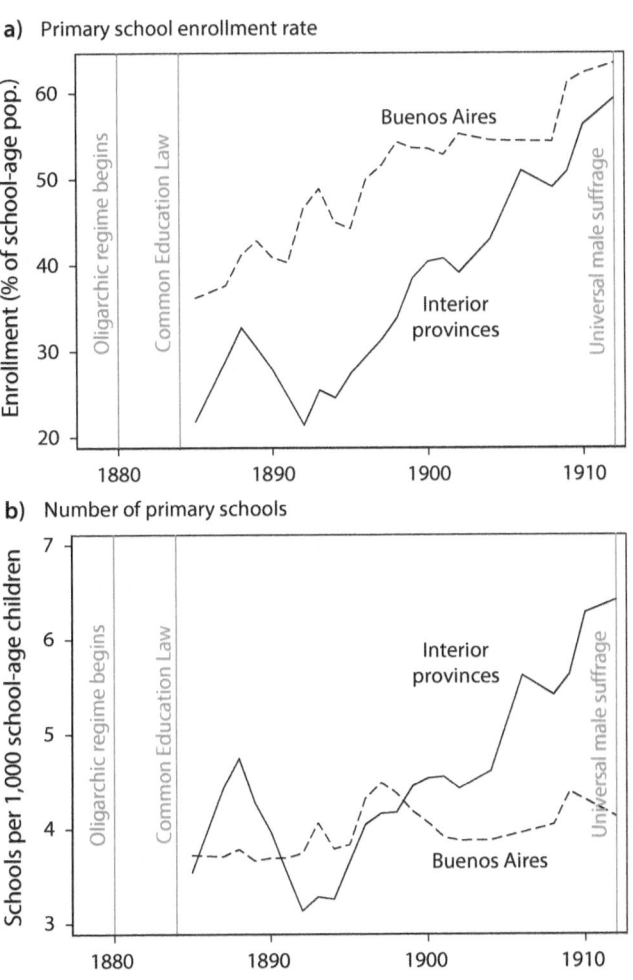

Figure 4.6. Number of primary schools and primary school enrollment rates in Buenos Aires compared to the Interior provinces of Argentina during the oligarchic regime, 1885–1912. "Buenos Aires" encompasses the City of Buenos Aires and the Province of Buenos Aires. See text and footnotes for sources and methodology.

with them civilized manners and an industrious spirit which would in turn contribute to transform Argentina into a peaceful and prosperous country. Crucially, national elites in the 1880s did not want to assimilate European immigrants; on the contrary, influenced again by Sarmiento's *Facundo* and other writings, they believed that the French, English, and Dutch belonged to a superior race compared to the Spanish and the "savage" indigenous populations who were the ancestors of the Argentine population. These immigrants would not need to be civilized. In fact, instead of creating schools to assimilate them, the 1884 Law of Common Education gave European immigrants considerable flexibility to set up their own schools. It was only in the 1910s—after a report published by the National Education Council concluded that the European immigrants who had come to Argentina came mostly from Spain and Italy and not from the "superior races" that Sarmiento and Roca had expected—that primary education was reformed to promote a strong and common national identity.[166]

Finally, interstate wars and industrialization, two common explanations of what drove the expansion of primary schooling, also deserve consideration as potential drivers of educational expansion in Argentina. In the case of interstate wars, Argentina fought wars with Uruguay, Brazil, and Paraguay between independence and 1870, thereafter entering a long period of relative international peace. Although its neighbors often received military support from France and the United Kingdom, in most cases Argentina emerged victorious from these conflicts. It is therefore not obvious why, when Roca assumed power in 1880, he would have had an interest in making costly investments in primary education with the goal of strengthening military capacity vis-à-vis its neighbors. Moreover, as mentioned earlier, primary schools did not begin to emphasize the inculcation of a national identity until the 1910s, suggesting that inoculating the population from foreign threats was not a priority during the period of rapid education expansion that began with Roca. One possibility is that Roca's government wanted to instill nationalist sentiments specifically in territories that Argentina had acquired in previous interstate wars and in provinces that were bordering its former enemies. If that had been the case, we should see greater expansion of primary schooling in the provinces of Corrientes, Entre Ríos, and Buenos Aires compared to the rest of the country. However, this is not what we see in the data. Educational expansion in Entre Ríos during the late nineteenth century was sharp, but Entre Ríos was a bastion of federalist *caudillos*, so it is difficult to infer from statistics alone whether the expansion of primary education in that province was driven by external conflict or by internal rebellions. More telling are the numbers for Corrientes, the only province that bordered all three external enemies. If

---

166. Bertoni (2001); Ceva (2018); Rock (2002); Biblioteca Nacional del Maestro (n.d.), "La escuela al servicio de la nación: El programa de Ramos Mejía"; Argentina (1898).

Roca had wanted to inoculate the population from external threats, we should see greater expansion of primary schooling in that province. However, educational expansion in Corrientes from the 1880s until the end of the oligarchic regime was unremarkable compared to the rest of the Interior. Together, these facts suggest that interstate wars were not a leading driver behind the development of a national primary education system.

With respect to the possibility that the national primary education system sought to promote industrialization, it is true that some of the habits that national elites sought to inculcate for the sake of promoting social order also happened to be good for forming docile workers. However, while some national elites pointed this out during the congressional debate of the 1884 Law of Common Education, arguments about the economic benefits of mass education were dwarfed by arguments about the value of moral education for social order and state-building.[167] Moreover, teaching the masses technical and scientific skills to bolster industrialization was not among the state's top reasons for providing primary education. In 1884, as the debate of the Law of Common Education advanced in Congress, the Minister of Justice, Worship, and Public Instruction, Eduardo Wilde, received numerous letters from educators in the Interior provinces who proposed orienting the curriculum toward practical content relevant to economic productivity. One such letter came from Eusebio Gómez, a school director from Santa Fé province, who wrote, "the country demands imperiously the formation of merchants, industrialists, farmers, engineers, and workers in general." He proposed subjects like industrial applied chemistry and agricultural practices, and the removal of theoretical subjects with no immediate economic benefit. The government ignored these proposals, leaving the teaching of productive skills to separate technical-vocational institutions known as *Escuelas de Artes y Oficios*, which as the legislation indicated were "intended for the formation of good workers" with "sufficient manual skills" and "technical knowledge."[168] This is not to say that primary schooling did not result in the acquisition of practical knowledge and skills that could enhance individual productivity. But as we will see in the next chapter, if it did, this was likely an unintended consequence of a curriculum adopted by national elites to promote the moral education of the masses.

---

167. Argentina, *Diario de Sesiones (Diputados)* of June 23, July 4, July 6, July 11, July 12, July 13, July 14, July 18, July 20, and July 23 of 1883, and Argentina, *Diario de Sesiones (Senado)* of August 18, September 30, and October 8 of 1881; August 28 of 1883; and July 26 of 1884.

168. Argentina (1938).

CONCLUSION

The idea that shaping children's moral character was important for political stability circulated in Western societies since the Enlightenment. However, political rulers' actual exposure to episodes of mass violence against the status quo increased the popularity of these ideas among national elites and drove central governments to take greater charge of and expand mass schooling. The cases of Prussia, France, Chile, and Argentina show that this logic of conflict-driven education reform with indoctrination goals in mind played out in very different types of non-democratic regimes across the long nineteenth century. In chapter 6 we will examine the limits and generalizability of the argument, a discussion that will help elucidate why the central governments of England and Mexico lagged behind other European and Latin American countries, respectively, in promoting primary education. Chapter 7 further probes the generalizability of the theory, examining whether a similar conflict-driven logic helps explain education reforms under democracies. Before we turn to these questions, however, let us look at how primary education systems in nineteenth-century Europe and Latin America were designed in order to accomplish the state's goal of social control.

CHAPTER FIVE

TEACHERS, INSPECTORS, AND CURRICULUMS AS INSTRUMENTS OF SOCIAL ORDER

How were primary education systems designed to shape the moral character of children and promote social order? When states in Europe and Latin America began to take an interest in the education of the popular classes, they did not just expand access but also increased the centralization of education. Because they wanted primary schools to produce well-behaved citizens who respected existing rules and authorities, state efforts to expand primary education were accompanied by new national laws and regulations designed to encourage student attendance and control what happened inside the classroom. By 1900, twenty-five European and Latin American countries had a comprehensive national primary education law that regulated many aspects of schooling. These laws are the focus of this chapter. In it, we will examine the content of the first comprehensive primary education law adopted during the nineteenth century in each of these countries.[1]

1. The twenty-five laws correspond to the first national primary education law passed in European and Latin American countries that passed such laws before 1900. The list includes: Prussia (1763 General Rural Schools Regulations); Austria (1774 General School Ordinance); Netherlands (1806 Education Act); Denmark (1814 School Acts); Norway (1827 Law Concerning the Peasant School System in the Country); France (1833 Law); Greece (1834 Law); Belgium (1842 Organic Law of Primary Instruction); Sweden (1842 Elementary School Statute); Cuba (1844 *Plan General de Instrucción Pública para las Islas de Cuba y Puerto Rico*); Peru (1850 *Primera Ley de Instrucción Pública*); Spain (1857 *Ley de Instrucción Pública*); Italy (1859 Casati Law); Chile (1860 *Lei de Instrucción Primaria*);

What kind of curriculum did these laws envision?[2] We will see that most of the laws established a mandatory curriculum determining the content and messages that the state wanted all primary school children to learn. Moral education occupied a central place in these curriculums, but two different models emerged for how to teach morality. In one model, the curriculum was circumscribed to teaching a narrow set of subjects, of which moral education rooted in religious doctrine was the dominant one. In the other model, moral principles were to be acquired through reasoning and abstract thinking, not religion, and the curriculum therefore included a broader set of subjects—such as algebra and science—that sought to develop students' reasoning skills for the purpose of enabling them to access universal moral principles.

To successfully expand primary education in accordance with the state's goals, states also needed a large number of teachers who had both the willingness and ability to implement the state's educational agenda—an "army of teachers." What was done to ensure that teachers would be loyal agents of the state inside the classroom? Here, central governments became directly involved in training aspiring teachers through state-controlled institutions often called Normal Schools, a name that alluded to their goal of normalizing or standardizing every aspect of teaching. In addition, most national laws of the nineteenth century established teacher certification requirements, including the requirement for aspiring teachers to show proof of their moral uprightness.

Most national laws also established provisions for the centralized inspection of schools. Inspectors served the dual purpose of disseminating information about the content of national education regulations among teachers and monitoring teachers' on-the-ground compliance with these

---

Costa Rica (1869 *Reglamento de Instrucción Primaria*); Colombia (1870 *Decreto Orgánico de Instrucción Pública*); Venezuela (1870 *Decreto de Instrucción Pública*); England (1870 Elementary Education Act); Ecuador (1871 *Ley Reforma de la Educación*); El Salvador (1873 *Reglamento de Instrucción Pública*); Guatemala (1875 *Ley Orgánica de Instrucción Pública Primaria*); Uruguay (1877 *Ley 1.350*); Brazil (1879 *Decreto 7.247*); Argentina (1884 *Ley 1.420 de Educación Común*); Jamaica (1892 Elementary Education Law). A copy of each law can be found in the online appendix.

2. Somewhat surprisingly, these questions have not received much attention in the social sciences, but one common argument that sociologists have made is that curriculum policies, and education policies more generally, looked, and still look, more or less the same, modeled after a common international recipe that is voluntarily adopted or imposed on countries as a condition for receiving international aid. In contrast to this view, I argue that the content of national primary school curriculums varied considerably as a result of domestic factors—specifically the relative balance of power between conservatives, who believed that the basis of morality was religious doctrine, and liberals, who believed that morality stemmed from science and reason.

regulations. Finally, to address inspectors' and national politicians' concern that parents would not be interested in sending their children to school, most laws included a compulsory schooling provision and stipulated penalties for parents who failed to comply.

AN ARMY OF TEACHERS

For states to even pursue the goal of moralization through mass education, they first needed to recruit large numbers of teachers. In the nineteenth century, this presented a major challenge. First, most of the population was illiterate and therefore unqualified to teach without adequate prior training. Second, men who *were* literate typically were of good social and economic standing and would demand high salaries. Given the vast quantity of teachers needed, most states could ill afford this strategy. Solutions to these problems varied. In some parts of Europe, such as Prussia under Frederick the Great, the state tried to recruit teachers among unemployed men such as soldiers returning from war. A far more popular and successful approach to large-scale, low-cost recruitment, prominent in the Americas, was to target educated women who, unlike educated men, typically lacked other job options. In fact, by 1900, more than two-thirds of teachers in Argentina, Chile, Uruguay, the United States, and Canada were women.[3] In several European countries including Spain, Italy, France, Finland, and the United Kingdom, the feminization of the teaching profession was also a deliberate policy choice that facilitated a more rapid expansion of primary schooling.[4]

Recruiting a sufficiently large corps of teachers was the first challenge; states then faced the challenge of establishing and retaining control over how these teachers behaved inside the classroom. Reformers like Guizot and Sarmiento were keenly aware that the success of their education plans depended on both the willingness *and* the ability of teachers to implement the state's educational agenda. To align the will and competency of teachers with the interests of the state, virtually all central governments turned to four main policy tools: teacher training, teacher certification, school inspections, and standardized curriculums.

---

3. Lindert (2004).
4. Lindert (2004); Cappelli and Quiroga Valle (2021).

TEACHER TRAINING

By 1900, almost all central governments in Europe and Latin America had become directly involved in training aspiring primary school teachers through state-controlled institutions often called Normal Schools, which focused exclusively on training teachers.[5] Normal Schools were regulated and often directly managed by the state and sought to shape a teacher's moral character as well as their capacity to implement the national curriculum. Sometimes, the state took advantage of existing institutions that trained teachers, such as teaching seminars set up by the Church, providing them with public funding in exchange for the implementation of the state's new teacher training curriculum. This was the case for the Berlin Normal School, to which Frederick II allocated an annual grant starting in 1753 while concurrently imposing a new curriculum. More frequently, however, states chose to create new Normal Schools from scratch. In France, for example, the Guizot Law of 1833 mandated every department to set up a Normal School to train teachers in accordance with national regulations. In Argentina, the central government during Sarmiento's presidency founded the country's first Normal School in 1870 in the province of Entre Ríos. When Roca assumed power in 1880, a total of eleven Normal Schools had already been established by the central government across eight provinces, and during Roca's presidency, another twenty-three were founded such that by 1888 every province had at least one state-run Normal School.[6] In Chile, the vast majority of public primary school teachers were trained in Santiago in Normal Schools established by the central government in 1842 and 1854, and then deployed to teach in other provinces, including the remote province of Atacama, which did not have its own Normal School until 1905.

Every aspect of the functioning of Normal Schools was carefully considered by national policymakers who wanted to ensure that a trained teacher would be able, but especially willing, to act as a loyal agent of the state. This included not only their curriculum, which was usually modeled after the national curriculum for primary schools, but also: admissions criteria, which often included mechanisms to screen applicants for their moral conduct; the architecture of schools, including such issues as how to design outdoor

---

5. The data come from Paglayan (2021). The exception is Bolivia, where the state began to provide teacher training to aspiring primary school teachers in 1909.
6. Alliaud (2007).

patios in order to facilitate the monitoring of students; and the day-to-day management of Normal Schools, which was subject to detailed regulations.

By design, the number of Normal Schools tended to be limited, which facilitated their control by the central government and implied that the vast majority of aspiring teachers lived in these institutions throughout the length of their training, typically lasting from two to four years. Guizot, Sarmiento, and other education reformers viewed the boarding school nature of Normal Schools as a crucial tool that allowed the state to carefully monitor and mold future teachers' behavior. Their belief was that by living in an environment controlled by the state, future teachers would acquire the very same values and habits of deference and obedience which later on they would be tasked with teaching children. In the regulations of the Normal School of Versailles, which served as inspiration to draft regulations for Normal Schools in other countries, this pivot was explicit: "It is necessary to learn to obey if one day one intends to command."[7] Normal School regulations tended to be very detailed and applied to every aspect of an aspiring teacher's life inside the school, from the moment they woke up to the time they went to sleep. This is exemplified by the following articles extracted from the regulations of the Normal School of Versailles, which touch on things as varied as wake-up routines, permissible and prohibited behaviors during class time, meals, recreation, bathroom breaks, physical appearance, and the need to obey and be silent under all circumstances:

- Art. 1: Discipline is in all respects entrusted to the director ... All movements are announced by a first ringing of the bell. If the student-teachers are in class or in the study area, they must prepare to leave work quietly ... If they are in recreation, they must approach the place where the lines are formed.
- Art. 6: *Studying*. The most absolute silence must reign during their studies. Leaning against tables or keeping desks open is prohibited. All student-teachers must be bareheaded unless the doctor has provided a special permission in writing to keep their hats on.
- Art. 7: Leaving one's place to consult with other student-teachers or passing notes is expressly forbidden. Borrowing classmates' notebooks to receive help with one's work is expressly prohibited.

---

7. Sarmiento (1849), pp. 172–173.

Art. 8: No student-teacher will be able to leave their studies unless they are feeling sick. Since study and class time are preceded and followed by recreation time, students must develop the habit to never interrupt their work. After the morning session, at 10am, students have ten minutes to satisfy their needs, forming lines in the courtyard before entering singing lessons.

Art. 12: The most absolute silence and tranquility must be observed when forming lines and moving from one place to another. Separating from these lines without permission is expressly prohibited.

Art. 15: During meals, one student-teacher will do an instructional reading designated by the director.

Art. 16: The most absolute silence must be observed during meals.

Art. 18: *Bedrooms*. The same silence must reign in the bedrooms. The least word is reprehensible there, more than anywhere.

Art. 22: Wake-up time is indicated by ringing bells at 5am in winter and 4am in summer. At the second ringing of the bell students descend forming a line and in silence ... At the last ringing all student-teachers must be in their place, on their knees, and do the morning prayer.

Art. 27: Running in the backyard is expressly prohibited.[8]

Again, the argument for directing the work of Normal Schools toward the development of the moral character of future teachers was straightforward: since the main goal of primary education was to shape children's moral character, and because children learn above all by example, national elites reasoned that good moral qualities must first be ingrained in teachers. This line of reasoning is captured in numerous essays and official reports across Europe and the Americas, including a study about Normal Schools in Europe and the United States commissioned by the Chilean government to José Abelardo Núñez in 1878. In his final report, based on three and a half years abroad observing Normal Schools in Germany, France, Belgium, Denmark, Norway, Sweden, the United Kingdom, and the United States, Núñez concludes:

> Moral education, the basis for the formation of the character of the child, is the first foundation of any good education system ... Religious

---

8. Sarmiento (1849), pp. 170–172.

sentiment, love of family and country, respect and obedience to the law, as well as a strict notion of duty and self-responsibility, constitute the fundamental principles that should be the subject of constant attention on the part of the teacher, and naturally they will have a very important part in the formation of students in Normal Schools ... For this reason, the Normal School [must] be an establishment ... of the strictest moral discipline ... Since the main goal of education must be ... directed towards raising the moral level of a people, the realization of such an ideal will naturally depend on the moral conditions in which children's instructors find themselves. The example of the teacher is the most eloquent of the lessons; and his word, whether through teaching or through counsel, will have double force if it is backed by the reputation of a moral and pure life.[9]

TEACHER CERTIFICATION

Concern for the moral character of teachers translated into increased state intervention not only in teacher training but also in the certification or licensing of new teachers. Certification refers to the process by which aspiring teachers are screened and granted permission to become teachers. Its aim was to ensure that only those teachers who would be loyal and competent carriers of the state's message and curriculum could enter the classroom. As such, it was a fundamental aspect of the state's education strategy.

When countries in Europe and Latin America first adopted a comprehensive national primary education law regulating various aspects of primary education, the large majority of these foundational laws stipulated that in order to be hired as a primary school teacher, individuals must first demonstrate suitable moral qualifications. This conclusion comes from assembling and examining the content of the first national primary education law adopted by twenty-five European and Latin American countries before 1900. The first column of figure 5.1 summarizes the results of this examination, indicating in black those cases where the law required aspiring teachers to show proof of their moral competency. Combing through these foundational laws, I found that twenty of the twenty-five

---

9. Núñez (1883), pp. 96–97.

190 | Chapter 5

Figure 5.1. Certification requirements for primary school teachers according to the first national primary education laws of European and Latin American countries. See text and footnotes for sources and methodology.

laws contained provisions requiring aspiring teachers to provide a certificate of good moral standing.[10]

Despite this commonality, there was considerable variation across countries both in the criteria used to screen applicants for moral competence and in the authorities deemed qualified to provide certificates of good

---

10. The laws that did *not* include such provisions are: Venezuela (1870 *Decreto de Instrucción Pública*); England (1870 Elementary Education Act); Uruguay (1877 *Ley 1.350*); Brazil (1879 *Decreto 7.247*); Jamaica (1892 Elementary Education Law).

morality to aspiring teachers. In 1760s Prussia, for example, teachers were required to obtain a letter from the local priest vouching for their moral character; in addition, Frederick II's regulations prohibited anyone who owned or worked at a tavern from being employed as a primary school teacher. In Austria, Denmark, Norway, and Sweden, too, priests were in charge of vouching for a job candidate's morality. In France, by contrast, the certification of teacher morality was left to secular authorities. The Guizot Law of 1833 required aspiring teachers to present "a certificate stating that the applicant is worthy, by his morality, to devote himself to teaching." This certificate had to be signed by the mayor of the municipality (or municipalities) where the applicant had resided during the previous three years, and was required of all teachers regardless of whether they sought to work in a public or a private primary school. The same law prohibited anyone "convicted of theft, swindling, bankruptcy, breach of trust or assault on morals" from becoming a teacher. In Italy too, the primary education law of 1859 required aspiring teachers to present a certificate of morality signed by the mayor. In Colombia and Guatemala, per decrees introduced in 1870 and 1875, respectively, the morality of aspiring teachers had to be certified by an examination committee. In Cuba, an 1844 education law established that in order to teach in a primary school, individuals had to present a certificate of "good behavior and pure bloodline" issued by the local education council. In Argentina, the 1884 Law of Common Education specified that no one could be employed as a public school teacher, teaching assistant, school director, or deputy director, without previously demonstrating their technical, moral, and physical capacity to fulfill these jobs. While the latter required a doctor's note, the usual (but not mandatory) way to prove technical and moral competency was to present a certificate of graduation from a Normal School accompanied by a letter from the Normal School's director speaking to the candidate's moral qualities.

Yet another policy tool used to ensure that new teachers had the moral qualifications for the job was to mandate graduation from a state-regulated Normal School as a condition to obtain a certificate or license to teach. This kind of regulation accorded the state monopoly control over teacher training, so that future teachers would be molded in accordance with the state's education goals and *only* with those goals. The precursor here was, again, Prussia. When in 1753 Frederick II allocated an annual grant to the Berlin Normal School, he simultaneously signed an order requiring all future school vacancies throughout Prussia to be filled with teachers trained in that school. By 1900, this norm had spread widely across Europe and Latin America. Of the twenty-five countries that first adopted a comprehensive national primary education law before 1900, fifteen included a provision within the law requiring aspiring teachers to hold a Normal School degree. This is shown in the second column of figure 5.1. Initially, this requirement was lightly enforced since Normal Schools had not yet produced sufficient graduates to staff the growing number of primary schools. But over time, as the number of Normal Schools and their alumni increased, it became the only possible pathway to enter the teaching profession—an arrangement that persists in many countries today.

SCHOOL INSPECTION

In addition to trying to mold teacher behavior *before* they entered the classroom by regulating both teacher training programs and teacher certification requirements, most states in the Western world also made efforts to control teacher behavior *inside* the classroom. To this end, not only did they pass detailed education regulations specifying how school time was to be used, but also created centralized school inspection systems to monitor and induce teacher compliance with the national curriculum and other regulations. In addition, inspectors played a key role in monitoring student attendance to enforce parental compliance with compulsory schooling laws.

To obtain a good picture of the policies and structures that central governments put in place to inspect schools, I again analyzed the content of the first comprehensive national primary education law adopted by European and Latin American countries before 1900, this time focusing on the provisions of the law that related to inspection. Three main questions guided the examination of these laws. First, did the law establish that a secular authority must inspect schools, or did it leave the inspection of schools to religious actors? Second, if a secular authority was involved in inspections, who did inspectors report to—local governments or the central government? Third, what was the function of school inspections? The answers to these questions are summarized in figure 5.2.

The analysis of landmark laws uncovers three patterns. First, virtually everywhere across Europe and Latin America, the first comprehensive primary education law adopted at the national level established that the inspection of primary schools must be conducted directly by inspectors appointed by a secular authority (indicated by a black box in the first col-

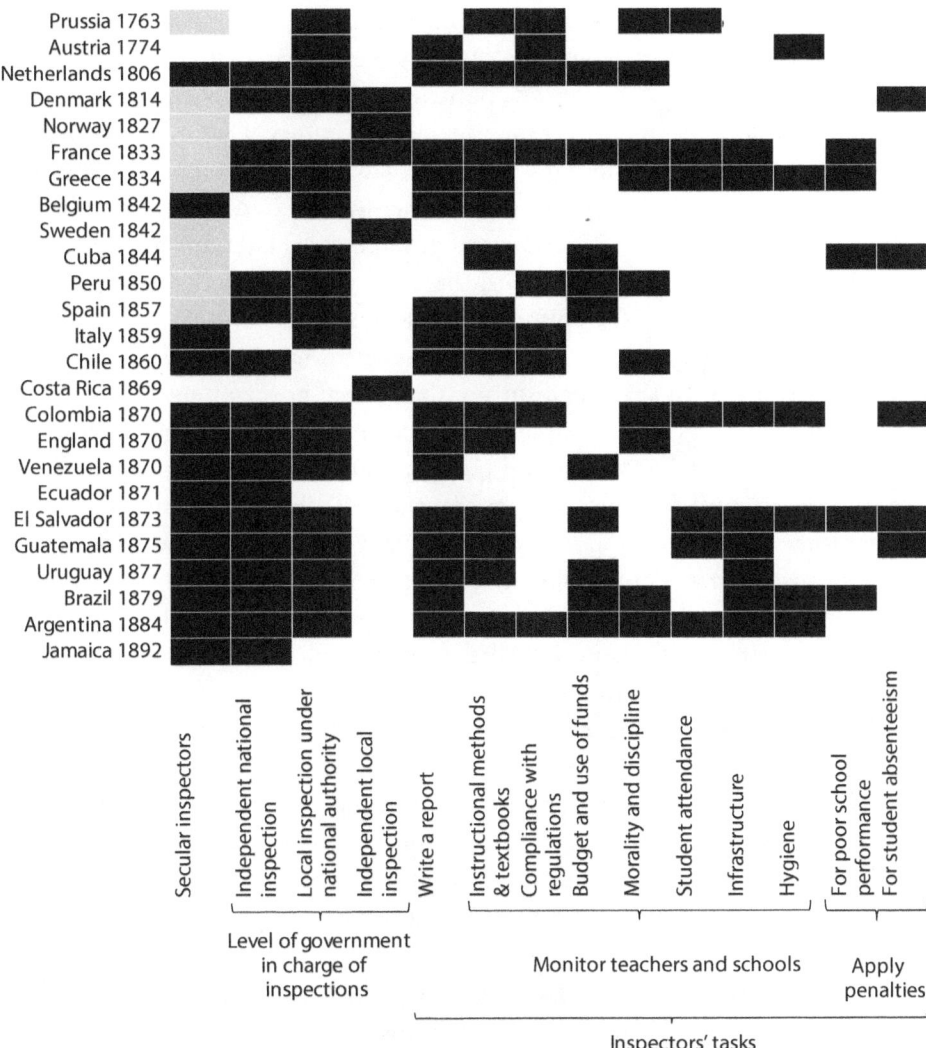

Figure 5.2. School inspection policies according to the first national primary education laws of European and Latin American countries. See text and footnotes for sources and methodology.

umn) or, if conducted by a priest or religious actor, must nonetheless be done on behalf of the government (indicated by a grey box). The notable exceptions were Austria's 1774 General School Ordinance, where inspection of primary schools was left entirely to religious actors, and Costa Rica's 1869 *Reglamento de Instrucción Primaria*, which did not specify whether a religious or secular actor must be in charge of inspections.

Second, in the vast majority of countries, the ultimate authority over school inspections rested with the central government. Beginning with the Netherlands in 1801, all European countries eventually established a centralized inspection system during the nineteenth century. The only European countries whose first landmark education law did not establish a centralized framework for inspection were Norway and Sweden, but even in these two cases, a centralized inspection system was created later during the nineteenth century. In some countries, the central government deployed its own inspectors across the country. In others, it relied on local inspection committees who appointed their own inspectors but reported to the central government. In several countries, the central government relied on a combination of its own inspectors and locally appointed inspectors who ultimately reported to the central government. In Latin America, too, virtually all states made efforts to create centralized school inspection systems to enforce teacher compliance with national education policies. However, school inspectorates in Latin America tended to be less resilient than those in Europe; over time, they developed a poor reputation, not least for the common practice of accepting bribes from schools in exchange for ignoring violations of education regulations.

Third, inspectors reporting to the central government visited schools around the country, observed and evaluated teachers, examined student notebooks, verified student attendance, and then produced detailed written reports on the quality of education, understood as the degree to which schools complied with education laws and regulations. Sometimes, as in France since the 1830s, school inspectors addressed these reports to the national Minister of Public Instruction; other times, as in England and Scotland, inspectors remained independent from the Ministry, reporting directly to the queen or king. Regardless of who they were written for, inspectors' reports were the primary source of information that central governments used to monitor the status of primary education and identify common issues that could require new regulations or policy reform. In addition to these monitoring and reporting functions, school inspectors also played a key role in maintaining schools and teachers informed about policy changes, serving as messengers of the central government around the country. Last, inspections could lead to sanctions for schools and teachers found to be in violation of existing regulations.

The penalties for teachers who failed to comply with existing education laws and regulations varied. The most common ones established by the law included withholding teacher salaries or school funding, suspension from the job, and eventually, dismissal. Indeed, this was the beginning of accountability systems designed to incentivize teachers and schools to comply with education laws and regulations, a practice still prevalent in education systems today.

COMPULSORY SCHOOLING

The kind of primary education system that most central governments envisioned in the nineteenth century posed a challenge: If its goal was not to improve the material well-being of the lower classes but to instill obedience and acceptance of the status quo, how could the state incentivize parents to send their children to school? Indeed, as we saw in chapter 4, the perception that parents would be reluctant to enroll their children in primary school—whether accurate or not—was a common concern voiced by school inspectors and politicians during the nineteenth century.

The main way by which central governments sought to address this concern was to make enrollment in primary education compulsory. Twenty-one of the twenty-five national primary education laws analyzed in this chapter contained a compulsory schooling provision. This is shown in figure 5.3. Moreover, two-thirds of the laws established specific penalties for failing to comply with this provision. In Prussia, the 1763 law prohibited children who did not attend primary school from receiving the religious confirmation. By far the most common type of penalty, however, was a monetary fine for parents whose children were not in school. In Sweden (1842), Spain (1857), and Uruguay (1877), parents first received a warning if their child was not in school; if the child continued to be absent, the law empowered the government to fine parents. In Denmark (1814), Norway (1827), Greece (1834), Colombia (1870), Ecuador (1871), Guatemala (1875), Brazil (1879), Argentina (1884), and Jamaica (1892), the fine could be issued at the first instance of recorded absenteeism, without a prior warning. In some cases, the law also stipulated more severe penalties for parents who failed to pay the corresponding fine: in Denmark (1814), this could lead to imprisonment or forced labor, while in Sweden (1842) it could result in the child's removal from their home and their placement under the state's supervision.

A small minority of countries sought to incentivize school attendance by relying on rewards instead of penalties. In Mexico, as we will see in

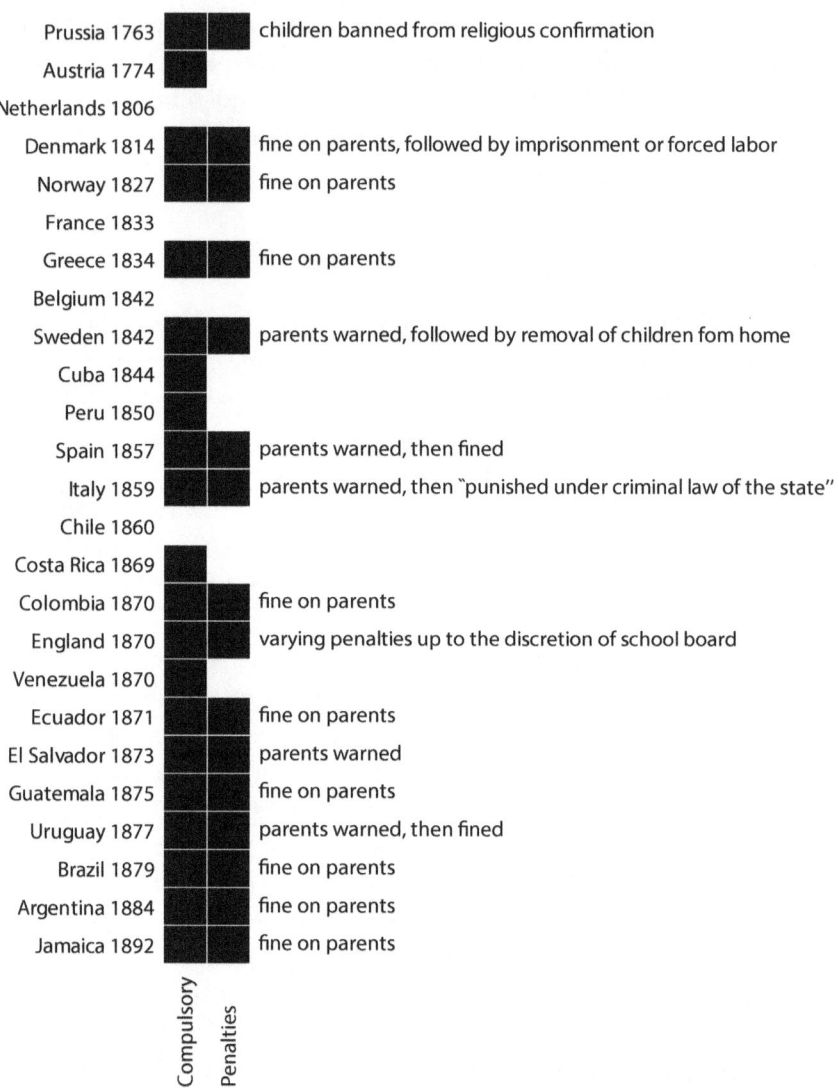

Figure 5.3. Compulsory schooling provisions included in the first national primary education laws of European and Latin American countries. See text and footnotes for sources and methodology.

chapter 6, the national government during the 1920s incentivized school attendance by providing free school meals. In the Netherlands, an education law passed in 1889 tied parental access to various public services to children's school attendance. In Chile, the central government relied on teachers to persuade parents to send their children to school, and the 1860 law stipulated an annual monetary prize to be awarded to the male and female teacher who had excelled at their job in each municipality.[11]

Education laws often charged inspectors with the duty to enforce compulsory schooling provisions by checking attendance and applying penalties to parents whose children were out of school. We do not know much about the extent to which these penalties were perceived as a real threat by parents, but their inclusion in landmark education laws is a sign that central governments were worried that, if left to parental demand alone, school attendance would be low.

NATIONAL CURRICULUMS FOR MORAL EDUCATION

One of the fundamental tools available to states seeking to shape children's education is the curriculum. A national curriculum determines the content of education by establishing the list of subjects that must be taught in schools, how much time should be allocated to each, and implicitly, what subjects should *not* be taught. By 1900, most countries in Western Europe and Latin America had a national curriculum for primary schools. The remainder of this chapter will take an in-depth look at these curriculums.

When public primary education systems emerged, regulating the curriculum was a means to address some national elites' fear that educating the less privileged could backfire by raising their aspirations and empowering them to demand deep change. In 1760s Prussia, as we saw in chapter 4, the king himself expressed concern that if peasants learned too much, they might reject their place in society and migrate to the cities in search of better economic opportunities. The solution, according to his policy advisers, was to establish separate mandatory curriculums for rural and urban schools so that what children learned in rural schools would prove worthless in getting a city job—an approach that was also adopted by other countries. Similar concerns surfaced in other countries. In Chile, while the vast majority of members of congress expressed support for the goals of the 1860 General Law of Primary Education, Máximo Arguelles, a conservative member and author of the book *Popular Education in Chile*, argued that teaching

---

11. By the turn of the century, Chilean congressmen began to voice concern that persuasion had been "entirely useless" in compelling the lower classes to send their children to school. Compulsory schooling, they argued, was needed to prevent these children from being raised "in a social context full of vices, bad examples and perverse customs, in a context well prepared for the germination of future criminals." Chile adopted compulsory schooling in 1925. See Egaña (1996), p. 17.

reading skills would "excite the people's passions," especially by enabling them to read the press, as had happened in Chile in the 1850s and in France in 1848.[12] In Argentina, too, a few congressmen expressed concern that transmitting "abundant knowledge can inadvertently produce generations who are physically and spiritually sick."[13]

Despite these concerns, most elites thought that the risk of empowering the masses could be successfully mitigated by carefully curating the content of education children received. To shape that content, states imposed a national curriculum and selected and distributed mandatory textbooks. This approach has lasted: In 2020, more than 95 percent of countries had a national curriculum and 75 percent had centrally approved school textbooks.[14] Even today, when national elites perceive that education systems have failed to attain their goals—for example, when new protests against the status quo emerge—a common response is not to roll back education provision but to reform the curriculum in hopes that a new curriculum will better accomplish the state's goals.

Precisely because national curriculums are at the core of what education systems do and of what goals they seek to accomplish, they have been the subject of some of the most heated policy debates in history. In some cases, curriculum debates hinge on whether education systems should primarily teach values or skills, and on whether they should primarily discipline children or empower them. But even when there is ample agreement about the general goals of education, there can be considerable disagreement about how to attain those goals and how to design the curriculum to that effect. The nineteenth-century curriculum debates in Europe and Latin America are illustrative of this. Even when national elites agreed that the main goal of primary education systems was a moralizing one, and that teaching values of discipline, obedience, and respect for authority was paramount, they often disagreed about what moral education entailed and, especially, whether it should contain religious teachings or be entirely secular.

The secular-religious divide was not the only point of contention in nineteenth-century debates about the curriculum; there was also disagreement on whether science education belonged in primary schools at all. This

---

12. Serrano, Ponce de León, and Rengifo (2012), p. 82.
13. *Diario de Sesiones* 1899, quoted in Alliaud (2007), p. 79.
14. Data from the Varieties of Political Indoctrination in Education and the Media (V-Indoc) Dataset (Neundorf et al. 2023).

was true even among elites who shared the view that the main goal of mass education was to teach moral principles. Some national curriculums prescribed a narrow set of subjects, of which moral education was the dominant one, followed by reading, writing, and basic arithmetic. In others, science education was also incorporated, not in addition to but *as part of* the state's moral education goals. These divergent approaches to mass education reflected different understandings of the roots of morality. Put simply, states adopted a narrow curriculum when elites were of the opinion that religion was the basis of morality, and a broader curriculum including considerable science and math when reasoning capabilities were thought to be crucial for learning moral principles. But before we get to the question of why the content of curriculums varied, let us look at what curriculums looked like.

DIFFERENCES AND SIMILARITIES IN NATIONAL CURRICULUMS

Of the twenty-five European and Latin American countries that adopted a comprehensive national primary education law before 1900, twenty-two countries imposed an official curriculum in their first comprehensive law.[15] I focus on the content of these initial curriculums both because of the book's interest in the foundational stages of primary education systems and because initial curriculums had a long-lasting influence. In Prussia, for example, the curriculum introduced by the 1763 General Rural School Regulations continued to apply until 1854—nearly a century! In France and Argentina, the curriculums imposed by the Guizot Law of 1833 and 1884 Law of Common Education, respectively, remained virtually unchanged for more than fifty years. Of the countries discussed in chapter 4, Chile was the one where the first national curriculum, introduced in 1860, lasted the least, but even in that case, it remained in place for twenty-five years.

What subjects were typically prescribed by the first national primary school curriculums of the nineteenth century? Figure 5.4 depicts the answer. In nine countries, including Greece, Brazil, and Uruguay, the law prescribed a single curriculum for all primary schools. In thirteen countries, including Prussia, France, and Costa Rica, the law prescribed a different curriculum for lower primary schools, which had to be established everywhere and were the only type of school available in rural areas, and upper primary

---

15. The exceptions were the laws of England (1870), Ecuador (1871), and Jamaica (1892), which did not stipulate the curriculum.

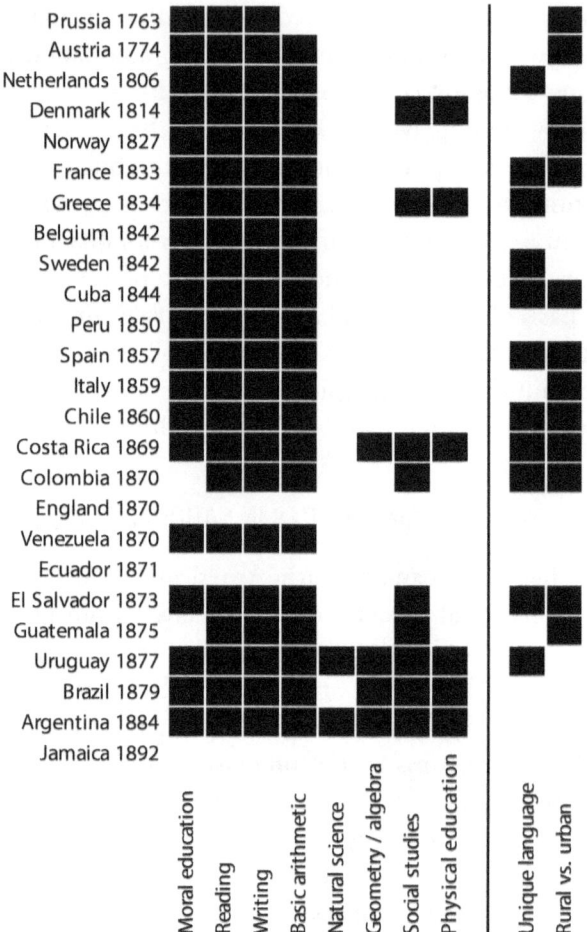

Figure 5.4. Mandatory subjects in the curriculum for lower primary schools according to the first national primary education laws of European and Latin American countries. The comprehensive primary education laws of England (1870), Ecuador (1871), and Jamaica (1892) did not contain a mandatory national curriculum. See text and footnotes for sources and methodology.

schools, which were circumscribed to urban areas. When such a distinction existed, figure 5.4 focuses on the curriculum for lower primary schools, as these were the most common and available type of school.[16]

16. The thirteen countries whose first national curriculum established a different set of mandatory subjects for rural versus urban schools are: Prussia (1763), Austria (1774), Denmark (1814), Norway (1827), France (1833), Cuba (1844), Spain (1857), Italy (1859), Chile (1860), Costa Rica (1869), Colombia (1870), El Salvador (1873), and Guatemala (1875).

An obvious pattern that emerges from comparing national primary school curriculums is the ubiquity of moral education. Not only did the teaching of moral principles have a standalone subject in almost every country, but also, it was often the first subject that appeared in national curriculums, followed by reading, then writing, and finally, arithmetic. Moreover, the teaching of morality was not restricted to the time spent in a moral education class. Typically, instruction in reading and writing aided the inculcation of moral principles and values drawn from religious doctrine or from secular sources. In Prussia, for example, reading instruction focused on reading the catechism. In France and Chile, too, the texts used to teach reading and writing contained numerous references to God's rewards and punishments for good and bad behavior. Denmark's 1814 Law dictated that "when reading, such books should presumably be used which could give rise to the formation of the children's mindset" as well as "impart to them knowledge which could serve to eradicate prejudice."[17] Similarly, Bolivia's 1827 curriculum specified that the teaching of reading and writing had to be done through moral and religious instruction and the use of "very compendious catechisms."[18] The pervasiveness and importance of moral education in national curriculums is consistent with the findings of previous chapters, where I highlighted its role in the development of national primary education systems.

Another important observation that stems from these laws is the absence of a systemic effort to teach a common language. Eleven of the twenty-two curriculums depicted in figure 5.4 specified that instruction must take place in a common language, such as French in the case of the Guizot Law of 1833, Castilian Spanish in the case of Spain's 1857 education law, or the "patriotic language" in the case of Chile's 1860 law. However, another eleven curriculums did not impose a common language: seven curriculums did not specify in any way what language should be taught in schools, and four curriculums encouraged or required instruction in multiple languages according to the characteristics of the local community.[19] To the extent

17. Denmark (1814a), *Anordning for Almue-Skolevæsenet paa Landet i Danmark*, Art. 23.
18. Bolivia (1827), *Ley de 9 de enero*, Art. 1.
19. The laws of the Netherlands (1806), France (1833), Greece (1834), Sweden (1842), Cuba (1844), Spain (1857), Chile (1860), Costa Rica (1869), Colombia (1870), El Salvador (1873), and Uruguay (1877) required instruction in a unique and specific common language. The laws of Austria (1774), Denmark (1814), Norway (1827), Peru (1850), Venezuela (1870), Guatemala (1875), and Brazil (1879) did not specify a language of instruction. The laws of Prussia (1763), Belgium (1842), Italy (1859), and Argentina (1884) encouraged or required instruction in multiple languages.

that inculcating a common language is a marker of nation-building efforts, these patterns suggest that nation-building was less important in explaining the emergence of state-regulated primary education systems than what has been argued in the past. Moral education was a more prevalent component of the first national curriculums than instruction in a common language.

Some readers may rightly note that the design of many national curriculum plans, with their focus on moral education and reading, could in principle reflect not the central government's indoctrination goals but the goals of the Church. This is a reasonable conjecture if we take curriculums in isolation. However, as we saw earlier in this chapter, the introduction of national curriculums was usually accompanied by additional policies that gave central governments the authority to train and certify teachers as well as the authority to inspect schools and apply sanctions to those who failed to comply with government directives. In other words, even in those cases where moral education included religious teachings, the teachers who imparted this education and the inspectors who oversaw them responded to the central government, not the Church. In fact, countries with an established official Church did not introduce a national curriculum any earlier—or any later—than those where religious actors lacked the same level of unity and political influence.

Although writing and arithmetic were also part of the official curriculum, it is important not to overstate their role. In many countries during the early nineteenth century, children often did not receive any instruction in writing and arithmetic despite their place in the official curriculum. In Prussia, for example, the law allowed children to stop attending primary school once they had received the Protestant or Catholic confirmation. In response to this type of provision and to pressure from parents who wanted their children to return to work, teachers often devoted the majority of school time to moral and religious education and to reading the catechism. By the time instruction in writing began, many children had already received the confirmation and their parents had removed them from school.[20] In Chile, the common practice among teachers was to begin by teaching moral education and reading, which were considered easier to learn. By the time they moved on to more complex subjects, such as writing and arithmetic, many children had already left school.[21]

20. Melton (2002).
21. Egaña Baraona (2000).

While the presence of moral education was one of the main similarities across national primary curriculums in the nineteenth century, the character of moral education and, in particular, whether it was religious or secular, did vary considerably across countries and over time. During roughly the first two-thirds of the nineteenth century, the large majority of initial primary education laws included religious teaching as part of moral education. During the last third of the nineteenth century, however, an increasing number of countries made moral education a secular subject. In these countries, religious instruction was either prohibited or made optional.

The shift from religious to secular moral education during the late nineteenth century was accompanied by another important change: the increasing prevalence in primary school curriculums of math subjects that went beyond basic arithmetic, such as geometry or algebra, and of natural science subjects such as chemistry or physics. Before 1870, only Costa Rica included geometry in its national curriculum, and no country's curriculum included natural science subjects. After 1870, geometry and/or algebra and natural science began to be gradually added into national curriculums. To be clear, no one event occurred in 1870 that accounts for these changes; 1870 is simply an arbitrary year chosen to facilitate the comparison between curriculums adopted earlier and later in the nineteenth century.

Another visible change toward the end of the nineteenth century was the increasing inclusion of physical education and of social studies subjects such as history and geography in national curriculums for primary schools. These subjects were typically used to foster patriotic sentiments and to prepare children, through physical exercises, to serve as future soldiers in wars with other states. What is interesting is that in Europe, which created state-regulated primary education systems, the first national education laws of only Denmark and Greece—passed in 1814 and 1834, respectively—included physical education and social studies as part of the curriculum. The general absence of these subjects in national curriculums prior to the 1870s provides additional evidence that inculcating nationalism and preparing for war were not among the main goals driving the emergence of mass education systems.

These changes in curriculum content over time emerge from comparing not just countries that adopted a national curriculum early versus late in the nineteenth century but also from comparing how national curriculums changed *within* countries. The cases of Prussia and France illustrate these trends. In Prussia, the 1763 curriculum for rural schools focused first on religious moral instruction, which included teaching the catechism, as well as prayer and religious chanting. After that, students began to be exposed to reading, typically taught using religious texts, and later on, if they were still in school, to writing instruction. Arithmetic was not mandatory. If numeracy skills were taught at all, they were very rudimentary and instruction took place at the very end of primary school and in extraordinary Winter sessions, not the regular school year. This model for primary education was more or less followed by France's Guizot Law of 1833 and by other countries that introduced national curriculums roughly before the 1870s. Later on, however, Prussia's curriculum underwent substantial reform, first in 1854 with the introduction of national history as a new mandatory subject, and then in 1872 with the addition of geometry, social studies, and gymnastics. In the case of France, after more than fifty years of very basic elementary instruction focused on moral and religious education, reading, writing, French, and the metric system—taught in that order of importance—a new curriculum was adopted in the 1880s as part of a set of education reforms known as the Ferry Laws. The new curriculum replaced moral and religious instruction with the secular subject moral and civic education, and added new mandatory subjects in natural sciences, mathematics, history, geography, gymnastics, and military exercises.

It may be tempting to interpret the foregoing discussion as proof of diffusion theory, which holds that countries will adopt the curriculum that is considered desirable by international standards, resulting in considerable similarity across curriculums.[22] From this perspective, the introduction of natural science in many curriculums toward the end of the nineteenth century would be explained by the emergence of a new international model of what a good curriculum looked like—one that included natural science—and the diffusion and influence of that model curriculum across countries. While there is no doubt that countries often looked to others to inform education policy back home, and still do so today, the limitation of diffusion theory is that it doesn't acknowledge that there is often more than one education model that countries can choose to emulate or draw inspiration

---

22. One of the most influential studies behind the argument that national curriculums tend to look alike actually finds more variation across curriculums than it admits. Based on an analysis of national curriculums from 1920 to 1986, the study reveals that the average proportion of time allocated to teaching natural science across countries was 5.2 percent of the total teaching time in 1920–1944, with a standard deviation of 4; and the average proportion allocated in 1945–1969 was 7.1 percent with a standard deviation of 4.6 (Benavot et al. 1991). See also Benavot (1992, 2004); McEneaney (2003); and Meyer, Kamens, and Benavot (2017).

from. Today, for example, there are two distinct approaches to promote high-quality teaching. The Finland model uses a highly selective process for admitting individuals into teacher education programs but gives teachers considerable autonomy in the classroom. The U.S. model makes it easier to become a teacher but gives teachers relatively little leeway to deviate from local and state education policies.

In the nineteenth century, too, two main models circulated. Both of them focused on how to promote discipline and obedience, but while one model emphasized the role of religious doctrine in teaching moral principles, the other emphasized the role of science and reasoning capabilities as a crucial component of a person's *moral* education. Because of the centrality of this conflict in nineteenth-century educational and moral debates, these two curricular approaches are the focus of the remainder of this chapter. I begin by summarizing these moral education models. I then compare the national curriculums of Argentina and Chile, two countries that, despite their many similarities, pursued different models. Drawing on transcripts from legislative debates to illustrate conservatives' and liberals' differing views about *how* to promote moral education, I argue that the balance of power between them had critical implications for which model of moralization was adopted in national curriculums.

THE ROOTS OF MORALITY: RELIGION VERSUS SCIENCE

The main source of moral teachings in premodern Europe was, without a doubt, the Church. Initially, the Catholic Church enjoyed an undisputed position in the moral education of the population. The Protestant Reformation eliminated this monopoly, but even within Protestantism, the Bible remained the source of moral teachings. Christianity advanced the view that we are born with a tendency to sin, but that we can save ourselves from an afterlife of eternal punishment by living in accordance with the moral lessons of the Bible, including the Ten Commandments—"thou shall not murder," "thou shall not steal," "thou shall not covet thy neighbor's house," etc. Starting in the fifteenth century, religious missionaries and other emigrants brought Christianity and its moral lessons to the Americas, replacing—or extinguishing—the religion of native populations. In both Europe and the Americas, separation between the Church and the State eventually became the norm, but the Church's legitimacy as a moral authority outlived the decline of its formal political power. Against this backdrop, when states developed national primary education systems to promote social order, a natural approach to teach future citizens how to behave was to take advantage of the moral authority of the Church by incorporating religious doctrine into the moral education curriculum. This is what Prussia, Chile, and many other countries did.

During the eighteenth and nineteenth centuries, however, powerful new ideas emerged about the roots of morality that did not rely on religious doctrine as the only or primary source of good moral behavior. Enlightenment philosophers argued that religion was not necessary for accessing moral principles, and that these could be accessed through reason. The German philosopher Immanuel Kant was perhaps the most influential voice behind this idea. Kant claimed that the grounding of moral principles lay in reason alone, and not the commands of religious authorities or even God. He argued that the supreme moral principle—that we should always act according to maxims that we would be willing to accept as a universal law—was discoverable by reason alone, unaided by religious teachings or empirical observation. With respect to the moral education of children, Kant argued in *Über Pädagogik* that the role of schools is to teach children their duties, both to themselves and to others, and to encourage them to abide by these duties; this, he wrote, is the way to build children's character. He suggested that children could gain much from reading a textbook containing "everyday questions of right and wrong" which would form the basis for careful thinking and consideration.[23] To be clear, Kant did not oppose the teaching of religion; he believed children are bound to encounter it in their lives and therefore should learn about it,[24] but did not think religion was the foundation of morality, writing: "But is man by nature morally good or bad? He is neither, for he is not by nature a moral being. He only becomes a moral being when his reason has developed ideas of duty and law."[25]

While Kant highlighted the role of deductive reasoning in accessing moral principles, another hugely influential philosophy in education debates was positivism, founded by French philosopher Auguste Comte, which stressed the relationship between morality and science. Writing during the first half of the nineteenth century, Comte was concerned that the French Revolution of 1789 had reduced the legitimacy of the Catholic Church but had failed

---

23. Kant (1900), p. 104.
24. Kant (1900), p. 110.
25. Kant (1900), p. 108.

to replace it with an alternative moral authority accepted by all. "The great political and moral crisis of existing societies," he wrote, stemmed from "the profound divergence that now exists among all minds, with regard to all the fundamental maxims whose fixity is the first condition of a true social order."[26] Comte argued that, in modern societies, science should and would occupy the void left by the decline of religion:

> As the sciences have become positive, and as—in consequence—they have made ever-increasing progress, a larger and larger mass of scientific ideas has entered our common education, at the same time as religious doctrines gradually lost their influence...The only influence religious doctrines have on our minds is that which stems from the fact that morality has remained attached to them. This influence will necessarily remain until the time when morality has undergone the revolution that has already occurred in all our particular branches of knowledge as they became positive.[27]

Comte was especially interested in the ability of science to organize and make sense of the physical and social worlds, to help individuals predict the consequences of their actions, and to discover universal laws or truths that, unlike religious doctrine, would become acceptable to all. He believed that the human mind, if properly cultivated, could "discover, by a well-combined use of reasoning and observation, the actual laws of phenomena,"[28] including not only natural but also social phenomena. He predicted that, in the future, science would be "the permanent spiritual basis of the social order, as long as our species remains active in the world."[29] At a practical level, Comte argued for instruction in mathematics, astronomy, physics, chemistry, and biology to provide "the scientific training which prepares the way for social studies," followed by instruction in sociology—a term he invented—and history, which, he claimed, would serve "as a basis for the systematization of moral truth."[30]

While Enlightenment theories and positivism were influential among liberal political elites during the nineteenth century, religion remained the preferred source of moral education among conservative politicians. As we

---

26. Comte (1988), p. 28.
27. Comte (1998a), pp. 32–33.
28. Comte (1988), p. 2.
29. Comte (1998b), p. 171.
30. Comte (1865), p. 267.

will see through the cases of Argentina and Chile, the balance of power between these two groups played a role in shaping whether, in pursuit of the common moralizing goals of primary education, the national curriculum would focus on a narrow set of subjects dominated by moral and religious education, or whether it would also include training in natural and social sciences.

TWO APPROACHES TO MORAL EDUCATION: CHILE VERSUS ARGENTINA

In previous chapters, we saw that mass violence gave way to the centralization and expansion of primary education in European and Latin American countries, and that in the Western world, internal conflict was a more important driver of educational expansion than democratization, industrialization, military threats, or the spread of ideas about the nation-building role of education. Through an in-depth look at Prussia, France, Chile, and Argentina, I also showed that the reason why central governments responded to concerns about mass violence by expanding primary education was not because they wanted to appease ordinary people by improving their economic well-being, but because national elites believed they could prevent future social disorder by teaching children to respect authority and be content with the status quo.

Despite the common goal behind Prussia's 1763 General Rural School Regulations, France's 1833 Guizot Law, Chile's 1860 General Law of Primary Education, and Argentina's 1884 Law of Common Education, these countries adopted different national curriculums for primary schools. Most notable were the differences between Chile and Argentina, two countries that, despite their many similarities, nonetheless adopted starkly different curriculums. Chile and Argentina had similar histories of Spanish colonial rule, gained independence at the beginning of the nineteenth century, and established oligarchic regimes that maintained the hierarchical structures of the colonial period. Both had a predominantly Catholic, rural, and illiterate population. Their resources and economies were also similar, based on heavily taxed commodities exports and reliance on foreign investment and loans to finance large public infrastructure projects. In both, extending the reach of the state and maintaining order in the periphery presented similar geographic challenges given their large north to south territories. Both were exposed to similar education ideas, among other reasons because of the influence of mass education advocate Domingo F. Sarmiento, a native of Argentina who also lived and worked in Chile for many years.

Finally, as I showed in chapter 4, both countries expanded primary education to shape the moral character of the masses and prevent the recurrence of mass violence. And yet, Chile and Argentina adopted very different national curriculums for primary schools. What did their curriculums look like, and why did they differ?

The comparison of the Chilean and Argentine curriculums echoes the review of national curriculums presented above. While both countries provided moral education in line with the main goal of primary education, moral education was religious in Chile but secular in Argentina. Moreover, while the Chilean curriculum included only basic arithmetic and no science education, the Argentine curriculum included more advanced math education as well as considerable training in the natural and social sciences. Table 5.1 provides a list of the mandatory subjects for primary schools and for Normal Schools in each country according to their first national education laws. As we can see, the national curriculum established by Chile's 1860 General Law of Primary Education included only four subjects: Christian doctrine and morality; reading and writing in Spanish; arithmetic; and the official measurement system. By contrast, Argentina's 1884 Law of Common Education established *secular* moral education, taught through three subjects: moral education, civic instruction, and urban studies, which was devoted to teaching children how to behave like the civilized populations of the cities that Sarmiento had praised in *Facundo*. Like the Chilean curriculum, Argentina's curriculum also included reading and writing in Spanish and arithmetic. However, the Argentine curriculum also included French; geometry; drawing; natural sciences; physics and chemistry; history; and geography. The curriculums for Normal Schools to train primary school teachers followed the same pattern, with the Argentine curriculum teaching moral education as a secular subject and covering more subjects and more science and math than the Chilean one.

The curriculum patterns introduced in 1860s Chile and 1880s Argentina lasted for more than half a century, creating differences between them that extended well into the twentieth century. These differences are inconsistent with the view that countries choose education policies following a common international model. Argentina and Chile made very different initial policy choices with respect to the content of education *despite* having the same exposure to European ideas about education and even a common advocate for mass education in Sarmiento. To explain the differences in curriculum policy between these two countries we need to look beyond the

Table 5.1. List of Mandatory Subjects in Primary Schools and Normal Schools in Argentina and Chile, circa 1880

	Argentina	Chile
Primary Schools	Reading and writing National language French Arithmetic Drawing Geometry Map drawing Natural sciences Physics and chemistry Moral education Civic instruction Urban studies History Geography Singing and gymnastics Home economics Housework	Reading and writing in the patriotic language Practical elements of arithmetic Legal measurement system Christian doctrine and morality
Normal Schools	Spanish language Grammar Notions of literature Composition exercises Reading and writing/composition Arithmetic Geometry Cosmography Physics Chemistry Natural history Philosophy Morals and manners Civic instruction Geography History Home economics and crafts Anatomy, physiology, and hygiene Drawing exercises Physical exercise Singing exercises Pedagogy Observation at the School of Application Practice at the School of Application	Reading and writing Practical elements of arithmetic Legal measurement system Elements of cosmography and physics Christian doctrine and morality Sacred history Religious and moral dogma History of the Americas and Chile Music Horticulture Drawing Pedagogical theory and practice

Note: For Argentina, the table shows the primary school curriculum as stipulated in the 1884 Law of Common Education and the curriculum for Normal Schools as stipulated in the National Decree of January 24, 1880. For Chile, both curriculums are from the 1860 General Law of Primary Education.

role of global ideas about education and into how domestic forces shaped curriculum policy decisions. In particular, we need to consider what conservative politicians, who were dominant in 1860s Chile, and secular liberals, who dominated in 1880s Argentina, argued was the appropriate curriculum to advance their shared goals of shaping the moral character of the masses and forging social order.

THE CONSERVATIVE APPROACH TO MORAL EDUCATION

The primary school curriculum established by the Chilean 1860 General Law of Primary Education was emblematic of the conservative approach to moral education. Conservatives argued that because religion was the basis of morality, the curriculum ought to rely heavily on religious doctrine. In the Chilean case, conservatives with strong ties to the Catholic Church controlled the presidency and a majority of seats in Congress between 1831 and 1861, a period known as the Conservative Republic or Authoritarian Republic. The 1860 education law, passed during this period of hegemonic rule by the Conservative Party, stipulated that moral education ought to be religious. The mandatory curriculum established Christian doctrine and morality as one of the few mandatory subjects. The official school textbooks that the Ministry of Public Instruction distributed during the 1860s to teach reading and writing heavily emphasized religious messages, making direct associations between submissive and obedient behavior on one hand and the precepts of Catholicism on the other. The widely used textbook *La conciencia de un niño*, for example, began by highlighting the importance of being obedient, and then taught that God's approval was the highest reward for good behavior, promised Heaven to children who accepted their lot on Earth, and alluded to Jesus's words to threaten children with punishment if they misbehaved:[31]

> Everything I have I owe to my parents. How can I express my gratitude? This is what I intend to do: I will behave in a way that always makes them feel satisfied. My parents only make commands that are useful to me. If I obey them, everyone admires me and says "what an excellent child." This way, I not only satisfy my parents but also everyone who doesn't know me. My parents send me to school, where I can learn

---

31. Sarmiento (1844).

useful and good things. There, an instructor teaches us how to behave so we will gain the love of our parents and everyone else.

I satisfy my parents by being good, kind, and very obedient. By behaving this way, I also satisfy God. Always invisible, always present, he sees and knows what I do and what I think in every instant. If I am good, he loves me. God will be the one who will reward me the most; it is for him that I must take advantage of what my teacher has to teach me.

If I am happy with what my parents give me to eat and drink; ... if I am nice to others, I will sow the seeds of my good behavior ... If I behave well and satisfy God, when I die I will go to Heaven.

Jesus said it: those who do not obey the Church are ungodly pagans and public sinners.

The religious approach to moral education also found support among conservatives in Argentina. Conservatives in Congress argued that the way to secure order was to emphasize religion and the Catholic idea that, if we behave well in this world, we will be rewarded in an afterlife. During the debate over the 1884 Law of Common Education that took place on July 6, 1883, in the Argentine House of Representatives, Pedro Goyena, a congressman who fervently opposed the secularization of the state and co-founded the *Catholic Union*, argued that the basis of all individual and social safety, of order and harmony, is religion, because religion dictates what constitutes moral behavior; therefore, public schools must teach religion to children because "to leave them without religious instruction would lead them to become dangerous citizens":

> Even when the state accomplishes its functions, especially those functions to guarantee that the activity of each individual does not disturb others, and society, instead of becoming anarchic, maintains order and harmony, the state won't accomplish those functions in a convincing way if it forgets the guarantee of all guarantees, the basis of all individual and social safety, the supreme law, that is, religion. ... There has been no society, anywhere, anytime, without religion or without God. When religious sentiment languishes, man reaches his lowest instincts. ... When we legislate on school issues, we legislate on the transformation of society, on the forces that will act on it; it is evident, then, that the law must promote those forces that are not blind, that

are conscious and driven by a superior principle of morality, and therefore must promote religion in public schools.... To leave a great number of children without religious education, children whom we have a special interest to educate and civilize, children who do not have the family means to become more civilized, to leave them without religious instruction would lead to them becoming dangerous citizens.[32]

Congressman Centeno was more succinct: "Children should be taught... 'one must not kill' 'one must not steal' because God has prohibited it."[33] Another conservative congressman, Tristán Achával Rodríguez, not only argued in favor of teaching religion as the basis of moral education and social order, but also specifically argued that science and human reasoning would not teach individuals not to kill or not to steal:

Education without religion will form... a generation of men without solid principles, without character, without conscience, weak, capable of the fall of the country.... It will be necessary for the child to know that he cannot kill, and why; that he cannot steal, and why; that he must respect private property, and why. And all this cannot be demonstrated scientifically; it cannot stem from human reasoning alone. These are truths that we know because they have been revealed from above and directly by God. It is not possible, then, to suppress religious teaching from schools.[34]

These truths [you shall not kill, you shall not steal], to be the basis of a moral order, must be rooted in the individual's intellect. But reason alone cannot take care of this; and therefore the Church says: it is not legitimate, even if we cannot prove it scientifically, to incline ourselves toward these mistaken behaviors; we must believe and submit ourselves to these revealed truths; we must believe there is an afterlife, because without it, all moral and social order will disappear.[35]

Finally, Argentine congressman Gallo, himself a secularist, aptly summarized Goyena and his co-partisans' arguments that, absent religious

---

32. Goyena, *Diario de Sesiones (Diputados)*, July 6, 1883, pp. 491–492.
33. Centeno, *Diario de Sesiones (Diputados)*, July 14, 1883, p. 634.
34. Achával Rodríguez, *Diario de Sesiones (Diputados)*, July 6, 1883, pp. 507–508.
35. Achával Rodríguez, *Diario de Sesiones (Diputados)*, July 14, 1883, p. 611.

education, criminal behavior, and eventually the downfall of society, would result:

> If we proceed [without religious education], we will form generations of criminals . . . Study history, and . . . what will you find? The disappearance, ruin and decadence of all those societies that did not maintain their religious sentiment . . . Our project begins by stating: "the teaching of morality will be mandatory." What does the study of morality entail? . . . It is based on God, it is based on the principle of an immortal soul which is the basis of human responsibility . . . The student will ask the teacher: why mustn't I kill? The teacher will respond: You mustn't kill because it is prohibited by God, . . . and if you did, you will be punished by God. This life on Earth is purely transitory; after it comes a life of eternal reward or punishment, based on good or bad behavior.[36]

THE LIBERAL APPROACH TO MORAL EDUCATION

While conservatives dominated Chilean politics during the debate of the 1860 law, liberals dominated national politics during the debate of Argentina's 1884 education law. It is important to understand that the liberals who ruled Argentina from 1880 to 1916 were liberals in the sense that they endorsed the secularization of state institutions,[37] yet they represented the elite and supported an oligarchic political regime with limited political participation.

In stark contrast to conservative arguments, liberal elites in Argentina believed that teaching Catholicism in public schools would engender social conflict between those who subscribed to this religion and those who did not. This, they argued, would defeat the very purpose of public schools to unite the population and promote peace and order. Influenced heavily by positivist philosophy, liberals maintained instead that what was needed was to teach children *universal truths* applicable to everyone, regardless of religious beliefs. It was by teaching these universal truths, including principles of geometry and physics, that schools could help create unity among citizens and thus reduce disorderly behavior in society. These ideas are well

---

36. Gallo, *Diario de Sesiones (Diputados)*, July 12, 1883, p. 538.

37. To advance this agenda, liberals in Congress passed the 1884 Law of Civil Registries, which established a civil registry of births, marriages, and deaths in an attempt to displace the Catholic Church from people's daily lives, replacing it with the state.

captured in one of the speeches delivered in Congress by the Minister of Justice, Worship, and Public Instruction, himself a liberal and part of President Roca's liberal administration:

> *History tells us that the state has specific ends. The state unites men* to one another so that they will pursue common goals. The Church unites men to God so that they will pursue individual goals.... The state has the *duty to form citizens*; not Jews, not Catholics, because that would go against the ends of the state and the freedom of consciousness. Schools must teach universal ideas, not dogmas, and much less to those who do not desire the teaching of principles that go against their own beliefs. *The ideas that must be taught in schools must be universal, and the Church is not universal, even if it pretends to be. The teaching of arithmetic, for example, is the same teaching for everyone; the teaching of geometry is the same for everyone, because its truths can be grasped by human intelligence; but the teaching of religion does not fall in that category ... The state's duty to instruct with a social goal is fulfilled by teaching what is true everywhere and for everyone, by providing universal knowledge.*[38]

The state, which governs inheritances, protects the lives and honor of its citizens, cannot neglect education; and with the same right that it can turn a child into a soldier, it can and must impose on children the duty to instruct themselves, because it matters for the wellbeing of the Nation.... *We mustn't create divisions inside schools; we mustn't separate the protestant child from the catholic ... because then we will engender fights and discord inside the school, and those will continue in the street*, and enter the family, and then go back again from the families to the street, taken there not by the children but by their parents or adults, helping sow irreparable seeds of division among the people.[39]

In addition to opposing the teaching of Catholic doctrine, or of any other religious dogma, liberals in Congress held that knowledge of what constitutes good and bad behavior precedes the emergence of Christianity; that morality is inherent to man, and that in order to enable men to access universal moral principles, the key was to develop their *capacity for abstraction, logic and reasoning*. This would form the basis of good behavior. The liberal

---

38. Minister of Justice, Worship, and Public Instruction, *Diario de Sesiones (Diputados)*, July 13, 1883, pp. 557, 581. Emphasis is mine.
39. Minister of Justice, Worship, and Public Instruction, *Diario de Sesiones (Diputados)*, July 13, 1883, p. 583. Emphasis is mine.

congressman Civit, for example, argued that morality is independent of religion:

> Philosophy demonstrates that morality is independent of religion, that the distinction between what is right and wrong, the distinction between rightful and wrongful doing, is a law inherent to man's nature. The teacher, for example, will tell its disciples: you shall not lie in the name of your own dignity, because if you lie others will think less of you, and so will you.[40]

As articulated by the Minister of Justice, Worship, and Public Instruction during the congressional debates of the 1884 Law of Common Education, liberals believed that "moral principles are abstract"; while religious doctrine could be a shortcut for individuals whose intelligence was not sufficiently developed to access moral principles, teaching science would be superior since learning science would help grasp abstract principles:

> We must teach morality. Moral principles are innate to men; things have been known to be moral since before the existence of Christianity. Some of those moral principles have been adopted by Christianity, but they are universal, and therefore civilizing, principles ... Morality can be taught without teaching religion because moral principles are abstract, they are present in all human minds, whereas religious principles refer to concrete things. Religious worship has external manifestations. There is no doubt that for certain levels of intelligence, it would be almost impossible to penetrate the mind with abstract principles. From that standpoint, the teaching of morality in schools will be deficient, but this difficulty is also present in all the sciences, and for that reason the teaching of science is so important.[41]

At best, liberals thought that teaching religion as the original source of morality was a useful, if suboptimal, shortcut. At worst, they thought that teaching religion would divide society and undermine order, while teaching science would unite the population and provide a more solid grounding for morality.

---

40. Civit, *Diario de Sesiones (Diputados)*, July 11, 1883, p. 515.
41. Minister of Justice, Worship, and Public Instruction, *Diario de Sesiones (Diputados)*, July 13, 1883, pp. 566, 581–582, 586.

In sum, Chile in the 1860s and Argentina in the 1880s both erected centrally controlled primary school systems in response to national elites' heightened concern for social order after episodes of civil war. Both systems sought chiefly to shape the moral character of the poor to promote long-term social order and political stability. National elites in both countries were exposed to the same global ideas about mass education. Why, then, did their national curriculums for primary and for Normal Schools differ so much? Two main models for teaching moral principles existed, each reflecting a different view about the roots of morality: one viewed religion as the basis of morality; the other viewed reason and scientific laws as the ultimate source of moral principles. Domestic politics, and in particular the greater power of conservatives in Chile and of liberals in Argentina, shaped which of these competing views of the roots of morality was more influential when each country adopted its first national curriculum for primary schools.

CONCLUSION

Focusing on European and Latin American countries, in the last two chapters we examined the role that mass violence against the status quo played in bringing about education reform. These reforms sought to expand primary education and increase the state's regulatory role. The training, certification, and monitoring of teachers as well as the school curriculum were crucial areas of state intervention. In the nineteenth century, most states established national curriculums and regulated the teaching profession to ensure that what happened inside the classroom aligned with the state's goal of teaching discipline, obedience, and acceptance of the status quo. These policies are important to consider because, as I explain in the book's conclusion, they continue to shape present-day education systems. But before we turn to the long-term legacy of nineteenth-century education policies, in the next two chapters I consider the limits of the argument I have advanced so far and its ability to explain education reform more broadly.

CHAPTER SIX
LIMITS AND POSSIBILITIES OF THE ARGUMENT

I have argued that governments are more likely to turn to mass education as an indoctrination tool to inculcate obedience when they are deeply concerned about the problem of internal disorder. This chapter discusses the generalizability of this argument, or how applicable the argument is in different contexts. In other words, what are the kinds of contexts where we should expect governments to invest in education as an indoctrination tool to forge internal order, and when might a government *not* invest in education for indoctrination purposes?

Politicians are likely to invest in mass education systems to teach obedience when four preconditions are in place. One, politicians believe that the masses' participation in violent events poses a serious risk to their ability to maintain power. Two, politicians believe that schools can indeed serve as an indoctrination tool that teaches people to stay put. Three, notwithstanding their concerns about their ability to remain in power, politicians expect to remain in power long enough to be able to reap the benefits of educating future citizens. Four, a minimum level of fiscal and administrative capacity is in place—enough to allow investments in education.

These four preconditions constitute what political scientists would refer to as the scope conditions of the book's argument. They are important to consider if we are to understand the generalizability and limits of the argument. They help explain why the pivotal moments in the history of education in Prussia, France, Chile, and Argentina occurred when they did and not earlier. They can also help us understand why England and Mexico lagged behind other European and Latin American countries, respectively, in promoting primary education. Finally, these scope conditions can help us predict the types of future contexts in which we are likely to see investments in education for indoctrination purposes. Let's unpack what each precondition means.

CONDITION 1: POLITICIANS BELIEVE THAT MASS VIOLENCE POSES A SERIOUS THREAT

Educating the masses is a costly investment with primarily long-term benefits when the goal is to maintain social order. For politicians to invest in educating future citizens to teach them to accept the status quo, they must want to maintain the status quo in the first place, and crucially, they must believe that the masses, in the absence of this education, will behave in violent ways that threaten the status quo. This statement has two corollaries. First, violence that threatens the status quo but does not involve mass participation is unlikely to lead politicians to invest in mass education. Episodes of intra-elite conflict in which the masses are not mobilized by any of the elites fighting each other, for example, may lead to a redoubling of repression such as jailing or killing opponents, but are unlikely to lead to investments in mass education. After all, why make the costly effort to educate the masses if they do not pose a threat? Second, mass violence that is not perceived to pose a threat to the status quo that politicians benefit from is also unlikely to lead elites to invest in educating the masses. Communal violence, conflict between different religious or ethnic groups, or any other internal conflicts that do not involve the central government and therefore do not pose a risk to it, even if they do involve mass participation, are unlikely to lead the government to invest in mass education. To be sure, the groups fighting one another might make their own efforts to provide education with the goal of cultivating the loyalty of children in their communities. However, the government is unlikely to expend the costly effort to educate the masses if these do not pose a threat to its power.

Notice that, according to this argument, what matters most is not whether the masses actually pose a real threat to the status quo, but whether politicians believe this to be the case. In the four cases we considered in chapter 4, central governments invested in primary education in response to widespread mass violence in the form of peasant revolts, food riots, and mass involvement in civil wars. However, a government that *anticipates* an escalation of mass violence could turn to education before violence unfolds or becomes widespread. Moreover, education efforts could be based on an exaggerated sense of the real threat posed by the masses. Some of the inaccuracy in politicians' perception might stem from the lack of reliable crime statistics and other statistics, but exaggerated perceptions about the level of crime also exist in countries with accurate statistics. In the United States, for example, most people believe that crime is increasing despite decades of dramatic improvement.[1] Politicians may be affected by the same biases that lead ordinary people to overestimate the level of crime and violence. Further, even in those cases where a politician knows what the facts are, they can still take advantage of others' exaggerated perceptions and fears to build support for education reform by presenting education as a solution to the perceived problem of law and order.

Of course, one could argue that all politicians at all times are concerned about the possibility of mass violence, and to some extent this is true. What matters from the perspective of the book's argument is whether this concern is salient in politicians' minds, and crucially, whether politicians believe that existing policy tools such as repression are sufficient to avoid or contain prospective mass violence, and whether they believe that making costly investments in education would improve their ability to curtail mass violence enough to outweigh these costs.

A wide range of events can heighten politicians' concern about mass violence and social disorder. The most obvious examples are large-scale violent events of the kind that drove education reform in 1760s Prussia, 1830s France, 1860s Chile, and 1880s Argentina, all of which involved mass violence against the status quo. However, smaller-scale episodes of violence may also motivate elites to educate the population as long as these episodes engender the perception—justified or not—that the problem of mass violence is imminent and that existing policy tools are insufficient to deal with it.

Sweden's School Act of 1842 provides an example of the creation of a national primary education system triggered by concerns about mass violence that existed not because of large-scale violence but because politicians interpreted small-scale violence as a sign of things to come if the moral character of the lower classes was not improved. The background for this reform was the major social and demographic change that occurred in

---

1. Esberg and Mummolo (2018).

Sweden as a result of the radical transformation of the agrarian economy and rapid population growth that took place starting in the mid-eighteenth century and, especially, during the first decades of the nineteenth century. Historically, land in Sweden had been cultivated in the open-field system; although each peasant owned and cultivated their own strip of land, decisions concerning what crops to grow or what technologies to use were made collectively at the village level. The enclosure reforms of 1803, 1807, and 1827 gradually eliminated this system first in some regions and, eventually, everywhere. While some peasants were able to profit from the reforms, which coincided with a period of high international grain prices, and overall agrarian productivity increased significantly, in the 1830s signs emerged that the enclosure reforms had brought about greater social division.[2] The main reasons were the dissolution of villages and the decline in living standards for a large and growing class of former peasants—and their children—who became landless and turned to salaried work to make ends meet.[3]

Although only twenty riots were registered in Sweden between 1825 and 1844—a minuscule number compared to the number in France at the beginning of the July Monarchy—a weak harvest in 1837 caused episodes of violent unrest that, while isolated and small in scale, nonetheless sparked fear among Swedish elites about the possibility of a revolutionary threat. In the 1830s and 1840s, we see an intensification of debates in both newspapers and parliament about "the social question," a term used by national elites to encapsulate their fear that the "dangerous lower classes" in the countryside would revolt and take power from the ruling classes. In parliament, national elites described the lower classes as "a lower and bad sort of person," "morally degenerate," "a criminal rabble, the dregs of mankind, a dangerous mob," "bestial," "too readily violent"—a class, in sum, that "must be controlled and disciplined" in order to prevent immorality, crime, disorderliness, drunkenness, vices, disobedience, begging, ignorance, social unrest, and political revolt.[4] Against this background, writes Swedish historian Johannes Westberg, popular education became part of the debate on the social question. Along with other policies, such as the introduction of solitary-confinement penitentiaries, poor relief, and Bible societies, "primary schools were perceived as a social strategy to prevent crime, and curb

---

2. Rojas (1991); Bergenfeldt (2008); Westberg (2019).
3. While Sweden's population doubled between 1750 and 1850, the landless class quadrupled during this period (Westberg 2019, p. 199).
4. Petersson (1983), pp. 4, 270.

immorality and potential rebellion, and instead foster a subservient and disciplined population." Swedish elites who advocated for the establishment of a primary school system quoted elites from other countries who argued that schooling was "a safeguard against the raw masses." One contemporary, for example, described the School Act of 1842 as "a response to a moral panic and a fear of the dreaded underclass."[5]

While this example from Sweden's history illustrates that elites' fear of the masses may intensify even in the absence of large-scale violent conflict, even when such conflict *does* occur it will not always produce fear of the masses. For episodes of violent conflict to create the perception that the masses pose a risk to political stability and elites' power, the masses must be somehow involved in the conflict.

Some readers may raise the objection that, while Europe experienced considerable social unrest in the nineteenth century, most of the internal conflict that occurred in Latin America took the form of intra-elite wars between liberals and conservatives, the Church and the state, or the central and local governments. There is truth to this claim, but what the intra-elite characterization of Latin America's civil wars misses is the fact that many of these wars, although initiated by elites who wanted to fight other elites, also relied heavily on the mobilization of the lower classes. In Argentina during the first six decades after independence, for example, *caudillos* or warlords outside Buenos Aires mobilized the rural population to fight against Buenos Aires elites. In Chile, the Atacama rebels of 1859 were led by some of the province's wealthiest mine owners and leaders of the Radical Party, but these elites recruited and armed thousands of peasants, mine workers, and artisans to fight against the conservative government in Santiago.

Chilean history illustrates the importance of distinguishing between intra-elite conflicts with and without popular involvement to predict the consequences of conflict for mass education. While the 1859 civil war created consensus among conservative and liberal elites in Santiago about the need to educate the lower classes through a system of primary schools controlled by the central government, the 1851 civil war did not spark a conversation among national elites about mass education. The reason is that the 1851 civil war was a true intra-elite conflict. What triggered it was a fight within the upper ranks of the Conservative Party over who should succeed conservative president Manuel Bulnes. When Bulnes pointed to Manuel

---

5. Westberg (2019), pp. 199–201.

Montt as his preferred candidate, another conservative with presidential aspirations, General José María de la Cruz, mounted a coup to take over the central government. De la Cruz found support from some army officials and members of the National Guard as well as members of the opponent Liberal Party, but he did not mobilize the popular classes.[6] Although de la Cruz's attempted coup represented a threat to Montt's individual power, the civil war of 1851 never threatened to overhaul political institutions or reduce the power of the central government.[7] Moreover, the government quickly suppressed the foci of rebellion against Montt's ascension to the presidency. For all these reasons, the 1851 civil war, unlike the 1859 civil war, did not increase national elites' fear of the masses and, therefore, did not turn elites' attention to policies designed to pacify them.

CONDITION 2: POLITICIANS BELIEVE THAT SCHOOLS CAN INDOCTRINATE PEOPLE

In order for politicians who are afraid of the masses to invest in education as an indoctrination tool, they must believe that schools do in fact have the ability to teach future citizens to obey the state and its laws. This precondition bounds the argument temporally because, as we saw in chapter 3, the idea that education could serve as a tool to create loyal and obedient citizens only began to circulate widely among European political rulers in the late eighteenth century, and from there spread to other parts of the world. This implies that most instances of intense political instability occurred too early in history to trigger the emergence and expansion of a state-regulated primary education system. Some examples include the popular revolts of late-medieval Europe, the English civil war of 1642–1651, and the Glorious Revolution of 1688, all of which occurred before Enlightenment philosophers and Pietist reformers began to spread the view that mass education could serve the interests of political rulers to prevent future disorder and political instability.

Although the idea that primary education could help indoctrinate future citizens to respect the status quo began to circulate in the late eighteenth century, different countries were exposed to this idea at different times. In Chile, for example, this idea only made its ways into elite circles in the 1840s,

---

6. Collier (2003), pp. 98–102; Wood (2002), pp. 465–467.
7. Ortega Martínez and Rubio Apiolaza (2006).

owing to the publication of influential books and essays such as Domingo F. Sarmiento's *Educación Popular* (1849) or the Amunátegui brothers' *On Primary Instruction in Chile: What It Is and What It Ought to Be* (1853). From this perspective, the Chilean civil war of 1829–1830 occurred too early, so to speak, to trigger mass education. In the years surrounding this civil war, Andrés Bello was one of the most influential education thinkers and policymakers in Chile, but his educational ideas and efforts focused on secondary and university education for elites, not primary education for the masses. Like other Chilean politicians in the 1830s, Bello believed that providing secondary and university education opportunities for elites was crucial to train qualified bureaucrats and politicians and promote the country's economic development. By contrast, his ideas about the role of primary education were significantly less developed.[8]

EDUCATION IS FREEDOM: EXPLAINING ENGLAND'S EDUCATIONAL BACKWARDNESS BEFORE 1870

The absence of ideas about the social control power of mass education can also help explain England's educational backwardness. In the history of primary education systems, England stands out for lagging considerably behind other countries in Europe. As we saw earlier, in 1850 it was the only European country whose primary school enrollment rate was in the single digits. It was only in 1870—a full century after the Industrial Revolution and the introduction of compulsory schooling in Prussia—that the English government began to make a considerable effort to regulate and expand primary schooling.

By most common accounts of the factors that lead governments to invest in mass education, England should have been a global leader in the expansion of primary schooling, and the fact that it was not is an enigma. Its leadership in the Industrial Revolution presumably should have created incentives for the state to educate the population in order to ensure the existence of a large, skilled, and docile workforce. The many wars it fought in the eighteenth and nineteenth centuries against Prussia, France, the United States, and other European countries and British colonies presumably should have encouraged the British government to invest in mass schooling in order to instill a strong national identity and to train skilled and loyal soldiers. Electoral reform in 1832 should have created greater incentives for

---

8. Kilgore (1961).

elected politicians to expand primary education. Yet, despite having sufficient fiscal capacity, neither industrialization nor interstate wars nor competitive elections provided sufficient incentives for the government to promote primary schooling.

England's educational backwardness during most of the nineteenth century ceases to be an enigma once we adopt the theoretical perspective proposed in this book. The argument I have advanced suggests that the explanation for England's educational backwardness lies both in its relative political stability compared to other European countries throughout most of the nineteenth century *and* in the late diffusion—compared to continental Europe—of the idea that education could be used to indoctrinate the masses and promote social order.

England's most intense period of social and political instability took place in the seventeenth century during the English Civil War of 1642–1651 and the Glorious Revolution of 1688. These events, as noted earlier, occurred too early in history to trigger the expansion of primary schooling because the idea that education could help pacify the masses was only beginning to be articulated at that time. Toward the end of the eighteenth and beginning of the nineteenth centuries, the enclosure reforms brought about social unrest in the countryside, and industrialization and urbanization created a new working class that began to organize and express its discontent through strikes, the destruction of machines, and other forms of protest. The next major period of instability and upsurge in mass violence took place in the 1820s and early 1830s, when demands for electoral reform intensified. Concerned about a revolutionary upheaval, the government responded by directly addressing these demands through the Reform Act of 1832.[9] In the realm of education, in 1833 the national government began to provide some funding to the Church to subsidize the provision of elementary education, but did not create a national primary education system. The Church retained authority over the choice of the curriculum and the selection of teachers, and parents retained authority over the decision whether to enroll their children in school.

An important explanation for why the government, despite the mass violence of the early 1830s (or earlier waves of social unrest), did not set up a

---

9. Davis and Feeney (2017); Aidt and Franck (2015). The reform redistributed parliamentary seats from boroughs that were controlled by a tiny elite to counties that had contested elections and where a large fraction of the population could vote (Ertman 2010, p. 1008).

centralized system of public schools to educate the poor, lies in the ideas about education that circulated among English politicians at the time. Although some education reformers called for the expansion of elementary schooling "in order to protect against the dangers of radicalism, and to prevent social unrest, particularly in poor, overcrowded urban areas,"[10] many members of the elite did not share the belief that education was an effective tool to control the popular classes. Within the aristocracy, educating the working class and the poor was viewed as a dangerous endeavor that would likely lead people to "despise their lot in life," "render them factious and refractory," "enable them to read seditious pamphlets, vicious books, and publications against Christianity," "render them insolent to their superiors," and force parliament "to direct the strong arm of power against them." Industrialists, for their part, opposed mass schooling because they feared it would lead to a decline in child labor and a consequent increase in wages. In addition, English politicians took pride in being different from continental Europe; the fact that Prussia and France had centralized mass education under the state's authority was all the more reason to oppose this course of action.[11]

The distinct educational ideas that circulated in England appeared not only in political debates but also in influential fiction books that formed part of English literature and mass culture. While during the early 1700s works of fiction rarely mentioned education or schooling, toward the end of the eighteenth century Romantic writers began to include more references to education in their work—characterizing it as a tool for individual self-discovery and self-development more than a tool that could have benefits for the state or society.[12] The belief in the ability of education to empower the *individual* led fiction writers—many of whom belonged to the same social circles as members of parliament and other politicians—to support mass education for the middle and upper classes and, simultaneously, to caution about the dangers of providing mass education to poor and working-class individuals.[13] For example, the English poet William Wordsworth, one of the founders of the Romantic literary movement, wrote that promoting literacy among the working class was "dangerous to the peace

---

10. Wright (2012), p. 23.
11. Green (2013), pp. 254–255, 204–296.
12. Brantlinger (1998); Martin (2023).
13. Martin (2023).

of society,"[14] while the writer and philanthropist Hannah More, in her novel *The Sunday School*, represents mass literacy "as a threat to national security."[15]

According to intellectual and political elites, the dangers mass education posed for social and political stability stemmed from two main sources. First, elites were concerned that education would lead poor and working-class individuals to develop aspirations for social mobility instead of teaching them to accept their place in the social hierarchy. Second, elites worried that common people would use the literacy skills taught in school to read "poisonous" books, newspapers, and pamphlets that would do "moral damage" to them.[16] They feared, for example, that the common inclusion of crime stories in novels would encourage working-class individuals to engage in criminal behavior, even when novels were trying to discourage crime.[17] They feared, too, that Radical politicians and labor unions would take advantage of mass literacy to spread subversive messages that would incentivize collective action against the status quo.[18]

As we will see in the next chapter, England would have to wait until the mid-nineteenth century for the idea of mass education as a destabilizing force to be replaced by the view that educating the poor and the working classes could help promote order and stability.

EDUCATIONAL IDEAS OVER TIME

Is the notion of education as an indoctrination tool still prevalent today? To assess the extent to which the book's argument is temporally bounded, we need to consider not only when political rulers in a given country first became aware of ideas about the indoctrination role of education but also, crucially, for how long these ideas continued to shape politicians' views about the benefits of education. I discuss next how ideas and discourse about education have changed over time, what were the main factors leading to the growing discourse around the economic benefits of education, and why in modern societies it is difficult to know what truly motivates politicians to invest in education.

Existing ideas and public discourse about the benefits of education have changed over time, increasingly embracing the view that education provi-

---

14. Martin (2023), p. 96.
15. Brantlinger (1998), p. 6.
16. Brantlinger (1998), pp. 1, 5–6.
17. Brantlinger (1998), pp. 5, 8.
18. Martin (2023).

sion has important economic benefits. In the agrarian economies of the eighteenth and early nineteenth centuries, parents in rural areas were often reluctant to send their children to school because they perceived the economic costs to outweigh the benefits. This reluctance was the reason why several countries introduced compulsory schooling laws; politicians in these countries simply did not trust parents to willingly educate their children the way the state wanted them to. Today, by contrast, many parents view schools as a useful investment to give their children the necessary skills to obtain a good job, climb the social ladder, and live prosperous lives. Moreover, "education" today not only evokes ideas about individual opportunity, social mobility, and fairness; when people talk about "educated countries," we immediately think about economically developed ones. This is because, in addition to thinking of education as an important tool to improve individual well-being, we also think of it as a tool to promote the wealth of nations. The very same skills that enable someone to get a good job can also help boost technological innovation and economic productivity. Indeed, basic education is often thought of as one of the few policy tools that can help advance both economic equality *and* efficiency. Thus, today, both families and governments may value education because of its potential to produce economic benefits.

The view that education systems could produce social mobility and economic growth gained strength during the second half of the twentieth century. At least three factors helped solidify this economic conceptualization of the benefits of education: the Cold War, new economic theories of the 1960s, and the increasing educational role of international organizations. Competition for economic, technological, and military supremacy during the Cold War contributed to new perceptions about the potential economic benefits of education. As politicians in the United States observed what their main rival was doing in the realm of education policymaking, they were struck by how much emphasis Soviet schools placed on teaching everyone technical and scientific skills to contribute to industrialization.[19] Domestic policy in general increasingly came to be debated in the United States through the lens of economics,[20] and policymakers in Washington came to view—or at least frame—the country's educational problems as a threat

---

19. U.S. Department of Health, Education, and Welfare. Office of Education (1959, 1960).
20. Popp Berman (2022).

to sustaining "the once unchallenged preeminence in commerce, industry, science, and technological innovation."[21]

New economic theories in the 1960s gave further impetus to the idea that schooling, by increasing individual skills and productivity, was one of the main determinants of individual earnings and economic growth. Two economists at the University of Chicago, Jacob Mincer and Gary Becker, were especially influential in making the connection between education and individual productivity and earnings.[22] In the 1980s, Paul Romer proposed that economic growth depends on the stock of human capital, a theory that earned him the Nobel Laureate in economics.[23] These theories cemented the view that schooling and the acquisition of literacy and numeracy skills go hand in hand, a view that today we know does not always match the facts.[24]

The World Bank, created at the end of World War II and heavily dominated by economists, played a role in spreading the view that education has economic benefits for individuals and societies. Economists' ascendancy began in the early 1960s, when then World Bank President George Woods appointed Chicago economist Milton Friedman as his economic adviser. By the early 1980s, the World Bank employed fewer than twenty non-economist social scientists on its staff.[25] Much of the language that has been used in recent decades to justify education interventions highlights the economic benefits of those interventions.[26] An example of this comes from the World Bank's agenda for promoting education in developing countries between 2010 and 2020, which underscores the increased "desire of many nations to increase their competitiveness by building more highly skilled workforces," argues that education systems ought to "prepare young people with the right skills for the job market," and claims not only that "educated individuals are more employable, able to earn higher wages, cope better with economic shocks," but also that "education is fundamental to development and growth."[27] This type of description and justification of the benefits of education interventions, with its focus on economic benefits, has

21. The National Commission on Excellence in Education (April 1983).
22. Becker (1964); Mincer (1958).
23. Romer (1990, 1987).
24. World Bank (2018).
25. Moloney (2022), pp. 38, 53.
26. For an analysis of World Bank documents showing the prevalence of economics jargon from 1950 to 2010, see Moretti and Pestre (2015).
27. World Bank (2010), pp. v, 1.

characterized the World Bank's discourse on education since the early 1960s and was institutionalized in 1963 by an internal policy that required both an education expert *and* an economist to appraise every potential education loan.[28]

In addition to economic arguments for the provision of education, the last several decades have seen an intensification of the argument that education is a basic human right. From this perspective, education is not a means of social control but a precondition for individual freedom and self-realization. Accordingly, education must be compulsory, not to safeguard the government's social control agenda but to protect children's right to an education. Two United Nations agencies, the United Nations Educational, Scientific and Cultural Organization (UNESCO) and the United Nations Children's Fund (UNICEF), have been especially active in embracing and spreading the view of education as a basic right,[29] a view that is enshrined in the 1989 Convention on the Rights of the Child, ratified by 196 countries.[30]

Given the changing discourse about education during the postwar period and the emphasis that international organizations have placed on the economic benefits of education, it has become increasingly difficult to tell what are the true motivations behind governments' provision of education. For decades, governments from developing countries seeking foreign aid or loans to fund education projects have stressed the benefits for economic development, poverty reduction, and individual well-being. Yet, precisely because this is what international organizations and donors want to hear, it is difficult to know whether governments genuinely believe that promoting skills and economic opportunities is a crucial goal of education, or whether this is simply a rhetorical device they use because they know their audience (and lenders).

The growth of political openness in the last several decades is another factor that hinders our ability to determine whether governments that frame education as a strategy to promote social mobility and economic growth really believe that these are the main goals of education, or whether this, again, is a communication strategy they use because they understand that this is what citizens want to hear. During the nineteenth century, absolutist kings in continental Europe and oligarchic presidents in Latin America ex-

---

28. Jones (2007), pp. 33, 39.
29. Jones and Coleman (2005).
30. All eligible states except for the United States ratified the Convention.

pressed their views about the goals of education without much concern that their choice of words might trigger public backlash. Newspapers reporting on what they had said, if they existed, reached elites alone, and the radio did not exist. By contrast, in most democracies today it would be political suicide to talk openly about the indoctrination goals of public education, or to refer to uneducated individuals as "bloodthirsty hordes," "savages," or "barbarians."

Still, even in democratic countries today, politicians often allude to the important role that schools play in teaching values, forming good citizens, and promoting social cohesion and peace. Indeed, the most heated education debates of the twenty-first century have been those that center on what moral and political values should be taught in school. That politicians continue to fight fervently over these values is a strong indication that teaching skills is not the only goal ascribed to schools, and that most politicians continue to believe in schools' ability to mold the moral character and political behavior of future citizens. To be sure, schools can teach values that are in contradiction with, or at least not supportive of, indoctrination goals. But we should not just assume that democratically elected governments do not indoctrinate. Whether or not they do is an important empirical question that we will examine in chapter 7.

For now, the bottom line is that in recent decades it has become politically incorrect to tout the indoctrination role of schools, and therefore, it has become incredibly challenging to assess whether efforts to expand or reform mass education have been at least partly motivated by governments' indoctrination goals. The challenge is that, if we were to ask politicians, "Do you believe that schools should indoctrinate children?," the answer would probably be "no," even if politicians believe that schools *should* teach children to blindly accept a set of principles, simply because politicians understand the likely negative repercussions of revealing their true beliefs in such terms. Assessing to what extent indoctrination continues to be an important goal of mass education today will require creative research approaches that can tap into politicians' genuine motivations for providing mass education.

CONDITION 3: POLITICIANS EXPECT TO BE IN POWER LONG ENOUGH TO BENEFIT FROM EDUCATING FUTURE CITIZENS

Not all governments that are afraid of mass violence and believe that primary education can help pacify the masses will invest in education. One of the reasons is that, as a means of promoting compliant and nonviolent behavior, education is primarily a long-term strategy. While repression and concessions typically target adults who participate in violent events in order to compel or encourage them to stop fighting, primary schools target children. To the extent that children also participate in violent events, primary schools can help reduce social disorder in the short term by keeping children off the streets. But most of the benefits of educating children accrue over time, once they enter adolescence and young adulthood and become well-behaved citizens who respect the state and the status quo. Given this particular feature of education, for a government to be willing to make investments in education for the sake of social order, it must have a sufficiently long time horizon to reap the expected political benefits of educating children.

The relationship between a government's expected probability of remaining in power and its willingness to invest in education to promote social order is most likely nonlinear. At one extreme, governments that are well-entrenched in power to the point that they do not fear being overthrown by the masses will have few incentives to invest in education; from their perspective, doing so would entail a cost and no benefit—in other words, an unnecessary waste of resources. At the other extreme, governments in an extremely insecure position who fear for their immediate survival, such as those in the midst of a civil war or revolution, are also likely to have few immediate incentives to invest in education if they believe there is a high probability that they will not be around long enough to benefit from those investments. The greatest incentives to invest in mass education are likely to emerge in settings where the government *is* afraid of the masses—perhaps because of the traumatic experience of a recent period of social upheaval or because of an exaggerated perception of the level of crime—but also has some confidence in its ability to remain in power long enough to secure the benefits of educating the lower classes.

Contexts where this condition is likely to hold include, for example, post-conflict settings in which the government is focused on reconstruction strategies to consolidate the fragile peace recently achieved, such as Chile after 1859 and Argentina after 1880; ongoing civil wars where the government expects to be victorious; and contexts where there is increased concern about a potential future revolution—perhaps because of a spike in crime or social unrest—but the government is still, for the time being, securely in power, such as Prussia in the mid-eighteenth century or Sweden in the 1830s and 1840s.

Governments facing chronic violence, on the other hand, are less likely to make heavy investments in education or other forms of state-building. In these contexts, the government will likely prioritize strategies that increase the probability of short-term survival, such as increasing public spending on the military and police, jailing dissidents, or distributing boxes of food or other subsidies in an attempt to buy off loyalty, at least in the short term. Once there is an end to the period of violence and the government can start thinking beyond its immediate survival, mass education is likely to become an attractive investment as a means to prevent future conflict from re-emerging. An example of these dynamics comes from Argentine history. From independence in 1816 to 1880, the country was immersed in a prolonged period of recurrent civil wars, not unlike the experience of some African countries since their own independence. Ideas about the ability of primary education to deter the masses from participating in the civil wars circulated among Argentine elites since at least the 1840s, as we saw in chapter 4, but investments in education remained limited while the civil wars were ongoing. It was only in 1880 that a clear resolution to the six-decade conflict was achieved and the central government, no longer worried about its immediate survival, began to invest heavily in primary education as part of a broader set of state-building strategies designed to consolidate its power.

The condition that politicians must expect to be in power long enough to reap the benefits of educating future citizens does not limit the book's argument to a particular type of political regime. In chapter 4 we saw examples from a wide range of non-democratic regimes, including an absolutist regime, a constitutional monarchy, an oligarchic regime led by conservatives, and an oligarchic regime led by secular liberals. What about other types of non-democratic regimes, such as hegemonic-party regimes or military regimes? Barbara Geddes and Beatriz Magaloni have shown that hegemonic- or one-party regimes tend to last longer than personalist dictatorships, which in turn are more durable than military regimes.[31] Taking this fact into consideration, the book's theory would predict that hegemonic-party regimes facing threats from below will be more likely than personalist dictatorships, and these more likely than military regimes, to turn to education to indoctrinate the population. This expectation finds support in new data on education indoctrination presented in figure 6.1.

31. Geddes (2003); Magaloni (2008).

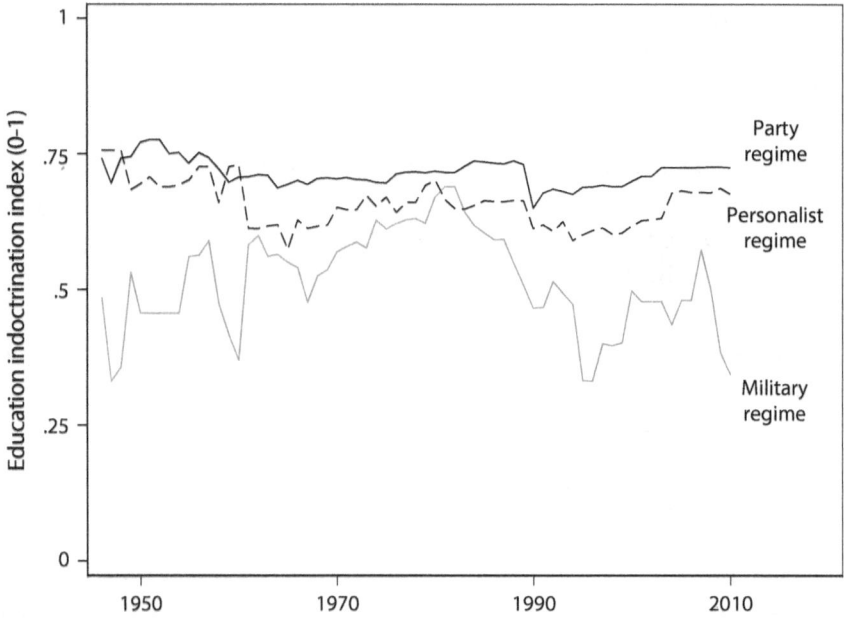

Figure 6.1. Average education indoctrination index around the world across different types of non-democratic regimes, 1946–2010. See text and footnotes for sources and methodology.

To explore how indoctrination varies across different types of non-democratic regimes, in figure 6.1 I combine Geddes's data on types of regimes[32] with a new cross-national dataset on education indoctrination that I collected with a team of social scientists led by Anja Neundorf.[33] The Varieties of Political Indoctrination in Education and the Media Dataset, or V-Indoc for short, covers more than 160 countries from 1945 to 2021 and includes an index of education indoctrination that ranges from 0 (low) to 1 (high). The index aggregates several variables contained in the V-Indoc dataset that capture three characteristics of education systems discussed in chapter 5 that are key for enabling governments to engage in indoctrination: first, whether the central government controls the curriculum and text-

---

32. Geddes, Wright, and Frantz (2014).
33. Neundorf et al. (2023). The construction of V-Indoc was conducted in partnership with the Varieties of Democracy Institute by surveying education experts in each country. On average, we surveyed 4.75 experts per country. V-Indoc was validated by comparing the responses of experts with the responses stemming from datasets that collected similar information but relied instead on education laws or content analysis of textbooks. See Neundorf et al. (2024) for additional information about these validation exercises.

books; second, the degree to which the curriculum seeks to mold political values as measured, for example, by whether primary schools are required to have a subject focused on inculcating moral and political values; and third, the extent to which the government exercises political control over teachers as measured, for example, by whether teacher hiring decisions take into consideration an applicant's moral aptitude and political behavior.[34] Figure 6.1 shows the average value of this index across three types of non-democracies: party, personalist, and military regimes. The pattern is clear: party regimes tend to have higher education indoctrination scores than personalist regimes, which in turn have higher indoctrination scores than military regimes. In additional analyses presented in the online appendix, I find complementary evidence that transitioning to a hegemonic- or single-party regime leads to an increase in education indoctrination, whereas transitioning to a military regime does not. These findings are consistent with the expectation that longer-lived regimes are more likely to engage in indoctrination than regimes with shorter time horizons.

To be clear, the type of political regime is just a proxy for its expected length; the latter is what really matters from the perspective of predicting whether a regime is likely to invest in education as an indoctrination tool. For example, while military regimes tend to be short-lived compared to other types of non-democratic regimes, a military regime that expects to be in power for a long time may have incentives to invest in education. An example of long-lasting military rule comes from Thailand. Since independence in 1932, there has been a military coup on average once every seven years, and the military has been in power two-thirds of the time. This history has made military coups and military rule a normal part of life. The military's most recent formal ascension to power took place in May 2014, when after months of political instability and mass demonstrations, the military mounted a coup, instituted a military junta, and established a new Constitution which gave the military the power to appoint all members of the Senate, in turn giving it an easy permanent route to choose the prime minister.[35] The regime's assessment of the mass violence of 2013–2014 was that educational deficiencies were partly to blame. While newspapers and education experts argued that the low quality of education in the countryside

---

34. For additional details about the construction of the Indoctrination Potential in Education index, see Neundorf et al. (2024).

35. Mérieau (2019); Freedom House (2022).

had contributed to persistent poverty which in turn fueled social unrest, the military junta had a different explanation. In a speech delivered soon after assuming power, Prayuth Chan-ocha, Thailand's prime minister and the leader of the military junta, complained that schools were doing a poor job of inculcating loyalty to the state and noted that "few Thai children could cite achievements of long-dead kings."[36] To address this problem, he drew up twelve values—including discipline; respect for laws, authorities, and elders; loyalty to the monarch; morality, integrity, and well-wishes toward others; moderation and self-restraint in consumption; shame for sins and for giving in to the dark force of desires; and public interest before personal interest—and ordered schools to teach them "to build the good character of the future generation."[37]

In some democracies, too, elected politicians may expect to be in power long enough to reap the benefits of investing in education to form well-behaved citizens—something I will return to in chapter 7.

CONDITION 4: SUFFICIENT FISCAL AND ADMINISTRATIVE CAPACITY

Even if a government *wants to* invest in education to promote long-term social order, it may be unable to do so if it lacks sufficient resources or administrative capacity. Constructing schools, printing and distributing textbooks, hiring teachers and school inspectors—all of these things require money. Moreover, while some of these are one-time investments, paying teachers and inspectors requires a permanent stream of public funding. Countries that lack a bureaucratic apparatus capable of raising sufficient tax revenues may be unable to provide education despite their intentions.

Other forms of administrative capacity, such as the existence of a census or railroads, can also matter for implementing some education reforms. In France, for example, the Guizot Law of 1833 required all municipalities with at least 500 inhabitants to maintain a school for boys. The central government could enforce this law because France at the time already had a national census. Several countries in Europe and Latin America had similar education laws which required the establishment of schools in areas with a population size above a certain threshold, and the existence of censuses

---

36. The Economist (2017).
37. Sangnapaboworn (2018).

typically preceded the passage of these laws.[38] The ability to deploy teachers and school inspectors hired and trained by the central government also often required the existence of a transportation network. In the nineteenth century, railroads facilitated the ability of inspectors to visit schools in disparate parts of the country. In Sweden, when parliament introduced a centralized school inspection system in 1861, student enrollment in primary schools—whose enforcement was charged to school inspectors—increased more in those localities that had a train station near them and could therefore be more easily accessed by inspectors.[39]

The availability of foreign loans has helped attenuate the extent to which a country's limited fiscal capacity precludes its ability to expand education. In 2018, a combined US$16 billion of international funding was devoted to education, including both loans from the World Bank and other development banks and direct aid. While this represents less than 1 percent of the total amount that governments around the world devoted to education in the same year, when we focus on low-income countries alone, foreign aid is responsible for close to one-fifth of total education spending.[40]

One of the central challenges in assessing a country's level of fiscal and administrative capacity is determining whether the absence of an education policy—such as education provision—is driven by a real lack of capacity or by insufficient will. Arguments pointing to a government's limited resources as a reason not to invest in education have been a constant throughout history. We saw an example of this in chapter 4 when we discussed the Chilean case: before the 1859 civil war, one common argument against the creation of a national primary education system was lack of funding; after the 1859 civil war, although the government's fiscal capacity had not increased, elites debated not *whether* the government could fund primary education but *how* it could do so. This example suggests that, when elites' fear of mass violence increases, so does their political willingness to invest existing resources on education even in the absence of an overall increase in the level of resources.

Solutions to the state's fiscal needs have been varied. In some cases, such as in France during the 1830s, the central government imposed on municipalities the need to raise taxes from the local population to maintain primary

---

38. Lopez (2020).
39. Cermeño, Enflo, and Lindvall (2022).
40. World Bank (2021).

schools. In others, such as France and Argentina during the 1880s, the central government assumed most or all of the costs of education provision. Many governments also thought of ways to cut the costs of education provision. In the United States, Southern Europe, and Latin America, governments hired female teachers as a means to save money because they understood that educated women, lacking other job opportunities, could be hired at a lower salary than educated men. Governments with the will to invest in education have often found ways to fund it despite having limited resources.

Of course, the very episodes of violence that might increase a government's interest in educating the masses may also destroy its fiscal capacity. France after the Revolution of 1789 provides a clear example of the adoption of education reforms with indoctrination goals followed by the failure to implement reform largely because of the dismal state of public finances. It is well known that the French Crown was already unable to pay its debts before the Revolution, but the revolutionary government's abolition of consumption taxes, their replacement with new direct taxes whose collection required a fiscal apparatus that the state lacked, the difficulty of obtaining new loans given the fear that the Revolution had inspired in owners of capital, and the need to wage foreign wars, further exacerbated France's fiscal deficit problems during the 1790s.[41] Fiscal troubles did not prevent the revolutionary government of the 1790s from debating education reform and passing laws that at the very least reflected the new ruling elite's educational goals. The most comprehensive of these was the Bouquier Law passed in December 1793 during Robespierre's Reign of Terror. The Jacobins were of the view that education had to indoctrinate future citizens in republican principles, and the punitive provisions of the Bouquier Law highlighted their insistence on education as a duty, not just a right. Although the original law stipulated that primary education should be free and universal, an amendment introduced a few months later also made it compulsory because, according to Robespierre and other powerful advocates of republican indoctrination, this was the only way to realize the moral and civic indoctrination goals of the state. Teaching all children to be good citizens and to obey the laws, members of the Reign of Terror's Committee on Public Safety argued, was a measure of revolutionary safety to crush

---

41. Levasseur (1894); Sargent and Velde (1995); White (1995).

counterrevolutionary tendencies.[42] In the end, despite these intentions, the Jacobins had more pressing issues to prioritize and lacked the funds to implement the Bouquier Law.[43] As we saw in chapter 4, primary education would have to wait until the next revolution in the 1830s before receiving a strong push from the state.

THE DISCONNECT BETWEEN POLITICAL WILLINGNESS AND CAPACITY: EXPLAINING MEXICO'S EDUCATIONAL BACKWARDNESS

The expansion of primary education in Mexico lagged considerably behind other countries in Latin America during the nineteenth century, and picked up pace only in the 1920s and 1930s. Unlike in England, whose educational backwardness compared to continental Europe can be explained by the national government's disinterest in educating the lower classes, the central government in Mexico passed several laws that signaled its interest in regulating and promoting primary education. However, limited state capacity prevented the implementation of these laws and delayed Mexico's expansion of primary schooling.

During the first century after its independence from Spain in 1822, Mexico was shaken by recurrent internal political conflicts and social turmoil that prevented the consolidation of a strong state, undermined economic development, and left an internally fragmented country more vulnerable to foreign invasion. Most of these internal conflicts pitted different groups of elites against one another—liberals against conservatives during the nineteenth century; urban businessmen, bureaucrats, and professionals against large landowners during the Mexican Revolution. But elites did not fight alone; they mobilized the large peasant and working classes to fight with them. The danger that any winning side in these successive internal conflicts faced was the possibility that the lower classes might organize on their own against the new regime or be mobilized, once again, by elites who opposed the regime.

As the central government sought to consolidate its control over Mexico's large territory during this century-long period, there was no shortage of education laws that signaled the government's interest in centralizing—within the limits of a federalist constitution—and promoting primary education. As in Argentina, and unlike the case of Chile, the main push toward

42. Vignery (1966).
43. Dwyer and McPhee (2002), pp. 88–89.

education centralization and expansion in nineteenth-century Mexico came from liberals and positivists who believed that religious doctrine, similar to superstition and ancient traditions, did not provide a solid moral foundation and were in fact signs of an inferior population in need of being civilized. Yet, despite the creation in 1833 of a centralized government agency devoted to regulating, promoting, and monitoring public schooling, and the subsequent passage of *twelve* education laws between 1843 and 1917,[44] Mexico's educational performance throughout that period remained lackluster relative to the rest of Latin America, owing largely to the federal government's limited administrative and fiscal capacity to implement these laws.[45]

Before the Mexican Revolution, the first signs of progress in expanding primary education were seen during the dictatorial regime of Porfirio Díaz, who assumed power in 1876 and was overthrown in 1911. The *Porfiriato*, as this period in Mexican history is known, ruled under the banner of "Order and Progress." This motto reflected the influence of positivist intellectuals' view that restoring and maintaining social order was a necessary precondition

---

44. The twelve laws are: the 1843 *Bases Orgánicas*, which establishes a common curriculum, stipulates how schools should be organized and what pedagogical methods should be used, and makes explicit the Mexican government's interest in controlling education; the 1856 *Estatuto Orgánico*, which establishes that the government has the authority to supervise that the education provided in private schools does not constitute a threat to the country's level of morality; the 1857 Constitution, which specifies that although private schools may exist, the state has the sole authority to determine the qualifications that individuals must have in order to teach in public or private schools; the education law of 1861, which proposes a unified curriculum for primary schools and the creation of new primary schools under the central government's authority; the 1865 *Ley de Instrucción Pública*, which establishes that primary education is compulsory, free for the poor, and will be supervised by the Ministry of Public Instruction; the 1867 and 1869 *Leyes Orgánicas de Instrucción Pública para el Distrito Federal y Territorios*, which affirms the need to form the future generation of Mexicans, reaffirms the principles of compulsory and secular schooling, and stipulates the creation of primary schools, and which was copied or closely imitated by many states; the 1879 *Reglamento de Escuelas Primarias Nacionales y Reglamento de Instrucción Pública*, which affirms the principle of secular education and introduces measures to ensure that schools teach values and behaviors that promote public hygiene; the education law of 1888, which gives the national state the authority to regulate education throughout the country, and reaffirms the principles of compulsory, free, and secular primary education; the 1891 *Ley Reglamentaria de la Instrucción Obligatoria en el Distrito Federal y territorios de Tepic y Baja California*, which affirms the same principles and calls for the creation of supervisory boards that monitor parental compliance with the compulsory schooling mandate, stipulates the creation of a primary school for boys and another one for girls for every 4,000 inhabitants, and creates the *Consejo Superior de Instrucción Primaria* to supervise, nominate teachers, and select textbooks; the 1908 *Ley de Educación Primaria para el Distrito y los Territorios Federales*; and the 1917 Constitution. See Solana, Cardiel Reyes, and Bolaños Martínez (1981).

45. Vaughan (1982), pp. 39–126.

to attract foreign capital and promote economic development.[46] In addition to relying on heavy-handed repression to restore and maintain order, the regime made considerable efforts to improve the morality and public behavior of the lower classes. Just like Sarmiento during the long period of Argentine civil wars, Mexican elites were concerned that the upbringing of the lower classes normalized the use of violence. They interpreted the persistence of crime as evidence that the lower classes were "immoral and socially undesirable."[47] They viewed popular customs as an excuse to binge on "tons of alcoholic beverages, spiced up with countless quarrels, fisticuffs, and a corpse here and there." They described the lower classes as *gente de trueno*—"rowdy folks"—whose behavior was characterized by "drunkenness, lack of discipline, roughness, and impudence."[48] Blaming workers' drinking habits for the rise of crime, they established anti-alcohol leagues to keep people out of taverns.[49] In Mexico City, the regime reorganized the police force to create a team of undercover agents who infiltrated taverns and social gatherings. It also banned bullfights because they "lowered the 'moral' level of the people" and "awakened their savage instincts."[50]

It was in this context of heightened concern about the morality and public behavior of the lower classes that primary education gained increasing interest among government officials and intellectuals with ties to Porfirio Díaz. In schools, morality was defined as "the formation of character through obedience and discipline" and entailed the eradication of "vices" such as ignorance, laziness, lack of punctuality, and the consumption of alcohol. The consequences of poverty, such as poor housing and malnutrition, were interpreted by the school program as moral sins for which the poor had to take personal responsibility. Two positivists, first Joaquín Baranda as head of the Secretary of Justice and Public Instruction (1882–1901), and then Justo Sierra as head of the Secretary of Public Education (1905–1911), played a key role in crafting a vision of primary education that highlighted its disciplinary goal. Disciplining the population, they argued, would help prevent crime and the recurrence of civil wars as well as promote economic growth by teaching the poor to work dutifully and accept their place in society. Under their leadership, the Mexican government defended the adoption of a unified

46. Schmitt (1966).
47. Beezley (2018); Vaughan (1982), pp. 26–28.
48. Beezley (2018).
49. Vaughan (1982), p. 27.
50. Beezley (2018).

curriculum for all schools and made the first efforts to train teachers who could teach this curriculum. Baranda equated primary schools to "civilizing propaganda" that prepares a large number of "good citizens,"[51] and warned that for Mexico to overcome internal threats and be able "to exist," the state and federal governments needed to invest in primary education to "regenerate society" and inculcate "love of the fatherland" and "love of peace." "Opening a school today," claimed Baranda, "means closing a prison for twenty years."[52] For Justo Sierra, too, "discipline was key to Mexico's survival." Having lived through the period of civil war and foreign invasion, Sierra viewed education primarily as a mechanism for forging social unity. Like most of his peers, "Sierra was anxious that political order replace the anarchy of Mexico's first half-century of independence" and viewed public schooling as "an alternative to socialism and worker agitation" because of its ability to develop habits of obedience, self-restraint, and altruism.[53]

Despite national elites' interest in expanding primary schooling to address long-standing problems of social order, the fraction of children enrolled in primary schools during the *Porfiriato* merely increased from 28 percent in 1880 to 33 percent in 1910.[54] The regime's ability to expand schooling in rural areas was especially restricted not only because of the resistance of local elites and parents to state intervention, but also because of the constraints imposed by limited fiscal and administrative capacity, poor roads infrastructure, and the absence of data about population size, enrollment, and the number of existing schools in remote areas.[55] During the Mexican Revolution, which lasted from 1910 to 1920, fiscal resources were put in the service of fighting the insurgency and became even less available for education, leading to a sharp reduction in public education spending, from 7 percent of total public expenditures in 1910 to less than 1 percent by 1919.[56]

When Alvaro Obregón took power in 1920, he began a process of state-building that entailed setting up centralized bureaucracies to regulate labor, commerce and industry, health, agriculture, social welfare, and education, as well as improving the state's fiscal apparatus.[57] New sources of fiscal revenue

---

51. Solana, Cardiel Reyes, and Bolaños Martínez (1981), p. 57.
52. Solana, Cardiel Reyes, and Bolaños Martínez (1981), pp. 59–60.
53. Vaughan (1982), pp. 23–27.
54. The data are from Lee and Lee (2016).
55. Solana, Cardiel Reyes, and Bolaños Martínez (1981), p. 65; Llinás Alvarez (1979), pp. 91–114, 120, 126–127.
56. Solana, Cardiel Reyes, and Bolaños Martínez (1981), p. 591.
57. Vaughan (1975).

were created in the early 1920s, and in 1924 the federal government introduced a new income tax.[58] Central government revenue during this decade almost tripled the level of revenue collected during the last decade of the *Porfiriato*.[59]

While the Revolution brought to power a new elite composed of small businessmen, lawyers, doctors, educators, and commercial farmers, the new elite faced the problem of containing organized peasants and workers, who during the Revolution fought for goals that were at odds with those of the elite. Peasants, not just workers, needed to be disciplined. Mass education became a key policy tool that the government used to restrain and coopt the popular classes.[60] José Vasconcelos was the person that Obregón chose to lead an unprecedented process of centralization and expansion of primary education. Vasconcelos drafted plans for the creation of a new Secretary of Public Education, or SEP, for its name in Spanish (*Secretaría de Educación Pública*), which became the first centralized agency with authority to regulate education everywhere in Mexico.[61] During the 1920s, the federal government established more than 3,300 federal primary schools, a sixfold increase relative to the number of federal schools toward the end of the *Porfiriato*.[62] Primary school enrollment increased from 30 percent in 1920 to 62 percent in 1925.[63] In contrast to the *Porfiriato*'s emphasis on expanding education in urban areas, Vasconcelos emphasized the expansion of schooling in rural areas, where the vast majority of the population lived, and which accounted for more than 80 percent of the new schools built by the federal government in the 1920s.[64] The new SEP also expanded its efforts to recruit "missionary" teachers who could spread the state's message to the popular classes, monitored more closely the work of teachers, distributed textbooks throughout the territory, and introduced a school breakfast program to encourage parents in rural areas to send their children to school.[65]

---

58. Aboites Aguilar (2003).
59. Historical data on fiscal revenues from 1825 to 2010 come from International Historical Statistics (2013).
60. Vaughan (1975).
61. Llinás Alvarez (1979).
62. Vaughan (1982), p. 153.
63. The data are from Lee and Lee (2016).
64. Vaughan (1982), p. 152.
65. Llinás Alvarez (1979); Vaughan (1982), pp. 125–164.

While it is reasonable to speculate that the federal government after the Mexican Revolution perhaps invested in mass education as a form of progressive redistribution to improve the material well-being of peasants and the working class, one of the strongest pieces of evidence against this hypothesis comes from the content of the curriculum. Just like during the *Porfiriato*, official textbooks continued to teach children to behave in orderly ways, be obedient, treat others with kindness, and resist the temptation to improve their material well-being. During the 1920s, the only history textbook published and used in schools was the one written by Justo Sierra for Porfirian schools. Further, Vasconcelos hired former members of the Porfirian school bureaucracy to write textbooks for other subjects. The new textbooks, despite being written after the Revolution, praised the government of Porfirio Díaz for its ability to maintain order, promote material progress, and bring about "civilization." Among the main values they promoted, the textbooks used in the 1920s emphasized the importance of "order," "obedience," "patience," "compliance" in the workplace, "respect," "silence," "solidarity," "benevolence," "tolerance," and "forgiveness," and condemned "disobedience," "maltreatment of others," "envy," "avarice," "vanity," and "cruelty."[66]

The continuity in the content and goals of education is an enduring legacy of the Porfirian regime that speaks to the ubiquitous concern among elites—be they traditional landowners or the petite-bourgeoisie—to control the masses' behavior. This interest was already present under the *Porfiriato*, but it was only in the 1920s that the government's fiscal and administrative capacity improved sufficiently to enable Mexico's primary education system to catch up with other Latin American countries after decades of lagging behind them.

CONCLUSION

Although previous chapters presented evidence that nineteenth-century non-democracies in Europe and Latin America often created national primary education systems and promoted the expansion of primary schooling in an attempt to indoctrinate the masses, this phenomenon is not unique to the nineteenth century, to Western societies, to a particular type of non-democratic regimes, or even—as we will see in the next chapter—to

---

66. Vaughan (1982), pp. 215–238, 280–281.

non-democracies alone. Yet the ability of the book's argument to explain educational expansion across a wide range of contexts does not imply that fear of the masses and indoctrination goals were at the heart of efforts to expand primary education in all countries at all times. The discussion in this chapter should help readers understand and predict the types of contexts in which we are likely to see education reform with indoctrination goals in mind, the contexts in which education investments for indoctrination reasons are likely to be absent, and the contexts in which politicians may invest in education to pursue goals different than those pursued by absolutist Prussia or oligarchic Argentina. Four conditions will increase the likelihood that politicians will invest in education as an indoctrination tool to teach obedience: first, politicians must fear the masses; second, they must believe that education can help promote social order by instilling obedience; third, they must be sufficiently well-entrenched in power; and finally, they must have sufficient fiscal and administrative capacity at their disposal. The absence of any one of these conditions will likely prevent the expansion of mass education *qua* indoctrination—and can explain, as we have seen, England's and Mexico's delay in expanding access to primary education compared to other countries in their respective regions.

We can use this framework to consider, for example, the applicability of the book's argument in recent civil wars. Three conditions discussed in this chapter have been less frequently found among recent wars than among the civil wars that took place in the nineteenth or early twentieth century. First, while all civil wars in Europe and Latin America before 1945 involved the state, the same is not true of recent civil wars in Africa or Asia, where twelve civil wars since 1945 have been intercommunal wars between ethnic groups but *without* state involvement.[67] Moreover, owing to changes in the technologies of war, a new class of civil wars has emerged in the twenty-first century that does not require a large paramilitary force.[68] When mass violence against the state is absent, it is less likely that civil war will trigger investments in education. Second, the civil wars of the post–World War II period have lasted longer and been more recurrent than the wars of the

---

67. I computed this figure using data from the Correlates of War Project, which provides information about the occurrence of intrastate wars from 1816 to 2014 and classifies each war into four categories: civil wars for central control (with state involvement), civil wars over local issues (with state involvement), regional internal wars (without state involvement), and intercommunal wars (without state involvement).

68. Walter (2022).

prewar period.[69] Governments that face extreme uncertainty about their ability to hold on to power, either because they are in the midst of fighting a civil war or because they face chronic civil wars, are unlikely to make long-term investments in education. Third, given the evolution of ideas about the benefits of education since World War II, even if we do observe that a recent civil war incentivized the government to invest in mass schooling, probing whether this was driven by a motivation to indoctrinate or to address economic grievances becomes especially important. Still, recent studies of 1950s Turkey and 1980s Zimbabwe find evidence that central governments responded to internal conflict precisely in the ways that my theory predicts.[70] Future research in the social sciences can help assess the generalizability of the theory I have outlined by testing whether it explains education reform elsewhere.

---

69. According to data from the Correlates of War Project, before 1945 the majority of civil wars lasted one or two years, less than 20 percent of wars lasted more than five years, only 8 percent lasted ten or more years, and except for a few notable cases including, as we saw, Argentina, most countries did not experience recurrent civil wars. By contrast, in the post-1945 period, less than one-fifth of civil wars have lasted one or two years, more than 40 percent have lasted more than five years, 25 percent have lasted ten or more years, and chronic civil wars have been a feature of politics in many African countries.

70. Bozçağa and Cansunar (2022); Liu (2024). For Zimbabwe, see also Foley (1982); Shizha and Kariwo (2011); Matereke (2012); Ndebele and Tshuma (2014).

CHAPTER SEVEN
INDOCTRINATION IN DEMOCRACIES

So far, I have illustrated the book's argument by discussing the emergence, expansion, and characteristics of primary education systems in various types of non-democracies. In this chapter I shift the focus to democracies and address two questions. First, are there examples of democracies where heightened fears of mass violence led the government to invest in education for indoctrination purposes? After spending most of the chapter answering this question in the affirmative, I then devote a section to understanding how common indoctrination is in democratic regimes, and how it compares to indoctrination in non-democracies.

An implication of chapter 6 is that nothing precludes the book's argument from explaining educational reform in democratic settings. By this I do not mean that all democracies will use education to indoctrinate. What I mean is that whether a government chooses to indoctrinate should not depend on whether it was elected democratically. As long as political elites fear the masses, believe that education can mold children into future obedient citizens, expect to be around long enough to secure the benefits of education, and have sufficient administrative and fiscal capacity, then they are likely to turn to mass education—conceived as indoctrination—as a means of promoting social order and political stability.

The idea that democratically elected politicians may expect to benefit from the long-term stability brought about by their education investments is perhaps not obvious. After all, these politicians could be ousted in the next election. Still, the reality is that in many democracies, even though in principle anyone can run for office, elected politicians come from a relatively small elite. Once in office they appoint bureaucrats who attended the same elite universities they did and enact policies that protect the political and economic power of elites.[1] When democracies have this bias in favor of elites, even though the specific individuals who hold office may change with a new election, elites *as a group* can expect to hold power for a long time. In those contexts, when violent protests demanding institutional change threaten to upend this balance of power between elites and the masses, the former may turn to education to strengthen the status quo by teaching the latter that good citizens respect the law and do not behave in violent ways.

I discuss examples of this dynamic in three democracies or partial democracies. The first example comes from the United States during the Early Republic, a period that today would not qualify as a democracy given the inability of women and non-white adults to vote, but that at the time was considerably more democratic than any country in Europe or Latin America.[2] The second example comes from England during the late 1860s, a period when mass violence led both to the expansion of voting rights for the working class and to the creation of a national primary education system. The third example comes from Peru during the first decade of the twenty-first century, a period marked by the return of democracy and the end of a twenty-year period of armed internal conflict between left-wing guerrilla groups and the Peruvian state. The choice of these three cases, separated by two centuries, is deliberate; it seeks to provide examples of the book's argument in democratic contexts across a wide time span.

After fleshing out how the book's argument maps onto these three cases, I take a step back to consider the broader question of whether, in general, democracies tend to indoctrinate less than autocracies. I answer this question with new data on the prevalence and characteristics of indoctrination efforts across education systems in more than 160 countries from 1945 to 2021. An examination of these data suggests that democracies and autocracies put similar amounts of effort into inculcating a specific set of political values through education systems. The main difference between

---

1. Carnes and Lupu (2023).
2. For example, while less than 2 percent of the population could vote in Chile during the 1860s, historians estimate that between 60 and 90 percent of adult white males were eligible to vote in the thirteen U.S. states by the end of the 1780s, with most states falling in the upper end of that range. See Ratcliffe (2013).

them lies in which specific values they emphasize and what is the notion of "good citizen" that they promote. As we saw in previous chapters, autocracies often seek to teach contentment with the status quo. Democracies, on the other hand, allow citizens to express discontent but *within the bounds* of what is considered appropriate behavior in a democracy. Their education systems focus on instilling respect for democratic norms and institutions, including the norm that discontent should be expressed not through violence but by voting in elections.

Moreover, while schools in democracies place more emphasis on developing critical thinking skills than those in autocracies, critical engagement with the core moral and political principles that are taught in school is rare even in democracies. From the United States during the Early Republic to Peru during the first decade of the twenty-first century, education systems in democratic contexts have often discouraged students from questioning the basic norms and institutions that schools teach them to respect.

REVISITING THE DEFINITION OF "INDOCTRINATION"

Before we examine whether democracies use education systems to indoctrinate children, it is worth reminding readers that throughout this book I define "indoctrination" the way the *Oxford American Dictionary* defines it, as "the process of teaching a person or group to accept a set of beliefs uncritically." The key word in this definition is "uncritically." Philosophers of education tend to agree that what defines indoctrination is not whether the beliefs that are taught are true or false. What defines it is that those beliefs are taught through a process that discourages or precludes critical thinking or *open-mindedness*—the willingness and ability to entertain the possibility that, under some circumstances, those beliefs could be false. For example, when schools teach students that democracy is the best form of government *without* simultaneously encouraging students to consider and assess the facts that critics of democracy stress, that constitutes indoctrination. Likewise, when teachers tell students that violence is never an acceptable way of expressing discontent, and they silence, ridicule, or punish students who articulate reasons for questioning this norm, that constitutes indoctrination. Usually, to discourage questioning, the teacher who indoctrinates will try to instill fear or a sense of shame for doubting these beliefs, and will attempt to create a deep emotional attachment to these beliefs such that questioning them would threaten the student's own understanding of who they are and how the world works.[3]

A common criticism of this definition of indoctrination, which conceptualizes the process of promoting critical thinking as its antithesis, is that promoting critical thinking also constitutes indoctrination—in liberal values and, especially, in the value of rational autonomy.[4] It is true that education institutions that promise to provide a liberal education tend to pride themselves in their efforts to promote critical inquiry. However, there are two problems with the argument that promoting critical thinking skills constitutes indoctrination. First, if this were true, then all forms of education would constitute indoctrination, making the term "indoctrination" meaningless. Second, and importantly, promoting critical thinking skills does not necessarily imply that individuals will in fact adhere to liberal values. While it is certainly possible for some so-called liberal education curricula to indoctrinate students in liberal values, a curriculum that truly promotes critical thinking is one that encourages students to question the core principles of liberalism, and makes it possible for students, as a result of this scrutiny, to *reject* these principles. The necessary pairing of liberalism and critical thinking runs into many counterexamples. Indeed, most people would be hard-pressed to dismiss Edmund Burke, Karl Marx, or Thomas Aquinas as lacking in critical thinking skills.

The type of indoctrination that this book focuses on is indoctrination in moral (secular or religious) and political beliefs that form the basis of an individual's moral character and political behavior. To be sure, education systems can indoctrinate children to believe a wide range of things. For example, a school could indoctrinate children in the idea that global warming is the by-product of human actions such as burning fossil fuels, *or* it could indoctrinate children in the idea that human beings are not responsible for long-term shifts in temperature and weather patterns. As important as this and many other subjects where indoctrination can occur are, my concern in this book is with indoctrination in a broader category of values and beliefs that shape how individuals behave in the public sphere and how they relate to existing institutions, rules, and authorities.

---

3. For a literature review and discussion of the definition of "indoctrination," see Callan and Arena (2009).

4. For example, Neundorf et al. (2024) argue that critical thinking constitutes a form of "democratic indoctrination."

Some may argue that a certain amount of indoctrination is needed to secure social order and the stability of states, including democratic ones. Whether this is indeed true is an important open question, and one that I hope social scientists and education scholars will study in the future. But whether a curriculum that promotes critical thinking skills constitutes a threat to the stability of states—in democracies or elsewhere—is beside the point. As in previous chapters, the question that I examine in the following pages does not concern the *consequences* of education or indoctrination, but rather the *motivations* for regulating and providing public primary education. Are democratically elected politicians interested in the education of young children at least partly because they view it as a useful policy tool to forge order and stability by molding children into law-abiding "good citizens"?

THE UNITED STATES DURING THE EARLY REPUBLIC

In his classic book on education in the United States during the Early Republic, Carl Kaestle argues that the Founding Fathers were concerned that a republican form of government in which the general will was represented, refined, and articulated by the best men would not be sustainable if the general population remained uneducated.[5] Following the American Revolution (1775–1783) through which the United States gained independence from Great Britain, the former revolutionaries faced the complex task of establishing and consolidating a new government. Although they had fought for individual liberty, political elites soon found themselves debating the importance of balancing liberty and order. The view that emerged as dominant saw "conformity as the price of liberty"[6] and popular education as one of the key policy tools to align the moral character of citizens with the goals of ensuring social order and the stability of the new republic.

Two rebellions intensified political elites' concern about social disorder and increased their interest in education as a long-term solution to this problem: Shays' Rebellion in Massachusetts (1786–1787) and the Whiskey Rebellion in Pennsylvania (1791–1794).[7] The first of these brought together struggling farmers and disgruntled former soldiers who had received little

---

5. Kaestle (1983).
6. Tyack (1966), p. 31.
7. Kaestle (1983); Koganzon (2012).

or no compensation for their service during the American Revolution and now faced high taxes and the threat of foreclosure. United by economic grievances and led by war veteran Daniel Shay, they protested against the taxes set by the Massachusetts state legislature and blocked county courts from ruling in favor of debt collectors. When state militia, instead of complying with the governor's order to quash the insurrection, sympathized with the protesters, the governor had to organize a private militia to defeat the rebels. Shays' Rebellion not only disrupted the state government of Massachusetts but also expanded to other parts of New England and led to a perception among elites that a stronger central government was needed in order to maintain order in the new nation. As George Washington wrote in a letter to David Humphrey while the latter tried to quash the expansion of Shays' Rebellion to Connecticut, the worry was that "commotions of this sort, like snow-balls, gather strength as they roll."[8]

Some elites attributed Shays' Rebellion and other incidents of violent protest against the government to protesters' selfishness; others, to their lack of reasoning capabilities. Whatever the explanation, support for popular education as an antidote for these behaviors grew, bolstered by the premise that education could enlighten the masses about the importance of protecting republican institutions. In the aftermath of Shays' Rebellion, in 1789 the Massachusetts legislature passed the first state law on common education. Other Northeastern states followed suit between the 1790s and 1820s.[9] Although there was some variation in the content of these state laws, they all called for the organization and public funding of "common schools," which were to teach a curriculum that was to some extent supervised by the state government.[10]

What was the goal of common schools during the Early Republic? Speaking to his classmates at Harvard University about the nature of society and politics just weeks after the onset of Shays' Rebellion in 1786, John Quincy Adams argued that "Education is one of the most important subjects that can engage the attention of mankind; a subject on which the welfare of States and Empires ... depend." According to Adams, "Civilization is to a State what Education is to an Individual," by which he meant that a state's success is determined by its level of civilization, which in turn rests on the

---

8. Washington (October 22, 1786).
9. Kaestle (1983).
10. Kaestle (1983); Paulsen, Scheve, and Stasavage (2022).

education of its inhabitants.[11] While Adams was firmly against a monarchical form of government, he did admire the education systems of European monarchies, whom he viewed as "the most civilized Nations" at that time.[12] For him and many of his contemporaries, European education systems became an object of admiration because of their ability to civilize the population and contribute to the long-term viability of the state.[13]

The idea that mass education could promote political stability by teaching future citizens to respect existing institutions was shared widely in elite circles. A year after Adams spoke about the benefits of education at Harvard, Shays' Rebellion now a few months behind, Thomas Jefferson wrote to James Madison reflecting on the rebellion and arguing that "the education of the common people" was a more effective strategy to preserve peace and order than repression. At the time, Jefferson was living in France and observed that there and in other European countries, the use of large armies "to crush insurrections" had not prevented the occurrence of violent rebellions—a sign, to him, of the inefficacy of repression to prevent disorder. In his words:

> Say finally whether peace is best preserved by giving energy to the government, or information to the people. This last is the most certain and the most legitimate engine of government. Educate and inform the whole mass of the people, enable them to see that it is their interest to preserve peace and order, and they will preserve it, and it requires no very high degree of education to convince them of this. They are the only sure reliance for the preservation of our liberty.[14]

All the influential educational thinkers of the Early Republic subscribed to the view that deficiencies of moral character were at the root of social disorder, crime, and poverty, and that correcting this character should be the main goal of public schooling.[15] A leader on education issues during the Early Republic and one of the signatories of the Declaration of Independence was Benjamin Rush, who in the midst of Shays' Rebellion warned that while the war against Britain was over, this was "far from being

---

11. Boonshoft (2015), p. 1.
12. Boonshoft (2015), p. 2.
13. Boonshoft (2015).
14. Jefferson (1787a, 1787b).
15. Kornfeld (1989), p. 159.

the case" for revolutions within the United States. "On the contrary," he argued in reference to internal uprisings, "nothing but the great drama is closed" and "it remains yet to establish and perfect our new forms of government." To do so, Rush advocated for a system of common schools to "conform" and "prepare the principles, morals, and manners of our citizens for these forms of government."[16] In an essay on education written in 1786 and addressed to the legislature and citizens of Pennsylvania, Rush argued that schools were essential for forming good citizens, by which he meant compliant ones. He believed that establishing schools where the authority of teachers was "absolute" would help form future obedient citizens:

> I am satisfied that the most useful citizens have been formed from those youth who have never known or felt their own wills till they were one and twenty years of age, and I have often thought that society owes a great deal of its order and happiness to the deficiencies of parental government being supplied by those habits of obedience and subordination which are contracted at schools.[17]

Another key proponent of the power of education to form law-abiding citizens was Noah Webster, who believed that "strict discipline" at home and in schools was "the best foundation of good order in political society."[18] Best known today for his contributions to the Merriam-Webster dictionary first published in 1828, Webster was already well known in the 1780s for the spelling, grammar, and reading compendium and textbooks he wrote for use in elementary schools. His textbooks included "moral tales carefully crafted for children," and his popular *American Spelling Book* "featured a 'Federal Catechism' from which children could memorize and recite the advantages of republican government."[19] Like Locke and other Enlightenment philosophers, Webster argued that the most effective way to secure order in the new republic was to target *children* through an education system designed to shape their moral values:

> Our legislators frame laws for the suppression of vice and immorality... And do laws and preaching effect a reformation of manners?

---

16. Kesler (1991), p. 102.
17. Rush (1786), *Thoughts upon the Mode of Education Proper in a Republic*, in Rudolph (1965), p. 16.
18. Webster (1790), *On the Education of Youth in America*, in Rudolph (1965), p. 58.
19. Kornfeld (1989), p. 162.

Experience would not give a very favorable answer to this inquiry. The reason is obvious: the attempts are directed to the wrong objects. Laws can only check the public effects of vicious principles but can never reach the principles themselves, and preaching is not very intelligible to people till they arrive at an age when their principles are rooted or their habits firmly established. An attempt to eradicate old habits is as absurd as to lop off the branches of a huge oak in order to root it out of a rich soil. The most that such clipping will effect is to prevent a further growth. The only practicable method to reform mankind is to begin with children, to banish, if possible, from their company every low-bred, drunken, immoral character.[20]

Inculcating support for a republican form of government among future citizens was a central goal of mass education during the Early Republic.[21] Rush argued that schools had to "convert men into republican machines";[22] teach students "that there can be no liberty but in a republic",[23] and "prepare our youth for the subordination of laws and thereby qualify them for becoming good citizens of the republic."[24] Webster's *American Spelling Book* edition of 1798 "told children of the advantage of republicanism and the defects of monarchy, aristocracy, and democracy."[25] Jefferson defended the prescription of textbooks to lay down "the principles which are to be taught" in schools, and to "guard against the dissemination of such principles among our youth" that could "poison" children with ideas contrary to a republican form of government. He argued that if "there is one branch in which we are the best judges," that is the form of government.[26]

Concerns about crime and social unrest were equally salient in the creation of a public school system during the Early Republic. Morality was emphasized "not as an end in itself but as the basis for civic security."[27] The

---

20. Webster (1790), *On the Education of Youth in America*, in Rudolph (1965), p. 63.
21. Tyack (1966) and Kesler (1991), among other historians, also use the term "indoctrination" to characterize the type of moral and civic education that Jefferson, Rush, Webster, and other leading educational thinkers of the Early Republic advocated for.
22. Rush (1786), *Thoughts upon the Mode of Education Proper in a Republic*, in Rudolph (1965), p. 17.
23. Rush (1786), *Thoughts upon the Mode of Education Proper in a Republic*, in Rudolph (1965), p. 15.
24. Rush (1786), *Thoughts upon the Mode of Education Proper in a Republic*, in Rudolph (1965), p. 16.
25. Tyack (1966), p. 36.
26. Jefferson, quoted in Tyack (1966), p. 40.
27. Hobson (1918), p. 14.

threat to the stability of the new republic that came from *within* was made "abundantly clear"[28] by Shays' Rebellion in the 1780s, the Whiskey Rebellion in the 1790s, and other episodes of mass violence. The arrival of new immigrants who were perceived to be selfish, more predisposed to crime, and "hard to govern," further exacerbated elite concerns about internal order.[29] Writing in 1786, for example, Benjamin Rush argued that "of the many criminals that have been executed within these seven years, four out of five of them have been foreigners." Instead of spending more on jails or restricting immigration, Rush preferred investing in public schools to educate immigrants and thus "prevent our morals, manners, and government from the infection of European vices."[30] All men who lack an education, he warned, "become savages or barbarians".[31]

> Fewer pillories and whipping posts and jails, with their usual expenses and taxes, will be necessary when our youth are properly educated ... I believe it could be proved that the expenses of confining, trying, and executing criminals amount every year, in most of the counties, to more money than would be sufficient to maintain all the schools that would be necessary in each county. The confessions of these criminals generally show us that their vices and punishments are the fatal consequences of the want of a proper education in early life.[32]

In addition to advocating for moral education to safeguard republican institutions and to prevent crime and social unrest, many proponents of a public school system during the Early Republic also supported the teaching of basic practical knowledge such as arithmetic and the principles of money. The reasons were both political and economic. Some, like Rush, held that stimulating the economy through education was a good political investment not only to grow the tax base and thus enlarge the wealth of the state, but also because commercial activity was "the best security against the influence of hereditary monopolies of land, and, therefore, the surest protection against aristocracy."[33]

---

28. Koganzon (2012), p. 416.
29. Hobson (1918), p. 10.
30. Rush (1786), *Thoughts upon the Mode of Education Proper in a Republic*, in Rudolph (1965), p. 23.
31. Rush (1786), *Thoughts upon the Mode of Education Proper in a Republic*, in Rudolph (1965), p. 4.
32. Rush (1786), *Thoughts upon the Mode of Education Proper in a Republic*, in Rudolph (1965), pp. 6–7.
33. Rush (1786), *Thoughts upon the Mode of Education Proper in a Republic*, in Rudolph (1965), p. 19.

A smaller minority of elites maintained that teaching practical knowledge would foster individual liberty and equal representation. A leading advocate of this liberal approach to mass education was the anti-Federalist Robert Coram. He argued that education should level the playing field between rural farmers and commercial and mercantile elites, and that schools should be public "1st. Because every citizen has an equal right to subsistence and ought to have an equal opportunity of acquiring knowledge."[34] Coram championed the view that public schools should impart knowledge to every child so "that they may be enabled to support themselves with becoming independency (sic.) when they shall arrive to years of maturity,"[35] and that schools "should also prevent people from falling into abject poverty."[36] He underscored that "an equal representation is absolutely necessary to the preservation of liberty. But there can never be an equal representation until there is an equal mode of education of all citizens."[37]

In this context of diverse possible goals, the vision of mass education that prevailed according to historians was one that placed order before liberty, submission and obedience before equal representation, and moral education before practical skills.[38] Most elites during the Early Republic shared Noah Webster's view that "the *virtues* of men are of more consequence to society than their *abilities*, and for this reason the *heart* should be cultivated with more assiduity than the *head*."[39] Indeed, when in 1797 the American Philosophical Society of Philadelphia organized an essay contest on the best system of public schooling for the United States, the cash award went to the essays written by Samuel Harrington Smith and Samuel Knox, both of whom "stressed the need for a homogeneous moral education to promote public good, rather than the individual development of the scholar."[40] For example, Smith's plan for public schooling proposed that children ages 5–10 years old should be instructed about "moral duties" and learn basic

---

34. Coram (1791), *A Plan for the General Establishment of Schools throughout the United States*, in Rudolph (1965), p. 138.
35. Coram (1791), *A Plan for the General Establishment of Schools throughout the United States*, in Rudolph (1965), p. 113.
36. Coram (1791), *A Plan for the General Establishment of Schools throughout the United States*, in Rudolph (1965), p. 120.
37. Coram (1791), *A Plan for the General Establishment of Schools throughout the United States*, in Rudolph (1965), pp. 135–136.
38. Rudolph (1965); Tyack (1966); Kornfeld (1989); Koganzon (2012).
39. Webster (1790), *On the Education of Youth in America*, in Rudolph (1965), p. 67. Emphasis in the original.
40. Kornfeld (1989), p. 160.

writing and arithmetic, leaving to later stages of education the teaching of "more correct knowledge of arithmetic" and practical skills for "agriculture and mechanics."[41]

Mass education in the Early Republic, then, took on a dual character. Although schools incorporated liberal elements designed to enable individuals to exercise their liberty and earn a decent living, they also embraced features modeled after the education systems of non-democratic Prussia and France. Specifically, American schoolchildren were free to think and question freely *as long as* their questioning was not aimed at the moral values or republican principles that schools sought to inculcate. The historian David Tyack calls this "the great paradox" of educational thought during the Early Republic; although they had fought for individual liberty during the American Revolution, in its aftermath political elites and intellectuals "argued for an indoctrination of citizens; an educational goal which clashed with the right to dissent and to make independent political and moral judgments."[42] This indoctrination in republican government, civic duties, and moral behavior was necessary, elites argued, to safeguard social order and protect the new republican form of government, which they considered a precondition for durable liberty.

The importance assigned to the goal of molding children into well-behaved future *citizens* is further evidence by the differential efforts that white elites made to provide education for free versus enslaved Black individuals. To the extent that white education reformers cared about the education of free Black children, it was because they understood that these children would eventually become citizens. For this reason, they created schools to instill in free Black children "values of respectability, order, deference, and industry." As in Prussia, France, or Chile, the "main thrust was moral education, and literacy was directed more to this purpose than to individual advancement." If this education resulted in upward mobility, it was accidental—the goal was to "elevate" free Black children *morally* so that they would "escape vice, criminal activity, and poverty." These efforts to school *free* Black children contrasted with the prohibitions that white elites put in place against schooling Black children of enslaved families. These

---

41. Smith (1797), *Remarks on Education*, in Rudolph (1965), p. 211.
42. Tyack (1966), p. 29.

children, according to elites, did not need to be taught how to exercise their political rights in the new republic because they simply had none.[43]

The tension between education and indoctrination goals that emerged in the Early Republic was a persistent one. During the Common School Movement of the late 1830s and 1840s, Horace Mann, arguably the main leader of this movement, insisted like Jefferson had done after Shays' Rebellion that children needed to be taught, above all, that voting, not violence, was the legitimate way to express discontent.[44] In his role as Secretary of the Massachusetts Board of Education, which he held from 1837 to 1848, Mann wrote *Annual Reports* where he reflected on the state of public elementary schooling, argued for its expansion, and made concrete proposals on how to accomplish this. It was in one of these reports where he coined the famous phrase that education should serve as "the great equalizer."[45] What is less known is that this report was in fact devoted to emphasizing the importance of providing a *moral* education to all future citizens as a means of eradicating violence. "Had the obligations of the future citizen been sedulously inculcated upon all the children of this Republic," Mann reasoned, "would the patriot have had to mourn over so many instances, where the voter, not being able to accomplish his purpose by voting, had proceeded to accomplish it by violence?"[46] Indeed, five decades after John Quincy Adams praised European education systems for their ability to civilize the population, Mann would similarly advocate for emulating Prussia's primary education system, arguing that just as schools in Prussia focused on indoctrinating children to respect the absolute monarch, so should schools in the United States focus on indoctrinating future citizens "for the support and perpetuation of republican institutions." According to Mann, the following "should be taught to all the children until they are fully understood":

---

43. Kaestle (1983), p. 39. Pervasive stereotypes about the inferiority of enslaved Black individuals also led many white elites to assume that these children could not be "civilized" through education. To some extent, these stereotypes also affected how *free* Black individuals were perceived, but in this case, Kaestle argues the schooling opportunities that Black communities funded for their children "helped to demonstrate to some whites the fallacy of the widespread belief in Negro inferiority" (Kaestle 1983, p. 38).
44. Massachusetts Board of Education, Horace Mann, National Education Association of the United States (1848), p. 12; Cubberley (1920).
45. Massachusetts Board of Education, Horace Mann, National Education Association of the United States (1848), p. 59.
46. Massachusetts Board of Education, Horace Mann, National Education Association of the United States (1848), p. 85.

> Especially, the duty of every citizen, in a government of laws, to appeal to the courts for redress, in all cases of alleged wrong, instead of undertaking to vindicate his own rights by his own arm; and ... the duty of changing laws and rulers by an appeal to the ballot, and not by rebellion.[47]

The tension in the character of education became the center of disputes among education philosophers and reformers during the Progressive Era. On one end of the debate were Edward Thorndike, Ellwood Cubberley, and other education reformers who believed that schools should primarily serve societal goals such as social order and industrialization, and that these goals could be best accomplished by increasing the centralization,[48] standardization, and bureaucratization of education systems.[49] On the other end of the debate was John Dewey, who criticized this approach as authoritarian and argued that schools could best prepare individuals for democratic life if the schools themselves were democratically organized. To Dewey, this meant that students should be able to influence what they learned—thus his emphasis on an individualized student-led curriculum—and that schools should strive to promote critical thinking, discussion, consultation, persuasion, and debate.[50] The resilience of the traditional approach over Dewey's progressive educational ideas is captured by Ellen Condliffe Lagemann, who began her 1988 Presidential Address to the History of Education Society as follows:

> I have often argued to students, only in part to be perverse, that one cannot understand the history of education in the United States during the twentieth century unless one realizes that Edward L. Thorndike won and John Dewey lost. The statement is too simple, of course, but nevertheless more true than untrue and useful ... If Dewey has

---

47. Massachusetts Board of Education, Horace Mann, National Education Association of the United States (1848), p. 12.
48. While education in the United States has a relatively decentralized governance structure in which most education policies are made at the school district or state levels, before the Progressive Era education was even more decentralized than today. In the cities, each ward could choose its own teachers. Citywide school boards charged with teacher recruitment across wards and district-level educational bureaucracies and authorities such as the Superintendent of Schools were created during the Progressive Era, and it was during this time, too, that states began to take a more active role in regulating the curriculum and teacher certification requirements. See Tyack (1974).
49. Levin (1991).
50. Dewey (1916).

been revered among some educators and his thought has had influence across a greater range of scholarly domains ... Thorndike's thought has been more influential within education. It helped to shape public school practice as well as scholarship about education.[51]

The duality in the goals and characteristics of public schooling remains visible to this day. It is an obvious feature—obvious at least to anyone who has completed part of their education in another country—that schools in the United States tend to have a relatively participatory classroom environment. Teachers encourage student participation by asking questions to check student understanding, having students work in small groups to work out a joint answer to a question, or setting up student debates. This participatory culture, however, coexists with regular rituals that seek to inculcate a specific set of political values and principles among children, such as the notion that voting is the most important duty of citizens, or that protest activities should always be peaceful. An example of a widespread ritual used to inculcate political principles is the daily recitation of the Pledge of Allegiance, which is required in forty-seven states. Hand on their heart, children as young as five years old pledge allegiance to "the flag of the United States and to the Republic for which it stands" even before they know how to spell their own name—and certainly well before they know what a republic is.

The education systems that emerged during the Early Republic began a long tradition in U.S. history in which public elementary schooling, in addition to teaching reading, writing, and arithmetic, assumed the crucial function of providing a moral and civic education to future citizens, teaching them about their political duties, stressing the importance of voting, and delegitimizing the use of violence to make demands. That function emerged, the historian Carl Kaestle and many others have argued, out of the Founding Fathers' fear for their own life, property, and the survival of the institutions that protected their elite status.

ENGLAND'S ELEMENTARY EDUCATION ACT OF 1870

As we saw in previous chapters, England was a latecomer to the transformation of primary education systems in Europe. Chapter 6 traced England's educational backwardness to its relative political stability and to the fact

---

51. Levin (1991), p. 71.

that the most disruptive episodes of mass violence—the English civil war, the Glorious Revolution, and the events leading up to the Reform Act of 1832—all *preceded* the diffusion among English elites of the idea that educating the lower classes could help promote social order and political stability. Until the mid-nineteenth century, English elites, unlike elites in continental Europe, tended to view mass education as a potentially destabilizing force. Following the Reform Act of 1832, political stability returned to England until the late 1860s. During this time, elementary education expanded through the action of the Church, and school enrollment remained voluntary. The combination of low parental demand for education in most parts of the country and the Church's practice of establishing schools in places with high parental demand resulted in an education system with limited reach. In the absence of mass mobilization against existing political institutions, national elites deemed this system good enough.

England began to catch up with other European countries in 1870 with the passage of the Elementary Education Act, also known as the Forster Act. This was England's first national primary education law, and as we saw in chapter 5, it trailed all national education laws in continental Europe. For the first time, the government set out to create a national primary education system and to ensure universal access to primary schooling. To accomplish this, the Act allowed Church-run schools to continue operating but supplemented these schools with a new system of public primary schools built and managed by locally elected school boards. The Forster Act charged these local boards with establishing and maintaining enough public schools to accommodate all children between the ages of 5 and 13 who otherwise lacked access to primary education. It also stipulated that these schools be non-denominational. If a board failed to ensure universal access, the Education Department could dissolve it and set up a new board. With this new system in place, primary school enrollment rates expanded rapidly after 1870, and in less than two decades England's primary education provision finally caught up with the rest of Europe.[52]

What led to the passage of the landmark Forster Act of 1870? As the book's argument predicts, the central government's interest in actively regulating and promoting primary education emerged in the late 1860s, when a new wave of social unrest led members of parliament to question the efficacy of delegating the education of children to the Church and voluntary associa-

---

52. See figure 2.2 in chapter 2.

tions. To be sure, English elites had sought for decades to frustrate the activism of working-class members and unions in industrializing areas, but strikes and mass demonstrations in 1866 in London's Hyde Park, Manchester, Leeds, and other parts of England created an unusual sense of alarm regarding the working class's "dogged determination that leads to violence,"[53] with *The Times* and other newspapers warning of revolution, moral degradation, and social danger.[54]

Educational ideas in England had started to change in the mid-nineteenth century as popular writers used their pens and personal connections to politicians to promote a view of mass schooling as a potential contributor to, rather than as a deterrent of, social and political stability.[55] Charles Dickens, Elizabeth Gaskell, Charles Kingsley, and Benjamin Disraeli (a novelist before he became a politician) were among those most influential to write that educating the poor could teach them to make better choices, thus restraining labor radicalism and supporting social stability. Disraeli articulated this view in his famous novel *Sybil*, published in 1845, where he depicted the difficult living conditions of the working class: "It is that increased knowledge of themselves that teaches the educated their social duties."[56] During the 1850s, Dickens campaigned to extend access to education to the working class using the argument—novel for England at the time—that "the existence of a large uneducated class was a physical danger to society." He also lectured actively to raise funds for education and wrote articles for *The Examiner*, *The Daily News*, and *Household Words*, where he reminded the public and his upper-class friends of the relationship between crime and ignorance.[57] But arguably the most influential intellectual in reshaping educational ideas in England was Matthew Arnold, whose efforts have earned him comparisons to Victor Cousin in France, Domingo F. Sarmiento in Argentina, and Horace Mann in the United States.[58] In addition to his work as a poet and literary critic, Arnold served as a school inspector from 1851

---

53. Snell-Feikema (2005), p. 33.
54. Snell-Feikema (2005).
55. Martin's (2023) analysis of how education was discussed in more than 500 fiction books authored by English writers between 1720 and 1920 suggests that between 1840 and 1860, there was a marked increase in the ratio of references associating education with societal and state goals relative to individualistic goals.
56. Martin (2023), p. 121.
57. Collins (1955), p. 126.
58. Rapple (1989).

to 1886.⁵⁹ In 1859, he convinced the government to send him to France, the Netherlands, and Switzerland to learn about the primary school systems of continental European countries, later extending his study to Germany.⁶⁰ Arnold's interest in education stemmed from his belief that the working and middle classes were dangerously obsessed with their own economic well-being and "fortune making."⁶¹ He believed that, to prevent anarchy, it was imperative for people to care about the consequences of their actions for others and for society,⁶² and argued that a state-regulated primary education system was the best way to inculcate this.⁶³

While the diffusion of educational ideas similar to those current in continental Europe—conceptualizing public primary education as a useful tool to promote social order—encountered a receptive audience among some politicians, until the late 1860s there was not enough support within parliament to create a national primary education system regulated by the state. Many members of parliament considered the existing framework of educational provision through the Church good enough. The Newcastle Report of 1861 offered validation; formed in 1859, the Newcastle Commission was tasked with investigating and reporting on the current state of "popular education" in England. Its final report, published in 1861, presented statistics—accepted at the time but questioned a few years later—that claimed that, of 2,655,767 children in England and Wales, only 120,305 had no instruction. The Report also highlighted the "rapid progress of elementary education in this country since the beginning of the century,"⁶⁴ and concluded based on these enrollment statistics that "the proportion of children receiving instruction to the whole population is, in our opinion, nearly as high as can be reasonably expected."⁶⁵

The mass demonstrations of 1866 produced a dramatic change in the attitudes of national politicians toward mass education. In early 1866, the prevailing diagnosis within the government—supported by the Newcastle Report—was that the system of government-subsidized Church schools and voluntary attendance had reached a large majority of children.⁶⁶ By 1868,

---

59. Arnold (1908).
60. Rapple (1989).
61. Brunell (1940), p. 4.
62. Arnold (1883).
63. Brunell (1940); Martin (2023).
64. Great Britain, Education Commission (1861), p. 294.
65. Great Britain, Education Commission (1861), p. 293.
66. Roper (1975), p. 183.

however, the dominant view affirmed that the existing system had resulted in an inadequate supply of elementary schools and insufficient school attendance, both of which countered the interests of the state.[67] An October 1866 report on the state of elementary education in Manchester helped cement the new view that many children, especially those of the poorer classes, did not receive any instruction, and that this was the cause for the unrest in Manchester and other parts of England earlier that year.[68]

Parliament's main response to the problem of social disorder that emerged in 1866 took the form of electoral and educational reform. In the short term, it sought to pacify the working class by extending voting rights through the Second Electoral Reform Act. Passed in August 1867 and implemented gradually over the next two years, the reform increased the franchise from 8.5 percent to 20 percent of the adult population.[69] One of the main architects of the reform, Benjamin Disraeli, who by then was the Conservative leader of the House of Commons, defended the reform by calling attention to "the working-class question," predicting that, "otherwise," if the government failed to extend the franchise, he saw "anarchy ahead."[70] At the same time, other members of parliament argued that extending the franchise without also reserving for government a central role in educating the poor and the working class would threaten the state's survival.

While Conservatives in parliament had historically sided with the Church's view that the operation of primary schools should be left to religious actors, by the late 1860s several prominent Conservatives joined Liberal politicians to support greater state intervention in primary education. Liberals argued that the lack of education among the lower classes was a product of the low supply of schooling and "the indifference, the selfishness, or avarice"[71] of parents. They worried that the existence of a large group of uneducated children constituted "the great social and political danger of the country."[72] Conservatives, too, spoke of "the necessity of education." They shared in the view that "there is a vast amount of educational deficiency in this country, and that although vast efforts have been made ... by voluntary associations and religious bodies to meet educational deficiencies, yet those

---

67. Roper (1975), p. 203.
68. Roper (1975), pp. 186–8.
69. I calculated this using the Varieties of Democracy Dataset.
70. Snell-Feikema (2005), p. 34.
71. Henry Fawcett, U.K. Parliament, HC Deb, 17 February 1870, vol. 199, cc438–98.
72. Earl de Grey and Ripon, U.K. Parliament, HL Deb, 25 July 1870, vol. 203, cc821–65.

efforts failed to reach a large number of our youthful population."[73] They argued that expanding mass education, especially moral education, was necessary to convert the "hearts of the disobedient to the wisdom of the just."[74]

One of the fiercest proponents of education reform was Robert Lowe, who in 1867 had strongly opposed electoral reform. Immediately after the passage of the Second Reform Act, Lowe called for the urgent creation of a national education system, whose function would be to teach the newly-enfranchised "ignorant barbarians"[75] of the working classes to respect existing institutions and thus ensure "the peace of the country."[76] The creation of such a system, he said, was "the first and highest of political necessities."[77] Speaking before the House of Commons soon after it approved the Reform Act of 1867, Lowe told members of parliament: "The time has arrived when it is our duty to vindicate for the state its real function" in education matters, because the state, he claimed, has "a vital interest in the education of every one of its members." Lowe argued that the existence of a sector of the population that was not reached by education institutions presented a danger to the state, and that reversing this situation was "a question of self-preservation—it is a question of our existence, even of the existence of our Constitution."[78] "From the moment that you can entrust the masses with power," said Lowe, "their education becomes an absolute necessity."[79]

In the aftermath of the 1866 demonstrations, then, both Liberal and Conservative politicians warned of the need to quickly build a national education system controlled by the state, and introduced education bills to this effect. The bill that eventually became law in 1870 was drafted in October 1867 by the Liberal William Forster, just two months after the passage of the Second Electoral Reform Act. The proposal, as described by Forster, created "a complete national system of education," making local educational authorities accountable to the central government for elementary education provision. It also introduced the principle of compulsory education because

---

73. Duke of Marlborough, U.K. Parliament, HL Deb, 25 July 1870, vol. 203, cc821–65.
74. The Earl of Shaftesbury, U.K. Parliament, HL Deb, 25 July 1870, vol. 203, cc821–65.
75. Marcham (1973), p. 186.
76. Wright (2012), p. 23. See also Hurt (1979).
77. Marcham (1973), p. 186.
78. Roper (1975), p. 197.
79. Sylvester (1974), p. 16.

"parents," he claimed, "neglect the education of their children."[80] Forster insisted to parliament that it "must not delay" in approving his bill. He argued that "upon the speedy provision of elementary education depends our industrial prosperity," "our national power," and crucially, since "Parliament has lately decided that England shall in future be governed by popular government," "the good, the safe working of our constitutional system." Seeking the support of members of parliament "who are swayed not so much by these general considerations," Forster emphasized that education "is a safeguard against calamity"; that "ignorance is weakness" which in turn "often leads to vice," leading "child after child—boys or girls—growing up to probable crime." He closed by asking, "Dare we then take on ourselves the responsibility of allowing this ignorance and this weakness to continue one year longer than we can help?"[81]

After the Forster Act of 1870, the organization of schools, the pedagogical methods, and the content of the curriculum and textbooks used in England all focused on advancing the shared interest of elites in "developing controllable subjects who would accept their place, rather than autonomous individuals who could think for themselves."[82] The emphasis on moral education, on "socializing the rising generation, and teaching the values that would form responsible citizens," was reflected in schools' insistence on discipline and good habits.[83] The guidelines that the Education Department distributed among schools "focused on moral training through the 'ordinary management of the school,'" an important aspect of which was a system of rewards and punishments to mold behavior.[84] The drill, a teaching method characterized by systematic repetition, was touted for its potential benefits in inculcating "habits of obedience, promptness, self-control, and silence."[85] Religious instruction entered the curriculum in large part to support the goal of shaping the moral character of children. The textbooks used to teach children how to read were infused with language that promoted patriotism; by stressing "a shared cultural heritage," Susannah Wright argues, "pupils were encouraged to love king and country, and

---

80. The 1870 law did not establish compulsory schooling for all children, but it enabled local school boards to establish compulsory schooling for children of the district governed by the board.
81. William E. Forster, U.K. Parliament, HC Deb, 17 February 1870, vol. 199, cc438–98.
82. Wright (2012), p. 23–4.
83. Wright (2012), p. 21.
84. Wright (2012), p. 25.
85. Wright (2012), p. 26.

to accept their place in the social hierarchy, and class or gender roles."[86] One of the most popular textbooks, *The Citizen Reader*, included a preface from William Forster that highlighted that "at a time when we have just added millions to the citizens who have the right of electing representatives," it was imperative "to instruct them in the duties of citizenship."[87] The same textbook, in a chapter titled "Education," taught children that the ultimate goal of schooling was to instill values of "cheerful obedience to duty, of consideration and respect for others, and of honor and truthfulness in word and act." These values, articulated by the Board of Education, were displayed in many schools and classrooms, and children were taught that learning them was "indeed more important than even reading and writing."[88]

In sum, throughout much of the nineteenth century, the combination of England's political stability and unique ideas about education implied that the national government did not see much reason to invest in educating the lower classes. As a result, England lagged behind other European countries in the provision of primary education. Intellectual elites began to embrace the view of education as a policy tool to promote social order around the middle of the nineteenth century, but this was insufficient to bring about education reform. The disruption to England's political stability in the late 1860s and national elites' heightened fear of the masses in the context of the 1866 demonstrations and the 1867 extension of the franchise were fundamental in forging a widespread coalition of support for proposals to create a national primary education system. These events led liberal and conservative politicians to update their beliefs surrounding mass education and created a sense of urgency about the need to instruct all working-class children in moral values that would prevent social revolution. This shared sense of urgency in a context of fragile relations between elites and the masses played a key role in explaining the Education Act of 1870 and how England caught up with its European neighbors.

PERU IN THE TWENTY-FIRST CENTURY

Peru in the early 2000s provides a recent example of a democratic government that advanced education reform in the aftermath of a period of violent internal conflict in order to prevent future conflict. Between 1980 and

---

86. Wright (2012), p. 27. See also Heathorn (1995).
87. Arnold-Forster (1887), p. i.
88. Arnold-Forster (1887), p. 180.

2000, Peru was immersed in a prolonged armed conflict between the state and the communist guerrilla group *Sendero Luminoso* (Shining Path), officially known as Communist Party of Peru (PCP-SL). PCP-SL was particularly embedded in rural areas and among peasant and indigenous communities where the state's presence ranged from weak to absent. Led by a former professor of philosophy, Abimael Guzmán, PCP-SL waged what it called a "people's war" to overthrow the government in Lima and institute a dictatorship of the proletariat. The government's primary response during the 1980s and 1990s focused on repression: it increased military spending, enlarged the military, created a unified National Police, and made considerable efforts to bolster its surveillance capacity. The capture of Guzmán in 1992 and of his successor, Oscar Ramírez, in 1999, led to the end of the conflict in 2000. That same year, President Alberto Fujimori fled to Japan facing accusations of electoral fraud, corruption, and human rights violations, and democratic elections were reinstated. In 2001, a transitional government established the Truth and Reconciliation Commission (*Comisión de la Verdad y Reconciliación* or CVR) to investigate the causes of the armed conflict and the extent of human rights violations from 1980 to 2000, and to recommend policies to compensate victims and institutional reforms to prevent future conflict. In line with the book's argument, one of the CVR's main recommendations focused on education reform.

The CVR's final report claimed that the state's "neglect of public education during a conflict that had important ideological and symbolic components"[89] had enabled guerrilla groups to recruit supporters by using schools and universities to spread its subversive ideology, "reach the youth," and "form future cadres."[90] The commission argued that the state needed to regain control over education and use schools to promote values of peace, respect for the state's authority, and respect for human rights and the lives of others. The Catholic Church agreed with the CVR on the importance of strengthening the moral education and disciplining function of schools.[91] The government's main educational efforts during the post-conflict period, the CVR argued, were to prioritize the rural areas that formed the bastion of PCP-SL to "prevent the reappearance of violence."[92]

---

89. Comisión de la Verdad y Reconciliación (2003), tome VIII, part 3, p. 339.
90. Comisión de la Verdad y Reconciliación (2003), tome VIII, part 3, p. 561.
91. Instituto de Democracia y Derechos Humanos de la Pontificia Universidad Católica del Perú (2007).
92. Comisión de la Verdad y Reconciliación (2003), tome IX, part 4, p. 133.

The chapter of the CVR's final report devoted to the links between PCP-SL and teachers is particularly telling of how national elites conceived the role of education in post-conflict Peru. In it, the CVR argues that mass education enables the state to be present throughout the entire territory. It further argues that, as paid employees of the state, teachers have the duty to "promote the interests of *the state and hegemonic sectors*" of society,[93] leaving no room for a discussion of whether the existing balance of power between elites and the popular classes should be reconsidered.

Following on the recommendations of the CVR report, soon after the end of the conflict the new democratic government quickly began to implement two core education reforms: first, it expanded the reach of the public education system, and second, it reformed the school curriculum. The expansion of schooling was facilitated by a 2003 Executive decree which declared an Educational Emergency, giving the National Ministry of Education the power to bypass municipal and regional authorities in order to expand schooling. Moreover, similar to the geographic patterns observed in France during the 1830s or Chile during the 1860s, an analysis of Peruvian education statistics conducted by Hillel Soifer and Everett Vieira shows that school enrollment rates in post-conflict Peru increased most in provinces that had posed the greatest threat to the central government between 1980 and 2000.[94] The increase in enrollment resulted both from the central government's effort to construct new schools and improve existing ones, and from its efforts to encourage school enrollment and attendance: In 2005, with the help of a World Bank loan, the government introduced a conditional cash transfer program that gave low-income families a monthly cash subsidy as long as their children attended school. Revealingly, the criteria used to distribute cash subsidies prioritized poor families in municipalities that had experienced the highest levels of violence during the years of armed conflict.[95]

The second component of the government's educational intervention was a reform of the national curriculum to enhance moral and civic education. In a document published in 2001 outlining the Ministry of Education's vision for the next five years, the Ministry "assumed the responsibility to educate for democracy and citizenship," and defined good citizenship as the

---

93. Comisión de la Verdad y Reconciliación (2003), tome III, Chapter 3, p. 560. Emphasis mine.
94. Soifer and Vieira (2019), pp. 109–131.
95. Perova and Vakis (2009).

ability to harmonize one's personal life with the broader well-being of the country.[96] Subsequently, the declaration of an Educational Emergency in 2003 led Congress to pass a new General Law of Education which explicitly declared the goals of education to "forge a culture of peace" and to form future citizens. A crucial article of this law, article 6, introduced mandatory "Ethics and Civics Education" in *all* education institutions—public and private—to teach students to fulfill their duties, know the Constitution, know their rights, and exercise their responsibilities and rights as citizens.[97] While the law also listed other educational goals such as equity, inclusion, democracy, creativity, and the promotion of an environmental conscience, the cultivation of ethical values and behaviors retained the top spot on the list of educational goals, reflecting the government's determination to "strengthen individuals' moral conscience" and make it feasible to have a society characterized by "the permanent exercise of citizen responsibilities."[98]

Following the CVR report's recommendations and the curriculum requirements of the 2003 General Law of Education, in 2005 the Ministry of Education established a new mandatory curriculum for all pre-primary, primary, and secondary schools.[99] The curriculum included two new subjects explicitly focused on forming good citizens: Social Person, covering history, geography, and citizenship education; and Tutoring and Educational Guidance, conceived as a weekly space for the teacher to lead conversations with students about individual choices, social development, community service, cultural values, school discipline, etc., with the ultimate goal of teaching students "the importance of basic norms of coexistence."[100]

A look at the textbooks distributed by the Ministry of Education for the new Social Person course provides insight into the Ministry's notion of "good citizen." The textbook is split into three parts corresponding to history, geography, and citizenship, with the part on citizenship further divided into three themes: peace-building, the State, and local government. In a nutshell, a good citizen is one who behaves peacefully and respects existing laws. The section on peace-building promotes a vision of society in which conflicts are resolved not through violence but through dialogue and the

---

96. Frisancho (2009), p. 13.
97. Perú (July 28, 2003), *Ley General de Educación (Ley Nro. 28044)*, Art. 6.
98. Perú (July 28, 2003), *Ley General de Educación (Ley Nro. 28044)*, Art. 8. See also Perú, Ministerio de Educación (2005a, 2005b).
99. Perú, Ministerio de Educación (2005a).
100. Perú, Ministerio de Educación (2005a), p. 21.

search for common ground and consensus. War is characterized as an entirely negative phenomenon caused by "greed or the excessive desire to possess more than one has" and by the opportunism of those who stand to gain economically from war at the expense of the most vulnerable members of society—poor and marginalized communities, women, and children.[101] The section on the State urges students to help construct "a culture of respect for the law and for other people's rights, a culture grounded in values, social peace," and encourages them to "comply with norms of coexistence to acquire habits of punctuality, honesty, and courtesy"—all with the overarching goal of developing "respect for the law and for authority."[102]

In addition to reforming the curriculum and introducing a standalone subject to form nonviolent and obedient future citizens, in 2005 the Ministry published a set of curriculum guidelines on how to teach ethics in schools. The guidelines stress that promoting ethical behavior should be a goal that cuts across all subjects and educational practices. In the introduction to the guidelines, a brief message from the Minister of Education Javier Sota Nadal tells readers that, given the "situation of violence" that affected the country in recent years, ethics education and the teaching of moral values is an "urgent priority." This education, continues the Minister, "cannot be delayed" and "constitutes the only effective defense against immorality and Violence."[103] The guidelines also state that while the urgency to teach moral values and form responsible future citizens stems from the need to prevent future violence, these teachings also provide an opportunity to build a more democratic society.[104] While the guidelines list numerous values that schools ought to teach, they can be summarized into three groups: respect for other people's life and rights, sense of duty and responsibility, and concern for the well-being of others and of society as a whole. If individuals develop these values, the guidelines argue, peace and democracy will prevail.

Many of the methods proposed in the Ministry's guidelines for how to teach ethics and moral education resemble methods proposed by education reformers since the nineteenth century. According to these guidelines, all educational practices, in particular disciplining practices, must "consider

---

101. Barrantes, Luna, and Peña (2009), p. 26.
102. Barrantes, Luna, and Peña (2009), p. 27.
103. Perú, Ministerio de Educación (2005b), p. 5.
104. Perú, Ministerio de Educación (2005b), p. 13.

that the goal is to shape citizens."[105] The guidelines state that using rewards and punishments is an effective way of inducing primary school children to accept and obey existing rules and norms. They also indicate—rightly, as we saw in previous chapters—that inducing moral feelings of shame, guilt, remorse, and kindness is a centuries-old method of molding the values and behavior of children.

A notable point of departure in the educational approach of the Peruvian government following the internal armed conflict is that it officially promoted a more participatory classroom environment than the traditional approach to moral and civic education inherited from the nineteenth century. According to the curriculum introduced in 2005, immersing students in a democratic educational culture was crucial to prepare them to be active citizens in a democratic society. Learning to deliberate, articulate one's point of view, and find common ground with others, the government argued, were important citizenship skills.

This participatory educational approach did not have a chance to thrive in the Peruvian context of the 2000s. A reflection on the evolution of the education system conducted by Susana Frisancho, a moral education expert who contributed to shape curriculum policy during the post-conflict period, and Félix Reátegui, who coordinated the CVR's final report, concludes that despite the inclusion of more participatory elements in the 2005 curriculum, the "traditional approach to education (based on rote learning, routine and obedience)" remained "pervasive" in Peru following the internal armed conflict.[106] Their study highlights three reasons behind the persistence of traditional methods. The first is the existence of a deeply engrained authoritarian school culture and notion of social order within schools, characterized by "the inculcation of obedience to rules and norms."[107] In this context, teachers tended "to give orders that students have to obey without questioning and mostly stick to school rules without analyzing them critically."[108] The second reason for the lack of change in pedagogical practices points to the Ministry of Education. While the Ministry established a new curriculum, it never trained teachers on how to implement it or how to use the new textbooks and other resources it distributed. Predictably, teachers resorted to teaching moral and civics education and other subjects

---

105. Perú, Ministerio de Educación (2005b), p. 33.
106. Frisancho and Reátegui (2009), p. 430.
107. Frisancho and Reátegui (2009), p. 434.
108. Frisancho and Reátegui (2009), p. 434.

using the traditional authoritarian approach they knew best. Finally, the Peruvian government further disincentivized deliberation and critical thinking by passing legislation that criminalized justifications of former rebels' activities. Teachers feared being accused of this crime, punishable with life in prison, and understandably refrained from encouraging critical thinking or classroom debate on controversial topics.

The persistence of an authoritarian school ethos in post-conflict Peru was especially salient in the impoverished departments of Ayacucho and Apurímac, which had served as the PCP-SL's regional strongholds. Interviews with primary school teachers conducted by a team of education experts in both departments reveal that the notion of citizenship that prevailed among them was one that emphasized the role of citizens in preserving order.[109] For example, teachers placed much more importance on instilling compliance with duties than on building students' capabilities to exercise their rights. A good student, according to teachers, is one who respects others, complies with duties, coexists with others in harmony and peace, and is committed to the community. What's more, discipline was considered an "overarching value" in the quest to guarantee compliance with duty,[110] as exemplified by the school rules displayed in a school in Ayacucho:

> We will arrive early to school
> We will properly wear our school uniform
> We will raise our hands to speak
> We will participate in the scheduled activities
> We will take care of school furniture
> We will maintain order and discipline at all times
> We will be prepared for the evaluations
> We will put our values into practice
> We will justify our absence
> We will accept sanctions in case of non-compliance
> We will fulfill our tasks[111]

Classroom observations in post-conflict Ayacucho and Apurímac have found that, of all the activities that teachers engaged in during class, behavior management to maintain order and discipline was the one to which they

---

109. Barrantes, Luna, and Peña (2009), p. 40.
110. Barrantes, Luna, and Peña (2009), p. 42.
111. Barrantes, Luna, and Peña (2009), p. 74.

devoted the most time. The strategies they used ranged from reminding students about school rules to threatening, humiliating, and shouting at students.[112] To maintain order, teachers also relied on a system of student "police officers" and "brigadiers." These were students of exemplary conduct who were tasked, respectively, with enforcing order in their classroom and in the entire school. For example, brigadiers could sanction students who arrived late or were not properly dressed, while police officers could do the same with students who damaged their desk or spoke without the teacher's permission.[113]

That a government in the twenty-first century would place so much emphasis on the moral and civic education of future citizens is to some extent startling yet also indicative of the resilience of these educational goals over time.

The three cases discussed so far are not meant to suggest that *all* democracies use education to indoctrinate future citizens. What they suggest is that democratically elected politicians who face heightened concerns about the problem of mass violence *can* attempt to prevent future violence by using schools to form citizens who respect existing rules and institutions. In other words, the argument developed earlier in the book need not apply only to non-democracies.

HOW ARE THE EDUCATION SYSTEMS OF DEMOCRACIES DIFFERENT?

How common is indoctrination in democratic regimes? Is it more or less prevalent than in autocratic ones? If some indoctrination does occur in democracies, are there nonetheless important differences between the content of education in democracies versus autocracies? To answer these questions we need information about the content of education across a large number of democratic and autocratic regimes and over time. Until recently, this information had not been collected; cross-national time-series datasets on education focused on student enrollment, number of teachers, total education spending, and other features of education systems that tell us little about their goals or the prevalence of indoctrination in schools. The Varieties of Political Indoctrination in Education and the Media (V-Indoc)

---

112. Barrantes, Luna, and Peña (2009), pp. 75–88.
113. Barrantes, Luna, and Peña (2009), pp. 54–56.

dataset, which I assembled with a larger team led by Anja Neundorf, contributes to fill this void. V-Indoc includes many variables that allow us to compare the content of education across more than 160 countries from 1945 to 2021. In this chapter I focus on a small subset of variables that illustrate the broader patterns that emerge from the dataset.[114] To understand how education systems compare across political regimes, I combined V-Indoc with the Varieties of Democracy dataset, which classifies regimes into four groups: closed autocracies, electoral autocracies, electoral democracies, and liberal democracies.

Before discussing the patterns that emerge from this descriptive analysis, it is worth saying a little more about how we constructed and validated V-Indoc. First, we administered a common questionnaire among education experts in each country. Expert surveys are a common method for gathering cross-national data, but experts are not always reliable sources. In particular, because the term "indoctrination" today carries a negative connotation, we may worry that experts' assessments regarding its prevalence will be clouded by their own judgment of the merits of a particular regime. To increase the reliability of V-Indoc, we identified and contacted 24,000 education scholars using membership lists of history of education associations, lists of faculty affiliated with Schools of Education, etc. Of the scholars we contacted, 1,400 expressed an interest in contributing to our data collection effort. We then vetted candidates to assess their country-specific education expertise, which narrowed the pool to 760 experts among whom we administered the questionnaire—an average of five experts per country. Next, to further validate the reliability of the responses, we contrasted experts' answers to those from other datasets that gathered similar data but relied on objective sources of information such as education laws and school textbooks. While these alternative datasets covered fewer countries and years, the high degree of convergence in responses between them and V-Indoc gives us confidence about the reliability of experts' responses.[115] Finally, whatever responses remained biased by experts' political opinions would likely be biased in favor of democracy, leading experts to underreport the degree of indoctrination that occurs in this type of re-

---

[114]. For a deeper descriptive analysis that takes advantage of a larger set of variables, see Paglayan, Neundorf, and Kim (2023). That study also uses generalized synthetic control methods to estimate the effect of democratization on the characteristics of education systems.

[115]. See Neundorf et al. (2024) for additional information about these validation exercises.

gime, and leading us to overestimate the degree to which democracies and autocracies differ in their indoctrination efforts.[116]

Three main patterns emerge from an analysis of the data. First, democracies and autocracies put a similar amount of effort into inculcating a specific set of moral and political values through schools.[117] Second, democracies and autocracies differ markedly on the type of social and political order these efforts seek to consolidate. While education systems in democracies make considerable efforts to inculcate adherence to democratic norms and respect for democratic institutions, those in autocracies tend to prioritize other values and societal models. Third, schools in democratic regimes tend to encourage more critical thinking than those in autocracies. Still, in most democracies, as in most autocracies, efforts to inculcate specific moral and political values have tended to exceed efforts to promote critical thinking.

Let's dive into the first pattern and assess the efforts made by primary education systems across the globe to teach moral and political values. As part of V-Indoc, we asked education experts to indicate whether the primary school curriculum includes a mandatory subject that focuses on teaching political values. We directed experts to include subjects such as ethics and civics, or moral and civic education, but not history. The upper left panel of figure 7.1 shows the percentage of democracies and autocracies where the answer was "yes." A separate question asked whether the history curriculum promotes a specific set of beliefs that are used to justify a particular social and political order. We told experts to answer "yes" if the history curriculum frequently refers to a particular societal model—such as socialism, democracy, fascism, etc.—and clearly interprets that model as superior to alternatives. The percentage of democracies and autocracies with answers of "yes" appears on the upper right panel of figure 7.1.

In addition to caring about *whether* education systems attempt to teach a specific set of moral and political values and beliefs, our second pattern addresses *which* values and beliefs they teach. To get at this question, V-Indoc examines the content of the history curriculum. Unlike other subjects where indoctrination may also take place (e.g., ethics or civic education), history today is taught virtually everywhere either as a standalone subject or as part

---

116. An additional step we can take to increase our confidence in the conclusions that emerge from V-Indoc is to restrict the analysis to country-years with at least three experts. The conclusions reported in the main text remain the same when we do this.
117. I group electoral and liberal democracies into a single group of "democracies," and closed and electoral autocracies into a single group of "autocracies."

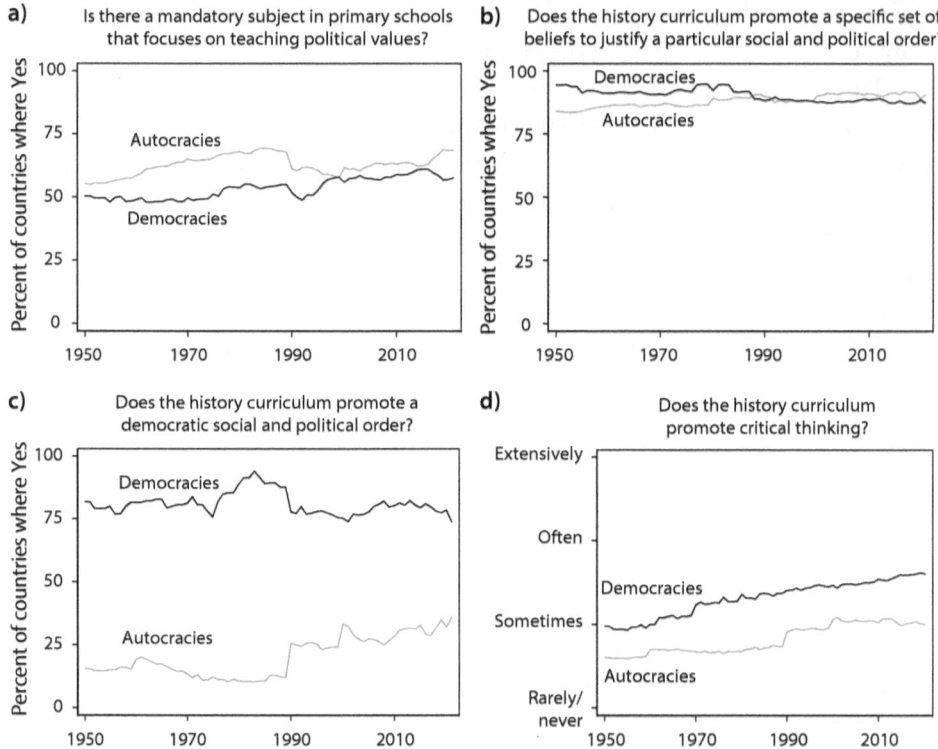

Figure 7.1. Indoctrination and critical thinking in the education systems of democracies and autocracies, 1950–2021. See text and footnotes for sources and methodology.

of social studies.[118] Specifically, in those cases where the history curriculum *does* promote a specific set of beliefs in order to justify a particular social and political order, V-Indoc also provides information about which social and political order the curriculum seeks to justify. Some education systems may use history lessons primarily to inculcate democratic norms such as the duty to vote and the right to express dissent through nonviolent means, or to teach respect for democratic institutions such as elections. Other systems may seek to inculcate different political norms, such as the notion that dissent is wrong even when peaceful, or to teach respect for non-democratic forms of government. The lower left panel of figure 7.1 shows the percentage of democracies and autocracies where the history curriculum focuses on teaching respect for *democratic* norms or institutions.

[118]. This differs from the first national primary education curricula that emerged in European and Latin American countries, where history was rarely a mandatory subject for primary schools.

Indoctrination efforts can coexist with efforts to promote critical thinking. For example, while a country's history curriculum may provide no room for students to challenge the notion that democracy is the best form of government, that same curriculum may allow students to challenge other lessons, such as those on the consequences of colonization or the causes of a war. To assess the prevalence of critical thinking in history lessons, we asked experts "To what extent do students have opportunities to discuss what they are taught in history classes? This question regards the degree to which students are de facto given the opportunity to engage in debates which question the material and content of their history classes, as well as being able to voice disagreement with each other." The response options were "0: Never or rarely," "1: Sometimes," "2: Often," and "3: Extensively." The bottom right panel of figure 7.1 shows the average response to this question across democracies and autocracies over time.

Now let's look at all the graphs jointly, paying attention to the size of the gap between democracies versus autocracies. The first pattern that emerges from figure 7.1 is that autocracies and democracies put similar effort into forming good citizens through primary education, as suggested by the relative proximity of the lines for democracies and autocracies in the upper left and upper right panels. They do so by including a mandatory subject focused on teaching political value and, further, by reinforcing the message of what constitutes a good citizen through the history curriculum. Specifically, between 1945 and 2021, 6 in 10 autocracies and 5 in 10 democracies required primary schools to have a standalone subject focused on teaching political values, and 9 in 10 autocracies *as well as* 9 in 10 democracies used history lessons to shape students' understanding of what are the political norms and institutions upheld by good citizens. The similarity across political regimes also appears when looking at additional measures of education systems' efforts to indoctrinate, such as whether the *secondary* school curriculum includes a standalone subject focused on teaching political values, *how intensive* are the efforts to teach a specific set of beliefs through the history curriculum, and whether schools promote student involvement in *extracurricular* civic or political activities. These measures are not shown in figure 7.1 for ease of exposition, but they provide further evidence that autocracies and democracies rely to a similar extent on education systems as a tool to mold future citizens' values and beliefs.

Where democracies and autocracies differ dramatically is in the notion of "good citizen" they portray, as shown in the lower left panel of figure 7.1. Eight in ten democracies use schools to promote the idea that good citizens are those who respect democratic norms and institutions. By contrast, only 2 in 10 autocracies teach democratic norms and institutions, this practice being more common in autocracies where elections exist than in those where they do not. A helpful example of such an electoral autocracy comes from Mexico, where the PRI ruled for 71 years uninterruptedly until 2000. During this period, the PRI held regular multiparty elections. High turnout and large victory margins in these elections helped boost the PRI's legitimacy and project an image of invincibility that dissuaded potential opponents from challenging the regime.[119] To encourage high turnout, the PRI targeted children. The national government distributed mandatory primary school textbooks that emphasized that voting in elections was the most important duty of citizens.[120] The share of autocracies that seek to instill respect for some subset of democratic norms or institutions has been on the rise since the 1990s. However, they still comprise a relatively small minority of autocracies.

Another difference between democracies and autocracies lies in how much they allow students to question what they are taught. On a scale from 0 to 3, where higher scores indicate more opportunities to discuss and challenge history lessons, democracies score on average 1.4 across the entire postwar period, while autocracies score just 0.8. In addition, while opportunities to engage critically with history topics have become more common in recent decades across both types of regimes, the expansion of opportunities has been greater in democracies. Still, there is considerable room for democracies to further promote critical thinking; when education experts were asked to compare the intensity of efforts to instill uncritical respect for a particular set of political values with the intensity of efforts to promote critical thinking, in most democracies the former outweighed the latter.

Some readers may wonder whether, despite putting similar amounts of effort into indoctrinating students, the overall quality of education in democracies is nonetheless better than in autocracies. This is a difficult question to answer because it requires first the very difficult task of defining what constitutes quality. What we do know is that the average reading comprehension, math, and science skills of students in democratic countries is similar to that of students in autocratic ones. This conclusion stems from a

---

119. Magaloni (2006); Klesner and Lawson (2001); Ames (1970).
120. Garfias and Paglayan (2020).

study conducted by Sirianne Dahlum and Carl Henrik Knutsen, who compared the performance of democracies and autocracies in international student exams such as the Programme for International Student Assessment (PISA).[121] PISA comparisons are valuable because, unlike many exams where teaching to the test is relatively easy, PISA is designed to test students' ability to apply concepts in new scenarios and evaluate data, claims, and arguments.

CONCLUSION

Maintaining social order is an essential function of all states—autocratic or democratic. During the eighteenth century, absolutist Prussia led the world in creating a centrally regulated primary education system in order to mold children into obedient subjects and thus consolidate the state's authority. It was not long before Prussia's primary education system became a model for other governments engaged in state-building. Non-democracies like France during the July Monarchy sent public officials to visit and learn about Prussian primary schools. So did more democratic countries like the United States and England. Across the Western world, primary schooling during the nineteenth century became conceived as a key policy tool to convert "savage" children into future citizens who respected rules, institutions, and authority—and who refrained from using violence. What varied across autocracies and democracies was the notion of "good citizen" that primary schools sought to impart. Moreover, in more democratic contexts, such as the United States during the Early Republic, the indoctrination role of schools was sometimes supplemented by additional goals, such as to teach children practical skills so that they could earn a decent living. Over time, democracies also expanded their efforts to promote critical thinking more so than autocracies. Yet as the case of twenty-first-century Peru and the analysis of cross-national data in this chapter suggest, primary schools in most democracies today continue to provide limited opportunities for children to question the basic moral and civic values that governments want to inculcate. Critical thinking in democracies is allowed so long as children do not question, for example, the norm that discontent should always be expressed through peaceful means—including voting—and never through violence.

121. Dahlum and Knutsen (2017).

John Dewey criticized the indoctrination role of education inherited from the nineteenth century and called it anti-democratic. To little avail, he proposed that students should participate in designing the rules of behavior to be followed in schools as preparation for exercising their political rights later on. Critics of Dewey's progressive education proposals argue that before individuals can exercise their own rights, they must learn their duties. Even if it were true that all states need to engage in some amount of indoctrination to be viable, it must be stressed that no moral or civic value is neutral. Some stand to gain, and others stand to lose, from the specific norms that education systems promote—and these norms are rarely chosen democratically.

CHAPTER EIGHT

DOES EDUCATION PROMOTE SOCIAL ORDER?

A central question that stems from this book—one that I hope will inspire a new wave of social scientific research—is whether mass education systems accomplished their goal of promoting social order and political stability. As fundamental as this question is, it remains severely understudied. This is unsurprising considering that the main paradigm of primary or basic education in the social sciences conceptualizes its provision as a policy tool that seeks to equip students with knowledge and skills that improve economic productivity and job opportunities. Accordingly, much research has gone into assessing whether schooling does indeed lead to improved skills, salaries, and economic growth. By contrast, we know relatively little about whether schools promote obedience and docility—in large part because these outcomes have not been at the top of social scientists' minds when thinking about the possible consequences of education.

The first two sections of this chapter seek to guide future research on how education shapes social order and political stability. The first section summarizes what we know so far about this question. It highlights common methodological challenges confronting researchers and then examines what studies that have found creative ways to address these challenges tell us about the impact of education on internal conflict, on crime, and on other individual values and behaviors like loyalty to the state. The second section offers a simple framework to think about the potential effects of mass schooling as a function of the features of education systems discussed in chapter 5. As the numerous historical examples suggest, social scientists would do well to move away from an exclusive focus on how years of schooling impact political outcomes and instead prioritize detailed studies of how the specific features of curriculum, teacher policies, and other education policies can impact these outcomes.

Following these considerations regarding the potential consequences of mass schooling, we come to the most important section of the chapter, where I clarify what role these consequences play in the overall argument of the book. As I anticipated in chapter 3, this is a book about the causes, not the consequences, of mass schooling. Some readers may be tempted to posit that if I am correct about what motivated politicians to regulate, expand, and reform primary education, then we should observe that education did in fact help strengthen internal order and political stability; otherwise, politicians would have learned that education was not an effective means of accomplishing these goals and would have stopped expanding mass education. This line of reasoning reflects a misunderstanding of the book's argument that deserves deeper attention. What we *should* observe if the book's argument is correct is evidence that politicians *believed* that mass schooling would produce social order, even if the evidence did not support such beliefs. Chapter 3 summarized the history of ideas that shaped politicians' beliefs about the consequences of mass education. In the third section of this chapter I complement that summary with an overview of the type of information that politicians gathered to track the consequences of education, the kinds of inferences they made with this information, and how they responded when these inferences led them to conclude—correctly or not—that education had failed to promote social order.

The collection of evidence presented in the third section of this chapter shows that, even when politicians concluded that education had failed to promote order and stability, they still held tightly to the conviction that mass education systems, if designed the right way, could be a stabilizing force. Because of this strong conviction, politicians did not move away from mass education when they observed signs that it had failed to accomplish their state-building goals. Instead, they reformed these systems hoping that a new approach for training teachers, a new curriculum, or some other education reform would help realize the supposed promise of mass education to form obedient citizens.

WHAT WE KNOW ABOUT THE EFFECTS OF EDUCATION ON SOCIAL ORDER AND POLITICAL STABILITY

While strong statements about the state-building power of education have abounded in policy circles for more than two centuries, their strength is not commensurate with the amount or quality of scientific evidence that exists on this topic. Speaking in September 1999 about the challenge of rebuilding conflict-afflicted societies, the then Secretary-General of the United Nations, Kofi Annan, affirmed: "My many years of service with the United Nations have convinced me that the first ingredient of political stability is an informed citizen ... Education is, quite simply, peace-building by another name. Education is the most effective form of defense spending there is." Yet roughly a decade later, in a report on the relationship between education and peace, the United Nations not only continued to insist on the importance of investing in education to prevent the recurrence of violence, but also admitted that the role of education in preventing violence "has received little systematic attention" in scientific research.[1]

Our limited knowledge stems not just from the fact that this question has not been salient in the minds of social scientists, but also from methodological challenges. Three main challenges hinder researchers. The first is the challenge of determining which consequences to consider, and then measuring them. Suppose we wanted to assess the extent to which primary schooling leads individuals to become more obedient or to internalize the moral values taught in school. These are difficult traits to observe, and therefore difficult to measure and study. One common approach to measure individual values is to ask individuals directly—for example, to ask them to what extent they think it is important to follow rules and respect authority, or to what extent they agree with a specific set of moral principles. The trouble with this approach is that respondents may *falsely report* allegiance to the "correct" values for fear of being judged or punished should they answer honestly. An alternative is to focus on observable behaviors like crime and violence against the state. But these are not without their own measurement problems. Should we consider all types of crimes—including, for instance, jaywalking—or should we restrict our analysis to crimes that threaten the state's viability, or perhaps to violent crimes alone? Similarly, what constitutes "violence against the state"? The evidence presented in previous chapters suggests that while it was often the case that large-scale

---

1. United Nations (2011), p. 160.

episodes of mass violence such as civil wars and social revolutions heightened politicians' fear of the masses, the decision to regulate and provide primary education sought to prevent *any* form of violence against the state. However, while data on the occurrence of large-scale forms of violence do exist, studying the effects of education on small-scale violence—e.g., painting graffiti or smashing the windows of a public building, etc.—would require assembling new datasets.

A second major challenge is establishing causality. Numerous studies have shown that individuals with fewer years of schooling are more likely to commit crimes,[2] and that countries with lower school enrollment rates tend to have more civil wars and other forms of large-scale violence.[3] Yet this does not necessarily imply that lower levels of schooling are what *cause* more crime or violence. The causal relationship could go the other way: incarceration often prevents individuals from getting more education, and civil wars may lead to the destruction of schools. What's more, some other factor could be responsible for the negative correlation between schooling and crime or violence. For example, perhaps having low-income parents or having a rebellious personality leads some individuals both to drop out of school and to engage in crime.

The third challenge, often underappreciated, is the fact that education reforms are usually part of a bundle of reforms, making it difficult to isolate the effect of any given measure. For example, a government pursuing a state-building agenda could simultaneously expand primary schooling, increase physical repression, and suspend the Church's power to register births and deaths. Even if this bundle of reforms led to a reduction in violence, it would be hard to identify how much of this reduction was caused specifically by the expansion of primary schooling.

While the challenges are many, some studies have found creative solutions that offer inspiration for future research. The most common approach is to identify contexts where the adoption of a new education policy impacted some cohorts of the population and some parts of the country more than others. This enables researchers to assess whether those impacted by the new policy experienced larger reductions in crime or violent conflict, or larger increases in loyalty to the state, than those not subjected to the reform. An-

---

2. For a summary of existing research on the effect of education on crime, see Lochner (2020), pp. 109–117; Bell, Costa, and Machin (2022); Lochner and Moretti (2004).

3. For a summary of existing research on the effect of education on civil war and other forms of violence, see Østby, Urdal, and Dupuy (2019).

other possible approach is to randomly assign educational opportunities across students, and then assess whether those who by pure chance received more schooling eventually became more likely to respect authority and less likely to engage in crime or participate in violent episodes. Random assignment of education interventions has become a popular approach for evaluating the effects of education. However, researchers have usually focused on how these interventions shape students' knowledge and skills and long-term employment and salaries, and only rarely have they taken the opportunity to assess also the effects of schooling on moral and political values, crime, and violent behavior.[4]

Taking stock of these studies, several conclusions emerge. First, we know exceedingly little about whether or how the creation and expansion of state-regulated primary education systems shaped patterns of internal social order. Although considerable evidence exists that countries with higher primary school enrollment rates tend to have fewer civil wars, for reasons discussed earlier this pattern cannot be used to conclude that higher access to schooling *leads to* a lower probability of civil war.[5] In an effort to determine the true extent to which primary schooling reduces internal conflict, a team of researchers examined the consequences of a large-scale primary school construction program rolled out by the Suharto regime in Indonesia during the 1970s, when the government built more than 61,000 primary schools. To estimate the impact of this program, the researchers took advantage of the fact that the government's construction efforts varied in intensity both across districts and within districts over time. They also assembled detailed information on the number of violent episodes and peaceful protests in each district from 1955 to 1994. They observed that while the number of violent episodes increased everywhere in Indonesia after the 1970s, violence increased *less* in those districts where more primary schools were constructed, suggesting that schooling lowered the probability of violent conflict. Notably, the researchers also found that the negative effect of schooling on violent conflict grew in magnitude over time, consistent with the notion that the impact of education tends to accrue in the long run. Moreover, the expansion of primary schooling reduced *all* types of violent conflict, regardless of whether the conflict was

---

4. A notable exception is Friedman et al.'s (2016) study of the consequences of a scholarship program in Kenya.
5. For a review of cross-country research on the effect of schooling on violent internal conflict, see Østby, Urdal, and Dupuy (2019).

driven by economic, ethno-religious, or political causes, but did not reduce the probability of *peaceful* protests.[6] Two main channels appear to explain why primary education led to a reduction of violence in Indonesia. First, with the explicit goal of promoting social order, the government of Suharto accompanied the expansion of primary schooling with the adoption of a new moral and civic education curriculum based on the state ideology (*Pancasila*), which emphasized respect for the Constitution, national unity, and religious tolerance.[7] Second, schooling also led to better-paid jobs, reducing the economic grievances that often fuel social unrest.[8] While the Indonesian case provides important insights, only the accumulation of evidence from other countries and time periods will help us build a better understanding of whether and how primary schooling shapes social order and violent conflict.

Another frequent goal of education is to reduce crime. As we saw in previous chapters, the view that schools can mold children into law-abiding adults and lower the long-term costs of the criminal justice system has been common in Western societies. For this outcome, we do have considerable and compelling evidence that schooling does indeed lead to large reductions in the prevalence of both property crimes (e.g., arson, theft, etc.) and violent crimes (e.g., murder, assault, etc.). In particular, studies of reforms that extended the number of years of compulsory schooling in Italy, England and Wales, Sweden, and the United States have consistently shown that these extensions had a sizeable negative impact on a wide range of types of crime. Furthermore, the crime-reducing effects of these reforms tend to be more pronounced in the long run than in the short term, and also reduce the criminal behavior of the sons of fathers who were affected by the extension of compulsory schooling, suggesting that the negative effect of schooling on crime does not just stem from the fact that attending school automatically removes people from the streets.[9] However, it is unclear whether schools reduce crime because they inculcate values of respect for existing laws, because attending school increases future earnings, or both.

While the evidence suggests that schooling does tend to reduce crime, its effect on other political behaviors and values is more varying. The most

---

6. Rochner and Saia (2020).
7. Nishimura (1995); Roth and Sumarto (2015); Rochner and Saia (2020).
8. Rochner and Saia (2020); Duflo (2001).
9. Buonanno and Leonida (2009); Hjalmarsson, Holmlund, and Lindquist (2015); Lochner and Moretti (2004); Machin, Marie, and Vujić (2011); Meghir, Palme, and Schnabel (2012).

commonly studied behavior is voter turnout. As we saw in chapter 7, education systems in democratic contexts often teach children that voting is the most important form of political participation and the primary means by which citizens should express their preferences and grievances. However, in the United States, where the effect of schooling on the propensity to vote during adulthood has been studied the most, social scientists disagree on whether additional schooling increases voter turnout. Some studies conclude that additional schooling boosts voter turnout,[10] while others find that it does not.[11]

When we turn our attention to how schools shape an individual's loyalty to the state, here again existing research suggests that schooling has sometimes strengthened, and other times eroded, loyalty. Examples of education reforms that were effective in promoting greater loyalty come from France and Prussia during the nineteenth century. In France, as we saw in chapter 4, the Guizot Law of 1833 required every town with at least 500 inhabitants to establish and maintain a primary school for boys, imposed a common curriculum, and increased the centralization of school inspections and teacher certification. To study the effects of this law, a team of economists compared long-run political outcomes in towns that in 1833 had just a few inhabitants short of 500 versus towns whose population was just above 500—that is, otherwise identical towns that were either exempted or affected by the law simply because of the arbitrary 500-inhabitant threshold. The researchers found that, just as the Guizot Law intended, the expansion of primary schooling led in the long run to stronger feelings of loyalty to the French state and increased support among citizens for the centralization of political authority.[12] In a similar effort to strengthen citizens' loyalty to the state, Prussia under Bismarck introduced a primary education reform that centralized the responsibility for funding schools and shifted the power to hire teachers from local to central authorities. The state used this reform to build new schools and recruit teachers who were aligned with its indoctrination agenda. Here, too, existing research suggests that the centralization of primary education contributed to strengthen citizens' loyalty and respect for the state's authority.[13]

---

10. Milligan, Moretti, and Oreopoulos (2004); Dee (2004); Sondheimer and Green (2010).
11. Tenn (2007); Kam and Palmer (2008); Berinsky and Lenz (2011).
12. Blanc and Kubo (2021).
13. Cinnirella and Schueler (2018).

Yet there are also examples where public schools have failed to accomplish the state's indoctrination goals, and have sometimes produced the opposite of what the state intended. In Kenya, for example, an experimental intervention that expanded girls' access to schooling led girls with more schooling to question the notion that "we should show more respect for authority" and increased their agreement with the view that violence is sometimes a legitimate tool to obtain what we want.[14] Another well-studied case where education failed to promote loyalty to the state comes from the United States during the 1920s. Before World War I, several states had allowed private schools to teach in both English and German. However, after the war, new state laws banned instruction in the German language in all schools, including private ones. While the goal of this education policy was to strengthen the allegiance of German American children to the United States, the reform backfired. Among other consequences, it reduced German Americans' willingness to volunteer for the U.S. Army during World War II.[15]

A FRAMEWORK FOR FUTURE RESEARCH ON THE EFFECTS OF EDUCATION

Because public school systems sometimes succeed and other times fail to promote nonviolent behavior, obedience, and respect for the state's authority, a fundamental question for social scientists interested in the consequences of education for state-building is: Under what conditions are these systems effective, and when and why do they fail to accomplish these goals? To inform future research on this question, I now turn to provide a framework that conceptualizes the potential effects of mass schooling as a function of three sets of education policies discussed in chapter 5: curriculum policies; teacher training and recruitment policies; and policies designed to align parents and students' behavior with the goals of the state.

THE ROLE OF THE CURRICULUM

The impact of primary schooling on social order and political stability will likely depend on what is taught in schools. In chapter 5 we saw that when central governments in Western societies first began to regulate primary

---

14. Friedman et al. (2016).
15. Fouka (2020).

schools, they established a mandatory curriculum stipulating the subjects that all primary schools should follow. An examination of these curriculums revealed the ubiquity of moral education—sometimes secular, sometimes religious. I argued in that chapter that, even though promoting good moral behavior was a common overarching goal, the curriculum that national governments adopted depended on politicians' beliefs about the basis of morality. In countries where a majority of the ruling class believed that the basis of morality was religious doctrine, governments adopted a narrow primary school curriculum focused on teaching moral and religious education and the rudiments of reading, writing, and arithmetic. By contrast, in countries where a majority of the ruling class believed that moral principles can be derived by reason, the curriculum also included subjects like algebra, geometry, and natural science. For liberal elites influenced by positivist philosophers like Auguste Comte, placing these subjects in the curriculum was important not to promote the skills of the population but to develop ordinary people's capacity to think abstractly and thus access universal moral principles.

In retrospect, it is not difficult to see how a moral education curriculum emphasizing math and science could have unintended consequences, emboldening instead of pacifying the population. Teaching math and science skills in primary schools could enable children to access higher-paying occupations than their parents, so that a peasant's son could become a factory worker or even a tailor or storekeeper, and his daughter, a seamstress or primary school teacher. As younger generations climb the social ladder, they may come to see themselves as members of a new working or middle class, and may develop aspirations for more political representation and power. Some could even take advantage of their wealth, skills, and social connections to organize others into new labor unions or political parties to push for institutional reforms that challenge the status quo.

The history of Argentina provides a textbook illustration of this dynamic.[16] As the national government centralized and expanded primary schooling after 1880 in an effort to "moralize" the masses and prevent a recurrence of civil war, a group of positivist intellectuals and liberal (anti-Church)

---

16. Additional examples of the importance of the curriculum in shaping the outcomes of education come from China and Egypt. In China during the late nineteenth century, the traditional approach to education, focused on the Confucian classics, was reformed to incorporate teaching in math and science. As a result of this reform, the wage premium of educated individuals increased notably (Yuchtman 2017). For similar evidence from a curriculum reform in 1950s Egypt, see Saleh (2016).

politicians crafted a primary school curriculum that, in addition to moral and civic education, also included algebra, geometry, physics, and chemistry, all with the purpose of developing people's ability to understand through reason, not religion, what constituted good moral behavior.[17] By the end of the nineteenth century, however, Argentina had become a symbol of social mobility, boasting the largest middle class in Latin America and making it the second most preferred destination in the world among European immigrants. In Buenos Aires, three-fourths of the working class and four-fifths of the middle class was composed of immigrants. Primary schools provided foreign-born individuals and their children with skills that were useful to climb the social ladder, moving from day laborer to baker, construction worker, shoemaker, or carpenter, and from there to storekeeper, professional, or civil servant.[18] This unintended consequence of schooling became a destabilizing political force, as members of the new working and middle classes formed professional associations and labor unions, joined disruptive strikes, and found political representation in a new party, the *Unión Cívica Radical* (UCR). Born in 1891 out of a student-led revolution to overthrow the oligarchic regime, the UCR organized additional revolutions in 1893 and 1905 which, though they failed to overthrow the regime, instilled deep fear among the ruling class.[19] In the early 1900s, the head of the National Education Council, José María Ramos Mejía, wrote a lengthy report in which he argued that the 1884 curriculum was partly responsible for the widespread labor strikes and social instability. By the time the government adopted a new curriculum, important societal and political changes were already underway. In 1912, Congress passed a universal male suffrage law, and in 1916, the UCR won the presidency in the country's first democratic elections. Exactly how much of this political transformation was caused by the primary education system created in the 1880s is difficult to ascertain, but to the extent that this system encouraged the formation of a middle class and led the working class to develop aspirations for social mobility, it inadvertently contained the seeds that contributed to undermine the very same oligarchic regime that three decades earlier had created it.

Of course, not all curriculums backfire. An example of a curriculum reform that attained its goals comes from China, where the central govern-

---

17. See chapters 4 and 5.
18. Pérez (2017); Rock (1985), p. 175.
19. Rock (1985), pp. 183–90.

ment in 2004 introduced a new politics textbook designed to promote "moral and ideological education." The new textbooks sought to legitimize the authority of the Chinese government and its officials by stressing that, as long as the country remained under the leadership of the Chinese Communist Party, law and order would prevail. A study by Davide Cantoni and others took advantage of the sequential rollout of the reform to study its impact on political attitudes by comparing the attitudes of those who were exposed to the old and new curriculums. The researchers found that, in line with the goals of the reform, those who were exposed to the new curriculum expressed more trust in the central government and were more likely to view government officials as civic-minded.[20]

While we still lack a deep understanding of how different curriculums shape long-term values and behaviors, a new generation of studies that examines the consequences of different curriculum plans is a promising trend.[21] One possibility suggested by the Argentine experience is that curriculums that teach considerable skills will fail to promote social order, since they equip the population with tools to challenge the status quo. But this is not an obvious prediction. We could instead expect that a curriculum that teaches not only values but also a good dose of skills is the best way to prevent revolutions, as enabling individuals to get well-paid jobs can lessen or eliminate the economic grievances that could otherwise lead individuals to rebel against the government. More research in this area could shed light on the impact of different types of curriculums.

THE ROLE OF TEACHERS

An education system's ability to accomplish its goals will likely depend not only on the curriculum but also on the motivation, knowledge, and skills of teachers to implement it. Since the nineteenth century, central governments have heavily regulated teacher training and certification to ensure that teachers are loyal and capable agents of the state. As explained in chapter 5, the creation of state-controlled Normal Schools—institutions exclusively devoted to training prospective teachers and often with monopoly power to issue teaching certificates—became a pervasive practice starting in the nineteenth century. These teacher training institutions sought to

---

20. Cantoni et al. (2017).
21. Garfias and Paglayan (2020); Cantoni et al. (2017); Bai and Li (2020); Clots-Figueras and Masella (2013); Voigtländer and Voth (2015).

imbue teachers with the same moral values that they were expected to teach their students. Many institutions operated as boarding schools in order to closely mold every aspect of future teachers' behavior, and had detailed regulations that heavily regimented the school day and prescribed a set of behaviors.

What policymakers failed to anticipate was that Normal Schools, by bringing future teachers together in a setting where they did not just study but also *lived* together, helped forge bonds among teachers that led to the emergence of a professional identity. This professional identity did not always coexist peacefully with the state. When teachers were not paid on time, when their meager salaries did not match the responsibilities that the state placed on them, when they resented school inspectors who constrained their pedagogical autonomy, they did not suffer in isolation but instead came together. Ironically, Normal Schools provided the first point of contact between teachers, facilitating the formation of professional associations and teacher unions. This was the case of France during the July Monarchy, an example of an ineffective attempt to control teachers. Less than three weeks following the passage of France's 1833 law of primary education, the Minister of Public Instruction, François Guizot, sent a copy of the law to every teacher along with a personal letter, signed by the minister himself, in which he described the importance of teachers' mission and explained that "universal primary instruction is from now on one of the guarantees of order and social stability."[22] It did not take long, however, before French school inspectors started noticing teachers' complaints about the Guizot Law. In particular, teachers were hostile toward the Church's ongoing—though declining—influence over primary schools. They joined professional associations, held pedagogical conferences to discuss challenges with the law's implementation, and turned to specialized journals to express their views. These conferences became crucial venues for building solidarity and a sense of collective identity among teachers. Normal Schools also became a breeding ground for the development of teachers' professional networks. In the words of French education scholar Nicholas Toloudis, "thus did the regime's mobilization of teachers, by way of the training institutions, beget the teachers' own use of those same institutions as a resource for their own political mobilization."[23]

---

22. Toloudis (2012), p. 37.
23. Toloudis (2012), pp. 63–64.

While French teachers' resistance was expressed through collective action, in other cases teachers resisted the implementation of the official curriculum through individual pedagogical decisions. The behavior of teachers during the first two presidencies of Juan Perón in Argentina is a well-studied case of how teachers can creatively undermine the official curriculum. Between 1946 and 1955, Perón's government turned to education as a means to teach a particular partisan ideology: it declared the Peronist Doctrine a National Doctrine to be taught in schools; replaced old textbooks with new ones designed to inculcate love and loyalty toward Perón and his wife, Evita; and mandated teachers to accurately implement the exercises contained in these textbooks, many of which encouraged students to reflect on the Peronist Doctrine and worship Evita. However, an analysis of children's notebooks conducted by Argentine education expert Silvina Gvirtz reveals that teachers often resisted the state's mandate through everyday pedagogical choices that were difficult for school inspectors to detect. For example, teachers would have students summarize Evita's autobiography, but would grade students' responses exclusively on spelling and grammar, not on the ideological substance of what they wrote. Similarly, they would have students write "Evita loves me" on their notebooks, but these phrases would appear accidentally by splitting the sentence into separate letters or words as part of an exercise designed to teach calligraphy.[24]

A similar example of unorganized teacher resistance comes from Venezuela under the government of Hugo Chávez. In 2007, the Chávez administration introduced a new "Bolivarian" national curriculum whose stated goal was to develop a "new citizen" who was socialized into values of liberty, cooperation, social equality, unity, and Latin American integration and solidarity. Accompanied by the distribution of new official textbooks, the new curriculum promoted a radically new understanding of Venezuelan history and identity. A study of the implementation of this reform shows that, in Caracas, teachers who perceived the new curriculum as a threat to their middle-class status and identity refrained from using any portions of the new textbooks that they found politically unpalatable.[25]

While the previous examples illustrate the challenges governments encounter in limiting teacher autonomy, governments sometimes do find effective ways to exert control. The Mexican experience is a case in point.

24. Gvirtz (1999).
25. Abbott, Soifer, and Vom Hau (2017).

Throughout most of the PRI regime, public school teachers and the union that organized them, the SNTE, operated as brokers of the PRI, mobilizing electoral support in their local community and monitoring how parents voted. The SNTE itself was controlled by PRI politicians, and teachers knew that their job depended on compliance with union and party directives. For example, in the 1990s, when the government introduced important curriculum and education governance reforms, the vast majority of teachers and the SNTE did not oppose it. To foment their allegiance, the government rewarded public school teachers with generous economic benefits. It established minimum working conditions across the country; earmarked states' education budgets to guarantee the uniformity of teachers' working conditions; agreed to nationwide teacher pension benefits; and increased real teacher salaries by 35 percent between 1988 and 1994, which resulted in teachers moving from being the lowest-paid group to the second-highest paid group of public sector employees.[26]

Motivation—whether for ideological or economic reasons—is not the only factor shaping teachers' implementation of the official curriculum; their skills matter, too. In a study of teachers in seven Sub-Saharan African countries which together represent close to 40 percent of the region's population, Tessa Bold and her coauthors found that only one in ten teachers have a minimum knowledge of general pedagogy. Part of this deficit stems from the limited pedagogical skills of those in charge of providing teacher training.[27] The problem of inadequate teaching skills is not unique to Sub-Saharan Africa. In Latin America, for example, Denise Vaillant has written extensively about the excessive focus of teacher training programs on education philosophy and pedagogical theory and, relatedly, the absence of practical opportunities to apply these theories and receive feedback from instructors.[28]

Understanding how education policies shape teachers' motivation, knowledge, and skills to implement a prescribed curriculum, and how these factors in turn affect social order and political stability, should be priorities in future research on the consequences of education.

---

26. Garfias and Paglayan (2020); Murillo (1999).
27. Bold et al. (2017).
28. Vaillant (2018); Vaillant and Manso (2022).

THE ROLE OF PARENTS AND STUDENTS

Another issue that may prevent education systems from accomplishing policymakers' intended goals is the resistance of parents, students, and civil society to the state's educational agenda. One common approach to understanding parents' schooling decisions considers the monetary costs and benefits of schooling: on one hand, enrolling children in school can result in short-term economic losses for families who formerly relied on children's work; on the other, schooling may increase a child's future income. The approach predicts that parents will enroll their children in school when the expected monetary benefits exceed the monetary costs of this decision.

The limitation of this approach is that, historically, primary schooling often did not seek to improve future incomes. As documented in previous chapters, politicians in Western societies often touted the power of primary schools to indoctrinate children, and declared that improving the economic situation of poor families was not the goal of schooling. To be sure, as illustrated earlier in the example of Argentina, there are cases where primary education may have inadvertently promoted upward social mobility. But when schooling did not have clear economic benefits, or was not expected by parents to have such benefits, why did some parents nonetheless choose to enroll their child in school?

Here, it is helpful to consider also the *non-monetary* costs and benefits of this decision. One potential non-monetary cost of enrolling a child in school includes the psychological distress suffered when submitting one's will to the will of the state. Recall from previous chapters that politicians from countries as diverse as absolutist Prussia and the United States during the Early Republic often claimed that a key goal of mass schooling was to break the child's will, molding this will to the interests of the state. Such efforts may cause varying levels of psychological distress across individuals. For parents of children who will grow up with little individual freedom regardless of whether they attend school, the indoctrination efforts of the state may be perceived as less costly. But even when it produces some psychological distress, schooling—and indoctrination—may also be perceived to bring about psychological benefits. As the sociologist Norbert Elias emphasizes in *The Civilizing Process*, throughout history, violent behavior has increasingly been labeled as improper, bringing about individual feelings of shame and remorse.[29] To avoid such feelings, individuals have voluntarily and gradually engaged in self-restraint and self-discipline. Parents who perceived primary schooling as a useful vehicle for teaching children the norms of "civilized" behavior may have willingly enrolled their children in school to save them from the shame of being labeled "savages."

Education reformers in the nineteenth century usually assumed that children would passively learn the set of values and behaviors prescribed by the state as long as they attended school. Their main concern was that parents would resist sending their children to school. The most common policy response to this perceived problem was the adoption of compulsory schooling laws which, as we saw in chapter 5, usually included a provision establishing penalties against parents who failed to comply. However harsh on paper, penalties for not enrolling children in school are more likely to encourage parental compliance when parents believe that these penalties will indeed be enforced. Yet central governments often lack the capacity to do so. Enforcement requires sufficient funds not just to construct schools and hire teachers, but also to hire and train school inspectors. Moreover, inspectors' ability to monitor parental behavior will depend, among other things, on whether they can reach remote areas and on the existence of population censuses or other administrative records that provide information about which parents have school-age children.

The case of Sweden illustrates the importance of state capacity for monitoring and aligning parental behavior with the interests of the state. Sweden adopted compulsory schooling in 1842. According to the law, parents found in violation of the compulsory schooling provision were first given a warning and then fined. If they failed to pay the fine, the law empowered state officials to remove children from their home and place them under state supervision. To encourage children to attend permanent public schools, in 1861 parliament decided to hire and deploy national inspectors throughout the entire territory. By 1868, there were thirty-six national school inspectors in charge of overseeing 174 localities. Some of these localities were more difficult to reach than others because, despite parliament's plans, the national railroad network had not been completed yet. In a study conducted by Alexandra Cermeño and others, the researchers found that the ability of inspectors to reach localities by train was a key determinant of their ability to monitor and enforce compliance with the state's directives. In those

---

29. Elias (1994).

localities that inspectors could reach by train, enrollment in permanent public schools increased by 17 percent compared to otherwise similar localities that did not yet have a train station.[30]

An interesting question is whether penalties are more or less effective than rewards in encouraging parental and student compliance with education regulations. Research on policies designed to assimilate immigrants—a different but related area of public policy—suggests that policies that *reward* individuals for some types of behavior are more likely to be effective in molding values and behaviors than policies that *prohibit* and *penalize* certain types of behavior.[31] The use of explicit rewards for school attendance was uncommon historically,[32] but it has become pervasive in recent decades with the rapid spread of conditional cash transfer programs that offer cash to low-income families who enroll their children in school.

Failure to enroll a child in school is not the only form of parental resistance to the state's educational agenda. Another option is to enroll children in private schools. In many countries, the national government's limited ability to attain universal primary schooling on its own has often led policymakers to allow private schools to operate, too.[33] To avoid an undue loss of control, governments have regulated the curriculum of private schools, required teachers in private schools to undergo the same training and certification procedures as public school teachers, and/or subjected private schools to similar inspection policies as public ones. In practice, however, compliance with regulations tends to be harder to enforce in private schools than in public ones. Private schooling may thus give parents an option to comply with the compulsory schooling mandate without actually educating their children in the state's prescribed curriculum.

Parents can also defy the goals of education policies through their actions at home or in other domains of the private sphere. For example, the adoption of an official curriculum that seeks to inculcate a specific set of unacceptable values may lead affronted parents to intensify their efforts to imbue their children with their preferred values. An example of this type of compensatory behavior comes from the United States in the 1920s, when several states banned the use of German in public and private primary schools

30. Cermeño, Enflo, and Lindvall (2022).
31. Fouka (2024).
32. A notable exception presented in chapter 5 comes from Mexico after the Revolution, when the central government offered free meals to children who attended school.
33. See chapter 4.

in an effort to increase German American children's loyalty to the United States. Vicky Fouka's investigation found that German parents responded by enrolling their children in Sunday schools operated by the Lutheran Church. Contrary to the goals of education policymakers, this led their children to develop stronger, not weaker, bonds with Germany.[34]

In sum, parental resistance, depending on the specific characteristics of the education policy, may counterbalance the state's efforts to shape children's values.

THE IMPORTANCE OF BELIEFS ABOUT THE CONSEQUENCES OF EDUCATION

The core of this book—its motivation, its analysis, and its conclusions—deals with the *causes* of mass schooling. While understanding the *consequences* of mass schooling is a significant question, it is important to keep in mind that it is also a separate question. We do not need to understand whether schools succeeded or failed to promote state-building in order to understand what motivated politicians to regulate and provide primary education in the first place. This can be somewhat counterintuitive. As emphasized earlier in the chapter, what we should observe if the book's argument is correct is evidence that politicians *believed* that mass schooling would produce social order, even if the evidence, strictly speaking, should not have supported such beliefs. I have presented considerable evidence from a wide range of countries that politicians who advocated for mass schooling believed—correctly or not—that educating the lower classes with an eye toward promoting good moral behavior (as defined by elites) would help pacify the population, prevent future crime, and reduce the probability of anarchy and revolution.

Were these beliefs based on the kind of evidence that social scientists today would consider rigorous enough to make a valid claim about how education impacted morality, crime, or anarchy? Certainly not. Both historically and today, the kinds of evidence that many politicians have relied on

---

34. Another example comes from Indonesia during the 1970s. When Suharto's regime expanded public primary schooling and adopted a secular curriculum, Islamic organizations responded by increasing the provision of religious secondary education. As a result, the government's school construction efforts led not only to increased enrollment in secular primary schools but also to increased enrollment in secondary Islamic schools, dampening the state's ability to diffuse secular values. See Bazzi, Hilmy, and Marx (2022).

to make inferences about the effects of specific education policies are often not adequate to justify those inferences. Yet that has not prevented them from using this evidence to reach their own conclusions, however misguided, about the benefits of a proposed policy.

What's more, time has proven the resilience of politicians' belief in the power of education to promote social order and political stability. Even when confronted with evidence that could suggest the opposite, politicians did not move away from education altogether, but instead reformed education systems with the conviction that a new curriculum, a new set of policies for training and recruiting teachers, or some other education reform would allow these systems to realize their promise.

Let's look at the types of evidence and reasoning that politicians during the nineteenth century relied on to assess whether an education system was effective in accomplishing its goals, and how they responded when they concluded that primary education had failed to promote the strength and stability of the state.

HOW GOVERNMENTS ASSESSED THE CONSEQUENCES OF EDUCATION

One of the most common types of evidence that nineteenth-century policymakers used to judge the efficacy of primary education systems were crime statistics. Both in Western Europe and Latin America, as national governments began to collect information about the level and types of crime, they regularly collected and published information about whether incarcerated individuals had received any kind of formal education. Although politicians often interpreted these statistics incorrectly, the mere fact that governments were interested in systematically measuring the relationship between crime and education, as well as the conclusions that politicians derived from these statistics—again, however misguided—provide strong evidence that politicians viewed primary education as a crucial policy tool to reduce crime.

Consider an example from Chile that is representative of the kinds of evidence and arguments about crime and education seen in many other countries. Starting in 1860, the same year Congress passed the General Law of Public Instruction, the Chilean government began to publish yearly the *Anuario Estadístico de la República de Chile*, an official compendium of national statistics covering a wide range of topics including demography, agriculture, commerce, education, crime, public sector employment, and other topics of interest to the government. The section of the report devoted to crime regularly featured information about the total number of people who had been imprisoned in the previous year, as well as how many of these new prisoners had any formal instruction. A typical report included a comparison of the proportion of new prisoners with formal instruction relative to the previous year, an example of which is shown at the top of figure 8.1. What is telling about these reports is how the government interpreted these data. Examples of these interpretations are shown at the bottom of the figure. In years when there was a decline in the proportion of new prisoners who had any instruction, such as between 1869 and 1870, the government saw evidence of the ability of education to reduce crime. Similarly, in years when there was an increase in the proportion of new prisoners who had any instruction, such as between 1868 and 1869, the government interpreted this as a "distressing result" that suggested that education was not "contributing to moralize" the population. In this as in other cases, however, the government did not conclude that education systems were an inherently ineffective policy tool to moralize the population. What it argued instead was that the education system was contributing to "malice" because it had become "distorted" and needed to be realigned with its mission.

An institutional feature that facilitated the collection of these statistics is that, in many countries, the responsibility to regulate and monitor schools and prisons originally fell under the same bureaucratic agency.[35] Sometimes called Ministry of Justice and Public Instruction, other times Ministry of Justice, Worship, and Public Instruction, these agencies reported to Congress on the state of law and order *and* education. They gathered statistics on the number and outcome of court trials, the number of incarcerations per year by type of crime and by demographic characteristics of the offender, the level of enrollment in primary and secondary schools and universities, and the number of public libraries. In Chile, for example, oversight over crime and education issues fell under the Ministry of Justice, Worship, and Public Instruction from 1837 to 1887, and then under the Ministry of Justice and Public Instruction until 1927, at which point the Ministry of Public Education was formed as a standalone agency. Even then, the Chilean government continued issuing an annual statistical compendium titled *Educación y Justicia*, containing both education and crime statistics, until 1969.

It was the French Ministry of Justice in 1828 that pioneered the practice of collecting detailed annual statistics about the level of instruction among

---

35. In Latin America alone, this includes Argentina, Bolivia, Chile, Dominican Republic, Mexico, Paraguay, and Uruguay.

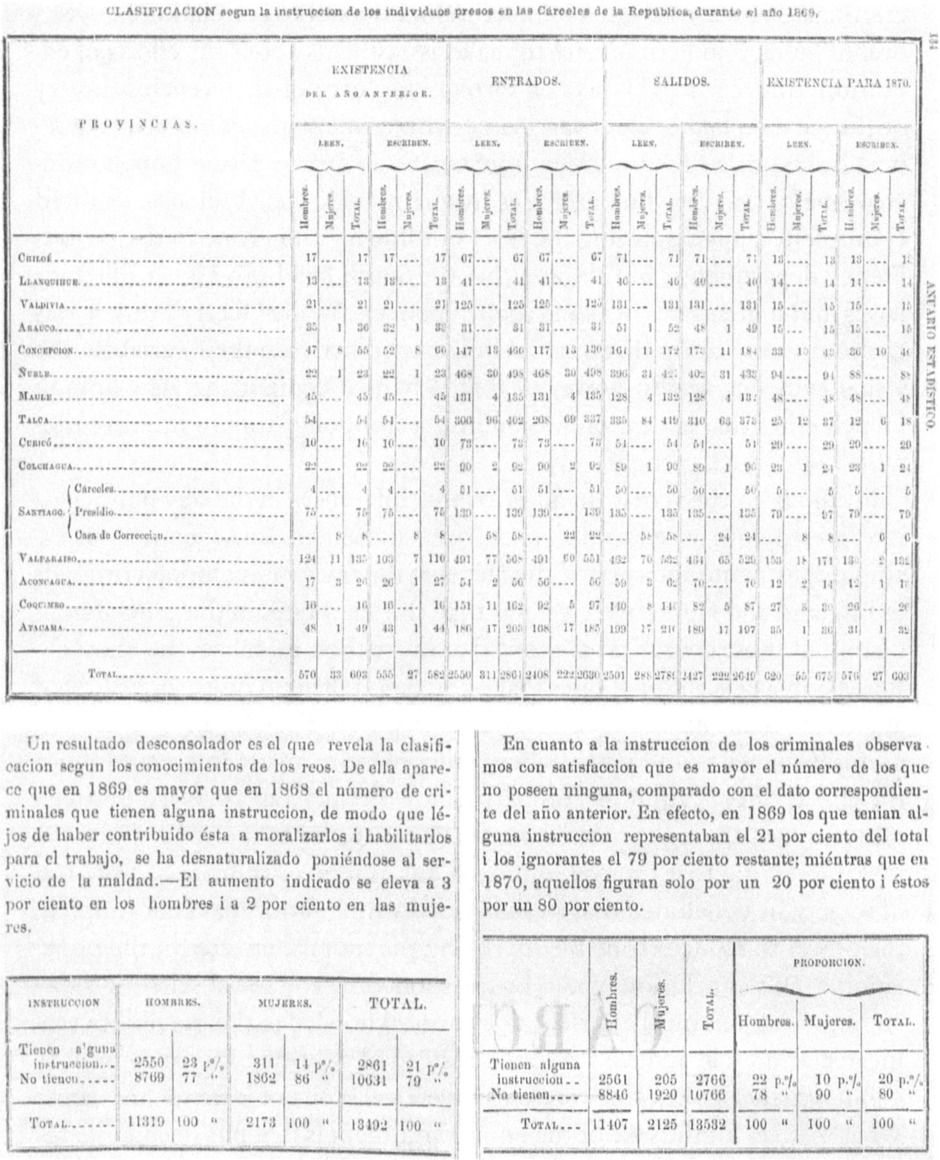

CLASIFICACION segun la instruccion de los individuos presos en las Cárceles de la República, durante el año 1869.

134

ANUARIO ESTADÍSTICO.

PROVINCIAS.	EXISTENCIA DEL AÑO ANTERIOR.						ENTRADOS.						SALIDOS.						EXISTENCIA PARA 1870.					
	LEEN.			ESCRIBEN.			LEEN.			ESCRIBEN.			LEEN.			ESCRIBEN.			LEEN.			ESCRIBEN.		
	Hombres.	Mujeres.	TOTAL.	Hombres.	Mujeres.	TOTAL.	Hombres.	Mujeres.	TOTAL.	Hombres.	Mujeres.	TOTAL.	Hombres.	Mujeres.	TOTAL.	Hombres.	Mujeres.	TOTAL.	Hombres.	Mujeres.	TOTAL.	Hombres.	Mujeres.	TOTAL.
CHILOÉ	17	....	17	17	....	17	67	....	67	67	....	67	71	....	71	71	....	71	13	....	13	13	....	13
LLANQUIHUE	13	....	13	13	....	13	41	....	41	41	....	41	40	....	40	40	....	40	14	....	14	14	....	14
VALDIVIA	21	....	21	21	....	21	125	....	125	125	....	125	131	...	131	131	....	131	15	....	15	15	....	15
ARAUCO	35	1	36	32	1	33	31	....	31	31	....	31	51	1	52	48	1	49	15	...	15	15	....	15
CONCEPCION	47	8	55	52	8	60	147	13	460	117	13	130	161	11	172	173	11	184	33	10	43	36	10	46
ÑUBLE	22	1	23	22	1	23	468	30	498	468	30	498	396	31	427	402	31	433	94	....	94	88	....	88
MAULE	45	....	45	45	....	45	131	4	135	131	4	135	128	4	132	128	4	132	48	....	48	48	....	48
TALCA	54	....	54	54	....	54	306	96	402	268	69	337	335	84	419	310	63	373	25	12	37	12	6	18
CURICÓ	10	....	10	10	....	10	73	....	73	73	....	73	54	....	54	51	....	51	29	....	29	20	....	20
COLCHAGUA	22	....	22	22	....	22	90	2	92	90	2	92	89	1	90	89	1	90	23	1	24	23	1	24
SANTIAGO. Cárceles	4	....	4	4	....	4	51	....	51	51	....	51	50	....	50	50	....	50	5	....	5	5	....	5
SANTIAGO. Presidio	75	....	75	75	....	75	139	....	139	139	....	139	135	....	135	135	....	135	79	....	97	79	....	79
SANTIAGO. Casa de Correccion	....	8	8	....	8	8	....	58	58	....	22	22	....	58	58	....	24	24	....	8	8	....	6	6
VALPARAISO	124	11	135	103	7	110	491	77	568	491	60	551	462	70	532	464	65	529	153	18	171	130	2	132
ACONCAGUA	17	3	20	26	1	27	54	2	56	56	....	56	59	3	62	70	....	70	12	2	14	12	1	13
COQUIMBO	16	....	16	16	....	16	151	11	162	92	5	97	140	8	148	82	5	87	27	3	30	26	....	26
ATACAMA	48	1	49	43	1	44	186	17	203	168	17	185	199	17	216	180	17	197	35	1	36	31	1	32
TOTAL	570	33	603	555	27	582	2550	311	2861	2408	222	2630	2501	288	2789	2427	222	2649	620	55	675	576	27	603

Un resultado desconsolador es el que revela la clasificacion segun los conocimientos de los reos. De ella aparece que en 1869 es mayor que en 1868 el número de criminales que tienen alguna instruccion, de modo que léjos de haber contribuido ésta a moralizarlos i habilitarlos para el trabajo, se ha desnaturalizado poniéndose al servicio de la maldad.—El aumento indicado se eleva a 3 por ciento en los hombres i a 2 por ciento en las mujeres.

INSTRUCCION	HOMBRES.		MUJERES.		TOTAL.	
Tienen alguna instruccion...	2550	23 p°/o	311	14 p°/o	2861	21 p°/o
No tienen.....	8769	77 "	1862	86 "	10631	79 "
TOTAL......	11319	100 "	2173	100 "	13492	100 "

En cuanto a la instruccion de los criminales observamos con satisfaccion que es mayor el número de los que no poseen ninguna, comparado con el dato correspondiente del año anterior. En efecto, en 1869 los que tenian alguna instruccion representaban el 21 por ciento del total i los ignorantes el 79 por ciento restante; miéntras que en 1870, aquellos figuran solo por un 20 por ciento i éstos por un 80 por ciento.

	Hombres.	Mujeres.	TOTAL.	PROPORCION. Hombres.	PROPORCION. Mujeres.	PROPORCION. TOTAL.
Tienen alguna instruccion..	2561	205	2766	22 p.°/o	10 p.°/o	20 p.°/o
No tienen....	8846	1920	10766	78 "	90 "	80 "
TOTAL...	11407	2125	13532	100 "	100 "	100 "

Figure 8.1. Chilean statistics of convicted criminals by literacy status. Source: *Anuario Estadístico de la República de Chile 1869 and 1870.*

criminals. France, too, was a pioneer in looking at the correlation between overall literacy and crime rates to make assessments about the effects of education. André-Michel Guerry, a former employee of the French Ministry of Justice who had become fascinated with crime statistics, published a report in 1833 titled *Essay on Morality Statistics in France*. This report, considered one of the very first exercises in quantitative social science, featured choropleth maps displaying the level of illiteracy and crime in the various French departments, and showed that the South had both higher illiteracy levels and higher rates of crime against persons. While Guerry himself was cautious not to claim that a causal link existed between these variables, the visual evidence was so powerful that it helped cement the view among French elites that education was an important policy tool to improve morality and reduce crime.[36]

Invalid or, at the very least, questionable inferences in the way politicians interpreted data on education and crime abounded. In Argentina, for example, Sarmiento interpreted the fact that illiteracy rates among criminals in England and France were greater than illiteracy rates in the general population of those countries as "proof that instruction moralizes the masses."[37] It was only in exceptional cases that politicians relied on more sophisticated analysis to make inferences about the consequences of education. One such example comes from France, where one politician made inferences about the effects of education by comparing how literacy rates evolved between 1828 and 1842 among convicted criminals compared to the general population. Observing that literacy improved less among criminals than the rest of society, he concluded that this provided strong proof that education has the power to reduce crime by improving the moral character of the population.[38] This conclusion would be questioned by any social scientist today, among other reasons because it does not acknowledge the possibility that incarceration may reduce schooling instead of the other way around.

But whether politicians' inferences were valid or not is beside the point. What matters for the sake of the book's argument is that politicians *believed* in the benefits of education for crime reduction, gathered evidence to assess the consequences of education, and interpreted this evidence in ways

---

36. Friendly (2007).
37. Sarmiento (1849), p. 55.
38. Sarmiento (1849), p. 55.

that reflected their conviction about the potential of education to reduce crime.

WHAT DID GOVERNMENTS DO WHEN EDUCATION "FAILED"?

When politicians concluded that the education system had failed to reduce crime or social disorder, they reformed those systems. They did not stop investing in mass schooling, but instead adopted a new curriculum, changed the procedures for training and recruiting teachers, or introduced changes in their inspection system, all with the hope that *this* time they would choose the right set of education policies to pacify the population.

A historical example of governments' tendency to reform a failing education system rather than foregoing mass schooling altogether comes from Germany after the 1848 Revolution. As in other parts of Western Europe, 1848 was a year of widespread popular discontent that escalated into full-blown social revolution against the established order. In the German case, the revolution failed. Although liberals were able to take control of the government for a few short months, as early as October 1848 their power was showing visible signs of erosion. By November 1850, conservatives were back in control and the old order had been fully restored. Conservatives blamed primary school teachers for the 1848 Revolution. In 1851, the conservative journalist and social critic Wilhelm Riehl described teachers as a "perverse" and "evil demon" and argued that they had inspired the peasantry to rise up. Although historians still debate the accuracy of this claim, in the 1850s, Riehl's diagnosis that teachers were key instigators of the revolution quickly acquired the status of an established truth.[39] For the conservative government, however, the problem was not education as such but rather the content and organization of education, both of which needed to be reformed in order for schools to effectively produce "loyalty of the citizen for the state" and "true obedience to the law."[40]

Following the restoration of the old order in 1850, the Prussian government introduced a series of ultra-conservative education reforms that further increased the state's control over popular education (*Volksschule*) vis-à-vis the

---

39. Welch (2001), pp. 25–26. For opposing views about the accuracy of Riehl's diagnosis see, on one hand, Nipperdey (1976) as an example of a historian who argues that "mass education was a vehicle of social unrest" (p. 172) in large part because "there was a revolutionary disposition among teachers" (p. 169) and, on the other hand, Skopp (1982) as an example of a historian who argues that the idea of the revolutionary teacher was just a myth, and "probably only around 1 percent of teachers were actively involved in the actual revolutionary movement" (p. 400).

40. Nipperdey (1976), pp. 162–166.

churches.[41] The historian Kenneth Barkin writes that "Prussia's leaders had come to see what a Trojan horse compulsory schooling could become if it were not tightly controlled."[42] The set of reforms introduced to tighten control over primary education included reforms of teacher training, the primary school curriculum, and the administration of schools. First, the Prussian government centralized the administration of teacher training seminars and imposed on these a rigid curriculum that emphasized that "teachers' main duty was to produce God-fearing patriotic subjects for the king."[43] Second, a new curriculum for primary schools was adopted in 1854. Unlike the preceding curriculums of 1763/5, the new curriculum provided more precise instructions regarding how many hours should be devoted to each mandatory subject, and imposed a unified curriculum for all primary schools regardless of whether they were located in rural versus urban or in Protestant versus Catholic regions. Third, in 1854 the administration of the *Volksschule* became increasingly centralized under the Ministry of Education as part of "a counterrevolutionary tactic in Prussia." In other parts of Germany, too, governments who "feared that the revolution had been nourished in the schools" responded by enhancing their control over primary education, thus reducing the educational authority of churches and local governments. Through these reforms, writes Douglas Skopp, "the *Volksschule* was re-dedicated as an institution designed to teach political loyalty and religious piety."[44]

The reforms in Prussia are illustrative of a general pattern whereby politicians who conclude that an education system is failing to accomplish its goals respond by reforming the system. Another illustration of this pattern comes from how politicians in Argentina responded to the problem of mass violence against the oligarchic regime that emerged at the turn of the century. Education policymakers blamed the violence on the national curriculum adopted in 1884. In their view, the curriculum had failed to promote social order because, while it placed a heavy emphasis on moral education, it did not do enough to assimilate the immigrant population. To fix the problem of violence they observed among immigrants and the working class, in 1910 the central government introduced a new national curriculum for primary schools which, it argued, would undo "the nation's moral decline"

41. Barkin (1983), p. 51.
42. Barkin (1983), p. 52.
43. Barkin (1983), p. 51.
44. Skopp (1982), p. 356.

and restore social order by forging national unity. Contrary to the previous curriculum, which respected the diverse identities of the immigrant population, the new curriculum was heavily focused on inculcating a shared national identity. It placed a greater emphasis on teaching Spanish, history, and geography; prescribed the teaching of patriotism in every single subject, from moral education and gymnastics to arithmetic and geometry; and eliminated many of the more complex subjects included in the previous curriculum, such as physics and chemistry.[45] Around this time, new rituals were also incorporated into the school day and calendar to celebrate national heroes and symbols.[46]

While in some cases the diagnosis that politicians made was that an ill-conceived curriculum was to blame for the failure of primary schools to promote social order, in other cases they concluded that the problem lay with teachers' failure to implement the prescribed curriculum. Pointing the finger at teachers usually went hand in hand with characterizations of teachers as disloyal or, in more extreme cases, subversive. The responses to this type of conclusion usually entailed reforms that affected the teaching career in various ways. Sometimes, policymakers sought to increase teachers' loyalty by targeting *existing* teachers through centralized school inspections or, in more extreme cases, teacher purges. Other times, they focused on enhancing *future* teachers' loyalty by reforming teacher training and certification policies. This was the approach not only in Prussia, as we saw earlier, but also in France after the 1848 Revolution. The French government concluded that teachers were partly responsible for the revolution and that existing policies were not doing an adequate job of training and recruiting teachers who would act as loyal agents of the state. To address this, the government reformed the curriculum of Normal Schools and narrowed down the requirements for earning a basic teaching certification to three things: moral righteousness, religious knowledge, and political docility.[47]

Teacher training reforms and government-led purges of the teaching corps have been common tools to reign in "subversive" teachers well beyond the nineteenth century. Countries as diverse as democratic Finland and dictatorial Chile during the 1970s opted to move the responsibility to train teachers to universities, abolishing teacher training seminars and Normal

---

45. Ramos Mejía (1910), t.I.
46. Bertoni (2001).
47. Toloudis (2012), p. 52.

Schools in part because politicians feared that these institutions were enabling the organization of radical left-wing students.[48] In Argentina during the first two presidencies of Juan Perón (1946–1955), the government increased the accessibility of teacher education programs in an effort to recruit into teaching more members of the working class that formed Perón's core constituency, and fired existing teachers who refused to swear allegiance to the Peronist Doctrine.[49] In Spain, Franco first fired those teachers who, because of their left-wing orientation, were perceived as a national security threat, and then, those teachers who, because of their traditional Catalan or Basque family names, were perceived as a threat to the strict type of nationalism that Franco's regime sought to inculcate.[50] Other recent examples include the mass purge of teachers in China during the Cultural Revolution as part of the Anti-Rightist Campaign of 1957–58;[51] the purge of Black teachers and school principals in the United States during the Civil Rights Movement;[52] and the teacher purges in Turkey in 2016 when, months after a failed attempt to overthrow Recep Erdoğan, the government fired 15,000 education workers accused of threatening the rule of law.[53]

History is replete with evidence showing that when governments believe their education systems are failing, they tend not to move away from investing in education, but instead tend to reform those systems with the hope that a new set of education policies will finally help attain the state's educational goals. Instead of giving up on the idea that mass education can strengthen existing political institutions, governments have reformed the curriculum, adding a renewed emphasis or a new twist in the way they go about teaching moral and civic values. Instead of accepting that some degree of teacher autonomy may be unavoidable, governments have frequently turned to more or new education reforms which, they hope, will better align teachers' behavior with the state's educational agenda.

At a general level, this response is no different from the response we see today among governments that hope their education systems will promote economic development but observe that schools are failing to promote basic

---

48. Furuhagen and Holmén (2017).
49. Bernetti and Puiggrós (1993).
50. Balcells and Villamil (2020).
51. Zeng and Eisenman (2018).
52. Fenwick (2022); Fultz (2004).
53. Kingsley (2016).

skills. The typical response of governments in this situation is not to stop investing in education, but rather to innovate in the sphere of education policy in hopes that more funding or a new curriculum or set of policies for recruiting, monitoring, or compensating teachers will promote more skills acquisition. We can view the tendency to reform a failing education system in a positive or negative light, depending on whether we think it reflects an entrepreneurial and steadfast spirit or an arrogant and stubborn attitude. However we judge it, this is as common a response today as it was a century ago.

CONCLUSION

In this chapter, I summarized what we know today about how education shapes social order and political stability and offered a framework for considering the potential consequences of mass schooling. I closed by discussing how the consequences of education policy for social order relate to the causes behind the rise and spread of mass education. Policymakers gathered information to track the consequences of education and interpreted this information in a way that is consistent with the book's argument. In the face of inadequate, scarce, and often misinterpreted information, they nonetheless remained convinced of the power of education systems to promote social order.

CHAPTER NINE
THE FUTURE OF EDUCATION

There is a coercive element present in mass education systems. This coercive element was built into these systems and has persisted over time. We often overlook its presence when thinking about the goals of education, in part because we confuse what ought to be the goals of education in a liberal society versus what goals education systems actually set out to accomplish. This book sheds light on the importance that governments throughout history have given to discipline, obedience, and acceptance of the status quo as key goals of mass education. It reconceptualizes the provision of mass education as a state-building policy tool designed to promote values, attitudes, and behaviors conducive to internal order and political stability, more so than as a progressive or economic policy tool designed to promote skills for social mobility and economic growth. The coercive roots of mass education continue to shape education systems and help explain why these systems do a poor job of promoting skills. Being aware of these roots is valuable for educators and education reformers, international organizations, and those committed to strengthening democracy and reducing inequality.

ENDURING LEGACIES AND MODERN CHALLENGES

Education systems today face a problem of low skills: While almost all countries have universal access to primary education, many children who have been in school for years lack basic reading, math, and science skills. The phenomenon is global. Roughly 40 percent of women in South Asia, North Africa, and the Middle East with exactly five years of primary schooling, and 50 percent in Sub-Saharan Africa, cannot read a single sentence. Again, despite *five years of schooling*.¹ While among Latin American countries this extreme form of illiteracy, though present, is less common, more than 40 percent of 15-year-olds who are *in school* still lack basic reading comprehension, math, and science skills.² Wealthy countries are not exempt; in the United States and other OECD countries, about 13 percent of 15-year-old students lack basic skills.³ In most countries, the acquisition of skills is particularly troublesome among children of low-income families.

The problem of low education quality constitutes one of the most serious obstacles to economic development today. It also threatens the stability of democracies. Foreign aid agencies and international organizations have coalesced around an agenda focused on addressing the issue, which UNESCO and the World Bank have labeled a "learning crisis."⁴ While a skilled workforce was unnecessary during the First Industrial Revolution, over time technological progress has become increasingly dependent on skills.⁵ Considerable evidence suggests that, today, the average level of literacy and numeracy skills is a much more significant determinant of economic development than the level of access to schooling.⁶ When schools fail to teach the kinds of knowledge and skills that enhance productivity and innovation, education systems also fail to realize their potential to bolster democratic stability⁷—it is well-documented that economic development prevents democracies from collapsing.⁸ In addition, schools have been blamed for failing to equip citizens with the ability to evaluate arguments and evidence, detect false claims, and identify politicians with authoritarian inclinations.

---

1. Le Nestour, Moscoviz, and Sandefur (2021).
2. The figure is based on the PISA 2018 results from Argentina, Brazil, Chile, Colombia, Costa Rica, Dominican Republic, Mexico, Panama, Peru, and Uruguay (OECD 2019). PISA stands for Programme for International Student Assessment, an international standardized test administered by the OECD every three years among a nationally representative sample of 15-year-old students who are in school in participating countries.
3. Based on PISA 2018 results (OECD 2019).
4. In 2018, the World Bank devoted its flagship *World Development Report* to the learning crisis (World Bank 2018). See also UNESCO (2014).
5. Galor and Moav (2000); Goldin and Katz (2008).
6. See Barro (2001); Hanushek and Woessmann (2008); World Bank (2018). For example, among countries with similar years of schooling, GDP per capita is considerably greater among those countries where students have better reading, math, and science skills. By contrast, among countries with similar student skills, more years of schooling are not associated with higher levels of GDP per capita.
7. For example, see Khalenberg and Janey (2016); Berner and Ross (2022); Van Sloun (2022).
8. Przeworski (2005).

In international development circles, the leading explanation for the problem of low education quality is that policymakers *do not know* what education policies work best to promote skills. Accordingly, the primary solution proposed to tackle the learning crisis is to address policymakers' ignorance by "evaluating what works and using that evidence to inform policy change."[9] In the words of economists Esther Duflo and Abhijit Banerjee, key proponents of this approach, policymakers choose policies that do not promote skills "*not out of bad intentions . . . but* simply because the policy makers had the wrong model"[10] of how to promote skills in mind. As Andrés Velasco, former Minister of Finance for Chile, has aptly noted, the idea that producing and disseminating evidence on "what works" is the key to solving the so-called learning crisis is premised on a simple "implicit model of policymaking: if you build it, they will come. Politicians, if confronted with strong evidence, will do the right thing."[11]

Departing from the common focus on the limitations of current education policies, this book offers a broader perspective that highlights the deep roots of modern education systems' dismal performance at teaching skills. It suggests that a fundamental reason behind this performance is that the very creation, initial design, and expansion of public primary education systems was not guided by a concern to improve the basic skills of the population, much less their critical thinking skills. Instead, the key reason why central governments set up and invested in these systems was to teach ordinary people to be obedient and well-behaved. Again, mass education was conceived not as a poverty reduction tool or as a tool to empower the masses, but as an essential component of the repertoire of state-building policies used to promote social order and political stability.

The reasons why politicians care about mass education have changed less than we may think since the nineteenth century. True, the explicit goals of education—as stated in laws and other official documents—have expanded over time, and many education systems today do have the goal of promoting skills, at least on paper. Even so, when in 2017 researchers at the Brookings Institution examined mission and vision statements and other official policy documents from Ministries of Education in 152 countries, they found that promoting "values" was a more common, explicit goal of education

---

9. World Bank (2010).
10. Banerjee and Duflo (2011), p. 16. Emphasis mine.
11. Velasco (2019).

than promoting "skills" or "knowledge."[12] In at least some countries, official documents and political speeches that mention "skills" as a key goal of education may simply be paying lip service to citizens, foreign aid agencies, and other actors who have come to expect this as a stated goal of schools; when the Center for Global Development surveyed 900 senior education officials from 35 low-income and lower-middle income countries in 2020, officials ranked "dutiful citizens" as the number one priority outcome of education, followed by secondary school completion, with basic literacy and numeracy skills last in their list of priorities.[13]

It is therefore unsurprising that the emphasis on "evaluating what works and using that evidence to inform policy change" has not lived up to its promise to address the so-called learning crisis. Hundreds of millions of dollars, dozens of experimental studies, and two decades later, we have amassed significant evidence on education interventions that have improved students' skills when implemented by NGOs. Yet this knowledge has failed to translate into government-endorsed systemwide education reforms. Why? In part, because policymakers value experimental studies less than development economists and international organizations had hoped.[14] But, more fundamentally, because governments often care more about teaching discipline and obedience than basic skills and critical thinking. A good example comes from Kenya. In 2010, a team of researchers partnered with the national government to study whether hiring public school teachers on fixed-term contracts instead of offering permanent civil service jobs could lead to improvements in students' English and math skills. The assumption, informed by previous experimental studies, was that hiring teachers on renewable as opposed to permanent contracts would induce teachers to put more effort into teaching knowledge and skills. The team found that this was indeed what occurred when implementation was in the hands of an international NGO, but that the program failed to promote skills when implementation was turned over to the government because the government put less effort than the NGO into monitoring whether teachers were indeed focusing on improving student skills.[15] The government's behavior was predictable: Contemporary observers note that "the Kenyan school

---

12. I am grateful to Brookings Institution for sharing the original data. See Care et al. (2018).
13. Crawfurd et al. (2021).
14. Crawfurd et al. (2021).
15. Bold et al. (2018). See also Muralidharan and Niehaus (2017); Bellés-Obrero and Lombardi (2022).

system is quite authoritarian"; it focuses on disciplining students and maintaining order in the classroom, and "challenges to teacher authority are not tolerated." Moreover, "learning is by rote, and creativity and critical thinking in the classroom are not highly prized."[16] Absent strong monitoring by an external actor concerned about promoting skills (such as an NGO), teachers continued behaving as usual inside the classroom.

What this book shows is that governments' persistent reliance on schools to mold children into well-behaved citizens has deep roots. Their relative disinterest in improving the skills of the population is *not* a crisis of contemporary times, nor is it unique to current developing countries. It is an enduring phenomenon born of the goals that drove the creation and expansion of mass education systems in the Western societies of Europe and the Americas.

In addition, the book explains that political elites are especially likely to become invested in the indoctrination role of schools if they believe that the masses pose a threat to social order and political stability. A wide range of factors of varying scale and severity can exacerbate elite fear of the "unruly" and "morally flawed" masses, from an influx of immigrants to the outbreak of food riots, peasant revolts, or civil wars.[17] Here again, while the book demonstrates that increased concern among elites about the possibility of anarchy and the breakdown of social order played a key role in prompting governments to invest in primary schooling during the long nineteenth century, it also discusses recent efforts to reform education driven by similar concerns.

One recent illustration of the book's argument is the wave of curriculum reforms proposed, and in many cases enacted, by Republican politicians following the Black Lives Matter (BLM) protests of summer 2020. I witnessed these protests with deep concern that—like in France or Chile during the nineteenth century, or Peru in the twenty-first century—they might prompt those politicians who felt most threatened by protester demands to turn to education reform as a mechanism of social control. These concerns began to materialize when at the end of summer 2020 the Trump administration created the 1776 Commission, charged with making educa-

---

16. Friedman et al. (2016).

17. For contemporary evidence that immigration exacerbates concerns about crime, even when it does not actually lead to an increase in crime, see Ajzenman, Dominguez, and Undurraga (2023). See also Tyack (1974) on the role of immigration in the late-nineteenth-century United States in exacerbating traditional elites' fear of crime and anarchy.

tion policy recommendations to promote "patriotic education," "better enable a rising generation to understand the history and principles of the founding of the United States," and "correct the distorted perspective" and "radicalized view" that racial inequalities are the product of laws and public policies.[18] After Trump left the presidency in January 2021, the efforts to reform and "de-radicalize" school curricula turned to the state level, where Republicans, who felt most threatened by the BLM movement's demand to reform existing institutions, enacted laws that ban public schools from teaching "divisive concepts" such as institutionalized racism.[19]

While we may be tempted to underscore the differences between this and the other cases in the book (indeed, there are differences across *all* cases), Republican elites' anxiety following the BLM protests and their subsequent effort to prohibit schools from teaching about institutionalized racism fits well with the ubiquitous phenomenon identified in this book: Elites threatened by mass protest turn to education to teach children to accept the status quo. Nineteenth-century autocrats in Europe were among the first to respond to social unrest in this way, but politicians in modern societies—democratic and not—have turned to similar tactics, too.

The historical origins of primary education systems also matter for our understanding of the present because the manner in which education systems are organized today owes much to the past. The emphasis on rote memorization and repetition instead of critical thinking is one example of the practices that emerged as central to the goals of education in the nineteenth century, and that have proved incredibly resilient over time. Relatedly, the contents that students have to memorize and internalize typically serve the interests of dominant groups in society, for instance an interpretation of history that glorifies "national heroes" and minimizes or altogether avoids mentioning the violence inflicted by elites against other members of society. Consider the map of the world shown in figure 9.1. It depicts country experts' answers to the question, "When historical events are taught in school, to what extent are students exposed to diverse views and/or interpretations of these events?" The data come from the Varieties of Political Indoctrination in Education and Media dataset discussed in more detail in chapter 7. The answers depicted in figure 9.1 correspond to experts' assessments for the year 2021 and draw on an average of five experts per country.

---

18. Gaudiano (2020).
19. Stout and Wilburn (2021).

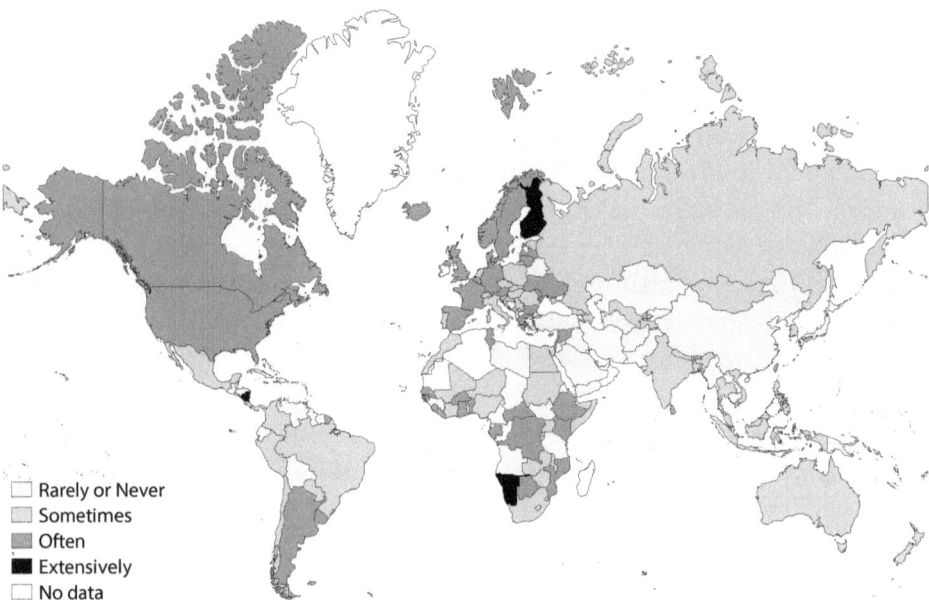

Figure 9.1. Frequency of student exposure to diverse viewpoints, by country, 2021. The map shows country experts' responses to the question: "When historical events are taught in school, to what extent are students exposed to diverse views and / or interpretations of these events?" See text and footnotes for sources and methodology.

What the data suggest is that schools expose students to different interpretations of history either often or extensively in less than one-third of countries. In seventy-one countries (43 percent), students are exposed to diverse viewpoints only sometimes, and in another forty-seven countries (28 percent) they are rarely or never exposed to a variety of viewpoints.

Another enduring feature of education systems is the presence of regimented curriculums and limited teacher autonomy. During the 1980s and 1990s, many countries adopted reforms that decentralized the responsibility for funding and/or managing schools from the central to subnational governments. However, rarely have centralized governments given up their power to determine the content of education. Also as part of the V-Indoc dataset, we asked country experts who determines the school curriculum—that is, the list of subjects taught and the amount of time devoted to each subject—as well as what proportion of school textbooks used to teach core subjects are approved by a national authority. We found that in 159 of the 166 countries for which we obtained responses, the curriculum as of 2021 was established either entirely or mostly by a national authority, and that in 121 countries (73 percent) *all* school textbooks are approved at the national level.

The persistence of education practices and institutions implies that, even when politicians *are* well-intentioned in the sense of wanting to promote skills, their efforts are constrained by the educational structures inherited from the past. Suppose, for example, that a government decides to adopt a new curriculum that places considerable emphasis on promoting literacy, numeracy, and critical thinking skills. Suppose also that the government prints and distributes new textbooks aligned with the new curriculum. Should we expect this curriculum and textbook reform to lead to an improvement in student skills? Probably not nearly as much as the government would want. One key constraint that most well-intentioned governments face is that the teachers responsible for implementing the new curriculum (or most other education reforms) have been poorly trained to promote skills.[20] From Latin America to Africa to the United States, education policy experts have noted that teacher training programs place considerable emphasis on training new teachers in classroom management strategies, history of education, and philosophy of education, yet fail to ensure that teachers have the subject matter knowledge they need to effectively teach language, math, or science. Even today, at a time when most members of society expect schools to successfully teach these subjects, teacher training programs have not adequately adapted to these expectations. It is no wonder that teachers in many countries spend a good portion of their classroom time on disciplining and managing student behavior. This is what they are best trained to do.

Another legacy that constrains well-intentioned education reforms is the architecture and design of classrooms. Most classrooms today are set up so that the teacher stands in front of the class and the students sit in rows facing the teacher. This design element deliberately sought to establish a clear hierarchy between teachers and students and to encourage respect for the teacher's authority. But when a teacher wants to promote debate and critical thinking, the traditional organization of classrooms gets in the way. Some of the favorite features championed by architecture firms that focus on designing student-centered classrooms are movable furniture that can accommodate a variety of activities, movable walls or a small meeting room

20. Bruns and Luque (2014); Bold et al. (2017).

within the classroom to support small group discussions, comfortable seating, project labs, and indoor-outdoor connection. The vast majority of classrooms around the world look very different.

All of this—rote memorization, regimented curriculum plans imposed by the central government, history lessons that teach the narrative of dominant groups, teacher-centered classrooms, and teacher education programs that do not adequately prepare teachers to teach skills—is accompanied by another enduring feature of education systems: the emphasis on disciplining students. According to the Oxford dictionary, to discipline is to "train someone to obey rules or a code of behavior." Historically as well as today, schools have relied on a combination of punishments and rewards to encourage obedience and good behavior. The list of punishments can range from public scolding and humiliation all the way to corporal punishment and school suspension. The rewards include public praise such as when a teacher recognizes a student's good behavior in front of the entire class, private praise in the form of stickers in a student's notebook or a note to their parents, and special privileges for well-behaved students.

To be sure, some schools have moved away from this traditional approach to education, especially schools that cater to students from wealthy backgrounds. However, these were never the students whom elites were concerned about. The students whom elites wanted to discipline were those from non-elite backgrounds—these were the students who, according to elites, had to be taught to respect the status quo. That this concern remains relevant to this day is made clear by how privileged versus non-privileged students are disciplined. There is extensive evidence that, for equivalent forms of misbehavior, schools apply harsher sanctions to students from non-privileged backgrounds, including low-income students and students from historically marginalized ethnic minorities.[21] In the United States, there are also entire chains of charter schools—such as Kipp Academy, Success Academy, and Achievement First—that are targeted at underprivileged students and operate under a "zero tolerance" and "no excuses" policy, with strict enforcement of rules and codes of conduct. The assumption of these schools,

---

21. For a review, see Welsh and Little (2018). The U.S. Department of Education under the presidency of Barack Obama issued guiding principles for school disciplining that sought to reduce the disparities in suspension and expulsion rates by ethnicity and disability status (U.S. Department of Education 2014). The focus on equity in disciplining methods was removed in a new set of guidelines for enhanced school safety issued during the Trump administration (Federal Commission on School Safety 2021).

just like the assumption of Prussian education reformers in the late eighteenth century, is that "in neighborhoods where violence and disorder are widespread,"[22] parents are not doing a good enough job of promoting good behavior, and the school must therefore step in to mold children into well-behaved and rule-abiding individuals.[23]

These examples illustrate that coercion—the practice of using threats or actual punishments to induce someone to behave in a specific way—remains part of the fabric of education systems to this day. The reason is not just inertia. As the previous discussion suggests, governments old and new have found the idea of using schools to mold children into obedient future citizens quite attractive. The preeminence of this over other possible goals of education both historically and today, and not the lack of knowledge about what policies work, is the most important challenge facing those who want education systems to better promote skills.

EDUCATION FOR PEACE OR SOCIAL CONTROL?

At times throughout the book, I have used the term "social control" to describe the goal pursued by governments interested in regulating and promoting mass education. In liberal societies today, this term has a negative connotation because it clashes with the value of individual autonomy that liberalism prizes. Some readers may question the choice of this term and suggest instead that we talk about education systems' goal of promoting "peace." Indeed, it could be argued that internal peace and order are necessary conditions for the exercise of the individual rights that are at the heart of liberal societies, including the right to govern one's own life. Put differently, in a society mired in social unrest, anarchy, or civil war, it is difficult for individuals to pursue their dreams. From this perspective, there is a place for education systems to promote peace and order without undermining, and in fact contributing to upholding, personal autonomy.

What distinguishes a benign peace education agenda from a social control agenda is that, in the latter, the specific values, attitudes, and behaviors that schools advance have been chosen by elites to preserve the existing balance of power within society. Elites throughout history have used mass

---

22. Boyd, Maranto, and Rose (2014).
23. For a critique of zero-tolerance, zero-excuses schools, see Skiba and Knesting (2002). For a defense of these schools, see Boyd, Maranto, and Rose (2014).

schooling to impose not only their preferred narrative about the country's history but also their preferred understanding of what constitutes good moral behavior and legitimate political action. This is true not just of autocratic rulers; even in democracies, elites often benefit from teaching ordinary citizens that voting, not rebelling or protesting, is the legitimate mechanism for expressing discontent with the status quo. Whenever schools disseminate values and attitudes to help those in power stay in power, education systems serve a *social control* purpose. This social control purpose is antithetical to the goal of promoting individual autonomy, as autonomy requires fostering critical thinking skills and, in particular, enabling students to question received truths.

Interest in the role of education as a tool to promote peace has intensified over the last decade among international organizations working in post-conflict settings. In 2011, UNESCO's annual flagship publication proposed "strengthening the role of education systems in preventing conflicts and building peaceful societies."[24] A year later, the United Nations launched the Global Education First Initiative, which proposed that the promotion of global citizenship become a key priority of education systems alongside providing education for all and improving the quality of education. According to this initiative, "While increasing access to education is still a major challenge in many countries," the "relevance of education is now receiving more attention than ever ... Beyond cognitive knowledge and skills, the international community is urging an education that will help resolve the existing and emerging global challenges menacing our planet," "with due emphasis on the importance of values, attitudes and skills that promote mutual respect and peaceful coexistence."[25] More recently, the United Nation's Sustainable Development Goals propose that schools should "promote a culture of peace and non-violence." Interest in post-conflict education has also grown quickly within universities, manifested in the creation of new courses, graduate programs, and conferences on the topic.

While there are clear echoes from the past in the peace-building agenda proposed by international organizations, with its emphasis on promoting social cohesion to prevent violence, we should hasten to highlight significant deviations from historical practice. Unlike traditional approaches, the type of citizenship education that international organizations advocate for

---

24. UNESCO (2011).
25. UNESCO (2014), p. 5.

also includes instruction in human rights, cosmopolitanism, and multiculturalism. Further, and in contrast to an approach that seeks to convince people to accept their place in society, both UNESCO and the World Bank view schools as a place to promote social mobility and address the economic inequalities that often lead to the onset of civil war.[26]

This book gives us reasons to be cautious about the success of this international agenda. It shows that the type of mass education that most states have supported in post-conflict settings is not the type of human rights–centered or multicultural education that the international development community has in mind. Whether we look at 1760s Prussia, 1880s Argentina, or even at more recent post-conflict settings such as Peru after 2000 or Thailand after 2014, the formation of students in conflict-afflicted countries has emphasized moral and political *duties* more than rights, and the legitimacy of *the state* as a supreme authority more than a cosmopolitan worldview, leaving little or no space to acknowledge or discuss the grievances of historically underprivileged groups.

Indeed, there is evidence that history is repeating itself. Several studies analyzing the content of national textbooks used to teach social studies, history, and civics in eighty countries since World War II have found that textbooks published in post-conflict settings are more likely to emphasize narratives of national unity and citizens' political duties, and less likely to discuss citizens' political rights or the rights of minorities, which are viewed as destabilizing or threatening to state legitimacy.[27] Education expert Garnett Russel has argued that this emphasis on citizens' political duties and national unity, and simultaneously, the rare mention of rights, diverse cultures, or the causes of past internal conflicts, reflect an irreconcilable tension between the national and global versions of citizenship education.[28]

The tendency of central governments in post-conflict settings to invest in mass education in order to strengthen the state's authority creates a major challenge for foreign aid agencies and international organizations, which fund education systems in developing countries but do not get involved in curriculum reform, much less the part of the curriculum that deals with social studies, history, or civics. The World Bank's financial support for education in 1990s Rwanda is a good case in point. Immediately after the

---

26. UNESCO (2011). See also https://www.worldbank.org/en/topic/education/brief/education-in-fragile-conflict-violence-contexts.
27. Russell and Tiplic (2014); Lerch (2016); Lerch, Russell, and Ramirez (2017).
28. Russell (2018).

Rwandan civil war of 1990–1994 and the genocide lasting from April to July of 1994, the government of Rwanda focused on reopening primary and secondary schools and initiated a program to rapidly expand primary education access by building new schools and repairing those damaged by the war. The new government also heavily revised the content of education in order to promote state- and nation-building. Civic education acquired a prominent role in an effort to create model citizens who would help sustain internal peace and respect the state.[29] In addition, after temporarily suspending the teaching of history in 1994, the Ministry of Education set out to teach future populations "the *true* history of Rwanda," blaming the civil war and genocide on past colonial policies, minimizing the existence of ethnic inequality and interethnic conflict, and giving scant attention to the violation of human rights.[30] Even as many teachers and education experts have denounced the role of schools in helping legitimize an authoritarian political regime, noting that the Rwandan curriculum acts as "a reflector of dominant government narratives from which deviation is not permitted,"[31] the World Bank continued to finance the government's education reforms. For example, a World Bank loan approved during the war and disbursed mainly between 1996 and 1998 contributed US$23.3 million toward the government's intervention in primary education following the civil war. Since 2000, the World Bank has committed close to US$1 billion toward Rwandan education.

To be sure, international organizations never explicitly offer loans or grants to design and implement indoctrination reforms. However, once education loans are disbursed, these organizations do not actively monitor precisely how the funds are used by the recipient government. Portions of a loan that are supposed to contribute to capacity-building within the Ministry of Education, for example, can easily be used by the government to commission, print, and distribute new textbooks. Portions that are supposed to contribute to teacher training can be repurposed to train new teachers in the government's new curriculum. World Bank staff generally choose to overlook these possibilities, in part because they lack the capacity, incentives, or contextual knowledge needed to evaluate the content of civic education, social studies, and history curriculums in each country, and in part

---

29. King (2013); Sundberg (2016).
30. King (2013); Russell (2018).
31. King (2013), p. 137.

because doing so would raise serious concerns about foreign interference with state sovereignty.

As complex as these issues are, the pattern of post-conflict education investments discussed in this book underscores the need for international organizations to engage deeply and consciously with uncomfortable questions: Should they fund education interventions in post-conflict contexts knowing that governments in these contexts are likely to use schools at least partly as an indoctrination tool? Should they revisit their practice of avoiding conversations about sensitive curriculum issues? Should they put in place stronger mechanisms to monitor that funds are being used in alignment with the original intent of the loan? These are crucial questions for international organizations, whose work moving forward is expected to focus increasingly on conflict-afflicted countries.[32]

THE PATH FORWARD

When I have presented portions of this book to people who have devoted their entire careers to improving education systems, a frequent response is that they found my work "depressing" and "demoralizing." Indeed, I often felt the same way while conducting my research. Yet over time, as the initial disillusionment subsided, I have come to see the book's findings as both crucial and empowering to those of us who care deeply about transforming education.

We cannot address the dismal performance of education systems at promoting skills without first understanding the root cause of this problem. Over the last two decades, the dominant explanation, coming from economics and pervading the work of international organizations, has focused on the *ignorance* of well-intended policymakers. To overcome the problem of low skills, goes the argument, we need to invest heavily in identifying education policies that do in fact promote skills, and in disseminating this knowledge among policymakers. Despite initial enthusiasm for this approach, its failure to stimulate systemwide education reforms suggests that the diagnosis was amiss. This book suggests that the key reason behind the problem of low skills is not the ignorance of governments but their

---

32. According to the World Bank, conflicts drive 80 percent of all humanitarian needs, and by 2030, up to two-thirds of the world's extreme poor will likely live in conflict-afflicted settings. See https://www.worldbank.org/en/topic/fragilityconflictviolence/overview.

disinterest in placing skills at the forefront of their education policy strategy. The long history of public primary education systems demonstrates that these systems emerged, were designed, and expanded first and foremost to mold children into obedient future citizens. This legacy has been sustained over time by policymakers who agree with its major tenets.

Why is this knowledge empowering? Because it enables us to focus our attention on what really matters—and what really matters is understanding the *motivations* of politicians to reform education systems. History is not destiny. Despite the prevalence of coercive elements across education systems today, there are countries whose education systems *have* undergone considerable transformation over time. Finland is perhaps the most famous case—a country that introduced compulsory schooling legislation to foster obedience and social order following the Finnish civil war, but whose education system after the Second World War underwent a gradual but deep transformation toward a more child-centered approach. Another example comes from Chile, where the initial approach toward primary education, with its narrow focus on indoctrinating future citizens to respect the state's authority, was reformed in the 1960s to give greater emphasis to math and science skills for economic development. Chile again underwent deep education reforms in the 2010s to better support social mobility.

The practical implication of this book's argument is that we need to understand what motivates a government, such as the governments of Finland and Chile, to deemphasize indoctrination and embrace an education policy agenda that teaches basic skills and critical thinking. International organizations tackling low education quality should redirect resources that today are invested in identifying education policies that work toward developing knowledge about what makes politicians tick. We have learned that evidence about "what works" does not. We have also learned that governments care deeply about the ability of education systems to promote internal order and political stability. The challenge ahead is to figure out the conditions under which governments that care about maintaining and consolidating their power are likely to invest in the kind of education that could empower individuals to challenge it.

REFERENCES

Abbott, Jared A., Hillel David Soifer, and Matthias Vom Hau. 2017. "Transforming the Nation? The Bolivarian Education Reform in Venezuela." *Journal of Latin American Studies* 49(4): 885–916.
Aboites Aguilar, Luis. 2003. *Excepciones y privilegios: Modernización tributaria y centralización en México, 1922–1972*. México, D. F.: El Colegio de México.
Acemoglu, Daron, and James A. Robinson. 2006. *Economic Origins of Dictatorship and Democracy*. Cambridge: Cambridge University Press.
Aghion, Philippe, Xavier Jaravel, Torsten Persson, and Dorothee Rouzet. 2019. "Education and Military Rivalry." *Journal of the European Economic Association* 17(2): 376–412.
Aidt, Toke S., and Raphaël Franck. 2015. "Democratization Under the Threat of Revolution: Evidence from the Great Reform Act of 1832." *Econometrica* 83(2): 505–547.
Ajzenman, Nicolás, Patricio Dominguez, and Raimundo Undurraga. 2023. "Immigration, Crime, and Crime (Mis)Perceptions." *AEJ: Applied Economics* 15(4): 142–176.
Albertus, Michael. 2015. *Autocracy and Redistribution: The Politics of Land Reform*. New York: Cambridge University Press.
Alesina, Alberto, Paola Giuliano, and Bryoni Reich. 2021. "Nation-Building and Education." *Economic Journal* 131(638): 2273–2303.
Alexander, Thomas. 1919. *The Prussian Elementary Schools*. New York: Macmillan.
Allen, R. C. 2003. "Progress and Poverty in Early Modern Europe." *Economic History Review* 56(3): 403–443.
Alliaud, Andrea. 2007. *Los maestros y su historia: Los orígenes del magisterio argentino*. Buenos Aires: Granica.
Alphabet des écoles primaires extrait de l'alphabet et premier livre de lecture autorisé par le Conseil royal de l'instruction publique et l'un des cinq manuels spécialement adoptés pour l'instruction primaire. 1841. Paris: L. Hachette.
Ames, Barry. 1970. "Bases of Support for Mexico's Dominant Party." *American Political Science Review* 64(1): 153–167.
Amunátegui, Miguel, and Gregorio Amunátegui. 1856. "De la instrucción primaria en Chile." Santiago: Imprenta del Ferrocarril.
Anderson, Benedict. 1983. *Imagined Communities: Reflections on the Origin and Spread of Nationalism*. London: Verso.
Anderson, Elisabeth. 2013. "Ideas in Action: The Politics of Prussian Child Labor Reform, 1817–1839." *Theory and Society* 42: 81–119.
Anderson, Elisabeth. 2018. "Policy Entrepreneurs and the Origins of the Regulatory Welfare State: Child Labor Reform in Nineteenth-Century Europe." *American Sociological Review* 83(1): 173–211.
Andersson, Jens, and Thor Berger. 2019. "Elites and the Expansion of Education in Nineteenth-Century Sweden." *Economic History Review* 72(3): 897–924.

Ansell, Ben W. 2010. *From the Ballot to the Blackboard: The Redistributive Political Economy of Education*. Cambridge: Cambridge University Press.
Ansell, Ben, and Johannes Lindvall. 2013. "The Political Origins of Primary Education Systems: Ideology, Institutions, and Interdenominational Conflict in an Era of Nation-Building," *American Political Science Review* 107(3): 505–522.
Ansell, Ben W., and David Samuels. 2014. *Inequality and Democratization: An Elite-Competition Approach*. New York: Cambridge University Press.
Archivo Nacional de Chile. "Ley General de Educación Primaria del 24 de Noviembre de 1860." http://www.archivonacional.cl/616/w3-article-28319.html.
Argentina. July 6, 1883. *Diario de Sesiones (Diputados)*.
Argentina. July 11, 1883. *Diario de Sesiones (Diputados)*.
Argentina. July 12, 1883. *Diario de Sesiones (Diputados)*.
Argentina. July 13, 1883. *Diario de Sesiones (Diputados)*.
Argentina. July 14, 1883. *Diario de Sesiones (Diputados)*.
Argentina. 1884. *Ley 1.420 de Educación Común*.
Argentina. 1898. "La educación común en 1898: informe presentado por el Presidente del Consejo Nacional de Educación." *El Monitor de la Educación Común*. Accessed July 1, 2020: http://repositorio.educacion.gov.ar:8080/dspace/handle/123456789/102702.
Argentina. Ministerio de Justicia e Instrucción Pública. 1938. "Escuelas de Artes y Oficios de la Nación." http://www.bnm.me.gov.ar/giga1/documentos/EL002889.pdf.
Arnold-Forster, H. O. 1887. *The Citizen Reader, With a Preface by the Right Hon. W. E. Forster, Formerly Vice-President of the Committee of Council on Education, For the Use of Schools*. Cassell & Company Ltd.
Arnold, Matthew. 1883. *Culture & Anarchy: An Essay in Political and Social Criticism; and Friendship's Garland, Being the Conversations, Letters, and Opinions of the Late Arminius, Baron von Thunderten-Tronckh*. New York: Macmillan. http://find.galegroup.com/openurl/openurl?url_ver=Z39.88-2004&url_ctx_fmt=info:ofi/fmt:kev:mtx:ctx&res_id=info:sid/gale:NCCO&ctx_enc=info:ofi:enc:UTF-8&rft_val_fmt=info:ofi/fmt:kev:mtx:unknown&rft.artnum=CGJPWR303235213&req_dat=info:sid/gale:ugnid.
Arnold, Matthew. 1908. *Reports on Elementary Schools 1852–1882*. Edited by F. S. Marvin. London: Her Majesty's Stationery Office.
Arola, Pauli. 2003. "Tavoitteena Kunnon Kansalainen: Koulun kansalaiskasvatuksen päämäärät eduskunnan keskusteluissa 1917–1924." Helsinki University Department of Education Research Paper 191, https://helda.helsinki.fi/bitstream/handle/10138/19795/tavoitte.pdf?sequence=2.
Austria. 1774. *General School Ordinance*.
Bai, Yu, and Yanjun Li. 2020. "Good bye Chiang Kai-shek? The Long-Lasting Effects of Education under the Authoritarian Regime in Taiwan." *Economics of Education Review* 78. https://www.sciencedirect.com/science/article/pii/S0272775720305306?casa_token=o4idlyrhoqEAAAAA:mf9aZBLFl8IthKPRM6adt8Vz2kP5RdE9cGXjvov8b1Tv_gC5vribPs5uBquy-0k_HTsYIvMa.
Baker, Richard. 2015. "From the Field to the Classroom: The Boll Weevil's Impact on Education in Rural Georgia." *Journal of Economic History* 75(4): 1128–1160.
Baker, Richard B., John Blanchette, and Katherine Eriksson. 2020. "Long-Run Impacts of Agricultural Shocks on Educational Attainment: Evidence from the Boll Weevil." *Journal of Economic History* 80(1): 136–174.
Balcells, Laia, and Francisco Villamil. 2020. "The Double Logic of Internal Purges: New Evidence from Francoist Spain." *Nationalism and Ethnic Politics* 26(3): 260–278.
Bandiera, Oriana, Myra Mohnen, Imran Rasul, and Martina Viarengo. 2019. "Nation-Building through Compulsory Schooling during the Age of Mass Migration." *The Economic Journal* 129(617): 62–109.
Banerjee, Abhijit V., and Esther Duflo. 2011. *Poor Economics: A Radical Rethinking of the Way to Fight Global Poverty*. New York: PublicAffairs.
Barkin, Kenneth. 1983. "Social Control and the Volksschule in Vormärz Prussia." *Central European History* 16(1): 31–52.

Barnard, Henry. 1851. *Normal Schools, and Other Institutions, Agencies, and Means Designed for the Professional Education of Teachers*, vol. 2. Hartford: Case, Tiffany. https://babel.hathitrust.org/cgi/pt?id=osu.32435028032308&view=1up&seq=11.
Barrantes, Rafael, Diego Luna, and Jesús Peña. 2009. "De las políticas a las aulas: Concepciones y prácticas de formación en ciudadanía en Huamanga y Abancay." In *Formación en ciudadanía en la escuela peruana: avances conceptuales y limitaciones en la práctica de aula*, edited by Felix Reátegui. Ch. 3, 19–96. Instituto de Democracia y Derechos Humanos de la Pontificia Universidad Católica del Perú. Accessed July 15, 2023: https://idehpucp.pucp.edu.pe/images/publicaciones/formacion_en_ciudadania_escuela_peruana.pdf.
Barro, Robert J. 2001. "Human Capital and Growth." *American Economic Review* 91(2): 12–17.
Bazzi, Samuel, Masyhur Hilmy, and Benjamin Marx. 2022. "Religion, Education, and Development." NBER Working Paper No. 27073.
Becker, Gary S. 1964. *Human Capital: A Theoretical and Empirical Analysis, with Special Reference to Education*. Cambridge, MA: National Bureau of Economic Research.
Becker, Sasha, and Ludger Woessman. 2009. "Was Weber Wrong? A Human Capital Theory of Protestant Economic History." *Quarterly Journal of Economics* 124(2): 531–596.
Beezley, William H. (ed.). 2018. "Porfirian Social Practices and Etiquette." In *The Oxford Encyclopedia of Mexican History and Culture*. New York: Oxford University Press.
Belgium. 1842. *Organic Law of Primary Instruction*.
Bell, Brian, Rui Costa, and Stephen Machin. 2022. "Why Does Education Reduce Crime?" *Journal of Political Economy* 130(3): 732–765.
Bellés-Obrero, Cristina, and María Lombardi. 2022. "Teacher Performance Pay and Student Learning: Evidence from a Nationwide Program in Peru." *Economic Development and Cultural Change* 70(4): 1631–1669.
Benavot, Aaron. 1992. "Curricular Content, Educational Expansion, and Economic Growth." *Comparative Education Review* 36(2): 150–174.
Benavot, Aaron. 2004. "A Global Study of Intended Instructional Time and Official School Curricula, 1980–2000." Paper commissioned for the Education For All Global Monitoring Report 2005, *The Quality Imperative*. https://unesdoc.unesco.org/ark:/48223/pf0000146625.
Benavot, Aaron, Yun-Kyung Cha, David Kamens, John W. Meyer, and Suk-Ying Wong. 1991. "Knowledge for the Masses: World Models and National Curricula, 1920–1986." *American Sociological Review* 56(1): 85–100.
Benavot, Aaron, and Phyllis Riddle. 1988. "The Expansion of Primary Education, 1870–1940: Trends and Issues." *Sociology of Education* 61(3): 191–210.
Bergenfeldt, Fredrik. 2008. "The Enclosure Movements—A Path towards Social Differentiation? Lessons from Southern Sweden in the 19th Century." Thesis, Lund University. Accessed August 24, 2022: https://www.lunduniversity.lu.se/lup/publication/1335979.
Berinsky, Adam, and Gabriel Lenz. 2011. "Education and Political Participation: Exploring the Causal Link." *Political Behavior* 33(3): 357–373.
Berner, Ashley, and Christina Ross. 2022. "Time to Refocus on Civics, for the Good of the Country—and Student Literacy." *The 74*, November 1. Accessed November 5, 2022: https://www.the74million.org/article/time-to-refocus-on-civics-for-the-good-of-the-country-and-student-literacy/.
Bernetti, J. L., and Adriana Puiggrós. 1993. "Los discursos de los docentes y la organización del campo técnico-profesional." In *Peronismo: Cultura política y educación (1945–1955)*. Buenos Aires: Galerna.
Bertoni, Lilia Ana. 2001. *Patriotas, cosmopolitas y nacionalistas: La construcción de la nacionalidad argentina a fines del siglo XIX*. Buenos Aires: Fondo de Cultura Económica.
Bertram, Christopher. 2023. "Jean Jacques Rousseau." *The Stanford Encyclopedia of Philosophy* (Summer 2023 Edition), edited by Edward N. Zalta and Uri Nodelman. https://plato.stanford.edu/archives/sum2023/entries/rousseau/.
Besley, Timothy, and Torsten Persson. 2008. "Wars and State Capacity." *Journal of the European Economic Association* 6(2): 522–530.

Biblioteca Nacional del Maestro. n.d. *Memoria e Historia de la Educación Argentina*. "Ley de Educación Común 1420." Accessed July 1, 2020: http://www.bnm.me.gov.ar/proyectos/medar/historia_investigacion/1880_1910/politicas_educativas/ley_1420.php.
Biblioteca Nacional del Maestro. n.d. *Memoria e Historia de la Educación Argentina*. "La escuela al servicio de la nación: El programa de Ramos Mejía." Accessed July 1, 2020: http://www.bnm.me.gov.ar/proyectos/medar/historia_investigacion/1910_1930/politicas_educativas/programa_ramos_mejia.php.
Blanc, Guillaume, and Masahiro Kubo. 2021. "French." Working Paper. Accessed October 18, 2022: https://www.guillaumeblanc.com/files/theme/BlancKubo_French.pdf.
Boix, Carles, Michael Miller, and Sebastian Rosato. 2013. "A Complete Data Set of Political Regimes, 1800–2007." *Comparative Political Studies* 46(12): 1523–1554.
Bold, Tessa, Deon Filmer, Gayle Martin, Ezequiel Molina, Brian Stacy, Christophe Rockmore, Jakob Svensson, and Waly Wane. 2017. "Enrollment Without Learning: Teacher Effort, Knowledge, and Skill in Primary Schools in Africa." *Journal of Economic Perspectives* 31(4): 185–204.
Bold, Tessa, Mwangi Kimenyi, Germano Mwabu, and Justin Sandefur. 2018. "Experimental Evidence on Scaling Up Education Reforms in Kenya." *Journal of Public Economics* 168: 1–20.
Boli, John, Francisco O. Ramirez, and John W. Meyer. 1985. "Explaining the Origins and Expansion of Mass Education." *Comparative Education Review* 29(2): 145–170.
Bolivia. 1827. *Ley de 9 de enero*.
Boonshoft, Mark. 2015. *Creating a 'Civilized Nation': Religion, Social Capital, and the Cultural Foundations of Early American State Formation*. PhD diss., Ohio State University.
Botana, Natalio. (1971) 2012. *El orden conservador; la política argentina entre 1880 y 1916*. Buenos Aires: Edhasa.
Bourguignon, François, and Thierry Verdier. 2000. "Oligarchy, Democracy, Inequality and Growth." *Journal of Development Economics* 62(2): 285–313.
Bowles, Samuel, and Herbert Gintis. 1976. *Schooling in Capitalist America: Educational Reform and the Contradictions of Economic Life*. New York: Basic Books.
Boyd, Alexandra, Robert Maranto, and Caleb Rose. 2014. "The Softer Side of 'No Excuses': A view of KIPP Schools in Action." *Education Next* 14(1): 48–54.
Bozçağa, Tugba, and Asli Cansunar. 2022. "The Education Dilemma: Favoring the In-Group or Assimilating the Out-Group?" Working Paper. Accessed December 12, 2023: https://static1.squarespace.com/static/5bfc07f15cfd79f62c9760b5/t/63223fdd504cb8530c733e5a/1663188959573/The_Education_Dilemma-11.pdf.
Brambor, Thomas, Johannes Lindvall, and Annika Stjernquist. 2017. "The Ideology of Heads of Government, 1870–2012." Version 1.5. Department of Political Science, Lund University.
Brantlinger, Patrick. 1998. *The Reading Lesson: The Threat of Mass Literacy in Nineteenth-Century British Fiction*. Bloomington: Indiana University Press.
Brazil. 1879. *Decreto 7.247*.
Brockliss, Laurence W. B., and Nicola Sheldon. 2012. *Mass Education and the Limits of State Building, c. 1870–1930*. Houndmills, U.K.: Palgrave Macmillan.
Brown, David S. 1999. "Reading, Writing and Regime Type: Democracy's Impact on Primary School Enrollment." *Political Research Quarterly* 52(4): 681–707.
Brown, David S., and Wendy Hunter. 1999. "Democracy and Social Spending in Latin America, 1980–92." *American Political Science Review* 93(4): 779–790.
Brown, David S., and Wendy Hunter. 2004. "Democracy and Human Capital Formation: Education Spending in Latin America, 1980 to 1997." *Comparative Political Studies* 37(7): 842–864.
Brownson, Orestes. 1839. "Decentralization: Alternative to Bureaucracy." *Boston Quarterly Review* 2: 393–418.
Brunell, Mary. 1940. "Matthew Arnold's Writings on Education in Relation to His Idea of Culture." Thesis, Loyola University.
Bruns, Barbara, and Javier Luque. 2014. *Great Teachers: How to Raise Student Learning in Latin America and the Caribbean*. Washington, DC: World Bank.

Buonanno, Paolo, and Leone Leonida. 2009. "Non-Market Effects of Education on Crime: Evidence from Italian Regions." *Economics of Education Review* 28(1): 11–17.
Callan, Eamonn, and Dylan Arena. 2009. "Indoctrination." *The Oxford Handbook of Philosophy of Education*. Oxford: Oxford University Press.
Campobassi, José. 1956. *Ley 1420*. Buenos Aires: Ediciones Gure.
Campobassi, José. 1975. *Sarmiento y su época*. Buenos Aires: Editorial Losada.
Cantoni, Davide, Yuyu Chen, David Y. Yang, Noam Yuchtman, and Y. Jane Zhang. 2017. "Curriculum and Ideology." *Journal of Political Economy* 125(2): 338–392.
Cappelli, Gabriele, and Gloria Quiroga Valle. 2021. "Female Teachers and the Rise of Primary Education in Italy and Spain, 1861–1921: Evidence from a New Dataset." *Economic History Review* 74(3): 754–783.
Cárdenas, Mauricio. 2010. "State Capacity in Latin America." *Economía* 10(2): 1–45.
Care, Esther, Helyn Kim, Alvin Vista, and Kate Anderson. 2018. "Education System Alignment for 21st Century Skills: Focus on Assessment." Brookings Institution. https://www.brookings.edu/wp-content/uploads/2018/11/Education-system-alignment-for-21st-century-skills-012819.pdf.
Carnes, Nicholas, and Noam Lupu. 2023. "The Economic Backgrounds of Politicians." *Annual Review of Political Science* 26: 253–270.
Carry, Alain. 1999. "Le compte satellite rétrospectif de l'éducation en France (1820–1996)." Série AF, no. 25 "Histoire économique quantitative," *Économies et Sociétés* no. 2–3 (Février-Mars). Paris: ISMÉA.
Carsten, Francis Ludwig. 1989. *A History of the Prussian Junkers*. Aldershot, Hants, U.K.: Scolar Press.
Centeno, Miguel Angel. 1997. "Blood and Debt: War and Taxation in Nineteenth-Century Latin America." *American Journal of Sociology* 102(6): 1565–1605.
Cermeño, Alexandra L., Kerstin Enflo, and Johannes Lindvall. 2022. "Railroads and Reform: How Trains Strengthened the Nation State." *British Journal of Political Science* 52(2): 715–735.
Ceva, Mariela, 2018. "Los inmigrantes y la escuela. Entre la centralización estatal y la descentralización social (1884–1914)." In *Identidades, memorias y poder cultural en la Argentina (siglos XIX al XXI)*, edited by María Bjerg and Iván Cherjovsky, 67–94. Bernal: Universidad Nacional de Quilmes.
Chamarbagwala, Rubiana, and Hilcías E. Moran. 2011. "The Human Capital Consequences of Civil War: Evidence from Guatemala." *Journal of Development Economics* 94(1): 41–61.
Charques, Richard Denis. 1932. *Soviet Education: Some Aspects of Cultural Revolution*. Available on Hathitrust: https://catalog.hathitrust.org/Record/007936776/Cite.
Chile. 1859a. *Documentos Parlamentarios. Discursos de Apertura en las Sesiones del Congreso i Memorias Ministeriales en los Dos Primeros Años del Segundo Quinquenio de la Administración Montt*. Santiago de Chile: Imprenta del Ferrocarril.
Chile. 1859b. *Documentos Parlamentarios. Discursos de Apertura en las Sesiones del Congreso i Memorias Ministeriales Correspondientes al Segundo Quinquenio de la Administración Montt*. Santiago de Chile: Imprenta del Ferrocarril.
Chile. 1860a. "Debate sobre Ley de Instrucción Primaria." *Monitor de las Escuelas Primarias* 10, tomo 8.
Chile. 1860b. *Lei de Instrucción Primaria*.
Chile. *Anuario Estadístico de la República de Chile*, multiple years.
Cinnirella, Francesco, and Erik Hornung. 2016. "Landownership Concentration and the Expansion of Education." *Journal of Development Economics* 121(1): 135–152.
Cinnirella, Francesco, and Ruth Schueler. 2018. "Nation Building: The Role of Central Spending in Education." *Explorations in Economic History* 67(1): 18–39.
Clark, Christopher M. 2006. *Iron Kingdom: The Rise and Downfall of Prussia, 1600–1947*. Cambridge, MA: Belknap Press of Harvard University Press.
Clark, G. 2005. "The Condition of the Working Class in England, 1209–2004." *Journal of Political Economy* 113(6): 1307–340.
Clots-Figueras, Irma, and Paolo Masella. 2013. "Education, Language and Identity." *Economic Journal* 123(570): F332–F357.

Collier, Paul, V. L. Elliott, Håvard Hegre, Anke Hoeffler, Marta Reynal-Querol, and Nicholas Sambanis. 2003. *Breaking the Conflict Trap: Civil War and Development Policy*. Washington, DC: World Bank.
Collier, Simon. 2003. *Chile: The Making of a Republic, 1830–1865*. New York: Cambridge University Press.
Collier, Simon, and William F. Sater. 2004. *A History of Chile, 1808–2002*. Cambridge: Cambridge University Press.
Collins, P. A. W. 1955. "Dickens and Adult Education." *British Journal of Educational Studies* 3(2): 115–127.
Colombia. 1870. *Decreto Orgánico de Instrucción Pública*.
Comin, Diego, and Bart Hobijn. 2009. "The CHAT Dataset." Harvard Business School Working Paper, 10–035: https://www.hbs.edu/ris/Publication%20Files/10-035.pdf.
Comisión de la Verdad y Reconciliación (Perú). 2003. *Informe Final*.
Comte, Auguste. 1865. *A General View of Positivism*. Translated by J. H. Bridges. London: Trübner & Co.
Comte, Auguste. 1988. *Introduction to Positive Philosophy*. Edited and translated by Frederick Ferré. Indianapolis, IN: Hackett Publishing.
Comte, Auguste. 1998a. "Summary Appraisal of the General Character of Modern History." In *Early Political Writings*, edited and translated by H. S. Jones, 5–46. Cambridge: Cambridge University Press.
Comte, Auguste. 1998b. "Philosophical Considerations on the Sciences and Scientists." In *Early Political Writings*, edited and translated by H. S. Jones, 145–186. Cambridge: Cambridge University Press.
Cooney, William, Charles Cross, and Barry Trunk. 1993. *From Plato to Piaget: The Greatest Educational Theorists From Across the Centuries and Around the World*. Lanham, MD: University Press of America.
Costa Rica. 1869. *Reglamento de Instrucción Primaria*.
Counts, George S. 1932. *Dare the School Build a New Social Order?* Speech delivered before the Progressive Education Association.
Cousin, Victor. 1833a. *Rapport fait à la Chambre des Pairs, par M. Cousin, au nom d'une commission spéciale chargée de l'examen du projet de la loi sur l'Instruction primaire. Séance du 22 juin, 1833.*
Cousin, Victor. 1833b. *Rapport sur l'Etat de l'instruction publique dans quelques pays de l'Allemagne et particulièrement en Prusse.* https://catalog.hathitrust.org/Record/006554030.
Crawfurd, Lee, Susannah Hares, Ayesha Khan, Ana Minardi, and Justin Sandefur. 2021. "What Do Developing Country Governments Learn from Aid? Evidence from Survey Experiments with 900 Education Policymakers in 36 Countries." Center for Global Development Working Paper. https://www.peio.me/wp-content/uploads/2021/papers/PEIOo21_paper_79.pdf.
Croke, Kevin, Guy Grossman, Horacio A. Larreguy, and John Marshall. 2016. "Deliberate Disengagement: How Education Can Decrease Political Participation in Electoral Authoritarian Regimes." *American Political Science Review* 110(3): 579–600.
Cuba. 1844. *Plan General de Instrucción Pública para las Islas de Cuba y Puerto Rico*.
Cubberly, Ellwood Patterson. 1920. *The History of Education: Educational Practice and Progress Considered as a Phase of the Development and Spread of Western Civilization*. Boston, MA: Houghton Mifflin, Riverside Press.
Cvrcek, Tomas, and Miroslav Zajicek. 2019. "The Rise of Public Schooling in Nineteenth-Century Imperial Austria: Who Gained and Who Paid?" *Cliometrica* 13(1): 367–403.
Dahlum, Sirianne, and Carl Henrik Knutsen. 2017. "Do Democracies Provide Better Education? Revisiting the Democracy–Human Capital Link." *World Development* 94: 186–199.
Darden, Keith, and Anna Grzymala-Busse. 2006. "The Great Divide: Literacy, Nationalism, and the Communist Collapse." *World Politics* 59(1): 83–115.
Darden, Keith, and Harris Mylonas. 2015. "Threats to Territorial Integrity, National Mass Schooling, Linguistic Commonality." *Comparative Political Studies* 49(11): 1446–1479.

Davis, Donagh, and Kevin C. Feeney. 2017. "Explaining British Political Stability After 1832." *Cliodynamics* 8(2): 182–228.
De Djin, Annelien. 2012. "The Politics of Enlightenment: From Peter Gay to Jonathan Israel." *Historical Journal* 55(3): 785–805.
Dee, Thomas S. 2004. "Are There Civic Returns to Education?" *Journal of Public Economics* 88(9–10): 1697–1720.
Denmark. 1814a. *Anordning for Almue-Skolevæsenet paa Landet i Danmark*.
Denmark. 1814b. *School Acts*.
De Pleijt, Alexandra. 2018. "Human Capital Formation in the Long Run: Evidence from Average Years of Schooling in England, 1300–1900." *Cliometrica* 12(1): 99–126.
Des merveilles de la nature, ou Lectures physico-morales à l'usage des écoles primaires; par J.-M. Martin, Inspecteur de l'instruction primaire du département du Morbihan. 1838. Paris: L. Hachette.
Dewey, John. 1916. *Democracy and Education: An Introduction to the Philosophy of Education*. New York: Free Press.
Dincecco, Mark. 2011. *Political Transformations and Public Finances: Europe, 1650–1913*. New York: Cambridge University Press.
Duflo, Esther. 2001. "Schooling and Labor Market Consequences of School Construction in Indonesia: Evidence from an Unusual Policy Experiment." *American Economic Review* 91(4): 795–813.
Dwyer, Philip G. 2014. *The Rise of Prussia 1700–1830*. London: Routledge.
Dwyer, Philip G., and Peter McPhee. 2002. *The French Revolution and Napoleon: A Sourcebook*. London: Routledge.
Ecuador. 1871. *Ley Reforma de la Educación*.
Edwards, Agustín. 1932. *Cuatro presidentes de Chile*. Valparaíso: Sociedad Imprenta y Litografía Universo.
Edwards Vives, Alberto, and Eduardo Frei Montalva. 1949. *Historia de los partidos políticos chilenos*. Santiago de Chile: Editorial del Pacífico.
Egaña, María Loreto. 1996. "La ley de Instrucción Primaria Obligatoria: un debate político." *Revista latinoamericana de estudios educativos* 26(4): 9–39.
Egaña Baraona, María Loreto. 2000. *La educación primaria popular en el siglo XIX en Chile: una práctica de política estatal*. Santiago: Ediciones de la Dirección de Bibliotecas, Archivos y Museos.
Elias, Norbert. 1994. *The Civilizing Process*. Oxford, U.K.: Blackwell.
Elis, Roy. 2011. "The Logic of Redistributive Non-Democracies." PhD diss., Stanford University.
El Salvador. 1873. *Reglamento de Instrucción Pública*.
Engerman, Stanley, and Kenneth Sokoloff. 2002. "Factor Endowments, Inequality, and Paths of Development Among New World Economics." NBER Working Paper No. 9259.
England. 1870. Elementary Education Act.
Ertman, Thomas. 2010. "The Great Reform Act of 1832 and British Democratization." *Comparative Political Studies* 43(8/9): 1000–1022.
Erxleben, Arnold. 1967. "The State, the Church, and Public Education in Eighteenth and Nineteenth Century Prussia." EdD diss., University of Nebraska.
Esberg, Jane, and Jonathan Mummolo. 2018. "Explaining Misperceptions of Crime." Working Paper, https://jmummolo.scholar.princeton.edu/sites/g/files/toruqf3341/files/esberg_mummolo_2018.pdf.
Federal Commission on School Safety. 2021. "Final Report of the Federal Commission on School Safety." https://www2.ed.gov/documents/school-safety/school-safety-report.pdf.
Fenwick, Leslie. 2022. *Jim Crow's Pink Slip: The Untold Story of Black Principal and Teacher Leadership*. Cambridge, MA: Harvard Education Press.
Fernández Abara, Joaquín. 2016. *Regionalismo, liberalismo y rebelión: Copiapó en la guerra civil de 1859*. Santiago: RIL Editores.
Filloux, Jean-Claude. 1993. "Émile Durkheim (1858–1917)." *PROSPECTS: Quarterly Review of Comparative Education* 23(1/2): 303–320.

Fitzpatrick, Sheila. 1979. *Education and Social Mobility in the Soviet Union, 1921–1934*. Cambridge: Cambridge University Press.
Flora, Peter. 1983. *State, Economy, and Society in Western Europe 1815–1975. A Data Handbook*, Volume I: The Growth of Mass Democracies and Welfare States. Chicago: St. James Press.
Foley, G. 1982. "The Zimbabwean Political Economy and Education, 1980–1982." Henderson Seminar Paper No. 52, University of Zimbabwe.
Ford, Guy. 1919. "The Prussian Peasantry Before 1807." *American Historical Review* 24(3): 358–378.
Foucault, Michel. 1995. *Discipline and Punish: The Birth of the Prison*. Translated by Alan Sheridan. New York: Vintage Books.
Fouka, Vasiliki. 2020. "Backlash: The Unintended Effects of Language Prohibition in U.S. Schools after World War I." *Review of Economic Studies* 87(1): 204–239.
Fouka, Vasiliki. 2024. "State Policy and Immigrant Integration." *Annual Review of Political Science* 27. https://www.annualreviews.org/content/journals/10.1146/annurev-polisci-051921-102651.
France. 1833. *Loi sur l'instruction primaire - Loi Guizot du 28 juin 1833*.
France. Assemblée Nationale (1871–1942). Chambre des députés, and France. Sénat. 1879. *Archives Parlementaires De 1787 à 1860*. Paris: Librairie administrative de Paul Dupont. SER2 V83 1833.
Freedom House. 2022. "Thailand Country Facts." *Freedom in the World 2022*. Accessed September 1, 2022: https://freedomhouse.org/country/thailand/freedom-world/2022.
Friedman, Willa, Michael Kremer, Edward Miguel, and Rebecca Thornton. 2016. "Education as Liberation?" *Economica* 83(329): 1–30.
Friendly, Michael. 2007. "A.-M. Guerry's 'Moral Statistics of France': Challenges for Multivariable Spatial Analysis." *Statistical Science* 22(3): 368–399.
Frisancho, Susana. 2009. "Formación en ciudadanía y desarrollo de la democracia. Una nota conceptual." In *Formación en ciudadanía en la escuela peruana: avances conceptuales y limitaciones en la práctica de aula*, edited by Félix Reátegui. Instituto de Democracia y Derechos Humanos de la Pontificia Universidad Católica del Perú. Chapter 2, pp. 11–18. Accessed July 15, 2023: https://idehpucp.pucp.edu.pe/images/publicaciones/formacion_en_ciudadania_escuela_peruana.pdf.
Frisancho, Susana, and Félix Reátegui. 2009. "Moral Education and Post-War Societies: The Peruvian Case." *Journal of Moral Education* 38(4): 421–443.
Furuhagen, Björn, and Janne Holmén. 2017. "From Seminar to University: Dismantling an Old and Constructing a New Teacher Education in Finland and Sweden, 1946–1979." *Nordic Journal of Educational History* 4(1): 53–81.
Fultz, Michael. 2004. "The Displacement of Black Educators Post-Brown: An Overview and Analysis." *History of Education Quarterly* 44(1): 11–45.
Gallego, Francisco A., and Robert Woodberry. 2010. "Christian Missionaries and Education in Former African Colonies: How Competition Mattered." *Journal of African Economies* 19(3): 294–329.
Galor, Oded, and Omer Moav. 2000. "Ability-Biased Technological Transition, Wage Inequality, and Economic Growth." *Quarterly Journal of Economics* 115(2): 469–497.
Galor, Oded, and Omer Moav. 2006. "Das Human-Kapital: A Theory of the Demise of the Class Structure." *Review of Economic Studies* 73(1): 85–117.
Garfias, Francisco. 2018. "Elite Competition and State Capacity Development: Theory and Evidence from Post-Revolutionary Mexico." *American Political Science Review* 112(2): 339–357.
Garfias, Francisco, and Agustina S. Paglayan. 2020. "When Does Education Promote Political Participation? Evidence from Curriculum Reforms." Working Paper presented at the 2020 Annual Meeting of the American Political Science Association.
Gatchel, Richard H. 1959. "Evolution of Concepts of Indoctrination in American Education." *Educational Forum* 23(3): 303–309.
Gaudiano, Nicole. 2020. "Trump creates 1776 Commission to promote 'patriotic education.'" *Politico*, November 2. https://www.politico.com/news/2020/11/02/trump-1776-commission-education-433885.
Gawthrop, Richard L. 1993. *Pietism and the Making of Eighteenth-Century Prussia*. New York: Cambridge University Press.

Geddes, Barbara. 2003. *Paradigms and Sand Castles: Theory Building and Research Design in Comparative Politics*. Ann Arbor: University of Michigan Press.
Geddes, B., J. Wright, and E. Frantz. 2014. "Autocratic Breakdown and Regime Transitions: A New Data Set." *Perspectives on Politics* 12(1): 313–331. DOI: 10.1017/S1537592714000851.
Gellner, Ernest. 1983. *Nations and Nationalism*. Ithaca, NY: Cornell University Press.
Goldin, Claudia, and Lawrence F. Katz. 2008. *The Race between Education and Technology*. Cambridge, MA: Belknap Press of the Harvard University Press.
Gollin, Douglas, Remi Jedwab, and Dietrich Vollrath. 2016. "Urbanization With and Without Industrialization." *Journal of Economic Growth* 21(1): 35–70.
Gómez Arévalo, Palevi. 2012. "Educación para la paz en el sistema educativo de El Salvador." *Ra Ximhai* 8(2): 93–126.
Gonnet, Paul. 1955. Esquisse de la crise économique en France de 1827 à 1832. *Revue d'histoire économique et sociale* 33(3): 249–292.
Gontard, Maurice. 1959. *L'Enseignement Primaire en France de la Révolution à la loi Guizot (1789–1833)*. Paris: Société d'Edition "Les Belles Lettres."
Great Britain, Education Commission. 1861. *Report of the Commissioners Appointed to Inquire into the State of Popular Education in England*. London: Her Majesty's Stationery Office.
Greece. 1834. *Education Law*.
Green, Andy. 2013. *Education and State Formation: Europe, East Asia and the USA*, 2nd ed. New York: Palgrave Macmillan.
Grew, Raymond, and Patrick J. Harrigan. 1991. *School, State, and Society. The Growth of Elementary Schooling in Nineteenth-Century France—A Quantitative Analysis*. Ann Arbor: University of Michigan Press.
Gryzmala-Busse, Anna. 2015. *Nations under God: How Churches Use Moral Authority to Influence Policy*. Princeton, NJ: Princeton University Press.
Grzymala-Busse, Anna. 2016. "Weapons of the Meek: How Churches Influence Public Policy." *World Politics* 68(1): 1–36.
Guatemala. 1875. *Ley Orgánica de Instrucción Pública Primaria*.
Guizot, François. 1816. *Essai sur l'histoire et sur l'état actuel de l'instruction publique en France*. Paris: Maradan.
Guizot, François. 1860. *Mémoires pour Servir à l'Histoire de Mon Temps*. Paris: Michel Lévy Frères.
Gvirtz, Silvina. 1999. "La politización de los contenidos escolares y la respuesta de los docentes primarios en los primeros gobiernos de Perón: Argentina 1949–1955." *Estudios Interdisciplinarios De América Latina Y El Caribe* 10(1): 25–35.
Haapala, Pertti, and Marko Tikka. 2013. "Revolution, Civil War, and Terror in Finland in 1918." In *War In Peace: Paramilitary Violence In Europe after the Great War*, edited by Robert Gerwarth and John Horne, 72–84. Oxford: Oxford University Press.
Hagen, William W. 2002. *Ordinary Prussians: Brandenburg Junkers and Villagers, 1500–1840*. Cambridge: Cambridge University Press.
Handlin, Oscar. 1982. "Education and the European Immigrant, 1820–1920." In *American Education and the European Immigrant, 1840–1940*, edited by Bernard J. Weiss. Urbana: University of Illinois Press.
Hanushek, Eric A., and Ludger Woessmann. 2008. "The Role of Cognitive Skills in Economic Development." *Journal of Economic Literature* 46(3): 607–668.
Heathorn, Stephen. 1995. "'Let Us Remember That We, Too, Are English': Constructions of Citizenship and National Identity in English Elementary School Reading Books, 1880–1914." *Victorian Studies* 38(3): 395–427.
Hjalmarsson, Randi, Helena Holmlund, and Matthew J. Lindquist. 2015. "The Effect of Education on Criminal Convictions and Incarceration: Causal Evidence from Micro-Data." *Economic Journal* 125(587): 1290–1326.
Hobbes, Thomas. 1991. *Man* and *Citizen (De Homine* and *De Cive)*. Indianapolis, IN: Hackett Publishing.
Hobbes, Thomas. 1994. *Leviathan*. Indianapolis, IN: Hackett Publishing.

Hobson, Elsie Garland. 1918. *Educational Legislation and Administration in the State of New York, 1777–1850*. PhD diss., University of Chicago.
Huntington, Samuel P. 1991. "Democracy's Third Wave." *Journal of Democracy* 2(2): 12–34.
Hurt, J. S. 1979. *Elementary Schooling and the Working Classes, 1860–1913*. London: Routledge.
Institut National de Recherche Pédagogique. n.d. "Texte des Ordonnances, Projets et Propositions de Loi Concernant L'Enseignement Primaire pendant la Période 1830–1833." Accessed August 20, 2021: http://www.inrp.fr.
Instituto de Democracia y Derechos Humanos de la Pontificia Universidad Católica del Perú. 2007. "Educación para la Democracia: Un Debate Necesario." *Democracia y Sociedad* 1.
International Historical Statistics. 2013. "North America: Central Government Revenue," downloaded and formatted by Jordan Scavo (November 18, 2013). Basingstoke: Palgrave Macmillan. Accessed October 17, 2022: https://gpih.ucdavis.edu/Government.htm.
Inter-university Consortium for Political and Social Research. 1992. "Social, Demographic, and Educational Data for France, 1801–1897." Ann Arbor, MI (ICPSR 48).
Israel, Jonathan. 2001. *Radical Enlightenment: Philosophy and the Making of Modernity, 1650–1750*. New York: Oxford University Press.
Israel, Jonathan. 2006. "Enlightenment! Which Enlightenment?" *Journal of the History of Ideas* 67(3): 523–545.
Italy. 1859. *Casati Law*.
Jaksić, Iván, and Sol Serrano. 1990. "In the Service of the Nation." *Hispanic American Historical Review* 70(1): 139–171.
Jamaica. 1892. *Elementary Education Law*.
Jasper, James. 2005. "Culture, Knowledge, and Politics." In *The Handbook of Political Sociology: States, Civil Societies, and Globalization*, edited by Thomas Janoski, Robert Alford, Alexander Hicks, and Mildred A. Scwartz. Ch. 5, 115–134. Cambridge, U.K.: Cambridge University Press.
Jedwab, Remi, and Dietrich Vollrath. 2015. "Urbanization Without Growth in Historical Perspective." *Explorations in Economic History* 58: 1–21.
Jefferson, Thomas. 1787a. "To James Madison." National Archives, December 20. Accessed September 9, 2022: https://founders.archives.gov/documents/Jefferson/01-12-02-0454.
Jefferson, Thomas. 1787b. "To Uriah Forrest with Enclosure." National Archives, December 31. Accessed September 9, 2022: https://founders.archives.gov/documents/Jefferson/01-12-02-0490.
Jones, Phillip W. 2007. *World Bank Financing of Education: Lending, Learning, and Development*. Abingdon, U.K.; New York: Routledge.
Jones, Phillip W., and David Coleman. 2005. *The United Nations and Education: Multilateralism, Development and Globalisation*. Abingdon, U.K.; New York: RoutledgeFalmer.
Kaestle, Carl. 1983. *Pillars of the Republic: Common Schools and American Society, 1780–1860*. New York: Hill and Wang.
Kam, Cindy D., and Carl L. Palmer. 2008. "Reconsidering the Effects of Education on Political Participation." *Journal of Politics* 70(3): 612–631.
Kandel, I. L. 1910. *The Training of Elementary School Teachers in Germany*. New York: Teachers College, Columbia University.
Kandel, I. L. 1933. *Comparative Education*. Boston, New York: Houghton Mifflin.
Kant, Immanuel. 1900. *Kant on Education (Über Pädagogik)*. Translated by Annette Churton. Boston: D. C. Heath & Co.
Kesler, Charles R. 1991. "Education and Politics: Lessons from the American Founding." *University of Chicago Legal Forum* 1991(1): 101–122.
Khalenberg, Richard D., and Clifford Janey. 2016. "Is Trump's Victory the Jump-Start Civics Education Needed?" *The Atlantic*, November 10.
Kilgore, W. J. 1961. "Notes on the Philosophy of Education of Andres Bello." *Journal of the History of Ideas* 22(4): 555–560.
King, Beatrice. 1937. *Changing Man: The Education System of the U.S.S.R.* New York: Viking Press. Available on Hathitrust: https://catalog.hathitrust.org/Record/001734115/Cite.

King, Elisabeth. 2013. *From Classrooms to Conflict in Rwanda*. New York: Cambridge University Press.
Kingsley, Patrick. 2016. "Turkey Sacks 15,000 Education Workers in Purge after Failed Coup." *The Guardian*, July 20. Accessed October 18, 2022: https://www.theguardian.com/world/2016/jul/19/turkey-sacks-15000-education-workers-in-purge.
Klesner, Joseph, and Chappell Lawson. 2001. "*Adiós* to the PRI? Changing Voter Turnout in Mexico's Political Transition." *Mexican Studies* 17(1): 17–39.
Koganzon, Rita. 2012. "'Producing a Reconciliation of Disinterestedness and Commerce': The Political Rhetoric of Education in the Early Republic." *History of Education Quarterly* 52(3): 403–429.
Kornfeld, Eve. 1989. "'Republican Machines' or Pestalozzian *Bildung*? Two Visions of Moral Education in the Early Republic." *Canadian Review of American Studies* 20(2): 157–172.
Kosack, Stephen. 2012. *The Education of Nations: How the Political Organization of the Poor, Not Democracy, Led Governments to Invest in Mass Education*. New York: Oxford University Press.
Laitin, David. 2007. *Nations, States, and Violence*. Oxford: Oxford University Press.
Lamberti, Marjorie. 1989. *State, Society, and the Elementary School in Imperial Germany*. New York: Oxford University Press.
Larreguy, Horacio, and John Marshall. 2017. "The Effect of Education on Civic and Political Engagement in Nonconsolidated Democracies: Evidence from Nigeria." *Review of Economics and Statistics* 99(3): 387–401.
Le Nestour, Alexis, Laura Moscoviz, and Justin Sandefur. 2021. "The Long-Term Decline of School Quality in the Developing World." Center for Global Development Working Paper.
Lee, Jong-Wha, and Hanol Lee. 2016. "Human Capital in the Long Run." *Journal of Development Economics* 122: 147–169.
León, Gianmarco. 2012. "Civil Conflict and Human Capital Accumulation: The Long-Term Effects of Political Violence in Peru." *Journal of Human Resources* 47(4): 991–1022.
Lerch, Julia C. 2016. "Embracing Diversity? Textbook Narratives in Countries with a Legacy of Internal Armed Conflict (1950 to 2011)." In *History Can Bite – History Education in Divided and Post-War Societies*, edited by D. Bentrovato, K. V. Korostelina, and M. Schulze, 31–43. Goettingen: Vandenhoeck & Ruprecht.
Lerch, Julia C., and Elizabeth Buckner. 2018. "From Education for Peace to Education in Conflict: Changes in UNESCO Discourse, 1945–2015." *Globalisation, Societies, and Education* 16(1): 27–48.
Lerch, Julia C., Susan Garnett Russell, and Francisco O. Ramirez. 2017. "Wither the Nation-State? A Comparative Analysis of Nationalism in Textbooks." *Social Forces* 96(1): 153–180.
Levasseur, Emile. 1894. "The Assignats: A Study in the Finances of the French Revolution." *Journal of Political Economy* 2(2): 179–202.
Levi, Margaret. 1988. *Of Rule and Revenue*. Berkeley: University of California Press.
Levin, Robert A. 1991. "The Debate over Schooling: Influences of Dewey and Thorndike." *Childhood Education* 68(2): 71–75.
Levitsky, Steven, and Lucan Way. 2022. *Revolution and Dictatorship: The Violent Origins of Durable Authoritarianism*. Princeton, NJ: Princeton University Press.
Lieberman, Evan S. 2005. "Nested Analysis as a Mixed-Method Strategy for Comparative Research." *American Political Science Review* 99(3): 435–452.
Lindert, Peter H. 2004. *Growing Public: Social Spending and Economic Growth Since the Eighteenth Century*. Cambridge: Cambridge University Press.
Lindert, Peter H. 2021. *Making Social Spending Work*. Cambridge: Cambridge University Press.
Lipset, M. Seymour. 1960. *Political Man: The Social Bases of Politics*. New York: Doubleday.
Liu, Shelley. 2024. *Governing after War: Rebel Victories and Post-war Statebuilding*. New York: Oxford University Press.
Llinás Alvarez, Edgar. 1979. *Revolución, educación y mexicanidad: La búsqueda de la identidad nacional en el pensamiento educativo mexicano*. Universidad Nacional Autónoma de México.
Lochner, Lance. 2020. "Education and Crime." In *The Economics of Education*, edited by Steve Bradley and Colin Green, 109–118. London; San Francisco: Academic Press.

Lochner, Lance, and Enrico Moretti. 2004. "The Effect of Education on Crime: Evidence from Prison Inmates, Arrests, and Self-Reports." *American Economic Review* 94(1): 155–189.

Locke, John. 1996. *Some Thoughts Concerning Education* and *Of the Conduct of the Understanding*. Edited by Ruth W. Grant and Nathan Tarcov. Indianapolis, IN: Hackett Publishing.

Lopez, David. 2020. "State Formation, Infrastructural Power, and the Centralization of Mass Education in Europe and the Americas, 1800 to 1970." Working Paper presented at the 2020 Annual Meeting of the American Political Science Association.

Machin, Stephen, Olivier Marie, and Sunčica Vujić. 2011. "The Crime Reducing Effect of Education." *The Economic Journal* 121(552): 463–484.

Magaloni, Beatriz. 2006. *Voting for Autocracy: Hegemonic Party Survival and Its Demise in Mexico*. Cambridge: Cambridge University Press.

Magaloni, Beatriz. 2008. "Credible Power-Sharing and the Longevity of Authoritarian Rule." *Comparative Political Studies* 41(4–5): 715–741.

Mann, Michael. 2012. *The Sources of Social Power*. New York: Cambridge University Press.

Manzano, Dulce. 2017. *Bringing Down the Educational Wall: Political Regimes, Ideology and the Expansion of Education*. Cambridge: Cambridge University Press.

Marcham, A. J. 1973. "Educating Our Masters: Political Parties and Elementary Education 1867 to 1870." *British Journal of Educational Studies* 21(2): 180–191.

Mariscal, Elisa, and Kenneth Sokoloff. 2000. "Schooling, Suffrage, and the Persistence of Inequality in the Americas, 1800–1945." In *Political Institutions and Economic Growth in Latin America: Essays in Policy, History, and Political Economy*, edited by Stephen Haber, 159–218. Stanford, CA: Hoover Institution Press.

Marshall, Alfred. 1890. *Principles of Economics*. London: Macmillan and Co. Accessed on HathiTrust, https://catalog.hathitrust.org/Record/008923638.

Martin, Cathie Jo. 2023. *Education for All? Literature, Culture and Education Development in Britain and Denmark*. New York: Cambridge University Press.

Massachusetts Board of Education, Horace Mann. 1844. "Seventh Annual Report of the Board of Education, Together with the Seventh Annual Report of the Secretary of the Board." Washington, DC.

Massachusetts Board of Education, Horace Mann, National Education Association of the United States. 1848. "Twelfth Annual Report of the Secretary of the Board of Education." *Annual Report, Together with the Report of the Secretary of the Board* v. 8–12. Washington, DC.

Matereke, K. P. 2012. "'Whipping into Line': The Dual Crisis of Education and Citizenship in Postcolonial Zimbabwe." *Educational Philosophy and Theory* 44(S2): 84–99.

McEneaney, Elizabeth H. 2003. "The Worldwide Cachet of Scientific Literacy." *Comparative Education Review* 47(2): 217–237.

Meghir, Costas, Mårten Palme, and Marieke Schnabel. 2012. "The Effect of Education Policy on Crime: An Intergenerational Perspective." NBER Working Paper No. 18145.

Melton, James Van Horn. 2002. *Absolutism and the Eighteenth-Century Origins of Compulsory Schooling in Prussia and Austria*. Cambridge: Cambridge University Press.

Meltzer, Allan H., and Scott F. Richard. 1981. "A Rational Theory of the Size of Government." *Journal of Political Economy* 89(1): 914–927.

Mérieau, Eugénie. 2019. "How Thailand Became the World's Last Military Dictatorship." *The Atlantic*, March 20.

Meyer, John W., David Kamens, and Aaron Benavot. 2017. *School Knowledge for the Masses: World Models and National Primary Curricular Categories in the Twentieth Century*. London: Routledge.

Meyer, John, Francisco Ramirez, Richard Rubinson, and John Boli. 1977. "The World Educational Revolution, 1950–1970." *Sociology of Education* 50(4): 242–258.

Meyer, John, Francisco Ramirez, and Yasemin Soysal. 1992. "World Expansion of Mass Education, 1870–1980." *Sociology of Education* 65(2): 128–149.

Milligan, Kevin, Enrico Moretti, and Philip Oreopoulos. 2004. "Does Education Improve Citizenship? Evidence from the United States and the United Kingdom." *Journal of Public Economics* 88(9–10): 1667–1695.

Mincer, Jacob. 1958. "Investment in Human Capital and Personal Income Distribution." *Journal of Political Economy* 66(4): 281–302.
Mitch, David. 1999. "The Role of Skill and Human Capital in the British Industrial Revolution." In *The British Industrial Revolution: An Economic Perspective*, edited by Joel Mokyr, 241–279. Boulder, CO: Westview Press.
Mitchell, Brian R. 2007. *International Historical Statistics 1750–2005*. Basingstoke: Palgrave Macmillan.
Mokyr, Joel. 2002. *The Gifts of Athena: Historical Origins of the Knowledge Economy*. Princeton, NJ: Princeton University Press.
Mokyr, Joel. 2005. "Long-Term Economic Growth and the History of Technology." In *Handbook of Economic Growth*, vol. 1, 1113–1180. Amsterdam: Elsevier.
Moloney, Kim. 2022. *Who Matters at the World Bank? Bureaucrats, Policy Change, and Public Sector Governance*. Oxford: Oxford University Press.
Montalbo, Adrien. 2020. "Industrial Activities and Primary Schooling in Early Nineteenth-Century France." *Cliometrica* 14(2): 325–365.
Moretti, Franco, and Dominique Pestre. 2015. "Bankspeak: The Language of World Bank Reports." *New Left Review* 92. Accessed August 29, 2022: https://newleftreview.org/issues/ii92/articles/franco-moretti-dominique-pestre-bankspeak.
Muralidharan, Karthik, and Paul Niehaus. 2017. "Experimentation at Scale." *Journal of Economic Perspectives* 31(4): 103–124.
Murillo, María Victoria. 1999. "Recovering Political Dynamics: Teachers' Unions and the Decentralization of Education in Argentina and Mexico." *Journal of Interamerican Studies and World Affairs* 41(1): 31–57.
Nash, Roy. 1990. "Bourdieu on Education and Social and Cultural Reproduction." *British Journal of Sociology of Education* 11(4): 431–447.
National Commission on Excellence in Education. 1983. *A Nation at Risk: The Imperative for Educational Reform, A Report to the Nation and the Secretary of Education*. April. Washington, DC.
National Research Council, Institute of Medicine. 2000. *From Neurons to Neighborhoods: The Science of Early Childhood Development*. Washington, DC: National Academy Press.
Ndebele, C., and R. Tshuma. 2014. "Ideology and the Curriculum: How Did Socialist Curriculum Development and Implementation in Zimbabwe from 1980 to 2004 Take Place Through the Social Studies Curriculum?" *Anthropologist* 18(1): 227–239.
Netherlands. 1806. *Education Act*.
Neundorf, Anja, Eugenia Nazrullaeva, Ksenia Northmore-Ball, Katerina Tertytchnaya, Aaron Benavot, Patrica Bromley, Wooseok Kim, Carl Henrik Knutsen, Philipp Lutscher, Kyle Marquardt, Agustina Paglayan, Dan Pemstein, and Brigitte Zimmer. 2023. "Varieties of Political Indoctrination in Education and the Media (V-Indoc) Dataset." DEMED Project. http://dx.doi.org/10.5525/gla.researchdata.1397.
Neundorf, Anja, Eugenia Nazrullaeva, Ksenia Northmore-Ball, Katerina Tertytchnaya, and Wooseok Kim. 2024. "Varieties of Indoctrination: The Politicization of Education and the Media around the World." *Perspectives on Politics*. First View: 1–28. https://doi.org/10.1017/S1537592723002967.
Nipperdey, Thomas. 1976. "Mass Education and Modernization—The Case of Germany 1780–1850," The Prothero Lecture delivered at the Royal Historical Society, printed in the *Transactions of the Royal Historical Society* 27: 155–172.
Nishimura, Shigeo. 1995. "The Development of Pancasila Moral Education in Indonesia." *Southeast Asian Studies* 33(3): 303–316.
Norway. 1827. *Law Concerning the Peasant School System in the Country*.
Nouveau manuel des écoles primaires, moyennes et normales, ou Guide complet des instituteurs et des institutrices . . . / par un membre de l'Université; et revu par Matter, Inspecteur-Général des études. 1836. Paris: Librairie Enciclopédique de Roret.
Núñez, José Abelardo. 1883. *Organización de Escuelas Normales. Informe presentado al Señor Ministro de Instrucción Pública de Chile*. Santiago: Imprenta de la Librería Americana.
OECD. 2019. "PISA 2018 Results (Volume I): What Students Know and Can Do." https://www.oecd.org/pisa/Combined_Executive_Summaries_PISA_2018.pdf.

Ortega Martínez, Luis, and Pablo Rubio Apiolaza. 2006. "La Guerra Civil de 1859 y Los Límites de la Modernización de Atacama y Coquimbo." *Revista de Historia Social y de las Mentalidades* 10(2): 11–39.
Østby, Gudrun, Henrik Urdal, and Kendra Dupuy. 2019. "Does Education Lead to Pacification? A Systematic Review of Statistical Studies on Education and Political Violence." *Review of Educational Research* 89(1): 46–92.
Oszlak, Oscar. 2012. *La formación del Estado argentino: orden, progreso y organización nacional*. Buenos Aires: Ariel.
Paglayan, Agustina S. 2021. "The Non-Democratic Roots of Mass Education: Evidence from 200 Years." *American Political Science Review* 115(1): 179–198.
Paglayan, Agustina S. 2022. "Education or Indoctrination? The Violent Origins of Public School Systems in an Era of State-Building." *American Political Science Review* 116(4): 1242–1257.
Paglayan, Agustina S., Anja Neundorf, and Wooseok Kim. 2023. "Democracy and the Politicization of Education." Available at SSRN: http://dx.doi.org/10.2139/ssrn.4395806.
Paulsen, Tine, Kenneth Scheve, and David Stasavage. 2022. "Foundations of a New Democracy: Schooling, Inequality, and Voting in the Early Republic." *American Political Science Review* 117(2): 518–536.
Pederson, Leland. 1965. "The Mining Industry of the Norte Chico, Chile." PhD diss. Department of Geography, University of California, Berkeley.
Pérez, Santiago. 2017. "The (South) American Dream: Mobility and Economic Outcomes of First- and Second-Generation Immigrants in Nineteenth-Century Argentina." *Journal of Economic History* 77(4): 971–1006.
Pérez, Santiago. 2018. "Railroads and the Rural to Urban Transition: Evidence from 19th-Century Argentina." Working Paper. Accessed September 24, 2021: http://seperez.ucdavis.edu/uploads/1/0/5/9/105905377/railroads_draft_april_2018.pdf.
Perova, Elizaveta, and Renos Vakis. 2009. "Welfare Impacts of the 'Juntos' Program in Peru: Evidence from a Non-Experimental Evaluation." World Bank Working Paper.
Perú. 1850. *Primera Ley de Instrucción Pública*.
Perú. 2003. *Ley General de Educación (Ley Nro. 28044)*, July 28.
Perú, Ministerio de Educación. 2005a. *Diseño curricular nacional de educación básica regular: proceso de articulación*. Lima: Ministerio de Educación del Perú.
Perú, Ministerio de Educación. 2005b. *Propuesta Pedagógica de Formación Ética*. Accessed online on July 13, 2023: http://www.minedu.gob.pe/minedu/archivos/a/002/02-bibliografia-comun-a-ebr-eba-y-etp/1-propuesta-pedagogica-par-la-formacion-etica.pdf.
Petersson, Birgit. 1983. "The Dangerous Classes." *Studies in Poverty and Crime in Nineteenth-Century Sweden*. Accessed August 24, 2022: https://www.diva-portal.org/smash/get/diva2:567669/FULLTEXT02.pdf.
Pigna, Felipe. 2009. *Los mitos de la historia argentina 2: De San Martín a "el granero del mundo."* Buenos Aires: Grupo Editorial Planeta.
Pilbeam, Pamela. 1976. "Popular Violence in Provincial France after the 1830 Revolution." *English Historical Review* 91(359): 278–297.
Pilbeam, Pamela. 1991. *The 1830 Revolution in France*. New York: St. Martin's Press.
Pinkney, David H. 1961. "A New Look at the French Revolution of 1830." *Review of Politics* 23(4): 490–506.
Plato. 1992. *Republic*. Translated by G.M.A. Grube. Indianapolis, IN: Hackett Publishing.
Plato. 2016. *Laws*. Translated by Tom Griffith. Cambridge: Cambridge University Press.
Ponce de León, Macarena. 2010. "La llegada de la escuela y la llegada a la escuela." *Historia* 43(2): 449–486.
"Poor Schools Are at the Heart of Thailand's Political Malaise." 2017. *The Economist*, January 19. Accessed March 25, 2024: https://www.economist.com/asia/2017/01/19/poor-schools-are-at-the-heart-of-thailands-political-malaise?utm_medium=cpc.adword.pd&utm_source=google&ppccampaignID=18156330227&ppcadID=&utm_campaign=a.22brand_pmax&utm_content=conversion.direct-response.anonymous&gad_source=1&gclid=Cj0KCQjwwYSwBhDcARIsA

OyL0fj9Pv7SClHUS29mCiatab5cbv0xqPhZwQZPPEjOAJsvecSw6qteDVEaAl00EALw_wcB&gclsrc=aw.ds.
Popp Berman, Elizabeth. 2022. *Thinking Like an Economist: How Efficiency Replaced Equality in U.S. Public Policy*. Princeton, NJ: Princeton University Press.
Post, John. 1984. "Climatic Variability and the European Mortality Wave of the Early 1740s." *Journal of Interdisciplinary History* 15(1): 1–30.
Projet de loi presenté par Guizot le 2 janvier 1833 et projet tel qu'il a ete modifié par la Chambre des Deputés dans sa Séance du 3 mai 1833. 1833.
Prost, Antoine. 1968. *Histoire de l'enseignement en France, 1800–1967*. Paris: Armand Colin.
Prussia. 1763. *General Rural School Regulations*.
Przeworski, Adam. 2005. "Democracy as an Equilibrium." *Public Choice* 123: 253–273.
Puiggrós, Adriana, and Sandra Carli. 1991. *Sociedad civil y Estado en los orígenes del sistema educativo argentino*. Buenos Aires: Editorial Galerna.
Queralt, Didac. 2022. *Pawned States: State Building in the Era of International Finance*. Princeton, NJ: Princeton University Press.
Ramirez, Francisco, and John Boli. 1987. "The Political Construction of Mass Schooling: European Origins and Worldwide Institutionalization." *Sociology of Education* 60(1): 2–17.
Ramírez, María Teresa, and Juana Téllez. 2006. "La educación primaria y secundaria en Colombia en el siglo XX." Banco de la República Working Paper. Accessed January 4, 2023: https://www.banrep.gov.co/docum/ftp/borra379.pdf.
Ramos Mejía, José María. 1899. *Las multitudes argentinas*. Buenos Aires: Félix Lajouane.
Ramos Mejía, José María. 1909. *La escuela argentina en el centenario: Proyectos del Presidente del Consejo Nacional de Educación Dr. José María Ramos Mejía*. Buenos Aires. Available at: http://www.bnm.me.gov.ar/giga1/libros/00006399/00006399.pdf.
Ramos Mejía, José María. 1910. *Historia de la instrucción primaria en la República Argentina 1810–1910 (atlas escolar) proyectada por el presidente del Consejo Nacional de Educación, Dr. José María Ramos Mejía, comp. y redactada por Juan P. Ramos*. Buenos Aires: Jacobo Peuser, tome I.
Ramsey, Paul J. 2002. "The War against German-American Culture: The Removal of German Language Instruction from the Indianapolis Schools, 1917–1919." *Indiana Magazine of History* 98(4): 285–303.
Ramsey, Paul J. 2006. "'Let Virtue Be Thy Guide, and Truth Thy Beacon-Light': Moral and Civic Transformation in Indianapolis's Public Schools." In *Civic and Moral Learning in America*, edited by Donald Warren and John J. Patrick, 135–151. New York: Palgrave Macmillan.
Ramsey, Paul J. 2009. "In the Region of Babel: Public Bilingual Schooling in the Midwest, 1840s–1880s." *History of Education Quarterly* 4(3): 267–290.
Rapple, Brendan. 1989. "Matthew Arnold and Comparative Education." *British Journal of Educational Studies* 37(1): 54–71.
Ratcliffe, Donald. 2013. "The Right to Vote and the Rise of Democracy, 1787–1828." *Journal of the Early Republic* 33(2): 219–254.
Reisner, Edward Hartman. 1922. *Nationalism and Education since 1789; A Social and Political History of Modern Education*. New York: Macmillan.
Renan, Ernest. 1871. *Le Réforme Intellectuelle et Morale*. Paris: Michel Lévy Frères.
Roberts, Margaret. 2018. *Censored*. Princeton, NJ: Princeton University Press.
Rochner, Dominic, and Alessandro Saia. 2020. "Education and Conflict: Evidence from a Policy Experiment in Indonesia." Working Paper. Accessed September 30, 2023: https://thedocs.worldbank.org/en/doc/5d41899bed6e401f94db2de247aee5ad-0050022021/original/Education-and-Conflict.pdf.
Rock, David. 1985. *Argentina, 1516–1982: From Spanish Colonization to the Falklands War*. Berkeley: University of California Press.
Rock, David. 2002. *State Building and Political Movements in Argentina, 1860–1916*. Stanford, CA: Stanford University Press.
Rojas, Mauricio. 1991. "The 'Swedish Model' in Historical Perspective." *Scandinavian Economic History Review* 39(2): 64–74.

Romer, Paul. 1987. "Crazy Explanations for the Productivity Slowdown." *NBER Macroeconomics Annual* 2: 163–202.
Romer, Paul. 1990. "Endogenous Technological Change." *Journal of Political Economy* 98(5): S71–S102.
Roper, Henry. 1975. "Toward an Elementary Education Act for England and Wales, 1865–1868." *British Journal of Educational Studies* 23(2): 181–208.
Ross, Michael. 2006. "Is Democracy Good for the Poor?" *American Journal of Political Science* 50(4): 860–874.
Roth, Christopher, and Sudarno Sumarto. 2015. "Does Education Increase Interethnic and Interreligious Tolerance? Evidence from a Natural Experiment." SMERU Working Paper. Accessed September 30, 2023: https://mpra.ub.uni-muenchen.de/64558/1/MPRA_paper_64558.pdf.
Rousseau, Jean-Jacques. 2019a. "Discourse on Political Economy." In *The Social Contract and Other Later Political Writings*, edited and translated by Victor Gourevitch, 3–38. Cambridge: Cambridge University Press.
Rousseau, Jean-Jacques. 2019b. "Considerations on the Government of Poland." In *The Social Contract and Other Later Political Writings*, edited and translated by Victor Gourevitch, 181–265. Cambridge: Cambridge University Press.
Rudolph, Frederick (ed.). 1965. *Essays on Education in the Early Republic*. Cambridge, MA: Harvard University Press.
Russell, S. Garnett. 2018. "Global Discourses and Local Practices: Teaching Citizenship and Human Rights in Post-Genocide Rwanda." *Comparative Education Review* 62(3): 385–408.
Russell, Susan Garnett, and Dijana Tiplic. 2014. "Rights-Based Education and Conflict: A Cross-National Study of Rights Discourse in Textbooks." *Compare: A Journal of Comparative and International Education* 44(3): 314–334.
Salazar, Gabriel, and Julio Pinto. 2018. *Historia contemporánea de Chile*. Santiago de Chile: LOM Ediciones.
Saleh, Mohamed. 2016. "Public Mass Modern Education, Religion, and Human Capital in Twentieth-Century Egypt." *Journal of Economic History* 76(3): 697–735.
San Román, Francisco J. 1894. *Reseña industrial e histórica de la minería i metalurjia de Chile*. Imprenta nacional.
Sangnapaboworn, Waraiporn. 2018. "The Evolution of Education Reform in Thailand." In *Education in Thailand*, edited by G. Fry, 517–554. Singapore: Springer.
Sargent, Thomas J., and François R. Velde. 1995. "Macroeconomic Features of the French Revolution." *Journal of Political Economy* 103(3): 474–518.
Sarmiento, Domingo F. (trans.). 1844. *La conciencia de un niño. Para el uso de las escuelas primarias*. Santiago de Chile: Imprenta del Progreso.
Sarmiento, Domingo F. 1845. *Facundo, Civilización y Barbarie*. Santiago: Imprenta del Progreso.
Sarmiento, Domingo F. 1849. *Educación Popular*. Santiago: Imprenta J. B.
Scheve, Kenneth F., and David Stasavage. 2016. *Taxing the Rich: A History of Fiscal Fairness in the United States and Europe*. Princeton, NJ: Princeton University Press.
Schleunes, Karl A. 1989. *Schooling and Society: The Politics of Education in Prussia and Bavaria, 1750–1900*. New York: Berg; distributed by St. Martin's.
Schmitt, Karl M. 1966. "The Mexican Positivists and the Church-State Question, 1876–1911." *Journal of Church and State* 8(2): 200–213.
Serrano, Sol, Macarena Ponce de León, and Francisca Rengifo. 2012. *Historia de la Educación en Chile (1810–2010)*, t. I. Santiago de Chile: Taurus.
Shemyakina, Olga. 2011. "The Effect of Armed Conflict on Accumulation of Schooling: Results from Tajikistan." *Journal of Development Economics* 95(2): 186–200.
Shizha, E., and M. T. Kariwo. 2011. *Education and Development in Zimbabwe. A Social, Political and Economic Analysis*. Sense Publishers.
Skiba, Russell J., and Kimberly Knesting. 2002. *Zero Tolerance, Zero Evidence: An Analysis of School Disciplinary Practice*. Jossey-Bass/Wiley.
Skopp, Douglas R. 1982. "The Elementary School Teachers in 'Revolt': Reform Proposals for Germany's Volksschulen in 1848 and 1849." *History of Education Quarterly* 22(3): 341–361.

Snell-Feikema, Michael D. 2005. "Popular Agitation and British Parliamentary Reform, 1866–1867." *Journal of Undergraduate Research at Minnesota State University, Mankato* 5, article 21.
Société pour l'instruction Elémentaire. 1833. "Circulaire du Recteur de l'Académie de Strasbourg aux principaux manufacturiers d'Álsace; Rèponse des manufacturiers." *Bulletin de la Société pour l'Instruction élémentaire* 52.
Soifer, Hillel David, and Everett A. Vieira. 2019. "The Internal Armed Conflict and State Capacity: Institutional Reforms and the Effective Exercise of Authority." In *Politics after Violence: Legacies of the Shining Path Conflict in Peru*, 109–131. Austin: University of Texas Press.
Solana, Fernando, Raúl Cardiel Reyes, and Raúl Bolaños Martínez (eds.). 1981. *Historia de la educación pública en México*. México, D. F.: Fondo de Cultura Económica.
Sondheimer, Rachel Milstein, and Donald P. Green. 2010. "Using Experiments to Estimate the Effects of Education on Voter Turnout." *American Journal of Political Science* 54(1): 174–189.
Spain. 1857. *Ley de Instrucción Pública*.
Squicciarini, Mara. 2020. "Devotion and Development: Religiosity, Education, and Economic Progress in 19th-century France." *American Economic Review* 110(11): 3454–3491.
Squicciarini, Mara, and Nico Voigtländer. 2015. "Human Capital and Industrialization: Evidence from the Age of Enlightenment." *Quarterly Journal of Economics* 30(4): 1825–1883.
Squicciarini, Mara, and Nico Voigtländer. 2016. "Knowledge Elites and Modernization: Evidence from Revolutionary France." NBER Working Paper No. 22779.
Stalin, Joseph. 1934. *The Political and Social Doctrine of Communism: Report of the Work of the Central Committee of the Communist Party of the Soviet Union*. Worcester, MA: Carnegie Endowment for International Peace, Division of Intercourse and Education. Available on Hathitrust: https://catalog.hathitrust.org/Record/102635323/Home.
Stasavage, David. 2005. "Democracy and Education Spending in Africa." *American Journal of Political Science* 49(2): 343–358.
Stout, Cathryn, and Thomas Wilburn. 2021. "CRT Map: Efforts to Restrict Teaching Racism and Bias Have Multiplied Across the U.S." *Chalkbeat*, June 9. https://www.chalkbeat.org/22525983/map-critical-race-theory-legislation-teaching-racism.
Sundberg, Molly. 2016. *Training for Model Citizenship: An Ethnography of Civic Education and State-Making in Rwanda*. London: Palgrave Macmillan.
Sweden. 1842. *Elementary School Statute*.
Swee, Eik Leong. 2015. "On War Intensity and Schooling Attainment: The Case of Bosnia and Herzegovina." *European Journal of Political Economy* 40: 158–172.
Sylvester, D. W. 1974. "Robert Lowe and the 1870 Education Act." *History of Education: Journal of the History of Education Society* 3(2): 16–26.
Tapia, Francisco B., and Julio Martinez-Galarraga. 2018. "Inequality and Education in Pre-Industrial Economies: Evidence from Spain." *Explorations in Economic History* 69(1): 81–101.
Tedesco, Juan Carlos. 1986. *Educación y sociedad en la Argentina: (1880–1945)*. Buenos Aires: Ediciones Solar.
Tenn, Steven. 2007. "The Effect of Education on Voter Turnout." *Political Analysis* 15(4): 446–464.
Tilly, Charles. 1990. *Coercion, Capital, and European States, AD 990–1992*. Cambridge, MA: Blackwell.
Tilly, Charles, and Raul Zambrano. 2006. "Violent Events in France, 1830–1860 and 1930–1960." Inter-university Consortium for Political and Social Research [distributor]. https://doi.org/10.3886/ICPSR09080.v1.
Toloudis, Nicholas. 2012. *Teaching Marianne and Uncle Sam: Public Education, State Centralization, and Teacher Unionism in France and the United States*. Philadelphia, PA: Temple University Press.
Toth, Carolyn R. 1990. *German-English Bilingual Schools in America: The Cincinnati Tradition in Historical Context*. New York: Peter Lang.
Tsurumi, E. Patricia. 1977. *Japanese Colonial Education in Taiwan, 1895–1945*. Cambridge, MA: Harvard University Press. Available on Hathitrust: https://catalog.hathitrust.org/Record/000723193.
Tuck, Richard. 1998. "Hobbes on Education." In *Philosophers on Education*, 159–167. London: Routledge.

Tyack, David. 1966. "Forming the National Character: Paradox in the Educational Thought of the Revolutionary Generation." *Harvard Educational Review* 36(1): 29–41.
Tyack, David B. 1974. *The One Best System: A History of American Urban Education*. Cambridge, MA: Harvard University Press.
Tyack, David. 2003. *Seeking Common Ground: Public Schools in a Diverse Society*. Cambridge, MA: Harvard University Press.
U.K. Parliament, HC Deb. 1870, February 17, vol. 199, cc438-98. Accessed at: https://api.parliament.uk/historic-hansard/commons/1870/feb/17/leave-first-reading.
U.K. Parliament, HL Deb. 1870, July 25, vol. 203, cc821-65. Accessed at: https://api.parliament.uk/historic-hansard/lords/1870/jul/25/elementary-education-bill.
UNESCO. 2011. "The Hidden Crisis: Armed Conflict and Education," *EFA Global Monitoring Report*. Paris: United Nations Educational, Scientific and Cultural Organization.
UNESCO. 2014. *Global Citizenship Education: Preparing Learners for the Challenges of the Twenty-First Century*. Paris: United Nations Educational, Scientific and Cultural Organization.
U.S. Department of Education. 1993. "120 Years of American Education: A Statistics Portrait." https://nces.ed.gov/pubs93/93442.pdf.
U.S. Department of Education. 2014. "Guiding Principles: A Resource Guide for Improving School Climate and Discipline." https://www2.ed.gov/policy/gen/guid/school-discipline/guiding-principles.pdf.
U.S. Department of Health, Education, and Welfare. Office of Education. 1959. *Soviet Commitment to Education. Report of the First Official U.S. Education Mission to the USSR*. Washington, DC: U.S. Government Printing Office.
U.S. Department of Health, Education, and Welfare. Office of Education. 1960. *Soviet Education Programs*. Washington, DC: U.S. Government Printing Office.
Uruguay. 1877. *Ley 1.350*.
Vaillant, Denise. 2018. *Estudio exploratorio sobre los modelos organizacionales y pedagógicos de instituciones dedicadas a la formación docente inicial: un análisis en clave comparada. Informe final*. Buenos Aires: INFOD e IIPE-UNESCO.
Vaillant, Denise, and Jesús Manso, 2022. "Formación inicial y carrera docente en América Latina: una mirada global y regional." *Ciencia y Educación* 6(1): 109–118.
Van den Berg, Axel, and Thomas Janoski. 2005. "Conflict Theories in Political Sociology." In *The Handbook of Political Sociology: States, Civil Societies, and Globalization*, edited by Thomas Janoski, Robert Alford, Alexander Hicks, and Mildred A. Scwartz, 72–95. Cambridge, U.K.: Cambridge University Press.
Van Sloun, Sherry. 2022. "The Future of American Education: It's Not All About STEM." *Council on Foreign Relations*, October 28. Accessed November 5, 2022: https://www.cfr.org/blog/future-american-education-its-not-all-about-stem.
Vaughan, Mary Kay. 1975. "Education and Class in the Mexican Revolution." *Latin American Perspectives* 11(2): 17–33.
Vaughan, Mary Kay. 1982. *The State, Education, and Social Class in Mexico, 1880–1928*. DeKalb: Northern Illinois University Press.
Velasco, Andrés. 2019. "Bipolar Economics." *Project Syndicate*, November 28.
Venezuela. 1870. *Decreto de Instrucción Pública*.
Vignery, Robert J. 1966. *The French Revolution and the Schools: Educational Policies of the Mountain, 1792–1794*. State Historical Society of Wisconsin for the Department of History, University of Wisconsin.
Voigtländer, Nico, and Hoachim Voth. 2015. "Nazi Indoctrination and Anti-Semitic Beliefs in Germany." *Proceedings of the National Academy of Sciences* 112(26): 7931–7936.
Vollmer, Ferdinand. 1918. *Die Preußische Volksschulpolitik Unter Friedrich dem Großen*.
Voltaire. 1901a. *The Works of Voltaire, Vol. IV (Philosophical Dictionary Part 2)*. Translated by William F. Fleming. New York: E. R. DuMont. https://oll.libertyfund.org/titles/353.
Voltaire. 1901b. *The Works of Voltaire, Vol. VI (Philosophical Dictionary Part 4)*. Translated by William F. Fleming. New York: E. R. DuMont. https://oll.libertyfund.org/titles/355.

Walter, Barbara F. 2022. *How Civil Wars Start: And How to Stop Them*. New York: Crown.
Wantchekon, Leonard, Marko Klašnja, and Natalija Novta. 2015. "Education and Human Capital Externalities: Evidence from Colonial Benin." *Quarterly Journal of Economics* 130(2): 703–757.
Washington, George. 1786, October 22. "To David Humphreys." National Archives, Accessed November 3, 2023: https://founders.archives.gov/documents/Washington/04-04-02-0272.
Weber, Elke. 2006. "Experience-Based and Description-Based Perceptions of Long-Term Risk: Why Global Warming Does Not Scare Us (Yet)." *Climatic Change* 77: 103–20.
Weber, Eugene. 1976. *Peasants into Frenchmen: The Modernization of Rural France, 1870–1914*. Stanford, CA: Stanford University Press.
Welch, Steven R. 2001. "Revolution and Reprisal: Bavarian Schoolteachers in the 1848 Revolution." *History of Education Quarterly* 41(1): 25–57.
Welsh, Richard O., and Shafiqua Little. 2018. "The School Discipline Dilemma: A Comprehensive Review of Disparities and Alternative Approaches." *Review of Educational Research* 88(5): 752–794.
Westberg, Johannes. 2019. "Basic Schools in Each and Every Parish: The School Act of 1842 and the Rise of Mass Schooling in Sweden." In *School Acts and the Rise of Mass Schooling: Education Policy in the Long Nineteenth Century*, edited by Johannes Westberg, Lukas Boser, and Ingrid Brühwiler, 195–222. Cham, Switzerland: Palgrave Macmillan.
White, Eugene Nelson. 1995. "The French Revolution and the Politics of Government Finance, 1770–1815." *Journal of Economic History* 55(2): 227–255.
Wood, James A. 2002. "The Burden of Citizenship: Artisans, Elections, and the Fuero Militar in Santiago de Chile." *The Americas* 58(3): 443–469.
Woodberry, Robert. 2012. "The Missionary Roots of Liberal Democracy." *American Political Science Review* 106(2): 244–274.
World Bank. 2010. *Education Sector Strategy for 2020*. Washington, DC: World Bank.
World Bank. 2018. *Learning to Realize Education's Promise. World Development Report*. Washington, DC: International Bank for Reconstruction and Development/ World Bank.
World Bank. 2021. *Education Finance Watch 2021*. Accessed September 1, 2022: https://thedocs.worldbank.org/en/doc/507681613998942297-0090022021/original/EFWReport2021219.pdf.
Wright, Susannah. 2012. "Citizenship, Moral Education and the English Elementary School." In *Mass Education and the Limits of State Building, C. 1870–1930*, edited by Laurence Brockliss and Nicola Sheldon. New York: Palgrave Macmillan.
Yuchtman, Noam. 2017. "Teaching to the Tests: An Economic Analysis of Traditional and Modern Education in Later Imperial and Republican China." *Explorations in Economic History* 63(1): 70–90.
Zeng, Zhaojin, and Joshua Eisenman. 2018. "The Price of Persecution: The Long-Term Effects of the Anti-Rightist Campaign on Economic Performance in Post-Mao China." *World Development* 109: 249–260.

INDEX

Note: Page numbers in **bold** indicate figures and tables.

Achával Rodríguez, Tristán, 213
Adams, John Quincy, 252–253, 259
administrative capacity. *See* state capacity
Africa: civil wars in, 233, 245, 246n69; data for, 42; democratization and primary education in North, 52; democratization and primary education in Sub-Saharan, 28, **52**, 53, 55n17; expansion of primary education lagging behind Latin America, 43; inadequate teaching skills in Sub-Saharan, 296; lack of reading skills in, 310; rise of postcolonial states in, 12
Aghion, Philippe, 73–74n55
Alexander, Thomas, 102n45, 125–126
Algeria, **49**, 64n35
Alliaud, Andrea, 167–168n133
American Philosophical Society of Philadelphia, 257
American Spelling Book (Webster), 254
Americas, the: access to primary education in, historical expansion of, 11–14, 38–86; compulsory schooling in, 195–197; democratization and state intervention in primary education in, 26, **49**; ideas about education in, 100–101, 106; industrialization and access to primary education in, 66–68; interstate wars and access to primary education in, **74**; religious education in, 205; school inspection policies in, 192–195; state intervention in primary education in, timing of, 8–11; teacher certification in, 189–192; teacher recruitment in, 185; teacher training in, 186–188. *See also specific countries*; Latin America
Amunátegui, Gregorio, 158–159, 165

Amunátegui, Luis, 158–59, 165
Andersson, Jens, 57n22
Annan, Kofi, 285
Ansell, Ben, 23n24, 26n36
Anuario Estadístico de la República de Chile, 162n123, 301–302, 303
Aquinas, Thomas, 250
Argentina: as case study, 124–25, 167–81; Chile and, comparison of expansion of primary education in, 60; civil war, 168–70; civil war and primary education, 80, 82n70, 167–179; curriculum for primary education in, 69; diplomatic rift with Chile, 173; first primary education law, timing of, **49**, **66**, 183n1; economic redistribution, 174; 1884 Law of Common Education, 45, 50, 124, 167–168, 171, 175–77, 180–181, 183n1, **190**, 191, **193**, 195, **196**, 199, **200**, 201n19, 208–212, 214, 216; fluctuation in the rate of expansion of primary schooling, 61, 166–167, **179**; geographic pattern of primary education expansion, 178, **179**; immigration and expansion of primary education, 178–180; industrialization and expansion of primary education, 177, 180–181; interstate wars and expansion of primary education, 71, 74n55, 75n56, 180–181; *Ley 1420* (*see* 1884 Law of Common Education under this heading); medical doctors, primary schooling and, 176n156; National Education Council (CNE), 167, 171, 175–177, 180, 292; Normal Schools for teacher training, 60, 161, 174–175, 177, 186, **190**, 191, 209, 210; number of primary schools, **179**;

Argentina (*continued*)
  Pedagogical Congress of 1882, 175; primary education statistics, earliest availability of, **49**; primary school enrollment rates, 44–45, **46**, **168**, 166–167, **179**; repression in, 173–174; right-wing support for educational expansion in, 56–57; state-building goal of primary education in, 170–177; timing of industrialization and adoption of landmark education legislation in, **66**. *See also* Catholic Church; Sarmiento, Domingo F.
Arguelles, Máximo, 197
Arnold, Matthew, 263–264
Asia: civil wars in, 245; data for, 42; democratization and primary education in, **52**; expansion of primary education lagging behind Latin America, 43; lack of reading skills in, 310; rise of postcolonial states in, 12
Australia, **49**, 64n35
Austria: access to primary schooling in authoritarian, 54; adoption of primary school policies prior to industrialization, 65; certification requirements for teachers in, **190**, 191; compulsory school provisions in, **196**; curriculum for primary schools in, **200**, 200n16, 201n19; data for, 11, **49**, 64n35; first primary education law, timing of, **49**, **66**, 183n1; enrollment rates in, 62, 82n69; Felbiger in, 106; reform in authoritarian, 115; school inspection policies in, 193; 1774 General School Ordinance, 183n1, **190**, 193, **196**, 200n16, 201n19
autocracies: comparison of school curriculum with democracies, 275–281; expansion of primary education under, 26, 31, 34, 35, 47–55, 58n23, 116; indoctrination by type of, **234**; left-wing and right-wing, 55–57; state-building through primary education in, 123–182; time horizon of, 233–236
Avellaneda, Nicolás, 169, 174

Baconnière de Salverte, Eusèbe, 144
Baker, Richard, 68n38
Banerjee, Abhijit, 312
banking crises, 86
Baranda, Joaquín, 241–242
Baraona, Loreto Egaña, 161
Barkin, Kenneth, 102, 306
Barnard, Henry, 59n24

Barrantes, Rafael, 272nn101–102, 274nn109–111, 275nn112–113
Barthe, Félix, 142–143
Becker, Gary, 229
Belgium, 22, **49**, 62, 66, 75n56, 186, **190**, **193**, **196**, **200**, 201n19
Bello, Andrés, 224
Benavot, Aaron, 41
Berger, Thor, 57n22
Biblioteca Nacional del Maestro, 167n133
Black Lives Matter (BLM), 314–315
Blanchette, John, 68n39
Boix, Carles, 48n11, 51n13, 107n60
Bold, Tessa, 296
Boli, John, 75
Bolivarian national curriculum, 295
Bolivia, **49**, 75n57, 82n70, 186n5, 201, 302n35
Bonaparte, Louis-Napoleon, 80
Bourdieu, Pierre, 6n6, 7n9
Bowles, Samuel, 25n31, 62n26
Brazil: Argentina, war with, 180; certification requirements for teachers in, **190**, 190n10; civil war and primary education in, 82n69; compulsory primary education in, 195, **196**; curriculum for primary schools, 199, **200**, 201n19; data for, 12, 64n35, 78; data on literacy, 311n2; democratization and primary education in, **49**; 1879 *Decreto 7.247*, 183n1, 190n10, **193**, **196**, 201n19; enrollment rates, 82n69; first primary education law, timing of, **49**, **66**, 184n1; interstate war and primary education in, 75n56; primary education in authoritarian, 55n18, 56; school inspection policies in, **193**
Britain. *See* England
Brownson, Orestes, 102
Bulgaria, **49**, 64n35
Bulnes, Manuel, 156, 122
Burke, Edmund, 250

Canada, 9, 13, 38, 43, **44**, **49**, 64n35, 75n56, 185
Cantoni, Davide, 293
Catholic Church: in Argentina, 60, 125, 171, 208, 212–216; in Chile, 60, 125, 164, 171, 208, 211–212; in France, 72, 125, 137–138, 149, 152–154; legitimacy of political rulers and, 94; mass education by, 22, 205; in Peru, 269; in Prussia, 48, 101, 107, 126, 134–135. *See also* religion
Centeno, Dámaso, 213
Center for Global Development, 313
Cermeño, Alexandra, 298

Chan-ocha, Prayruth, 236
Chávez, Hugo, 295
Chile: Argentina and, comparison of expansion of primary education in, 60; as case study, 124–125, 155–167; civil war of 1829–1830, 156, 224; civil war of 1851, 156, 222–223; civil war of 1859 and primary education in, 80, 82n69, 85, 155–167, 222, 237; curriculum for primary education in, 69, 162–164, 199–202, 205, 208–212; diplomatic rift with Argentina, 173; 1860 General Law of Primary Education (*Lei de Instrucción Primaria*), 69, 73, 124, 156, 160–165, 183n1, **190**, **193**, **196**, **200**, 200n16; first primary education law, timing of, **49**, **66**, 183n1; geographic pattern of primary education expansion in, 162–163; industrialization and adoption of landmark education legislation in, **66**; interstate wars and primary education in, 71, 75n56, 165; mining industry and expansion of primary education in, 165–166; Normal Schools for teacher training, 159, 161, 186, 188–189, **190**, 209–210, 217; number of primary schools in, 162–163, 165–166; primary education statistics, earliest availability of, **49**; primary school enrollment rates in, 45, 162–163; repression in, 157, 162–163; state-building goal of primary education in, 157–62; state capacity in, 166–167, 237. *See also* Catholic Church; Montt, Manuel
China, People's Republic of, **49**, 50, 64n35, 291n15, 292–293, 308
Citizen Reader, The, 268
Civil Rights Movement, 308
civil wars: in Argentina, 20, 168–170, 172–175, 217, 222, 233; in Brazil, 78; in Chile, 155–160, 162, 165, 167, 217, 222, 237; in Colombia, 78, 81–82; concessions to the Church following a, 23n25; education during, 77, 232, 286; in El Salvador, 81; in England, 94, 223, 225, 262; enrollment rates and, 14–15, 15, 61, 78–80, 78–86, 286–287; in Europe, 78–80 (*see also* country names under this heading); failed states and, 109; in Finland, 81, 324; in Latin America, 73, 78–80, 222 (*see also* country names under this heading); long-term consequences of, 119; in Mexico (Mexican Revolution), 239–240, 242, 244; post-World War II, characteristics of, 245–246; pre-World War II, characteristics of, 246n69;

in Rwanda, 322; in Spain, 78; state capacity and, 119–120; as type of internal conflict, 14–15, 77–78, 286, 314; in Uruguay, 45. *See also* internal conflict
Civit, Emilio, 216
Cold War, 84, 228
Colombia: certification requirements for teachers in, **190**, 191; civil war and primary education in, 80–83; compulsory primary education in, 195, **196**; curriculum for primary schools in, **200**, 201n19; data on literacy in, 211n2; 1870 *Decreto Orgánico de Instrucción Pública*, 183n1, **190**, **193**, 195, **196**, 200n16, 201n19; first primary education law, timing of, **49**, **66**, 183n1; fluctuation in the rate of expansion of primary schooling in, 61; interstate wars and primary school enrollment rates in, 75n56; *La Violencia*, period of, 78; primary education statistics, earliest availability of, **49**; primary school enrollment rates in, 44–45, **46**; school inspection policies, **193**
Comín, Diego, 64
Comisión de la Verdad y Reconciliación (Truth and Reconciliation Commission; CVR), 269–270
Communist Party of Peru / Sendero Luminoso (Shining Path; PCP-SL), 269–270, 274
compulsory primary education: across countries, 10, 185, 192, 195–197; collection of data on, 40; effect on crime of, 288; in Finland, 81, 85, 324; introduction of, 59; laws requiring (*see* laws regulating primary education); in Mexico, 240n44; parental resistance and, 57, 120, 228, 298; in Prussia, 48, 59, 68, 72, 102, 126, 128, 136, 306; in Soviet Russia, 69–70; in Sweden, 298; in the United States, 29, 59
Comte, August, 206–207, 291
Condliffe Lagemann, Ellen, 260
Confucian, 291n16
Connecticut, 252
Conservative Party (Chile), 156, 158, 211–213, 222–223; fusion with Liberal Party, 158–159
construction of schools: collection of data on, 39; in Argentina, **179**; in Chile, **163**; in France, **147**, **150**
Convention on the Rights of the Child (1989), 230
Coram, Robert, 257

Correlates of War Project, 77–78, 245n67, 246n69
Costa Rica, 12, 45, **49**, 82n69, 184n1, **190**, 193, **196**, 199, 200, 201n19, 203, 311n2
Counts, George S., 5n5
Cousin, Victor, 141, 263
Cuba, **49**, 55–56, 75n56, 82n69, 183n1, **190**, 191, 193, **196**, **200**, 200n16, 201n19
Cubberley, Ellwood, 260
Cultural Revolution, 308
curriculum for primary education: across countries, 197–205; catechism in, 107, 126n4, 127, 201–2, 204; in Chile, 69, 162–164, 199–202, 205, 208–12; Christian doctrine in, 96, 164, 209, 210, 211; Churches and timing of, 202; collection of data on, 40, 197, **200**; comparison in autocracies and democracies, 275–81; conservative model of teaching moral principles, 35, 211–214; diffusion theory and, 204–205; in France, 72–73, 144n70, 145, 152–154, 199–201, 203–204; industrialization and content of, 68–69; liberal model of teaching moral principles, 35, 214–217; math and science skills in, 3, 27, 199, **200**, 203–204; moral education in, 3, 21, 201–203; nation-building and, 3, 27, 201–204; in Prussia, 68, 126–127, 197, 199–204, 306; religious versus secular moral education, 23, 35, 198, 205–217; rural versus urban, 28, 68, 152, 197, **200**, 200n16, 306. *See also* moral education; skills
Czech Republic, **49**, 64n35

data: availability of official statistics on primary schooling, beginning of, 40–41, **49**; expansion of primary education, measures of, 39–43; focus on civil wars as one type of internal conflict, 77–78; internal conflict and, 31–32; onset of industrialization, problems presented by, 63–65; primary school enrollment rates, 41–43, 73–74n54; timing of state intervention in primary education, statistics on, 40–41
Dahlum, Sirianne, 281
De la Cruz, José María, 223
democracy / democratization: comparison of school curriculum with autocracies, 275–281; definitions of, 48, 51n13; and economic development, 311; and economic redistribution, 24; expansion of primary education and, 38–39, 47–55, 58n23; indoctrination through primary education in, 115, 231, 249–282, 320; time horizon of elites under, 116, 236, 247–248; as theory of education, 2, 24–26, 47. *See also* autocracies; England; Peru; United States
Denmark, **49**, 54, 59; 1814 School Acts, 66, 183n1, **190**, 191, 193, 195, **196**, 200–201, 203
Dewey, John, 99–100, 260–261, 282
Dickens, Charles, 263
diffusion theory: crises of internal order according to, 29; evidence for, 29, 58–60, 106; as an explanation for the expansion of primary education, 24–25; limitations of, 25, 29–30, 34, 60–61, 204–205, 204n22; state-building theory of education distinct from, 30
Disraeli, Benjamin, 263, 265
Dominican Republic, **49**, 82n69, 84, 302n34, 311n2
Duflo, Esther, 312
Durkheim, Émile, 6n6

Earl de Grey and Ripon (George Frederick Samuel Robinson, 1st Marquess of Ripon), 265
economic redistribution, 24, 33, 57; primary education in Chile and, 164; primary education in France and, 140–141, 152. *See also* social mobility
Ecuador, **49**, 65, 66, 75n56, 82n69, 183n1, **190**, 193, 195, **196**, 199n15, **200**
education: expansion of primary (*see* expansion of primary education); reform of moral character and (*see* moral character; moral education)
education theories, 24–32. *See also* diffusion theory; human capital; indoctrination; industrialization; nation-building; interstate wars; democracy / democratization; social control; state-building
Egypt, **49**, 50, 64n35, 291n15
1848 Revolution, 48, 80, 83, 305, 307
Elias, Norbert, 7n9, 297–298
Elías Calles, Plutarco, 57
elites / upper classes
  in Argentina: agreement about goals of mass education among, 177, 179, 181; civil wars and, 169–170; concern about mass violence among, 174; conflict among, 222; Sarmiento's ideas about the cause of civil war well received by, 171–174
  in democracies: 248, 320
  in Chile: civil war of 1859 and, 156–158; conflict among, 222–223; moral educa-

Index | 349

tion of the masses, concern about, 156; perception of parental demand for education, 165; support for schooling of the masses among, 158–159, 161, 237
in England: dangers of mass education according to, 226–227, 262; fear of working-class activism among, 263, 268; support for mass education among, 267, 268
in France: support for schooling of the masses among, 140, 144, 238, 304
in Mexico: concern about moral character of the lower classes among, 242, 244; conflict among, 239, 242; resistance to education intervention, 242
in Peru: role of education according to, 270;
in Prussia: concern about moral character of the lower classes among, 130; erosion of power among 129–130, 132; failure to contain disobedient peasants, 131–132; reforms targeting nobility, 130n21; support for schooling of the masses, 136
in Sweden: fear of the lower classes among, 220–222; goals of mass education according to, 222
in the United States: concern about mass violence among, 251–252, 256, 314n17, 315; goals of mass education according to, 253, 257–258, 261; efforts to provide education to Black children among, 258–259; support for schooling of the masses among, 251, 258
El Salvador, **49**, 75n56, 80–81, 82n69, **83**, 85, 184n1, **190**, **193**, **196**, 200, 201n19
England: Church provision of primary education in, 225, 262, 264; civil war of 1642–1651, 94, 223, 225, 262; as an educational laggard, 62–63, 224–227; 1870 Forster Education Act, 45, 50, 63, 183n1, 190n10, **193**, **196**, **200**, 266–268; first primary education law, timing of, **49**, 66, 183n1; Glorious Revolution of 1688, 223, 225, 262; ideas about mass education in, 225–27, 261–267; industrialization and adoption of landmark education legislation in, **66**; industrialization and expansion of primary education in, 62–63; internal conflict and expansion of primary education in, 225–227, 262–266; interstate wars and primary education in, 75n56; political consensus on mass education in, 265–266; primary education statistics, earliest availability of, **49**; primary school enrollment rates in, 44–45, **46**; Prussia and, comparison of rates of industrialization and primary schooling expansion in, 62–63; Reform Act of 1832, 225, 262; Second Reform Act (1867), 265–266; timing of industrialization and adoption of landmark education legislation in, **66**
enrollment rates: across countries and regions, 43–47; in Argentina, 167–68, **168**; child labor in agriculture and, 68n38; in Chile, 162, **163**; civil war and, 78–86 (see also internal conflict and mass education; specific countries); collection of data on, 39, 41–43; distinguishing between Western and Non-Western, 73–74n54; in France, 73n52, 137, 146, **147**, 149, **150**, 153n87; industrialization in Western countries and, 67n37; interstate wars and, 73–75; in Latin America, **168**; non-democratic regimes and, 50–54; prior to democratization, **51**, 51–53; in Prussia, 73n52
Erdoğan, Recep, 308
Ericksson, Katherine, 68n38
Europe: access to primary education in, historical expansion of, 11–14, 38–86, **44**; civil war and primary school enrollment rates in, 78–86 (see also internal conflict and mass education); compulsory schooling in, 195–197; democratization and state intervention in primary education in, 26, **49**; diffusion of ideas about education from, 59–60, 105–106, 159, 173, 188, 253, 259, 264; expansion of primary education systems, as the world leader in, 58–59; industrialization and access to primary education in, 66–68; industrialization and adoption of landmark education legislation in, 65–66; interstate wars and access to primary education in, 74; primary education laws, timing of first, **49**; primary education statistics, timing of earliest availability of, **49**; primary school enrollment rates in, 43–47; primary school enrollment rates prior to democratization in, 53; right-wing support for educational expansion in, 56; teacher certification in, 189–192; teacher training, as the world leader in, 59; teacher training in, 186–188; teacher recruitment in, 185; school inspection policies in, 192–195; state intervention in primary education in, timing of, 8–11, **49**. See also specific countries

350 | Index

expansion of primary education: across countries and regions, 43–47; Argentina as case study, 167–181 (*see also* Argentina); Chile as case study, 155–167 (*see also* Chile); democratization as an explanation for, 47–55, 58n23 (*see also* democracy / democratization); the diffusion argument as an explanation for, 58–61 (*see also* diffusion theory); economic motivations for (*see* economic redistribution); economic redistribution / social mobility as an explanation for, 141 (*see also* social mobility); England as case study, 224–227, 261–268 (*see also* England); explanations for, 24–32, 38–39; France as case study, 137–155 (*see also* France); industrialization as an explanation for (*see* industrialization); internal conflict as an explanation for (*see* internal conflict); interstate wars as an explanation for, 24–25, 28, 71–75 (*see also* interstate wars); left-wing / right-wing autocracies and, 55–58; measures of, 39–43; Prussia as case study, 124–137 (*see also* Prussia); unpopular among the masses, 57–58, 165; variation in the rate of, 45, 47. *See also* enrollment rates

expenditures on / funding of education: in Chile, 159; collection of data on, 40; in France, 145–146, **147**, 148, 151

Fawcett, Henry, 265
Felbiger, Johann, 103–107, 114, 128, 135
Finland: civil war and primary school enrollment rates in, 80–82, 82n69, **83**, 85; data for, **49**; democratization and primary education, **49**; education reform after World War II, 324; enrollment rates in, 44–45, **46**; feminization of the teaching profession in, 185; industrialization and primary education in, 64n35, **66**; interstate wars and primary school enrollment rates in, 75n56; as primary education laggard, 44–45; religion and primary education in, 22; teacher recruitment in, 205; teacher training in, 307
fiscal capacity. *See* state capacity
Flora, Peter, 42
Ford, Guy, 131
Foucault, Michel, 6n6, 7n9, 91–92
Fouka, Vasiliki, 300
France: as case study, 124–125, 137–155; Bouquier Law, 238–239; Catholic Church and primary education during July Monarchy,

149, 152–155; compulsory schooling in, adoption of, 59; curriculum for primary education in, 152–154, 199–201, 203–204; diffusion of ideas about education in, 59–60; enrollment data for, 42n6, 73n52; expenditure on primary education in, 145–148, 151; Falloux Law, 45, 80; fiscal capacity and expansion of primary education in, 149, 151; first primary education law, timing of, 28, **49**, 50, **66**, 183n1; fluctuation in the rate of expansion of primary schooling in, 61; geographic pattern of primary education expansion in, 148–150; Guizot Law, 45, 50, 137–138, 142–146, 148–149, 151–152, 154–155, 154–55, 183n1, **190**, **193**, **196**, 200n16; industrialization and expansion of primary education in, 152; interstate wars and primary school enrollment rates in, 73, 75n56; Jules Ferry Laws, 28, 72–73, 73n52, 204; *Loi sur l'instruction primaire* (*see* Guizot Law under this heading); Normal Schools for teacher training in, 186–188, **190**, 294, 307; number of primary schools in, 149, **150**; parental demand for education in, 58n22, 149, 151; primary education statistics, earliest availability of, **49**; primary school enrollment rates in, 44–45, **46**, 50–51, 149, **150**; primary schooling and democracy in, 50–51, 54; repression in, 138–140; Revolution of 1848, education reform after, 80, **83**, 307; Revolution of 1789, education reform after, 137, 238–239; social mobility not a goal of Guizot Law, 140–142; timing of industrialization and adoption of landmark education legislation in, 65–66, **66**; universal male suffrage in, 50
Francke, August Hermann, 103, 133–135
Franco-Prussian War, 28, 72–73
Frederick II "the Great" (king of Prussia), 33, 48, 59, 72, 81, 100–101, 103, 105–106, 115, 125, 127–128, 130–134, 137, 185–186, 191
Frederick William I (king of Prussia), 47
Frederick William III (king of Prussia), 105
free primary schooling for the poor, 40
Friedman, Milton, 229
Friedman, Willa, 287n4, 290n14
Frisancho, Susana, 273
Fujimori, Alberto, 269
Fürstenberg, Carl Egon von, 136

Gallo, Delfin, 213–214
Gallo, Pedro León, 157

Gaskell, Elizabeth, 263
Geddes, Barbara, 233–234
Gellner, Ernest, 27, 61, 63, 68
Germany: data for, 11, **49**; democratization and primary education in, **49**, 54; education reform after the 1848 Revolution, 305–306; enrollment rates, 44, 75n56; parental influence, education policy and, 300; studies of educational system in, 60, 188, 264. *See also* Prussia
Ghana, **49**, 55–56
girls' education, 143n64
Gintis, Herbert, 25n31, 62n26
Global Education First Initiative (United Nations), 320
Gómez, Eusebio, 181
Gontard, Maurice, 144
Goyena, Pedro, 212–213
Gramsci, Antonio, 25n31
Great Britain. *See* England
Greece, **49**, 59, 65, **66**, 75n56, 82n69, 83–84, 183n1, **190**, **193**, 195, **196**, 199, **200**, 201n19, 203
Grew, Raymond, 73n52
Grzymala-Busse, Anna, 23n25, 24n29
Guatemala, **49**, 82n69, 184n1, **190**, 191, **193**, 195, **196**, 200n16, 201n19
Güemes, Miguel María, 161–162, 164
Guerry, André-Michel, 140, 304
Guizot, François, 137, 139–144, 146, 151–155
Guizot Inquiry *(L'enquête Guizot)*, 146
Guizot Law. *See* France, Guizot Law
Guzmán, Abimael, 269
Gvirtz, Silvina, 295

Harrigan, Patrick, 73n52
Hecker, Johann, 103, 107, 128, 133–135
Hobbes, Thomas, 87, 94–97, 100
Hobijn, Bart, 64
Honduras, **49**, 82n69
human capital, 24, 26, 32–33, 229
Humphrey, David, 252
Hungary, **49**, 64n35, 74n56, 106

ideas about mass education: changes during the second half of the twentieth century, 228–231; during the Enlightenment, 94–99; global diffusion of, 105–107; as indoctrination, 89–91; in Latin America, 91; Pietism and, 102–103, 133–135; positivist *(see* positivism / positivist); in Prussia, 100–105, 132–137; as state-building, 100; in social contract theories, 93–100

immigration: as a trigger of nation-building, 25, 29; as an explanation for the expansion of primary education, 28–29; and education reform in Argentina, 29, 176n161, 178–180, 306–307; and education reform in the United States, 29, 256, 292; effect of education on assimilation of, 299; internal conflict and, 31–32, 314
India, **49**, 64n35
indoctrination: conditions conducive to, 36, 121, 218–219, 223, 231, 236, 239, 245, 314; deemphasizing, 324; definition of, 5, 249–251, 255n21; in democracies, 36, 231, 247–249, 258–259, 275, 282; education as, 3, 31–32, 118, 227, 231, 282; goals, 122, 182, 202, 231, 238, 245; international organizations and, 322–324; mechanisms of, 89–91; in non-democratic regimes, 116, 233–236; as a policy tool, 109–110, 112, 218, 223; prevalence of, global dataset indicating, 36, 275–281, 315; psychological consequences of, 297–298; as a strategy to maintain social / political order, 3–4, 20, 89–91, 251, 282, 289–290
Indonesia, **49**, 64n35, 287–288, 300n33
industrialization: content of the curriculum in non-Western countries and, 69–71; content of the curriculum in Western countries and, 68–69; data identifying the onset of, problems presented by, 63–65; enrollment rates in Western countries and, 67n37; expansion of primary education and, 38, 61–63, 66–68, 71; expansion of primary education in Argentina and, 180–181; expansion of primary education in Chile and, 165–166; expansion of primary education in England and, 25–26, 224–226, 263, 267; expansion of primary education in France and, 152, 155; expansion of primary education prior to, 38–39; expansion of primary education in the Soviet Union and, 69–70, 228; as an explanation for the expansion of primary education, 2, 24–28, 61–62; internal conflict and, 31–32; timing of adoption of landmark education legislation and, 65–66, **66**
inspection of schools: in France, 143, 145–146, 153–154, 289; local versus centralized, 194, 307; to monitor enrollment, **10**, 40; in the Netherlands, 194; policies for, 3, 35, 50, 92, 118, 120, 184, 192–195, 299; priests' involvement in, 113, 143, 145, 153, 193; in Prussia, 126; in Sweden, 194, 237

352 | Index

internal conflict: armed conflict in Peru, 268–269; banking crises, distinct from, 86; Black Lives Matter (BLM), 314–315; challenge posed by studying, 76–77; Civil Rights Movement, 308; civil war in Argentina, 168–170, 172–174; civil war in Chile, 155–160 (*see also* Chile), 162; civil wars, focus on, 77–78; common belief that there is no connection between expansion of primary education and, 75–76; expansion of primary education and, 39, 58, 61, 78–86; mass violence in France, 138–43, 148–149, **150**, 151, 155; peasant rebellions in Prussia, 128–132, 136; rebellions in the United States during the Early Republic, 251–253, 256, 259; in Sweden, perception of, 221

internal conflict and mass education: theory linking, 2–3, 19–20, 30–32, 108–123; Argentina as case study, 167–181 (*see also* Argentina); cases providing evidence for the theory of, 124–125, 248; Chile as case study, 155–167 (*see also* Chile); England as case study, 261–68 (*see also* England); evidence of expansion of primary education and, 14–15, 58, 61, 75–86; France as case study, 137–155 (*see also* France); Peru as case study, 268–275 (*see also* Peru); predictors of, 123; Prussia as case study, 125–137 (*see also* Prussia); United States as case study, 251–261 (*see also* United States)

interstate wars: in Argentina, 180–181; in Chile, 165; curriculum to train soldiers for, 203–204; in England, 225; as an explanation for the expansion of primary education, 24–26, 28, 31–32, 71; and primary school enrollment rates, 2, 28, 38, 71–75; in Prussia, 126–128

investment in education. *See* expenditures on / funding of education

Iran, **49**, 64n35

Ireland, **49**, 59, 62, 64n35, 65

Israel, Jonathan, 98–99n35

Italy, 22, **49**, 64n35, **66**, 75n56, 82n69, 180, 183n1, 185, **190**, 191, **193**, **196**, **200**, 200n16, 201n19, 288

Jamaica, **49**, 183n1, 190n10, **193**, 195, **196**, 199n15, **200**

Japan, **49**, 54, 64n35, 70–71, 269

Jefferson, Thomas, 253, 255, 259

Juárez Celman, Miguel Angel, 178n160

Kaestle, Carl, 251, 259n43, 261
Kant, Immanuel, 96, 98, 206
Kenya, **49**, 287n4, 290, 313–314
Kingsley, Charles, 263
Kleist, Conrad, 131–132
Knox, Samuel, 257
Knutsen, Carl Henrik, 281
Korea, Republic of (South), **49**, 64n35
Kosack, Stephen, 55n18

La conciencia de un niño (A Child's Conscience), 164, 211
Lastarria, José, 159
Latin America: civil war and primary school enrollment rates in, 78–86; European influence on ideas about education, 60; interstate wars and expansion of primary education in, 71; primary education laws, timing of first, **49**; primary school enrollment rates in, 43–47, **168**; primary school enrollment rates prior to democratization in, 53; right-wing support for educational expansion in, 56–57; timing of industrialization and adoption of landmark education legislation in, 65–66, **66**. *See also specific countries*

laws regulating primary education
Argentina: 1884 Law of Common Education, 45, 50, 167–168, 171, 175–177, 180–181, 183n1, **190**, 191, **193**, 195, **196**, 199, **200**, 201n19, 208–210, 212, 214, 216; *Ley 1420* (*see* 1884 Law of Common Education under this heading)
Austria: 1774 General School Ordinance, 183n1, **190**, 193, **196**, 200n16, 201n19
Belgium: 1842 Organic Law of Primary Instruction, 183n1, **190**, 193, **196**, 201n19
Brazil: 1879 *Decreto 7.247*, 183n1, 190n10, **193**, **196**, 201n19
Chile: 1860 General Law of Primary Education (*Lei de Instrucción Primaria*), 156, 160–162, 183n1, **190**, **193**, **196**, **200**, 200n16; collection of data on, 40; compulsory schooling laws, 59 (*see also* compulsory primary education)
Colombia: 1870 *Decreto Orgánico de Instrucción Pública*, 183n1, **190**, **193**, 195, **196**, 200n16, 201n19
Costa Rica: 1869 *Reglamento de Instrucción Primaria*, 183n1, **190**, **193**, **196**, 200n16, 201n19
Cuba: 1844 *Plan General de Instrucción Pública para las Islas de Cuba y Puerto*

Rico, 183n1, **190**, 191, **193**, **196**, 200n16, 201n19

Denmark: 1814 School Acts, 66, 183n1, **190**, **193**, **196**, 200n16, 201, 201n19, 203

Ecuador: 1871 *Ley Reforma de la Educación*, 183n1, **190**, **193**, 195, **196**, 199n15, **200**

El Salvador: 1873 *Reglamento de Instrucción Pública*, 183n1, **190**, **193**, **196**, 200n16, 201n19

England: 1870 Forster Education Act, 45, 50, 63, 183n1, 190n10, **193**, **196**, **200**, 266–268

France: 1848 Falloux Law, 80; 1833 Guizot Law, 45, 50, 137–138, 142–146, 148–149, 151–152, 154–155, 183n1, **190**, **193**, **196**, 200n16; 1881/82 Jules Ferry Laws, 28, 72–73, 73n52, 204; 1833 *Loi sur l'instruction primaire* (*see* 1833 Guizot Law under this heading)

opposition to: in Chile, 165; in France, 152, 155; in Prussia, 127

Greece: 1834 Law, 183n1, **190**, **193**, 195, **196**, 199, 201n19, 203

Guatemala: 1875 *Ley Orgánica de Instrucción Pública Primaria*, 183n1, **190**, **193**, 195, **196**, 200n16, 201n19

Italy: 1859 Casati Law, 183n1, **190**, 191, **193**, **196**, 200n16, 201n19

Jamaica: 1892 Elementary Education Law, 183n1, 190n10, **193**, 195, **196**, 199n15, **200**

Mexico: 240n44

Netherlands: 1806 Education Act, 183n1, **190**, **193**, **196**, 201n19

Norway: 1827 Law Concerning the Peasant School System in the Country, 183n1, **190**, **193**, 195, **196**, 200n16, 201n19

Peru: 1850 *Primera Ley de Instrucción Pública*, 183n1, **190**, **193**, **196**, 201n19; 2003 General Law of Education (*Ley General de Educación*), 271

Prussia: 1763 General Rural School Regulations, 50, 72, 125–128, 134–135, 183n1, **190**, **193**, 195, **196**, 199, 200n16, 201n19, 203, 208, 306

Spain: 1857 *Ley de Instrucción Pública*, 183n1, **190**, **193**, 195, **196**, 200n16, 201

Sweden: 1842 Elementary School Statute / School Act, 69, 183n1, **190**, 195, **193**, **196**, 201n19, 220, 222, 298

Uruguay: 1877 *Ley 1.350*, 45, 183n1, 190n10, **193**, 195, **196**, 201n19

Venezuela: 1870 *Decreto de Instrucción Pública*, 183n1, 190n10, **193**, **196**, 201n19

timing of earliest, **49**, 50, 60

timing of landmark and industrialization, lack of a clear pattern linking, 65–66, **66**

"learning crisis," 7, 32, 311–13

Lee, Hanol, 11–12, 40, 42–43, 64, 74n55

Lee, Jong-Wha, 11–12, 40, 42–43, 64, 74n55

Leguizamón, Onésimo, 175, 176n154

Levi, Margaret, 3n1

Levitsky, Steven, 116

Lieberman, Evan S., 124n1

Lindert, Peter H., 73n52, 75

Lindvall, Johannes, 23n24

Lipset, Seymour Martin, 32n44

Lleras Camargo, Alberto, 82

Locke, John, 96–98, 103, 254

López Mateos, Adolfo, 57

Lowe, Robert, 266

Luna, Diego, 272nn101–2, 274nn109–11, 275nn112–13

Madison, James, 253

Magaloni, Beatriz, 233

Mann, Horace, 17, 60, 106, 107n60, 259, 263

Mann, Michael, 33n48

Manzano, Dulce, 55n18

Maria Theresa (queen of Austria), 106, 115

Marlborough, George Charles Spencer-Churchill, 8th Duke of, 266

Marshall, Alfred, 25n31

Martin, Cathie Jo, 66

Martínez, Maximiliano Hernández, 81

Marx, Karl, 25n31, 250

Massachusetts, 59, 251–252

Massachusetts Board of Education, 259

masses, the: breakdown of social order / crisis in rural authority among the, 128–132, 136–137; lower classes in France, 138–140, 151; lower classes in Sweden, 221–222; moral degradation among, perception of, 130 (*see also* moral character); peasants and factory workers in Finland, 81; peasants and indigenous communities in El Salvador, 81; peasant and working classes in Mexico, 239; peasants in Prussia, 128–132, 136–137, 305; peasants, workers, and artisans in Chile, 156; rural and indigenous groups in Peru, 269; rural masses in Argentina, 172–176; in the United States, 252; working class in England, 225–227, 263–266. *See also* elites / upper classes

Melton, James, 72, 128, 131–132

Mexico: as case study, 239–244; civil war and primary school enrollment rates in, 82n69; curriculum for primary education in, 69, 244; data for, 302n34; data on literacy for, 311n2; democracy and primary schooling in, 54; electoral autocracy in, 280; first primary education law, timing of, **49, 66**, 183n1, 240n44; expansion of primary education after the Mexican Revolution, 242–243; expansion of primary education under the *Porfiriato*, 240–242; incentives for school attendance in, 195–196, 299n31; indoctrination of the masses in, 116, 242, 244; industrialization and primary education, 64n35, **66**; internal conflict in, 239; as primary education laggard, 20, 36, 47, 122, 182, 218–219, 239–245; primary education statistics, earliest availability of, **49**; primary school enrollment rates, 44–45, **46**; right-wing support for educational expansion in, 57; state capacity in, 240, 242–244
Meyer, John, 75
Middle East, 52, 310
military rivalry / military interpretations of primary school expansion. *See* interstate wars
Miller, Michael, 48n11, 51n13
Mincer, Jacob, 229
Mitchell, Brian, 41–42, 73–74n54
Mitre, Bartolomé, 169, 174
Mokyr, Joel, 25n31, 27n38, 62nn26–27, 64n33
Montalivet, Marthe Camille Bachasson Comte de, 142–143
Montt, Manuel, 157, 159–160
moral character: certification of required for aspiring teachers, **190**, 191; conservative model of teaching moral principles, 35, 211–214; liberal model of teaching moral principles, 35, 214–217; mass education and, 123; mass education in Argentina to shape, 168–169, 172–176; mass education in Chile to shape, 158, 160–162, 165; mass education in France to shape, 144–146, 152, 153–154; mass education in Prussia to shape, 136–137; of the masses in Argentina, 172–175; of the masses in France, 140–142, 148; Ten Commandments as guide for, 205; in the training of teachers, 3, 188–189. *See also* moral education
moral education: in Argentina, 177, 181, 208–211; in Chile, 156, 164, **200**, 201–202, 206, 208–211; by the Church, 18–19, 23, 94, 112, 153, 202, 205–206; competing models of, 23, 88, 120, 184, 203–217, 291; consequences for social order, 291, 306; as a goal of primary education systems, 6, 21, 22, 27, 30, 35, 117–118, 120, 202; emphasized in national curriculums for primary education, 3, 21, 120, 184, 197–208; in England, 266–268; in France, 22, 144, 153, **200**, 201; in Peru, 269, 272–273; in Prussia, 68, 101, 104–106, 136, **200**, 201, 206, 306–307; in the United States, 60, 256–259. *See also* moral character
modernization, 32, 121, 151
More, Hannah, 227

Napoleon III (emperor of France), 50
National Commission on Excellence in Education, 229
nation-building: diffusion theory and, 25, 30, 58–61; education as, 20, 58, 71, 90; expansion of Argentine schooling and, 178–180, 306–307; expansion of Prussian schooling and, 126–128; immigration waves as a trigger of, 25, 29; language of instruction and, 22, 100, **200**, 201–202; military rivalry and, 71, 127–128; relative low priority as a reason for mass education, 20, 22, 89–90, 100, 201–202, 208; in Rwanda, 322; theories of education based on, 24–26, 30. *See also state-building*
Netherlands, the, **49**, 60, 62, 64n35, 65, **66**, 75n56, 178, 183n1, **190, 193**, 194, 196, **200**, 201n19, 264
Neundorf, Anja, 234, 276
Newcastle Report of 1861, 264
Nicaragua, **49**, 75n56, 82n69
Nipperdey, Thomas, 305n39
Nkrumah, Kwame, 56
Normal School of Berlin, 48, 134, 186, 191
Normal School of Versailles, 187
Normal Schools: 184, 186, 293–294; in Argentina, 60, 174, 175, 177, 186, 209, **210**; in Chile, 60, 159, 161, 186, 209, **210**; degree from required to obtain a certificate or license to teach, **190**, 191–192; in Europe, 59; first state-sponsored, 134; formation of teacher organizations from within, 294; in France, 143n67, 186, 307 (*see also* Normal School of Versailles); monopoly over teacher training by, 21, 59; in Prussia, 59 (*see also* Normal School of Berlin); state regulation of, 186–88; in the United States, 59, 60

Norway, 11, 22, **49**, 59, 62, 64n35, 65, **66**, 75n56, 183n1, 188, **190**, 191, **193**, 194–95, **196, 200**, 200n16, 201n19

Obama, Barack, 318n21
Obregón, Alvaro, 242–243
OECD (Organisation for Economic Co-operation and Development), 7, 38, 311n2

Panama, **49**, 311n2
Pancasila (Indonesia), 288
Paraguay, **49**, 75n56, 82n69, 180, 302n34
peasant rebellions, 128–132, 136–137. *See also* internal conflict
Peña, Jesús, 272nn101–102, 274nn109–111, 275nn112–113
Pennsylvania, 251, 254
Pérez Mascayano, José, 161
Périer, Casimir, 139
Perón, Eva "Evita," 295
Perón, Juan Domingo, 56, 295, 308
Peronist Doctrine, 295, 308
Peru: as case study, 268–275; Catholic Church in, 269; certification requirements for teachers in, **190**; civil war and primary school enrollment rates in, 82n69, 270; compulsory schooling provisions, **196**; *Comisión de la Verdad y Reconciliación* (Truth and Reconciliation Commission; CVR), 269–270; Communist Party of Peru / Sendero Luminoso (Shining Path; PCP-SL), 269–270, 274; curriculum for primary schools in, **200**, 201n19, 270–273; data on literacy, 311n2; Educational Emergency of 2003, 270; 1850 *Primera Ley de Instrucción Pública*, 183n1, **190, 193, 196**, 201n19; first primary education law, timing of, **49, 66**, 183n1; indoctrination in democratic, 248–249, 268–274, 281, 314, 321; industrialization and primary education in, 64n35, **66**; internal conflict and curriculum reform in, 270–273; internal conflict and expansion of primary education in, 270; interstate wars and primary education in, 75n56; moral education in, 269, 272–273; primary education statistics, earliest availability of, **49**; school inspection policies in, **193**; teachers in, 270, 273–275; 2003 General Law of Education (*Ley General de Educación*), 271
Pietism, 93, 102–103, 125, 133–136, 223
Pilbeam, Pamela, 138
Plato, 93–94, 97–98

Pledge of Allegiance, 261
Polity Project, 48n11, 51n13
Ponce de León, Macarena, 159
Porfirio Díaz (José de la Cruz Porfirio Díaz Mori), 240–241, 244
Portugal, **49**, 59, 64n35, 66, 75n56
positivism / positivist, 206–207, 214, 240–241, 291–292
PRI (*Partido Revolucionario Institucional*), 57, 280, 296
primary education, expansion of. *See* expansion of primary education
Programme for International Student Assessment (PISA), 281
Prost, Antoine, 144
Prussia: as case study, 124–137; Church-State relations in, 23, 125; civil war and primary school enrollment rates in, 80; compulsory primary education in, 48, 59, 68, 72, 102, 126, 128, 136, 306; curriculum for primary education in, 68, 126–127, 197, 199–204, 306; England and, comparison of rates of industrialization and primary schooling expansion in, 62–63; first primary education law, timing of, 28, **49**, 59, 72, 128, **66**, 183n1; French study of the education system in, 141; ideas about education, diffusion of, 17, 59–60, 105–107; industrialization and adoption of landmark education legislation in, **66**; interstate wars and expansion of primary education in, 72, 126–128; mass education to shape moral character, 136–137; as model for state-building, 93, 281; moral education in, 68, 101, 104–106, 136, **200**, 201, 206, 306–307; nation-building and primary schooling expansion in, 126–128; non-democratic roots of primary education in, 47–48; Normal Schools for teacher training in, 48, 59, 134, 186, 191; peasant rebellions in, 128–132, 136–137, 148n77; Pietism and education in, 93, 102–103, 125, 133–136, 223; primary school enrollment rates in, 43–44, **44**, **46**, 73n52; reform of education in, 132–137, 305–306; religion and education reform in, 134–135; Revolution of 1848, education reform after, 80, 305–306; 1763 General Rural School Regulations, 50, 72, 125–128, 134–135, 183n1, **190, 193**, 195, **196**, 199, 200n16, 201n19, 203, 208, 306; teachers in, 48, 134. *See also* Felbiger, Johann; Frederick II "the Great"; Hecker, Johann

Quiroga, Juan Facundo, 171–172

Radical Party (Chile), 158, 222, 227
railroads: in Argentina, 170, 174; implementation of education reforms and, 236–237, 298; in Sweden, 237, 298
Ramirez, Francisco, 75
Ramos Mejía, José María, 176n156, 292
Reátegui, Félix, 273
religion
  Catholic Church (*see* Catholic Church)
  Church-State relations: 23, 107, 112–113; in Argentina, 23, 125, 171; in Chile, 23, 125, 156; in France, 23, 125, 138, 143–145, 153–155; in Prussia, 23, 125
  educational reform and: in Chile, 162, 164; in Prussia, 134–135
  Pietist, 93, 102–103, 125, 133–136, 223
Renan, Ernest, 72n51
Rengifo, Francisca, 159
revolutions of 1848, 48, 80, 83, 305, 307
Riddle, Phyllis, 41
Riehl, Wilhelm, 305
Roca, Julio A., 61, 170–171, 175–176, 178, 180–181
Rochner, Dominic, 288nn6–8
Romania, **49**, 64n35
Romer, Paul, 229
Rosas, Juan Manuel de, 171–173, 176n154
Rosato, Sebastian, 48n11, 51n13
Rostow, Walt Whitman, 62n29, 64–65
Rousseau, Jean-Jacques, 17, 94, 96–100
Rush, Benjamin, 253–256
Russia, **49**, 50, 54–56, 64n35, 69. *See also* Soviet Union (Union of Soviet Socialist Republics, USSR)
Rwanda, 321–322

Saia, Alessandro, 288nn6–8
Sarmiento, Domingo F., 60, 91, 106, 114, 158–159, 169, 171–180, 185–187, 208–209, 224, 241, 263, 304
Schlabrendorff, Ernst Wilhelm von, 136
Schleunes, Karl, 130, 135–136
Secretary of Public Education (SEP; Mexico), 241, 243
Serrano, Sol, 159, 161
Seven Years' War, 28, 72, 126–28
Shaftesbury, Anthony Ashley-Cooper, 7th Earl of, 266
Shays' Rebellion, 251–253, 256, 259
Sierra, Justo, 241–242, 244
skills: citizenship, 273; critical thinking, 249–251, 281, 291, 317, 320, 324; curriculum, place in, 198, 291; demand for, 62; economic concerns / job market, 229–230, 311; failure to teach / prioritize, 1, 3, 7, 22, 27–28, 32, 37, 66, 68–69, 71, 181, 231, 257–258, 308–314, 323–24; math / science, 22, 181, 184, 204, 228, 280, 291, 310–311, 324; for the military, 71; potential for teaching, 16, 20, 24–25, 34, 283, 287, 317–319; reading, 154, 164, 198, 227, 311; reasoning, cultivation of, 107, 184; social mobility and, 36, 228–229, 291–292 (*see also* social mobility); social order and the teaching of, 293; of teachers, 293, 296, 317–318
Skopp, Douglas, 305n39, 306
Smith, Samuel Harrington, 257–258
SNTE (Mexico), 296
social control: education as a policy tool for, 6–7, 17, 32, 125, 230, 314, 319–320; failure of, 75 (*see also* internal conflict); in Prussia, 102
social mobility: in Argentina, 292, 297; in Chile, 324; democratization and demands for, 24; education as contributor to, 121, 140–41, 228, 230, 310, 321; primary schools and, 57, 141; refraining from promoting, 6, 16, 35, 57, 105, 141, 227. *See also* economic redistribution
Soifer, Hillel, 270
Soininen, Mikael, 81
Sota Nadal, Javier, 272
South Africa, **49**, 64n35
Soviet Union (Union of Soviet Socialist Republics, USSR), 70, 228. *See also* Russia
Spain: certification requirements for teachers in, **190**; Chile, war with, 165n125; compulsory primary education in, 195, **196**; curriculum for primary education in, **200**, 201; data for, 12, 42n6; democratization and primary education in, **49**; 1857 *Ley de Instrucción Pública*, 183n1, **190**, **193**, 195, **196**, 200n16, 201; enrollment rate in, 62–63, 82n69; feminization of the teaching profession in, 185; immigration to Argentina from, 180; independence of colonies from, 60, 168, 239; industrialization and primary education in, **66**; interstate war and primary education in, 75n56; Normal Schools, 59; primary education in pre-industrial, 65; religion and primary education in, 22; Sarmiento's travel to, 60; school inspection policies in, **193**; teachers purged by Franco, 308
Spener, Phillip Jacob, 103

Spinoza, Baruch de, 98n35
Squicciarini, Mara, 151
Stalin, Joseph, 69–70n42
state, the / central government. *See* state-building; state capacity
state-building: in Argentina, 170–171, 233; in Chile, 158; chronic violence as an inhibitor of, 233; definition of, 3, 88n1; education as a tool for, 2–3, 16, 20, 30, 34, 87–89, 107, 158, 171, 284, 300, 310, 312; efficacy of education as a tool for, 285–290, 300; ideas about mass education as, 89–100; in France, 22; internal threats as a motivation for, 39, 108–122 (*see also* internal conflict and mass education); interstate wars as a motivation for, 2–3, 33; in Mexico, 242–243; need for, 116; policy tools for, 3–4, 310, 312; process of, 2–3; Prussia as a model for, 93, 281; relative high priority as a reason for mass education, 20, 22, 89–90, 100, 181, 201–202; as a theory of education reform, 2–3, 16–23, 29–30, 33, 87–89, 93, 108–122, 218–220, 223, 231–233, 236, 244–246; Tilly's theory of, 2–3, 3n1, 33. *See also* expansion of primary education; indoctrination; laws regulating primary education; moral education; nation-building; social control
state capacity: administrative capacity, 36, 121, 218, 236–237, 245, 247, 298; collaboration with the Church due to limited, 23; fiscal capacity, 19, 36, 121, 218, 236–237, 245, 247; military / repressive capacity, 3, 94; minimum level of as precondition for the expansion of primary education, 36, 121, 218, 236–247; railroads and (*see* railroads); relationship with civil war, 119–120; in Chile, 166–167; in England, 225; in France, 149, 151, 238; in Mexico, 240, 242, 244; in Sweden, 298–299
Stowe, Calvin, 59
Sustainable Development Goals (United Nations), 320
Sweden: certification requirements for teachers in, **190**, 191; compulsory primary education in, 59, 195, **196**; crime-reducing effects of primary education in, 288; curriculum for primary education in, 69, **200**, 201n19; 1842 Elementary School Statute / School Act, 69, 183n1, **190**, 195, **193**, **196**, 201n19, 220, 222, 298; expansion of schooling despite lack of parental demand, 57–58n22; first primary education law, timing of, **49**, **66**, 183n1; Normal Schools in, 188; primary education statistics, earliest availability of, **49**; primary schooling and democracy in, 54; railroads and school inspection / enrollment rates in, 237, 298–299; school inspection policies in, **193**, 194–195; small-scale violence and primary education in, 220–222, 232; timing of industrialization and adoption of landmark education legislation in, 65–66, **66**
Switzerland, **49**, 60, 64n35, **66**, 264

Taiwan, **49**, 54, 55n18, 64n35, 70–71
teachers
  certification of: across countries, 50, **190**; in Argentina, 177; in Chile, 164–165; collection of data on, 8, 40; in France, 143n67, 145, 154, 191; policies for, 3, 4, 9–10, 21, 184–185, 189–192
  moral requirements for: across countries, **190**; in Argentina, 177; in Austria, 191; in Colombia, 191; in Cuba, 191; in Denmark, 191; in France, 154, 191; in Guatemala, 191; laws establishing, 189–192; in Norway, 191; in Prussia, 126n4; in Sweden, 191
  purges of: 307–308
  recruitment of: 185, 237–238
  training of (*see also* Normal Schools): in Argentina, 167, 177; in Chile, 159, 164–165; collection of data on, 8, 40; first teacher training institution in Central Europe, 133n29; in France, 145; Normal Schools for, 59–60, 184, 186, 191–192, 293–294; policies for, 3, 9–10, 21, 184–189, 191; in Prussia, 48, 134; state monopoly over, 48, 164, 167, 191, 293; in Western countries, 50, 184–189, **190**
Tedesco, Juan Carlos, 168–169
Thailand, **49**, 64n35, 235–236, 321
Thorndike, Edward, 260–261
Tilly, Charles, 33, 149n82
Torres, José María, 175
Trump, Donald, 315
Tsurumi, E. Patricia, 70
Tuck, Richard, 94
Tunisia, **49**, 64n35
Turkey, **49**, 64n35, 246, 308
Tyack, David, 258

Unión Cívica Radical (Argentina; UCR), 292
United Kingdom, **49**, 180, 185, 188. *See also* England; Wales
United Nations, 4, 84, 230, 285, 320

United Nations Children's Fund (UNICEF), 230
United Nations Educational, Scientific and Cultural Organization (UNESCO), 12, 41–42, 230, 311, 320–321
United States: Black children in, efforts to educate, 258–259; Black teachers in, purges of, 308; boll weevil and enrollment rates in the South, 68n38; as case study, 251–261; Common School Movement, 259–260; compulsory schooling laws in, 29, 59; curriculum for common schools during the Early Republic, 254–255, 257–258; curriculum reforms after Black Lives Matter (BLM) protests, 314–315; democracy and primary education in, 47, 53; education for leveling the playing field in, 257–258; European influence on ideas about education, 17, 59–60, 253, 259–260; expansion of primary education in, timing of, 38; first state education laws in, 252; goals of mass education during the Early Republic, 251, 253, 257–258, 261; immigration and education reform in, 29, 256, 292; indoctrination through elementary education in, 5, 251–261, 314–315; military conflict and expansion of primary education in, 71; Normal Schools in, 59–60; primary education statistics, earliest availability of, **49**; primary school enrollment rates in, 43, **44**; Progressive Era, education debates during, 260–261; Prussian influence on ideas about education, 17, 259–260; rebellions during the Early Republic, 251–253, 256, 259; reports on Soviet education system, 70; tension between indoctrination and liberal education goals in, 257–261. *See also* Adams, John Quincy; Coram, Robert; Dewey, John; Jefferson, Thomas; Mann, Horace; Rush, Benjamin; Webster, Noah
universal access to schooling: collection of data on, 40
Uruguay: Argentina, war with, 180; certification requirements for teachers, **190, 193**; compulsory primary education, 195, **196**; curriculum for primary education, 199, **200**, 201n19; data for, 64n35, 302n34; data on literacy rates, 311n2; democratization and primary education, **49**; 1877 *Ley 1.350*, 45, 183n1, 190n10, **193**, 195, **196**, 201n19; enrollment rates, 44, **46**, 82n69; feminization of the teaching profession, 185; industrialization and primary education, **66**; as a regional leader in primary education, 45

Vaillant, Denise, 296
Vargas, Getúlio, 56
Varieties of Political Indoctrination in Education and the Media Dataset (V-Indoc), 234, 275, 315
Vasconcelos, José, 243–44
Vaughan, Mary Kay, 240n45, 241n47, 241n49, 242n53, 242n57, 243n60, 243n62, 243nn64–65, 244n66
Velasco, Andrés, 312
Venezuela, **49**, 64n35, 65, **66**, 184n1, **190, 193, 196, 200**, 201n19, 295
Vieira, Everett, 270
Voitgländer, Nico, 151
Voltaire (François-Marie Arouet), 96
Volksschule (Prussia), 305–6

Wales, 264, 288
Washington, George, 252
Way, Lucan, 116
Weber, Eugene, 24n29, 25n32
Webster, Noah, 254–55, 257
Westberg, Johannes, 221
Western countries: explaining the expansion of primary education in, 38–39; industrialization and enrollment rates in, 67n37; industrialization and expansion of primary education in, 67. *See also* Americas, the; Europe
Whiskey Rebellion, 251, 256
Wilde, Eduardo, 176, 181
Woods, George, 229
Wordsworth, William, 226
World Bank, 7, 32, 84, 229–230, 237, 270, 311, 321–322, 323n32; education, pressure to increase, 84. *See also* "learning crisis"
Wright, Susannah, 267–268

Zambrano, Raul, 149n79
Zimbabwe, **49**, 64n35, 246

The Princeton Economic History of the Western World

JOEL MOKYR, SERIES EDITOR

Recent Titles

The Wealth of a Nation: Institutional Foundations of English Capitalism, Geoffrey M. Hodgson

The Corporation and the Twentieth Century: The History of American Business Enterprise, Richard N. Langlois

Pioneers of Capitalism: The Netherlands 1000–1800, Maarten Prak and Jan Luiten van Zanden

Pawned States: State Building in the Era of International Finance, Didac Queralt

Pliny's Roman Economy: Natural History, Innovation, and Growth, Richard Saller

The Israeli Economy: A Story of Success and Costs, Joseph Zeira

Plagues upon the Earth: Disease and the Course of Human History, Kyle Harper

Credit Nation: Property Laws and Institutions in Early America, Claire Priest

The Decline and Rise of Democracy: A Global History from Antiquity to Today, David Stasavage

Trade in the Ancient Mediterranean: Private Order and Public Institutions, Taco Terpstra

The European Guilds: An Economic Analysis, Sheilagh Ogilvie

Going the Distance: Eurasian Trade and the Rise of the Business Corporation 1400–1700, Ron Harris

Dark Matter Credit: The Development of Peer-to-Peer Lending and Banking in France, Philip T. Hofman, Gilles Postel-Vinay, and Jean-Laurent Rosenthal

The Winding Road to the Welfare State: Economic Insecurity and Social Welfare Policy in Britain, George R. Boyer

The Mystery of the Kibbutz: Egalitarian Principles in a Capitalist World, Ran Abramitzky

Unequal Gains: American Growth and Inequality since 1700, Peter H. Lindert and Jeffrey G. Williamson

Uneven Centuries: Economic Development of Turkey since 1820, Şevket Pamuk

The Great Leveler: Violence and the History of Inequality from the Stone Age to the Twenty-First Century, Walter Scheidel

The Rise and Fall of American Growth: The U.S. Standard of Living since the Civil War, Robert J. Gordon

Brazil in Transition: Beliefs, Leadership, and Institutional Change, Lee J. Alston, Marcus André Melo, Bernardo Mueller, and Carlos Pereira

The Vanishing Irish: Households, Migration, and the Rural Economy in Ireland, 1850–1914, Timothy W. Guinnane

Fragile by Design: The Political Origins of Banking Crises and Scarce Credit, Charles W. Calomiris and Stephen H. Haber

The Son Also Rises: Surnames and the History of Social Mobility, Gregory Clark

Why Did Europe Conquer the World?, Philip T. Hofman

Lending to the Borrower from Hell: Debt, Taxes, and Default in the Age of Philip II, Mauricio Drelichman and Hans-Joachim Voth

Power to the People: Energy in Europe over the Last Five Centuries, Astrid Kander, Paolo Malanima, and Paul Warde

Cities of Commerce: The Institutional Foundations of International Trade in the Low Countries, 1250–1650, Oscar Gelderblom

Why Australia Prospered: The Shifting Sources of Economic Growth, Ian W. McLean

The Chosen Few: How Education Shaped Jewish History, 70–1492, Maristella Botticini and Zvi Eckstein

Creating Wine: The Emergence of a World Industry, 1840–1914, James Simpson

Distant Tyranny: Markets, Power, and Backwardness in Spain, 1650–1800, Regina Grafe

The Evolution of a Nation: How Geography and Law Shaped the American States, Daniel Berkowitz and Karen B. Clay

The Roman Market Economy, Peter Temin

States of Credit: Size, Power, and the Development of European Polities, David Stasavage

Power over Peoples: Technology, Environments, and Western Imperialism, 1400 to the Present, Daniel R. Headrick

Unsettled Account: The Evolution of Banking in the Industrialized World since 1800, Richard S. Grossman

A Farewell to Alms: A Brief Economic History of the World, Gregory Clark

Power and Plenty: Trade, War, and the World Economy in the Second Millennium, Ronald Findlay and Kevin H. O'Rourke

War, Wine, and Taxes: The Political Economy of Anglo-French Trade, 1689–1900, John V. C. Nye

Cultures Merging: A Historical and Economic Critique of Culture, Eric L. Jones

The European Economy since 1945: Coordinated Capitalism and Beyond, Barry Eichengreen

Feeding the World: An Economic History of Agriculture, 1800–2000, Giovanni Federico

Understanding the Process of Economic Change, Douglass C. North

The Strictures of Inheritance: The Dutch Economy in the Nineteenth Century, Jan Luiten van Zanden and Arthur van Riel

Farm to Factory: A Reinterpretation of the Soviet Industrial Revolution, Robert C. Allen

Quarter Notes and Bank Notes: The Economics of Music Composition in the Eighteenth and Nineteenth Centuries, F. M. Scherer

The Big Problem of Small Change, Thomas J. Sargent and François R. Velde

The Great Divergence: China, Europe, and the Making of the Modern World Economy, Kenneth Pomeranz

Black '47 and Beyond: The Great Irish Famine in History, Economy, and Memory, Cormac Ó Gráda

Growth in a Traditional Society: The French Countryside, 1450–1815, Philip T. Hofman

GPSR Authorized Representative: Easy Access System Europe - Mustamäe tee 50, 10621 Tallinn, Estonia, gpsr.requests@easproject.com